C++ Memory Management

Write leaner and safer C++ code using proven
memory-management techniques

Patrice Roy

C++ Memory Management

Portfolio Director: Kunal Chaudhari

Publishing Product Manager: Samriddhi Murarka

Program Manager: K. Loganathan

Book Project Manager: Ashwin Kharwa

Content Engineer: Rounak Kulkarni

Technical Editor: Kushal Sharma

Copy Editor: Safis Editing

Proofreader: Rounak Kulkarni

Indexer: Manju Arasan

Production Designer: Nilesh Mohite

Growth Lead: Mansi Shah

First published: March 2025
Production reference: 2070725

Published by Packt Publishing Ltd.
Grosvenor House
11 St Paul's Square
Birmingham
B3 1RB, UK.

ISBN 978-1-80512-980-6
www.packtpub.com

This book was written with love, and I was fortunate to write it from a loving home with the encouragement of my wife, Isabelle (Za), and my children, Marguerite, Calypso, Amandine, Viktor, and Ludo. Oh, and lots of animals.

My participation in the ISO C++ Standards Committee has allowed me to get a deeper understanding of the workings of the amazing language that is C++. There are too many to thank for this, but I will at least mention Michael Wong, who invited me to participate in this enlightening adventure; Jon Kalb, who made it possible for me to meet these fine folks and gave me an opportunity to teach to a wider audience; and, of course, Bjarne Stroustrup, who gave us this language, which has been my primary tool for decades now. If you enjoy this book, know that they are indirectly responsible for it too.

– Patrice Roy

Foreword

Back in 2014, when Patrice Roy first joined our Canadian C++ standardization delegation team, I noticed something distinctive about his approach. He had this remarkable ability to untangle complex technical concepts and present them with striking clarity – a skill that would serve him well in crafting this book.

I've had the pleasure of collaborating with Patrice within the C++ standardization community since 2014, during which time he has contributed to ISO C++, CPPCON, and my SG14 group actively. His expertise and ability to clearly articulate complex technical concepts are evident throughout this work. This book isn't merely a collection of rules; it's an exploration of the core principles governing how C++ interacts with memory. From the foundational definition of an "object" to the intricacies of pointers and references, Patrice meticulously guides readers through the essential building blocks. He tackles challenging topics such as object lifetime, memory alignment, and the potential pitfalls of undefined behavior with clarity and precision.

Memory management lies at the core of modern C++ programming, yet it remains one of the most challenging areas to master. When Patrice approached me about this book, I immediately knew he was the perfect person to tackle such a vital topic. Having worked closely with Patrice for years, I've witnessed his exceptional ability to distill complex ideas into accessible, actionable knowledge. His technical expertise, coupled with his passion for teaching, sets him apart as a thought leader and educator in the C++ world. He is also one of the most genuine, kind, and honest people I have ever met.

This book, *C++ Memory Management*, is a testament to Patrice's passion for dissecting complex topics and presenting them in an accessible way. It's not just a dry recitation of rules and best practices; it's a journey into the very heart of how C++ interacts with memory. From the fundamental definition of an "object" – a concept often taken for granted but surprisingly nuanced – to the often-misunderstood relationship between pointers and references, Patrice guides you through the essential building blocks. He doesn't shy away from the tricky bits either, tackling the thorny issues of object lifetime, alignment, padding, and the ever-present danger of memory leaks.

This book reflects Patrice's gift for progressive enlightenment. He begins with fundamental concepts – what exactly is an object in C++? How do pointers and references truly differ? These seemingly basic questions have nuanced answers that impact how we write code. From there, he ventures into trickier territory: object lifetime, alignment requirements, padding bytes, and the eternal challenge of preventing memory leaks.

Having spent years working on C++ atomics and memory models, I especially appreciate how the book builds understanding from first principles. *Chapter 1* lays crucial groundwork for objects and memory representation. *Chapter 2* bravely tackles undefined behavior and other pitfalls that can trap even experienced developers. This mirrors my own experience implementing transactional memory in C++ – understanding edge cases is vital.

As someone who has spent over two decades working on C++ compilers, language design, safety, AI, and particularly parallel computing and memory models, I appreciate the careful balance this book strikes between practical guidance and theoretical foundations. The progression from fundamental concepts in *Chapter 1* through increasingly sophisticated memory management techniques mirrors the journey that many C++ developers must take.

I have had the privilege of working with Patrice for years, and I can confidently say that his approach to teaching and writing reflects the traits of a seasoned expert who deeply understands both the intricacies of C++ and the challenges faced by those who wield it. With his clear explanations and practical insights, this book is not just about memory management – it's about writing better, safer, and more expressive C++ at every level of abstraction.

What sets this book apart is how it builds knowledge methodically, layer by layer, always connecting low-level details to high-level design principles. The sections on casts and const-correctness in *Chapter 3* go far beyond syntax, illustrating how to express intent clearly in code and leverage the type system as a safety net. *Chapter 4* delves into destructors and the RAII idiom, showcasing why C++ remains one of the most powerful tools for managing resources, allowing developers to write code that is both robust and clean.

The book's treatment of smart pointers and RAII in later chapters reflects modern C++ at its finest – showing how we can harness the type system and object lifetime semantics to write code that is both safer and more elegant. This exemplifies the philosophy that has guided my work chairing various C++ standardization groups: that C++ should offer powerful abstractions while still giving developers precise control when they need it.

As a long-time contributor to the evolution of C++ standards and a leader in the development of parallel and heterogeneous programming models, my own journey has revolved around navigating the delicate balance between high-level abstractions and low-level optimizations. Whether working on **high-performance computing** (**HPC**) systems, pushing the boundaries of AI/ML frameworks, or designing robust programming models for safety-critical systems, I've often found myself returning to the fundamental questions: *How do we manage resources efficiently?* and *How do we write code that is both powerful and maintainable?*

Whether you're a student learning C++, a professional developer looking to deepen your expertise, or an experienced programmer wanting to better understand the language's memory model, this book is an invaluable resource. Patrice has created something special here – a thorough yet approachable guide to one of C++'s most important topics.

This book is not just a technical manual – it is a conversation with a mentor. I consider Patrice to also be my mentor. Patrice writes with the voice of someone who has navigated the sharp edges of C++ and emerged with a deep respect for its potential. His examples are not contrived; they are drawn from the real world.

So, dive in. Embrace the journey. And let Patrice's expertise guide you to new heights in your C++ mastery.

– Michael Wong

Distinguished Engineer, ISO C++ Standards Founding Directions Group Chair, C++ Foundation Founding Director, Chair of SG14 (Games Dev/Low Latency/Financial, Embedded), SG19 (Machine Learning), Editor Concurrency TS2, Transactional Memory TS1/TS2, Canada's All Programming Languages (SC22) and Automotive Functional Safety for self-driving cars (TC22/SC32) Chair

Contributors

About the author

Patrice Roy has been playing with C++ professionally, for pleasure, or (mostly) both for over 30 years. After a few years doing R&D and working on military flight simulators, he moved on to academics and has taught computer science since 1998. Since 2005, he has been involved more specifically in helping graduate students and professionals from the fields of real-time systems and game programming develop the skills they need to face today's challenges.

Patrice has been a participating member of the ISO C++ Standards Committee since late 2014. He has five children, and his wife ensures that their house is home to a continuously changing number of cats, dogs, birds, and other animals.

About the reviewers

Dr. Martin Reddy is an IEEE fellow, an AAIA fellow, and an ACM Distinguished Engineer. He has published over 40 professional articles, 10 patents, and 2 books, including *API Design for C++*. Dr. Reddy was co-founder and CTO of the AI technology company PullString, which was acquired by Apple in 2019. At Apple, he was a software architect and designed major components of the Siri virtual assistant. Martin also spent 6 years at Pixar Animation Studios where he worked on the Academy Award-winning films *Finding Nemo*, *The Incredibles*, *Ratatouille*, and *Wall-E*. Before that, Dr. Reddy worked for 5 years at SRI International on distributed 3D terrain visualization technologies.

Kevin Carpenter, an experienced software engineer, excels in crafting high-availability C++ solutions for Linux and Windows, with expertise in transaction software, financial modeling, and system integration. As a lead project engineer, he ensures secure, high-speed credit card transactions. In his prior position, he played a lead role in developing an interest rate risk model for large credit unions, enhancing legacy code, and optimizing ERP data integration.

Kevin actively engages in the C++ community, volunteering at conferences such as ACCU, CppCon, C++ on Sea, and SwiftCraft, where he holds key positions such as speaker liaison and volunteer coordinator/chair. His diverse contributions to the C++ community showcase his commitment to excellence and drive for collaborative growth, leaving a lasting impact in the tech world.

Faezeh Sadat Zolfaghari began her journey into technology and robotics in late elementary school, driven by her passion for innovation and problem-solving. In middle school, she joined an elite national program for C++ programming, completing its 5-year curriculum as the top graduate among only 5 final participants out of 40. She then pursued a degree in computer science with a focus on cybersecurity. Since graduating, she has been working as a software engineer. Her curiosity spans areas such as biology, neuroscience, and robotics, inspiring her to explore the intersection of computing and interdisciplinary research. Her interests include algorithm optimization, HPC, and mathematics, all aimed at solving complex challenges.

Table of Contents

Part 2: Implicit Memory Management Techniques

6

Writing Smart Pointers   111

Part 3: Taking Control (of Memory Management Mechanisms)

7

Overloading Memory Allocation Operators   141

8

Writing a Naïve Leak Detector 163

9

Atypical Allocation Mechanisms 187

10

Arena-Based Memory Management and Other Optimizations 211

11

Deferred Reclamation 239

Part 4: Writing Generic Containers (and a Bit More)

12

Writing Generic Containers with Explicit Memory Management   263

13

Writing Generic Containers with Implicit Memory Management   303

Preface

Programs regularly have to allocate and manage memory, no matter what programming language they are written in. Why and how we do this depends on the language and the application domain, however: real-time systems, embedded systems, games, and conventional desktop applications all have different needs and constraints, and there is no single, universal best approach to all problems.

This book shows how modern C++ lets programmers write simpler and safer programs, but also how that language makes it possible to take control of memory allocation mechanisms and make sure programs respect the constraints they face. Starting from the language's basic concepts of objects' lifetimes and memory organization, you will learn how to write your own containers and your own allocators, and to adapt the very behavior of allocation operators to suit your needs. Depending on your needs, you will be able to make programs that are smaller, faster, more predictable... and safer.

Who this book is for

This book is written for individuals who have some programming experience and who enjoy both high-level and low-level programming. Having prior experience with generic programming and concurrent programming will lead to a more pleasant reading experience.

More specifically, this book is written for you if (a) you think managing memory in C++ is difficult but are willing to take a fresh look at it, (b) you want better control over the way your programs manage memory, or (c) you want your programs to be smaller, faster, and safer. You might benefit from this book if you come from a C++ background, of course, but also if you normally program in other languages and would like to look at what C++ allows you to do. This book will be helpful to any programmer, but you might find it particularly useful if you program in constrained environments (such as embedded systems or game consoles) or in other application domains where you need tight control over resource allocation mechanisms. Who knows, you might even enjoy it!

What this book covers

Chapter 1, Objects, Pointers, and References, discusses the basic concepts of the object model in the C++ language, providing us with a common basic vocabulary.

Chapter 2, Things to Be Careful With, looks at some of the tricky aspects of C++, with a more specific examination of low-level programming maneuvers that can lead us into trouble; we will examine what kind of trouble these can lead us to.

Chapter 3, Casts and cv-qualifications, examines the tools at our disposal to coerce the type system to our needs and discusses how to use these sometimes sharp tools in reasonable ways.

Chapter 4, Using Destructors, looks at this important aspect of C++ that makes it possible to write objects that are responsible for the management of resources in general and of memory in particular.

Chapter 5, Using Standard Smart Pointers, provides a look at how we can benefit from this important part of contemporary C++ programming, which inscribes responsibility over memory into the type system.

Chapter 6, Writing Smart Pointers, looks at ways in which we write homemade versions of the standard smart pointers as well as how we can design our own smart pointers to cover niches that are not yet covered by those provided by the standard library.

Chapter 7, Overloading Memory Allocation Operators, shows some of the many ways in which we can provide our own versions of memory allocation operators and explains why it can be a good idea to do so.

Chapter 8, Writing a Naïve Leak Detector, puts our new memory management skills to use to write a working (if simple) tool to detect memory leaks in a way that is essentially transparent to user code.

Chapter 9, Atypical Allocation Mechanisms, takes a tour of some unusual applications (and overloads) of the standard memory allocation operators, including non-throwing versions and others that handle "exotic" memory.

Chapter 10, Arena-Based Memory Management and Other Optimizations, uses our memory management skills to make programs execute more quickly and behave more deterministically, benefitting from domain-specific or application-specific knowledge.

Chapter 11, Deferred Reclamation, explores ways in which we can write programs that automatically reclaim dynamically allocated objects at chosen moments during program execution.

Chapter 12, Writing Generic Containers with Explicit Memory Management, explains how to write two efficient generic containers that manage memory themselves and discusses exception-safety and complexity tradeoffs of this practice.

Chapter 13, Writing Generic Containers with Implicit Memory Management, revisits the containers written in the previous chapter to see the impacts of moving from an explicit memory management approach to an implicit one that relies on smart pointers.

Chapter 14, Writing Generic Containers with Allocator Support, revisits our homemade containers to see how memory management can be customized through allocators, covering allocators from before C++11 to contemporary allocators, as well as PMR allocators.

Chapter 15, Contemporary Issues, looks toward the near future and examines some recent (as of the book's writing) features of C++ that pertain to memory management as well as some interesting candidate additions to the language in C++26 and C++29.

Annexure: Things You Should Know, provides some technical background that can help you get the most out of this book but that might not be common knowledge. Refer to it as needed, it's there for you!

To get the most out of this book

You will need a contemporary C++ compiler, ideally one that supports at least C++20 and ideally C++23. This book does not require other tools, but you are of course welcome to use your favorite code editor and experiment with the examples you will meet as you progress.

Care was taken to keep to standard C++ from a portable and safe perspective. The few places where you will meet examples that use non-portable code are identified as such.

Code examples have been tested on three distinct compilers and the samples on the book's GitHub repository all contain, in addition to the actual source code, links to online versions (in comments) that compile and that you can modify and adapt as you wish.

If you are using the digital version of this book, we advise you to type the code yourself or access the code from the book's GitHub repository (a link is available in the next section). Doing so will help you avoid any potential errors related to the copying and pasting of code.

I hope you enjoy the experience and find the examples to be an interesting starting point for your own explorations.

Download the example code files

You can download the example code files for this book from GitHub at `https://github.com/PacktPublishing/C-Plus-Plus-Memory-Management`. If there's an update to the code, it will be updated in the GitHub repository.

We also have other code bundles from our rich catalog of books and videos available at `https://github.com/PacktPublishing/`. Check them out!

Conventions used

There are a number of text conventions used throughout this book.

`Code in text`: Indicates code words in text, database table names, folder names, filenames, file extensions, pathnames, dummy URLs, user input, and Twitter handles. Here is an example: "The whole body of `f()` could legitimately be rewritten by your compiler as `return g(*p)` in this case, with the `return *p` statement being turned into unreachable code."

A block of code is set as follows:

```
int g(int);
int f(int *p) {
    if(p != nullptr)
        return g(*p); // Ok, we know p is not null
    return *p; // oops, if p == nullptr this is UB
}
```

When we wish to draw your attention to a particular part of a code block, the relevant lines or items are set in bold:

```
class X {
public:
    // #0 delegates to #1 which delegates to #0 which...
    X(float x) : X{ static_cast<int>(x) } { // #0
    }
```

Any command-line input or output is written as follows:

```
Verbose(0)
Verbose(2)
Verbose(6)
Verbose(7)
```

> **Tips or important notes**
> Appear like this.

Get in touch

Feedback from our readers is always welcome.

General feedback: If you have questions about any aspect of this book, email us at customercare@packtpub.com and mention the book title in the subject of your message.

Errata: Although we have taken every care to ensure the accuracy of our content, mistakes do happen. If you have found a mistake in this book, we would be grateful if you would report this to us. Please visit www.packtpub.com/support/errata and fill in the form.

Piracy: If you come across any illegal copies of our works in any form on the internet, we would be grateful if you would provide us with the location address or website name. Please contact us at copyright@packt.com with a link to the material.

If you are interested in becoming an author: If there is a topic that you have expertise in and you are interested in either writing or contributing to a book, please visit authors.packtpub.com.

Share Your Thoughts

Once you've read *C++ Memory Management*, we'd love to hear your thoughts! Scan the QR code below to go straight to the Amazon review page for this book and share your feedback.

https://packt.link/r/1805129805

Your review is important to us and the tech community and will help us make sure we're delivering excellent quality content.

Part 1:
Memory in C++

In this part, we will develop a common vocabulary on some key aspects of the object model in C++. This includes a discussion of ideas such as what an object is, what a reference is, and how C++ represents memory; a look at some of the risky or delicate maneuvers we sometimes need to do when writing low-level code (and the consequences that stem from doing them inappropriately); and how to coerce the type system to our needs in ways that do not come back to harm us. The knowledge gathered in this part will serve as a basis from which later chapters will be built.

This part has the following chapters:

- *Chapter 1, Objects, Pointers, and References*
- *Chapter 2, Things to Be Careful with*
- *Chapter 3, Casts and cv-qualifications*

1

Objects, Pointers, and References

Before we start discussing memory management in C++, let's make sure we understand each other and agree on a common vocabulary. If you're a long-time C++ programmer, you probably have your own ideas about what pointers, objects, and references are. Your ideas will stem from a wealth of experience. If you are coming to this book from another language, you might also have your own ideas as to what these terms mean in C++ and how they relate to memory and memory management.

In this chapter, we are going to make sure we have a common understanding of some basic (but profound) ideas so that we can build on this shared understanding for the rest of our adventure together. Specifically, we will explore questions such as the following:

- How is memory represented in C++? What exactly is that thing we call memory, at least in the context of the C++ language?

- What are objects, pointers, and references? What do we mean by those terms in C++? What are the lifetime rules of objects? How do they relate to memory?

- What are arrays in C++? In this language, arrays are a low-level but highly efficient construct represented in a way that directly impacts memory management.

Getting the most out of this book – get to know your free benefits

Unlock exclusive **free** benefits that come with your purchase, thoughtfully crafted to supercharge your learning journey and help you learn without limits.

Here's a quick overview of what you get with this book:

Next-gen reader

Our web-based reader, designed to help you learn effectively, comes with the following features:

Multi-device progress sync: Learn from any device with seamless progress sync.

Highlighting and notetaking: Turn your reading into lasting knowledge.

Bookmarking: Revisit your most important learnings anytime.

Dark mode: Focus with minimal eye strain by switching to dark or sepia mode.

Figure 1.1: Illustration of the next-gen
Packt Reader's features

Interactive AI assistant (beta)

Our interactive AI assistant has been trained on the content of this book, so it can help you out if you encounter any issues. It comes with the following features:

Summarize it: Summarize key sections or an entire chapter.

AI code explainers: In the next-gen Packt Reader, click the **Explain** button above each code block for AI-powered code explanations.

Note: The AI assistant is part of next-gen Packt Reader and is still in beta.

Figure 1.2: Illustration of Packt's AI assistant

DRM-free PDF or ePub version

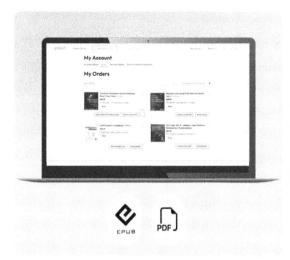

Learn without limits with the following perks included with your purchase:

- Learn from anywhere with a DRM-free PDF copy of this book.

- Use your favorite e-reader to learn using a DRM-free ePub version of this book.

Figure 1.3: Free PDF and ePub

Unlock this book's exclusive benefits now

Take a moment to get the most out of your purchase and enjoy the complete learning experience.

Note: Have your purchase invoice ready before you begin.

UNLOCK NOW

https://www.packtpub.com/
unlock/9781805129806

Technical requirements

This book assumes that readers have some basic knowledge of C++ or of syntactically similar languages such as C, Java, C#, or JavaScript. For this reason, we will not explain the basics of variable declarations, loops, `if` statements, or functions.

We will, however, use some aspects of the C++ language in this chapter that some readers might be less comfortable with. Please refer to *Annexure: Things You Should Know*, before reading this book.

Some of the examples use C++20 or C++23, so make sure that your compiler supports this version of the standard to get the most out of them.

The code for this chapter can be found here: `https://github.com/PacktPublishing/C-Plus-Plus-Memory-Management/tree/main/chapter1`.

Representation of memory in C++

This is a book on memory management. You, readers, are trying to figure out what it means, and I, as the author, am trying to convey what it means.

The way in which the standard describes memory can be seen in [`wg21.link/basic.memobj`]. Essentially, memory in C++ is expressed as one or more sequences of contiguous bytes. This opens up the possibility of memory expressed as a set of discontinuous blocks of contiguous memory because, historically, C++ has supported memories made of various distinct segments. Every byte in a C++ program has a unique address.

Memory in a C++ program is populated with various entities such as objects, functions, references, and so on. Managing memory efficiently requires grasping what these entities mean and how programs can make use of them.

The meaning of the word byte is important in C++. As detailed in [`wg21.link/intro.memory`], bytes are the fundamental storage unit in C++. The number of bits in a byte is implementation-defined in C++. The standard does state, however, that a byte has to be wide enough to contain both the ordinary literal encoding of any element of the basic literal character set and the eight-bit code units of the UTF-8 encoding form. It also states that a byte is made of a contiguous sequence of bits.

What often surprises people is that in C++, a byte is not necessarily an octet: a byte consists of at least eight bits but could be made of more (something that's useful on some exotic hardware). This might change in the future, as the standard committee might constrain that definition someday, but this is the situation at the time of the publication of this book. The key idea here is that a byte is the smallest addressable unit of memory in a program.

Objects, pointers, and references

We tend to use words such as object, pointer, and reference informally, without thinking too much about what they mean. In a language such as C++, these words have precise meanings that define and delimit what we can do in practice.

Before we get our hands dirty, so to speak, let's examine the formal meaning of these terms in C++.

Objects

If we polled programmers working with different languages and asked them how they would define the term object, we could probably expect such answers as "something that groups together variables and related functions" or "an instance of a class," which correspond to traditional takes on that term from the realm of object-oriented programming.

C++ as a language tries to provide homogeneous support for user-defined types such as structs or classes. It also provides support for fundamental types such as `int` or `float`. Thus, it probably should not be surprising that, for C++, the definition of an object is expressed in terms of its properties, not in terms of what the word means, and that this definition includes the most fundamental types. The definition of an object in C++ is described in [`wg21.link/intro.object`] and takes the following factors into account:

- How the object is created explicitly, such as when defining the object or constructing it through one of the many variations of `operator new`. The object may also be created implicitly such as when creating a temporary object as the result of some expression or when changing the active member of a `union`.

- The fact that an object is somewhere (it has an address) and occupies a region of storage of non-zero size, from the start of its construction to the end of its destruction.

- Other properties of an object, including its name (if it has one), its type, and its storage duration (`automatic`, `static`, `thread_local`, and so on.).

The C++ standard explicitly calls out functions as not being objects, even if a function has an address and occupies storage.

From this, we can infer that even a humble `int` is an object, but a function is not. You can see already, dear reader, that the book you're reading will touch on fundamental topics, since lifetime and the storage occupied by objects are part of the fundamental properties of these entities we use in our programs every day. Such things as lifetime and storage are clearly part of what memory management is about. You can convince yourself of that fact with this simple program:

```
#include <type_traits>
int main() {
    static_assert(std::is_object_v<int>);
    static_assert(!std::is_object_v<decltype(main)>);
}
```

What is an object? It's something that has a lifetime and occupies storage. Controlling these characteristics is part of the reasons why this book exists.

Pointers

There are numerous (around 2,000) mentions of the word "pointer" in the text of the C++ standard, but if you open an electronic copy of that document and search through it, you'll find that a formal definition is surprisingly hard to come by. This can be surprising given the fact that people tend to associate that idea with C and (by extension) C++.

Let us try to offer a useful yet informal definition, then: a pointer is a typed address. It associates a type with what is found at some location in memory. For that reason, in code like the following, one reads that n is an `int` object and that p points to an `int` object that happens to be the address of the n object:

```
int n = 3; // n is an int object
char c;
// int *p = &c; // no, illegal
int *p = &n;
```

> 💡 **Quick tip**: Enhance your coding experience with the **AI Code Explainer** and **Quick Copy** features. Open this book in the next-gen Packt Reader. Click the **Copy** button (**1**) to quickly copy code into your coding environment, or click the **Explain** button (**2**) to get the AI assistant to explain a block of code to you.
>
> ```
> function calculate(a, b) {                    Copy      Explain
>   return {sum: a + b};                          1          2
> };
> ```
>
> 🔒 **The next-gen Packt Reader** is included for free with the purchase of this book. Unlock it by scanning the QR code below or visiting `https://www.packtpub.com/unlock/9781805129806`.
>
>

It's important to understand here that p indeed points to an `int`, unless p is left uninitialized, p points to `nullptr`, or programmers have played tricks with the type system and made p point to something else deliberately. Of course, pointer p is an object, as it respects all the rules to that effect.

Much of the (syntactic) confusion about pointers probably comes from the contextual meaning of the * and & symbols. The trick is to remember that they have different roles when they appear in the introduction of a name and when they are used on an existing object:

```
int m = 4, n = 3;
int *p; // p declares (and defines) a pointer to an int
        // (currently uninitialized), introducing a name
p = 0; // p is a null pointer (it does not necessarily
```

```
           // point to address zero; 0 as used here is
           // just a convention)
p = nullptr; // likewise, but clearer. Prefer nullptr to
           // literal 0 whenever possible to describe
           // a null pointer
p = &m; // p points to m (p contains the address of m)
assert(*p == 4); // p already exists; with *p we are
           // accessing what p points to
p = &n; // p now points to n (p contains the address of n)
int *q = &n; // q declares (and defines) a pointer to an
           // int and &n represents the address of n, the
           // address of an int: q is a pointer to an int
assert(*q == 3); // n holds 3 at this stage, and q points
           // to n, so what q points to has value 3
assert(*p == 3); // the same holds for p
assert(p == q); // p and q point to the same int object
*q = 4; // q already exists, so *q means "whatever q
           // points to"
assert(n == 4); // indeed, n now holds value 4 since we
           // modified it indirectly through q
auto qq = &q;   // qq is the address of q, and its type is
           // "pointer to a pointer to an int", thus
           // int **... But we will rarely - if ever -
           // need this
int &r = n; // declaration of r as a reference to integer n
           // (see below). Note that & is used in a
           // declaration in this case
```

As you can see, when introducing an object, * means "pointer to." On an existing object, it means "what that pointer points to" (the pointee). Similarly, when introducing a name, & means "reference to" (something we will discuss imminently). On an existing object, it means "address of" and yields a pointer.

Pointers allow us to do arithmetic, but that's (legitimately) seen as a dangerous operation, as it can take us to arbitrary locations in a program and can therefore lead to serious damage. Arithmetic on a pointer depends on its type:

```
int *f();
char *g();
int danger() {
   auto p = f(); // p points to whatever f() returned
   int *q = p + 3; // q points to where p points to plus
              // three times the size of an int. No
              // clue where this is, but it's a bad,
```

```
                        // bad idea...
    auto pc = g(); // pc points to whatever g() returned
    char * qc = pc + 3; // qc points to where pc points
                        // to plus three times the size
                        // of a char. Please don't make
                        // your pointers go to places you
                        // don't know about like this
}
```

Of course, accessing the contents of arbitrary addresses is just asking for trouble. This is because it would mean invoking undefined behavior (described in *Chapter 2*), and if you do that, you're on your own. Please do not do such things in real code, as you could hurt programs – or worse, people. C++ is powerful and flexible, but if you program in C++, you're expected to behave responsibly and professionally.

C++ has four special types for pointer manipulation:

- `void*` means "address with no specific (type-related) semantics." A `void*` is an address with no associated type. All pointers (if we discount the `const` and `volatile` qualifiers) are implicitly convertible to `void*`; an informal way to read this is as "all pointers, regardless of type, really are addresses." The converse does not hold. For example, it's not true that all addresses are implicitly convertible to `int` pointers.

- `char*` means "pointer to a byte." Due to the C language roots of C++, a `char*` can alias any address in memory (the `char` type, regardless of its name, which evocates "character", really means "byte" in C and, by extension, in C++). There is an ongoing effort in C++ to give `char` the meaning of "character," but as of this writing, a `char*` can alias pretty much anything in a program. This hampers some compiler optimization opportunities (it is hard to constrain or reason about something that can lead to literally anything in memory).

- `std::byte*` is the new "pointer to a byte," at least since C++17. The (long-term) intent of `byte*` is to replace `char*` in those functions that do byte-per-byte manipulation or addressing, but since there's so much code that uses `char*` to that effect, this will take time.

For an example of conversion from and to `void*`, consider the following:

```
int n = 3;
int *p = &n; // fine so far
void *pv = p; // Ok, a pointer is an address
// p = pv; // no, a void* does not necessarily point to
//            an int (Ok in C, not in C++)
p = static_cast<int *>(pv); // fine, you asked for it, but
                            // if you're wrong you're on
                            // your own
```

The following example, which is somewhat more elaborate, uses `const char*` (but could use `const byte*` instead). It shows that one can compare the byte-per-byte representation of two objects, at least in some circumstances, to see whether they are equivalent:

```cpp
#include <iostream>
#include <type_traits>
using namespace std;
bool same_bytes(const char *p0, const char *p1,
                std::size_t n) {
    for(std::size_t i = 0; i != n; ++i)
        if(*(p0 + i) != *(p1 + i))
            return false;
    return true;
}
template <class T, class U>
    bool same_bytes(const T &a, const U &b) {
        using namespace std;
        static_assert(sizeof a == sizeof b);
        static_assert(has_unique_object_representations_v<
            T
        >);
        static_assert(has_unique_object_representations_v<
            U
        >);
        return same_bytes(reinterpret_cast<const char*>(&a),
                          reinterpret_cast<const char*>(&b),
                          sizeof a);
    }
struct X {
    int x {2}, y{3};
};
struct Y {
    int x {2}, y{3};
};
#include <cassert>
int main() {
    constexpr X x;
    constexpr Y y;
    assert(same_bytes(x, y));
}
```

The `has_unique_object_representations` trait is true for types uniquely defined by their values, that is, types exempt of padding bits.. That's sometimes important as C++ does not say what happens to padding bits in an object, and performing a bit-per-bit comparison of two objects might yield surprising results. Note that objects of floating point types are not considered uniquely defined by their values as there are many distinct values that qualify as NaN, or "not a number".

References

The C++ language supports two related families of indirections: pointers and references. Like their cousins, the pointers, references are often mentioned by the C++ standard (more than 1,800 times) but it's hard to find a formal definition for them.

We will try once again to provide an informal but operational definition: a reference can be seen as an alias for an existing entity. We deliberately did not use object, since one could refer to a function and we already know that a function is not an object.

Pointers are objects. As such, they occupy storage. References, on the other hand, are not objects and use no storage of their own, even though an implementation could simulate their existence with pointers. Compare `std::is_object_v<int*>` with `std::is_object_v<int&>`: the former is `true`, and the latter is `false`.

The `sizeof` operator, applied to a reference, will yield the size of what it refers to. Consequently, taking the address of a reference yields the address of what it refers to.

In C++, a reference is always bound to an object and remains bound to that object until the end of the reference's lifetime. A pointer, on the other hand, can point to numerous distinct objects during its lifetime, as we have seen before:

```
// int &nope; // would not compile (what would nope
//             // refer to?)
int n = 3;
int &r = n; // r refers to n
++r; // n becomes 4
assert(&r == &n); // taking the address of r means taking
//                 // the address of n
```

Another difference between pointers and references is that, contrary to the situation that prevails with pointers, there is no such thing as reference arithmetic. This makes references somewhat safer than pointers. There is room for both kinds of indirections in a program (and we will use them both in this book!), but for everyday programming, a good rule of thumb is to use references if possible and to use pointers if necessary.

Now that we have examined the representation of memory and taken a look at how C++ defines some fundamental ideas such as a byte, an object, a pointer, or a reference, we can delve a little deeper into some important defining properties of objects.

Understanding the fundamental properties of objects

We saw earlier that in C++, an object has a type and an address. It also occupies a region of storage from the beginning of its construction to the end of its destruction. We will now examine these fundamental properties in more detail in order to understand how these properties affect the ways in which we write programs.

Object lifetime

One of C++'s strengths, but also one reason for its relative complexity, arises from the control one has over the lifetime of objects. In C++, generally speaking, automatic objects are destructed at the end of their scope in a well-defined order. Static (global) objects are destructed on program termination in a somewhat well-defined order (in a given file, the order of destruction is clear, but it's more complicated for static objects in different files). Dynamically allocated objects are destructed "when your program says so" (there are many nuances to this).

Let's examine some aspects of object lifetime with the following (very) simple program:

```
#include <string>
#include <iostream>
#include <format>
struct X {
   std::string s;
   X(std::string_view s) : s{ s } {
      std::cout << std::format("X::X({})\n", s);
   }
   ~X(){
      std::cout << std::format("~X::X() for {}\n", s);
   }
};
X glob { "glob" };
void g() {
   X xg{ «g()» };
}
int main() {
   X *p0 = new X{ "p0" };
   [[maybe_unused]] X *p1 = new X{ "p1" }; // will leak
   X xmain{ "main()" };
   g();
   delete p0;
   // oops, forgot delete p1
}
```

When executed, that program will print the following:

```
X::X(glob)
X::X(p0)
X::X(p1)
X::X(main())
X::X(g())
~X::X() for g()
~X::X() for p0
~X::X() for main()
~X::X() for glob
```

The fact that the number of constructors and destructors do not match is a sign that we did something wrong. More specifically, in this example, we manually created an object (pointed to by p1) with operator new but never manually destructed that object afterward.

One common source of confusion for programmers unfamiliar with C++ is the distinction between pointer and pointee. In this program, p0 and p1 are both destructed when reaching the end of their scope (by the closing brace of the main() function), just as xmain will be. However, since p0 and p1 point to dynamically allocated objects, the pointees have to be explicitly destructed, something we did for p0 but (deliberately, for the sake of the example) neglected to do for p1.

What happens to p1's pointee then? Well, it has been manually constructed and has not been manually destructed. As such, it floats in memory where no one can access it anymore. This is what people often call a memory leak: a chunk of memory your program allocated but never deallocated.

Worse than leaking the storage for the X object pointed to by p1, however, is the fact that the pointee's destructor will never be called, which can cause all sorts of resource leaks (files not closed, database connections not closed, system handles not released, and so on). In *Chapter 4, Using Destructors*, we will examine how it is possible to avoid such situations and write clean, simple code at the same time.

Object size, alignment, and padding

Since each object occupies storage, the space associated with an object is an important (if low-level) property of C++ types. For example, look at the following code:

```
class B; // forward declaration: there will be a class B
         // at some point in the future
void f(B*); // fine, we know what B is, even if we don't
            // know the details yet, and all object
            // addresses are of the same size
// class D : B {}; // oops! To know what a D is, we have
                   // to know how big a B is and what a
                   // B object contains since a D is a B
```

In that example, trying to define the D class would not compile. This is because in order to create a D object, the compiler needs to reserve enough space for a D object, but a D object is also a B object, and as such we cannot know the size of a D object without knowing the size of a B object.

The size of an object or, equivalently, of a type can be obtained through the `sizeof` operator. This operator yields a compile-time, non-zero unsigned integral value corresponding to the number of bytes required to store an object:

```
char c;
// a char occupies precisely one byte of storage, per
// standard wording
static_assert(sizeof c == 1); // for objects parentheses
                              // are not required
static_assert(sizeof(c) == 1); // ... but you can use them
static_assert(sizeof(char) == 1); // for types, parentheses
                                  // are required
struct Tiny {};
// all C++ types occupy non-zero bytes of storage by
// definition, even if they are "empty" like type Tiny
static_assert(sizeof(Tiny) > 0);
```

In the preceding example, the `Tiny` class is empty because it has no data member. A class could have member functions and still be empty. Empty classes that expose member functions are very commonly used in C++.

A C++ object always occupies at least one byte of storage, even in the case of empty classes such as `Tiny`. That's because if an object's size was zero, that object could be at the same memory location as its immediate neighbor, which would be somewhat hard to reason about.

C++ differs from many other languages in that it does not standardize the size of all fundamental types. For example, `sizeof(int)` can yield different values depending on the compiler and platform. Still, there are rules concerning the size of objects:

- The size reported by operator `sizeof` for objects of type `signed char`, `unsigned char` and `char` is 1, and the same goes for `sizeof(std::byte)` as each of these types can be used to represent a single byte.

- Expressions `sizeof(short)>=sizeof(char)` and `sizeof(int)>=sizeof(short)` will hold on all platforms, which means that there might be cases where `sizeof(char)` and `sizeof(int)` are both 1. In terms of width (i.e., bits used in the value representation) of fundamental types, the C++ standard limits itself to stating the minimum width for each type. The list can be found at [wg21.link/tab:basic.fundamental.width].

- As we have already said, expression `sizeof(T)>0` holds for any type T. In C++, there are no zero-sized objects, not even objects of empty classes.

- The size occupied by an object of any `struct` or `class` cannot be less than the sum of the size of its data members (but there are caveats).

This last rule deserves an explanation. Consider the following situation:

```
class X {};
class Y {
    X x;
};
int main() {
    static_assert(sizeof(X) > 0);
    static_assert(sizeof(Y) == sizeof(X)); // <-- here
}
```

The line marked `<-- here` might be intriguing. Why would `sizeof(Y)` be equal to `sizeof(X)` if every Y object contains an X object? Remember that `sizeof(X)` is greater than 0 even though X is an empty class because every C++ object has to occupy at least one byte of storage. However, in the case of Y, which is not an empty class, each Y object already occupies storage due to its x data member. There's no reason to somewhat artificially add storage space to objects of that type.

Now, consider this:

```
class X {
    char c;
};
class Y {
    X x;
};
int main() {
    static_assert(sizeof(X) == sizeof(char)); // <-- here
    static_assert(sizeof(Y) == sizeof(X)); // <-- here too
}
```

The same reasoning applies again: an object of type X occupies the same amount of storage space as its only data member (of type `char`), and an object of type Y occupies the same amount of storage space as its only data member (of type X).

Continuing this exploration, consider this :

```
class X { };
class Y {
    X x;
    char c;
};
int main() {
```

```
        static_assert(sizeof(Y) >= sizeof(char) + sizeof(X));
}
```

This is the rule we mentioned earlier but expressed formally for a specific type. In this situation, supposing that `sizeof(X)` being equal to `1` is highly probable, one could even reasonably expect that `sizeof(Y)` would be equal to the sum of `sizeof(char)` and `sizeof(X)`.

Finally, consider this:

```
class X { };
class Y : X { // <--   private inheritance
    char c;
};
int main() {
    static_assert(sizeof(Y) == sizeof(char)); // <-- here
}
```

We moved from having an object of class X being a data member of Y to X being a base class of Y. This has an interesting consequence: since the base class X is empty, and since we know from definition that objects of the derived class Y will occupy at least one byte of storage, the base class can be flattened into the derived class for Y objects. This is a useful optimization called the **empty base optimization**. You can reasonably expect compilers to perform this optimization in practice, at least in the case of single inheritance relationships.

Note that since the presence of an X in a Y is an implementation detail, not something that participates in the interface of class Y, we used private inheritance in this example. The empty base optimization would apply with public or protected inheritance too, but in this case, private inheritance preserves the fact that the X part of a Y is something that only the Y knows about.

Since C++20, if you think composition would be more appropriate than inheritance to describe the relation between two classes such as X and Y, you can mark a data member as `[[no_unique_ address]]` to inform the compiler that this member, if it is an object of an empty class, does not have to occupy storage within the enclosing object. Compilers are not forced to comply, since attributes can be ignored, so make sure to verify that your chosen compilers implement this before writing code that relies on this:

```
class X { };
class Y {
    char c;
    [[no_unique_address]] X x;
};
int main() {
    static_assert(sizeof(X) > 0);
    static_assert(sizeof(Y) == sizeof(char)); // <-- here
}
```

All of the examples so far have been very simple, using classes with zero, one, or two very small data members. Code is rarely so simple. Consider the following program:

```
class X {
    char c; // sizeof(char) == 1 by definition
    short s;
    int n;
};
int main() {
    static_assert(sizeof(short) == 2); // we suppose this...
    static_assert(sizeof(int) == 4);   // ... and this
    static_assert(
        sizeof(X) >= sizeof(char)+sizeof(short)+sizeof(int)
    );
}
```

Supposing that the first two static assertions hold, which is probable but not guaranteed, we know that `sizeof(X)` will be at least 7 (the sum of the sizes of its data members). In practice, however, you will probably see that `sizeof(X)` is equal to 8. Now, this might seem surprising at first, but it's a logical consequence of something called **alignment**.

The alignment of an object (or of its type) tells us where that object can be placed in memory. The `char` type has an alignment of 1, and as such one can place a `char` object literally anywhere (as long as one can access that memory). For an alignment of 2 (which is likely for type `short`), objects can only be placed at addresses that are a multiple of 2. More generally, if a type has an alignment of n, then objects of that type must be placed at an address that is a multiple of n. Note that alignment has to be a strictly positive power of 2; not respecting this rule incurs undefined behavior. Of course, your compiler will not put you in that position, but you might put yourself in such trouble if you're not careful, given some of the tricks we will be using in this book. With great control comes great responsibility.

The C++ language offers two operators related to alignment:

- The `alignof` operator, which yields the natural alignment of a type T or of an object of that type.

- The `alignas` operator, which lets programmers impose the alignment of an object. This is often useful when playing tricks with memory (as we will) or when interfacing with exotic hardware (the term "exotic" here can be taken in a very broad sense). Of course, `alignas` can only reasonably increase the natural alignment of a type, not reduce it.

For some fundamental type T, one can expect the assertion that `sizeof(T)` is equal to `alignof(T)` to hold, but that assertion does not generalize to composite types. For example, consider the following:

```
class X {
    char c;
    short s;
```

```
    int n;
};
int main() {
    static_assert(sizeof(short) == alignof(short));
    static_assert(sizeof(int) == alignof(int));
    static_assert(sizeof(X) == 8); // highly probable
    static_assert(alignof(X) == alignof(int)); // likewise
}
```

Generally speaking, for a composite type, the alignment will correspond to the worst alignment of its data members. Here, "worst" means "biggest." For class X, the worst-aligned data member is n of type int and as such, X objects will be aligned on boundaries of `alignof(int)` bytes.

You might wonder now why we can expect the assertion that `sizeof(X)` is equal to 8 to hold if `sizeof(short)==2` and `sizeof(int)==4`. Let's look at the probable layout for objects of the X type:

Figure 1.1 – Compact layout of an object of type X in memory

Each box in this figure is a byte in memory. As we can see, there's a ? between c and the first byte of s. That comes from alignment. If `alignof(short)==2` and `alignof(int)==4`, then the only correct layout for an X object places its n member at a boundary of 4. This means that there will be a padding byte (a byte that does not participate in the value representation of X) between c and s to align s on a two-byte boundary and to align n on a four-byte boundary.

What might seem more surprising is that the order in which data members are laid out in a class impacts the size of the objects of that class. For example, consider the following:

```
class X {
    short s;
    int n;
    char c;
};
int main() {
    static_assert(sizeof(short) == alignof(short));
    static_assert(sizeof(int) == alignof(int));
    static_assert(alignof(X) == alignof(int));
    static_assert(sizeof(X) == 12); // highly probable
}
```

That often surprises people, but it's true, and something to think about. With this example, the probable layout for an X object would be as follows:

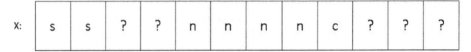

Figure 1.2 – Less compact layout for an object of type X in memory

By now, the two ? "squares" between s and n are probably clear, but the three trailing ? "squares" might seem surprising. After all, why add padding at the end of an object?

The answer is *because of arrays*. As we will soon discuss, elements of an array are contiguous in memory, and for that reason, it is important that each element of an array is properly aligned. In a case such as this, the trailing padding bytes in an object of class X ensure that if an element in an array of X objects is properly aligned, then the next element will be properly aligned too.

Now that you know about alignment, consider that just changing the order of elements from one version of class X to another resulted in a memory consumption increase of 50% for each object of that type. That hurts your program's memory space consumption and its speed all at once. C++ compilers cannot reorder your data members for you, as your code sees the addresses of objects. Changing the relative position of data members could break users' code, so it's up to programmers to be careful with their chosen layouts. Note that keeping objects small is not the only factor that can influence the choice of layout in an object, especially in multithreaded code (where sometimes keeping two objects at a distance from one another can lead to better cache usage), so one should remember that layout is important, but not something to take on naïvely.

Copy and movement

At this point, we need to say a few words about copy and movement, two fundamental considerations in a language such as C++ where there are actual objects.

The C++ language considers six member functions as special. These functions will be automatically generated for your types unless you take steps to prevent it. These are as follows:

- **The default constructor**: It's probably the least special of all six, as it's only implicitly generated if you write no constructor of your own.
- **The destructor**: This is called at the end of an object's lifetime.
- **The copy constructor**: It is called when constructing an object with a single object of the same type as argument.
- **The copy assignment**: It is called when replacing the contents of an existing object with a copy of the contents of another object.

- **The move constructor**: It is called when constructing an object from a reference to an object one can move from. Examples of movable-from objects include objects one could not refer to anymore, such as the (anonymous) result of evaluating an expression or one being returned by a function. The program can also explicitly make an object movable-from with `std::move()`.

- **The move assignment**: It behaves like copy assignment but is applied when the argument passed to the assignment operator is something one can move from.

When a type does not explicitly manage any resources on its own, one can usually write none of these special functions, as the ones generated by the compiler will be exactly what one wants. For example, consider the following:

```
struct Point2D {
    float x{}, y{};
};
```

Here, type `Point2D` represents a 2D coordinate that has no invariants (all values are fine for its `x` and `y` data members). Since we used default initializers for `x` and `y` that set these data members to 0, a default `Point2D` object will represent coordinate `(0,0)` and the six special member functions will behave as expected. The copy constructor will call the data members' copy constructors, the copy assignment will call their copy assignment operators, the destructor will be trivial, and move operations will behave like copy operations since the data members are of fundamental types.

Should we decide to add a parametric constructor to explicitly let user code initialize the `x` and `y` data members to other values than our chosen defaults, we can do so. However, this will cost us our implicit default constructor:

```
struct Point2D {
    float x{}, y{};
    Point2D(float x, float y) : x{ x }, y{ y } {
    }
};
void oops() {
    Point2D pt; // does not compile, pt has no default ctor
}
```

We can of course fix this. One way to do so is by writing the details of a default constructor explicitly:

```
struct Point2D {
    float x, y; // no need for default initializations
    Point2D(float x, float y) : x{ x }, y{ y } {
    }
    Point2D() : x{ }, y{ } { // <-- here
    }
};
```

```
void oops() {
    Point2D pt; // Ok
}
```

Another approach is to delegate work from the default constructor to the parametric constructor:

```
struct Point2D {
    float x, y; // no need for default initializations
    Point2D(float x, float y) : x{ x }, y{ y } {
    }
    Point2D() : Point2D{ 0, 0 } { // <-- here
    }
};
void oops() {
    Point2D pt; // Ok
}
```

Another even better approach is to inform the compiler that we want to retain the default behavior even though we did something (writing another constructor) that would otherwise prevent it:

```
struct Point2D {
    float x{}, y{};
    Point2D(float x, float y) : x{ x }, y{ y } {
    }
    Point2D() = default; // <-- here
};
void oops() {
    Point2D pt; // Ok
}
```

The latter option will usually lead to the best generated code, as compilers are really good at getting maximal results from minimal effort when they understand the programmer's intent. In this case, =default makes the intent very explicit: *please do what you would have done normally if my code had not interfered.*

A note about these constructors

We added parametric constructors to Point2D for the sake of this example, but it's not necessary in this case as Point2D is an aggregate. These types have special initialization support, but that's beside the point for our illustration. Aggregate types are types that comply with several restrictions (no user-declared or inherited constructors, no private non-static data members, no virtual bases classes, and so on) and that usually have no invariants to maintain, but can be initialized very efficiently by your compiler.

When a class explicitly manages resources, the default-generated special functions rarely do what we would want. Indeed, how could the compiler know about our intents in such a situation? Suppose we make a naïve `string`-like class of our own, starting with the following (incomplete) excerpt:

```cpp
#include <cstring> // std::strlen()
#include <algorithm> // std::copy()
class naive_string { // too simple to be useful
    char *p {}; // pointer to the elements (nullptr)
    std::size_t nelems {}; // number of elements (zero)
public:
    std::size_t size() const {
        return nelems;
    }
    bool empty() const {
        return size() == 0;
    }
    naive_string() = default; // empty string
    naive_string(const char *s)
        : nelems{ std::strlen(s) } {
        p = new char[size() + 1]; // leaving room for a
                                  // (convenient) trailing 0
        std::copy(s, s + size(), p);
        p[size()] = '\0';
    }
    // index-wise access to characters, const and non-const
    // versions: the const version is useful for const
    // naive_string objects, whereas the non-const version
    // lets user code modify elements
    // precondition: n < size()
    char operator[](std::size_t n) const { return p[n]; }
    char& operator[](std::size_t n) { return p[n]; }
    // ... additional code (below) goes here
};
```

Naïve as it is, this class clearly does explicit resource allocation by allocating a chunk of `size()+1` bytes to hold a copy of the sequence of characters starting at p. For that reason, the compiler-provided special member functions will not do the right thing for our class. For example, the default-generated copy constructor will copy pointer p, but that means we will have two pointers (the original p and p in the copy) sharing a common pointee, which is probably not what we want. The default-generated destructor will destroy the pointer, but we also want to deallocate the pointee and avoid a memory leak, and so on.

In a case such as this, we want to implement the so-called rule of three and code the destructor as well as the two copy operations (the copy constructor and the copy assignment). Before the arrival of move semantics in C++11, that was sufficient to properly implement resource management for our types. It technically still is today but considering move semantics too will help us get a more efficient type in many ways. In contemporary code, when discussing code that implements the two move operations in addition to the rule of three, we typically speak of the rule of five.

Destruction

As our `naive_string` type does resource management with the dynamically allocated array pointed to by p, the destructor for that class will be simple, as its role will be limited to deallocating the chunk of memory pointed to by p:

```
// ...
    ~naive_string() {
        delete [] p;
    }
// ...
```

Note that there is no need to check that p is non-null (`delete nullptr;` does nothing in C++ and is inherently non-dangerous). Also note that we are using `delete []`, not `delete`, as we allocated the chunk of memory with `new []`, not `new`. The nuances between these operations will be explained in *Chapter 7*.

Copy operations

The copy constructor is the function called when constructing an object of the `naive_string` class with an argument that is another object of that class. For example, consider the following:

```
// ...
void f(naive_string); // pass-by-value
void copy_construction_examples() {
    naive_string s0{ "What a fine day" };
    naive_string s1 = s0; // constructs s1 so this is
                          // copy construction
    naive_string s2(s0); // ...this too
    naive_string s3{ s0 }; // ...and so is this
    f(s0); // likewise because of pass-by-value
    s1 = s0; // this is not a copy construction as s1
             // already exists: this is a copy assignment
}
```

For our `naive_string` class, a correct copy constructor could be written as follows:

```
// ...
    naive_string(const naive_string &other)
        : p{ new char[other.size() + 1] },
          nelems{ other.size() } {
        std::copy(other.p, other.p + other.size(), p);
        p[size()] = '\0';
    }
// ...
```

Copy assignments could be written in numerous ways, but many of them are complicated or just plain dangerous. For example, consider the following example…but do not write your assignment operator like this!:

```
// ...
    // bad copy assignment operator
    naive_string& operator=(const naive_string &other) {
        // first, release the memory held by *this
        delete [] p;
        // then, allocate a new chunk of memory
        p = new char[other.size() + 1]; // <-- note this line
        // copy the contents themselves
        std::copy(other.p, other.p + other.size(), p);
        // adjust the size and add the trailing zero
        nelems = other.size();
        p[size()] = '\0';
        return *this;
    }
// ...
```

Now, this might seem reasonable (if a bit long-winded), but if we look at the line where memory allocation is performed, one has to wonder: what will happen if this fails? Indeed it could. For example, it might fail if the process is running low on available memory and `other.size()` is too much for whatever resources are left. In C++, by default, allocation with `operator new` throws an exception on failure. This would complete the execution of our copy assignment function, leaving `*this` in an incorrect (and dangerous!) state whereby p is non-null and `nelems` is non-zero but p points to what most would call garbage: memory we do not own and whose contents would lead to undefined behavior if used.

We could claim that we can do better and write even more code trying to fix this bug. The recommendation to avoid writing your copy assignment operators like this holds also in this case:

```
// ...
    // another bad copy assignment operator
    naive_string& operator=(const naive_string &other) {
        // first, allocate a new chunk of memory
        char *q = new char[other.size() + 1];
        // then release the memory held by *this and make
        // p point to the new chunk
        delete [] p; // <-- pay attention to this line
        p = q;
        // copy the contents themselves
        std::copy(other.p, other.p + other.size(), p);
        // adjust the size and add the trailing zero
        nelems = other.size();
        p[size()] = '\0';
        return *this;
    }
// ...
```

This looks safer on the surface, as we do not try to clean up the existing state of *this until we are sure that the allocation has worked. It might even pass most of your tests – until someone crafts the following test:

```
void test_self_assignment() {
    naive_string s0 { "This is not going to end well..." };
    s0 = s0; // oops!
}
```

With this use case, our copy assignment will behave very badly. After allocating a properly sized chunk of memory pointed to by q, it will delete what p points to. Unfortunately, this also happens to be what other.p points to, destroying the actual source data we are aiming to copy from. What follows that step reads from memory we do not own anymore, and the program stops making sense.

We can still try to patch this, and even make it work, but beware:

```
// ...
    // this works, but it's getting complicated and
    // is a sign we're doing something wrong
    naive_string& operator=(const naive_string &other) {
        // prevent self-assignment
        if(this == &other) return *this;
        // then, do that sequence of steps
```

```
    char *q = new char[other.size() + 1];
    delete [] p; // <-- pay attention to this line
    p = q;
    std::copy(other.p, other.p + other.size(), p);
    nelems = other.size();
    p[size()] = '\0';
    return *this;
}
// ...
```

This fix is a pessimization, since we will be making every copy assignment call pay for that `if` branch that, in practice, should almost never be used. Brute-force problem-solving led us to complicated code that works (though it's not necessarily self-evident) and that will need to be reconsidered with every resource-managing class we write.

> **About the word pessimization**
>
> The word *pessimization* is generally used as the opposite of *optimization*, referring to a programming maneuver or technique that makes program behavior less efficient than it should be. The preceding case is a well-known example of such a maneuver: everyone will pay for the potential branch introduced by the `if` statement even though it's only required for rare and degenerate cases – things that should not happen.
>
> When faced with a "pessimization" opportunity, it's often worth it to take a step back and reconsider. Maybe we've been taking the wrong angle when approaching the problem.

Luckily, there is a well-known idiom in C++ called the **safe assignment idiom**, colloquially known as copy-and-swap. The trick is to recognize that the assignment is made of two parts: a destructive part that cleans up the existing state owned by the destination object (the left side of the assignment) and a constructive part that copies the state from a source object (right side of the assignment) to the destination object. The destructive part is generally equivalent to the code found in the type's destructor, and the constructive part is generally equivalent to the code found in the type's copy constructor.

The informal copy-and-swap name for that technique comes from the fact that it is usually implemented through a combination of the type's copy constructor, its destructor, and a `swap()` member function that swaps member variables one by one:

```
// ...
    void swap(naive_string &other) noexcept {
        using std::swap; // make the standard swap function
                         // available
        swap(p, other.p); // swap data members
        swap(nelems, other.nelems);
    }
```

```
    // idiomatic copy assignment
    naive_string& operator=(const naive_string &other) {
        naive_string { other }.swap(*this); // <-- here
        return *this; // yes, that's it!
    }
// ...
```

That idiom is extremely useful to know and use as it's exception-safe, simple, and works for almost all types. The line that does all the work performs three steps:

- First, it constructs an anonymous copy of other using that type's copy constructor. Now, that might fail if an exception is thrown, but if it does, *this has not been modified and thus remains uncorrupted.

- Second, it swaps that anonymous temporary's contents (holding what we want to put in *this) with the destination object's contents (putting the now-unneeded state in that anonymous temporary object).

- Finally, the anonymous temporary object is destroyed at the end of the expression (being anonymous), leaving *this holding a copy of the state of other.

This idiom even works safely for self-assignment. It incurs an unneeded copy, but it trades an if branch that every call would have paid but almost none would have benefitted from for a copy that will rarely be useless.

You might notice noexcept preceding the opening brace of the swap() member function. We will return to this later, but for now, the important point is that we can claim that this function (swapping objects of fundamental types as it does) will never throw an exception. This information will help us achieve some precious optimizations later in this book.

Move operations

Our naive_string, which is augmented by its destructor, copy constructor, and copy assignment member functions, now manages resources appropriately. It could, however, be made faster, and sometimes even safer.

Consider the following non-member string concatenation operator that someone could want to add to complement our class:

```
// returns the concatenation of s0 and s1
naive_string operator+(naive_string s0, naive_string s1);
```

An operation like this could be used in user code such as the following:

```
naive_string make_message(naive_string name) {
    naive_string s0{ "Hello " },
                 s1{ "!" };
    return s0 + name + s1; // <-- note this line
}
```

The expression that follows the `return` statement first performs a call to `operator+()` and creates an unnamed `naive_string` object from the concatenation of `s0` and name. Then, that unnamed object is passed as the first argument to another call to `operator+()` that yields another unnamed object created from the concatenation of the first unnamed object and `s1`. With our current implementation, each unnamed object incurs an allocation, a copy of the data held in its buffer, a destruction, and more. It's more costly than it looks at first glance and is made even worse by the fact that each allocation could throw an exception.

Still, it works.

Since C++11, we can make such code significantly more efficient through move semantics. In addition to the traditional rule of three functions we just discussed, one can augment a class such as `naive_string` with a move constructor and a move assignment operator. These will kick in implicitly when the compiler operates on objects it knows will not be used anymore. Consider the following:

```
// ...
    return s0 + name + s1;
// ...
```

This translates to the following:

```
// ...
    return (s0 + name) + s1;
//          ^^^^^^^^^^^ <-- anonymous object (we cannot
/                               refer to it afterward)
// ...
```

It then translates to the following:

```
// ...
    ((s0 + name) + s1);
// ^^^^^^^^^^^^^^^^^^^^ <-- anonymous object (idem)
// ...
```

When one thinks about it, the reason for copy operations is to keep the source object intact in case we need it later. Temporary objects that have no name do not need to be preserved from further modifications as they cannot be referred to later. For that reason, we can be more aggressive with these and essentially move their contents instead of copying them. The rule we are asked to follow by the standard is to leave the moved-from object in a valid-yet-indeterminate state. Essentially, the moved-from object has to be in such a state that it can be safely destroyed or assigned to, and its invariants should still hold. In practice, that often amounts to leaving the moved-from object in something equivalent to its default state.

For our `naive_string` type, a move constructor could look like this:

```
// ...
   naive_string(naive_string &&other) noexcept
      : p{ std::move(other.p) },
        nelems{ std::move(other.nelems) } {
      other.p = nullptr;
      other.nelems = 0;
   }
// ...
```

The calls to `std::move()` in this specific case could be avoided (moving objects of fundamental types is equivalent to copying them), but it's probably more hygienic to make sure that the intent to move those objects is inscribed explicitly in the source code. We'll look cursorily at `std::move()` later in this section, but the important thing to remember is that `std::move()` does not move anything. It marks an object as movable in the eyes of the compiler. In other words, *it's a cast*.

The important things to note with our move constructor are as follows:

- The argument is of type `naive_string&&`. This means it is a reference to an `rvalue`, with `rvalue` itself informally meaning "something one could find on the right side of an assignment operator."

- Like `swap()`, it is marked `noexcept` to express the fact that no exception will be thrown during its execution.

- It's effectively transferring state from the source object, `other`, to the object under construction, `*this`. After the completion of this transfer, we leave `other` in a valid state (equivalent to what we would have with a default `naive_string` object), respecting the standard's recommendation.

One could write this function in a slightly terser manner with a small but quite useful function found in the `<utility>` header and named `std::exchange()`. Indeed, consider the following expression:

```
a = std::exchange(b, c);
```

This expression means "assign to a the value of b but replace the value of b with the value of c." This is a very common sequence of operations in real code. With this function, our move constructor becomes the following:

```
// ...
    naive_string(naive_string &&other) noexcept
        : p{ std::exchange(other.p, nullptr) },
          nelems{ std::exchange(other.nelems, 0) } {
    }
// ...
```

That form is idiomatic C++ and can lead to some interesting optimizations in some circumstances.

What about the move assignment? Well, we can take note of the idiomatic copy assignment we discussed at some length earlier and express it as follows:

```
// idiomatic copy assignment
naive_string& operator=(naive_string &&other) noexcept {
    naive_string { std::move(other) }.swap(*this);
    return *this;
}
```

Following the path set by our copy assignment operator, we expressed the move assignment operator as a combination of swap(), a destructor, and a move constructor. The general logic behind both idioms is the same.

Arrays

We have used arrays in our preceding examples, but we have not really provided a formal definition for that useful-yet-low-level construct. Note that in this section, the term "array" refers to raw, built-in arrays, not to other very useful but higher-level constructs such as std::vector<T> or std::array<T,N>.

Quite simply, in C++, an array is a contiguous sequence of elements of the same type. Thus, in the following excerpt, the a0 object occupies 10*sizeof(int) bytes in memory, whereas the a1 object occupies 20*sizeof(std::string) bytes:

```
int a0[10];
std::string a1[20];
```

The number of bytes between elements at indices i and i+1 in an array of some type T is precisely equal to sizeof(T).

Consider the following expression, which would be used in C++, as in C, for some array arr:

```
arr[i]
```

It evaluates to the same address as the following:

```
*(arr + i)
```

Since pointer arithmetic is typed, the + i part in this expression means "plus i elements" or "plus i times the size of an element in bytes."

Array sizes are positive but cannot be 0 unless the array is dynamically allocated:

```
int a0[5]; // Ok
static_assert(sizeof a0 == 5 * sizeof(int));
enum { N = sizeof a0 / sizeof a0[0] }; // N == 5
// int a1[0]; // not allowed: the array would be at the
               // same address as the next object in memory!
int *p0 = new int[5]; // Ok, but you have to manage the
                       // pointee now
int *p1 = new int[0]; // Ok, dynamically allocated; you
                       // still have to manage the pointee
// ...
delete [] p1; // good
delete [] p0; // good; be responsible
```

Each call to `operator new[]` has to yield a different address, even if the array's size is 0. Each call technically returns the address of a different object.

Summary

In this chapter, we took a look at fundamental ideas of the C++ language such as: what is an object? What are pointers and references? What do we mean when we talk about the size and alignment of an object or of a type? Why are there no zero-size objects in C++? What are the special members of a class and when do we need to write them explicitly? This non-exhaustive list of topics gave us a common vocabulary from which to build what you, dear reader, will find in the chapters to come.

With this, we are ready to get our hands dirty, so to speak. We have given ourselves a set of low-level tools and ideas from which to build higher-level abstractions, but we have to give ourselves some measure of discipline.

The next chapter will discuss some things we need to avoid. Those include undefined behavior, implementation-defined behavior (to a lesser extent), ill-formed no-diagnostic-required code, buffer overflows, and other unrecommendable behaviors.

Then, we will follow with a chapter describing C++ casts, and how they can help us express clear ideas even when we feel the need to eschew some of the rules set out for us by the language's type system.

After that, we will start to build beautiful and powerful abstractions that will help us with our stated goal of safely and efficiently managing resources in general and managing memory in particular.

2

Things to Be Careful With

So, you decided to read a book about memory management in C++ and are as ready to look at the high-level approaches and techniques as you are willing to "get your hands dirty", so to speak, in order to get fine-grained control over the memory management process. What an excellent plan!

Since you know that you are going to be writing very high-level code, but also very low-level code, there are a few things we need to make sure you are aware of such that you do not get in trouble or write code that seems to work but does not, at least not portably.

In this chapter, we will point out some aspects of C++ programming that will come into play throughout this book, but that you should be careful with. This might look like a (very) small compendium of bad practices or an encouragement to get in trouble, but please consider what follows as ways to use somewhat dangerous or tricky features well. You're using C++, you have significant freedom of expression, and you get access to features that are useful if you know and understand them well.

We want code that's clean and efficient, and we want responsible programmers. Let's try to get there together.

In this chapter, we will learn about the following:

- We will cover some of the ways in which one can get into trouble with C++ code. Indeed, there are things a compiler cannot reliably diagnose, just as there are things for which the C++ standard does not say what will happen, and writing code that does such things is a recipe for disaster – or at the very least surprising or non-portable behavior.

- In particular, we will explore how one can get in trouble with pointers. Since this book discusses memory management, we will use pointers and pointer arithmetic quite often, and being able to distinguish appropriate uses thereof from inappropriate ones will be valuable.

- Finally, we will discuss what kinds of type conversions we can do without resorting to type casts (the main subject of *Chapter 3*), and how rarely that's a good idea, contrary to popular belief.

Our overall goal will be to learn things we should not do (even though we will do some maneuvers that resemble them, on occasion), and avoid them thereafter, hopefully understanding why we do so. With that out of the way, we'll have many chapters to look at things we *should* do, and how to do them well!

Different kinds of evil

Before delving into some actual practices that require care, it's interesting to look at the main categories of risks we could run into if our code does not respect the rules of the language. With each such category comes a form of unpleasantness we should strive to avoid.

Ill-formed, no diagnostic required

Some constructs in C++ are said to be **Ill-Formed, No Diagnostic Required (IFNDR)**. Indeed, you will find quite a few occurrences in the standard of *"if [...], the program is ill-formed, with no diagnostic required."* When something is IFNDR, it means your program is broken. Bad things could happen, but the compiler is not required to tell you about them (indeed, sometimes, the compiler does not have sufficient information to diagnose the problematic situation).

One Definition Rule (ODR) violations, to which we will return in the *The ODR* section later in this chapter, fall under IFNDR. However, there are other such cases, such as having a global object that has different alignment requirements (through `alignas`) in different translation units (different source files, essentially), or having a constructor that delegates to itself either directly or indirectly. Here is an example:

```
class X {
public:
    // #0 delegates to #1 which delegates to #0 which...
    X(float x) : X{ static_cast<int>(x) } { // #0
    }
    X(int n) : X{ n + 0.5f } { // #1
    }
};
int main() {}
```

Note that your compiler might give a diagnostic; it's just not required to do so. It's not that compilers are lazy – they might even be unable to provide a diagnostic in some cases! So, be careful not to write code that leads to IFNDR situations.

Undefined behavior

We mentioned **Undefined Behavior (UB)** in *Chapter 1*. UB is often seen as a source of headaches and pain for C++ programmers but it refers to any behavior for which the C++ standard imposes no requirement. In practice, this means that if you write code that contains UB, you have no idea what's going to happen at runtime (at least if you're aiming for somewhat portable code). Canonical examples of UB include dereferencing a null pointer or an uninitialized pointer: do that and you'll be in serious trouble.

To compilers, UB is not supposed to happen (code that respects the rules of the language does not contain UB, after all). For that reason, compilers "optimize around" code that contains UB, to sometimes surprising effect: they might begin removing tests and branches, optimizing loops away, and so on.

The effects of UB tend to be local. For instance, in the following example, there is a test that ensures that p is not null before using *p in one case, but there is at least one access to *p that is unchecked. This code is broken (the unchecked access to *p is UB), so the compiler is allowed to rewrite it in such a way that all tests to verify that p is not null are effectively removed. After all, the damage would be done if p were nullptr, so the compiler is entitled to assume that the programmer passed a non-null pointer to the function!

```
int g(int);
int f(int *p) {
    if(p != nullptr)
        return g(*p); // Ok, we know p is not null
    return *p; // oops, if p == nullptr this is UB
}
```

The whole body of f() could legitimately be rewritten by your compiler as return g(*p) in this case, with the return *p statement being turned into unreachable code.

The potential for UB hides in various places in the language, including signed integer overflow, accessing an array out of bounds, data races, and so on. There are ongoing efforts to reduce the number of potential UB cases (there's even a study group, **SG12**, dedicated to this effort), but UB will likely remain part of the language for the foreseeable future, and we need to be aware of it.

Implementation-defined behavior

Some parts of the standard fall under the umbrella of **implementation-defined behavior**, or behavior that you can count on with a specific platform. This is behavior that your platform of choice is supposed to document, but that is not guaranteed to be portable to other platforms.

Implementation-defined behavior occurs in many situations and includes such things as implementation-defined limits: the maximum number of nested parentheses; the maximum number of case labels in a switch statement; the actual size of an object; the maximum number of recursive calls in a constexpr function; the number of bits in a byte; and so on. Other well-known cases of implementation-defined behavior include the number of bytes in an int object or whether the char type is a signed or an unsigned integral type.

Implementation-defined behavior is not really a source of evil, but it can be problematic if one strives for portable code but depends on some non-portable assumptions. It is sometimes useful to spell one's assumptions in code through static_assert when the assumption can be validated at compile-time or some similar, potentially runtime mechanisms in order to realize—before it's too late—that these assumptions are broken for a given target platform.

For example:

```
int main() {
    // our code supposes int is four bytes wide, a non-
    // portable assumption
    static_assert(sizeof(int)==4);
    // only compiles if condition is true...
}
```

Unless you are convinced that your code will never need to be ported to another platform, strive to rely as little as possible on implementation-defined behavior, and if you do, make sure that you validate (through `static_assert` if possible, at runtime if there's no other choice) and document this situation. It might help you avoid some nasty surprises in the future.

Unspecified behavior (not documented)

Where implementation-defined behavior is non-portable but documented for a given platform, unspecified behavior is a behavior that, even for a well-formed program given correct data, behaves in a way that depends on the implementation but does not need to be documented.

Some cases of unspecified behavior include the state of a moved-from object (said to be **valid but unspecified**, thus more of an unspecified state than an unspecified behavior), the order of evaluation of subexpressions in a function call, that is, whether `f(g(),h())` will evaluate `g()` or `h()` first, the values in a newly allocated chunk of memory, and so on. This latter example is interesting to our study; a debug build might fill newly allocated chunks of memory with a recognizable bit pattern to help in the debugging process, and an optimized build with the same toolset could leave the initial bits of a newly allocated chunk of memory "uninitialized", with the bits it held at the time when the allocation was performed, to get speed improvements.

The ODR

The ODR, simply summarized, states that there shall be only one definition of each "thing" (function, object in a scope, enumeration, template, and so on) in a translation unit, although there can be multiple declarations of that thing. Consider the following example:

```
int f(int); // declaration
int f(int n); // Ok, declaration again
int f(int m) { return m; } // Ok, definition
// int f(int) { return 3; } // not Ok (ODR violation)
```

In C++, avoiding ODR violations is important, as these "evils" can escape the compiler's scrutiny and fall into the realm of IFNDR situations. For example, due to the separate compilation of source files, a header file containing the definition of a non-`inline` function will lead to that definition being replicated in each source file that includes that same header. Then, each compilation might succeed, and the fact that there are multiple definitions of that function in the same build might be detected later (at link time) or just left undetected and cause havoc.

Erroneous behavior

Ongoing security-related efforts in C++ have led to discussions on a new kind of "evil" tentatively named *erroneous behavior*. This new category is meant to cover situations that could have been UB in the past, but for which we could issue diagnostics and provide well-defined behavior. The behavior would still be incorrect, but erroneous behavior would, in a way, provide boundaries to the consequences. Note that work on erroneous behavior is ongoing as of this writing, and this new wording feature might target C++26.

One use case envisioned for erroneous behavior is reading from an uninitialized variable, where the implementation could (for safety reasons) provide a fixed value for the bits read, and the conceptual error that stems from reading that variable would be something that implementations are encouraged to diagnose. Another use case would be forgetting to return a value from a non-void assignment operator.

Now that we've looked at the large "families" of unpleasantness that might hit our programs if we don't behave, let's delve into some of the main facilities that could get us in trouble and see what we should avoid doing.

Pointers

Chapter 1 looked at pointers in C++ in the sense of what they represent and what they mean. It described what pointer arithmetic is, and what it allows us to do. We will now examine practical uses of pointer arithmetic, with both proper and improper uses of this low-level (but sometimes precious) tool.

Uses of pointer arithmetic within an array

Pointer arithmetic is a nice and useful tool, but it's a sharp one that tends to be misused. With raw arrays, the following two loops, labeled A and B, behave in exactly the same way:

```
void f(int);
int main() {
    int vals[]{ 2,3,5,7,11 };
    enum { N = sizeof vals / sizeof vals[0] };
    for(int i = 0; i != N; ++i) // A
      f(vals[i]);
```

```
        for(int *p = vals; p != vals + N; ++p) // B
            f(*p);
}
```

You might wonder about the vals + N part in loop B, but it's valid (and idiomatic) C++ code. You can observe the pointer just past the end of an array, even though you're not allowed to observe what it points to; the standard guarantees that this specific one-past-the-end address is accessible to your program. However, no such guarantee is provided for the following address, so be careful!

As long as you respect the rules, you can use pointers to jump back and forth within an array. If you overreach and use a pointer to go further than one past-the-end, you will end up in UB territory; that is, you might be trying to access an address that's not in your process' address space:

```
int arr[10]{ }; // all elements initialized to zero
int *p = &arr[3];
p += 4; assert(p == &arr[7]);
--p;    assert(p == &arr[6]);
p += 4; // still Ok as long as you don't try to access *p
++p; // UB, not guaranteed to be valid
```

Pointer interconvertibility

The C++ standard defines what it means for an object to be **pointer-interconvertible** with another. Pointer-interconvertibility means that one can use a pointer to one as a pointer to the other, normally through reinterpret_cast (we will expand on this in *Chapter 3*), as they have the same address. Broadly speaking, the following points hold true:

- An object is pointer-interconvertible with itself

- A union is pointer-interconvertible with its data members, as well as their first data member if they are compound types

- With some restrictions, x and y are pointer-interconvertible with one another if one is an object and the other one is of the same type as the first non-static data member of that object

Some examples are included here:

```
struct X { int n; };
struct Y : X {};
union U { X x; short s; };
int main() {
    X x;
    Y y;
    U u;
    // x is pointer-interconvertible with x
```

```
    // u is pointer-interconvertible with u.x
    // u is pointer-interconvertible with u.s
    // y is pointer-interconvertible with y.x
}
```

If you try to apply `reinterpret_cast` in a way that does not respect pointer-interconvertibility rules, your code is technically incorrect and is not guaranteed to work in practice. Don't do that.

We will occasionally use the pointer-interconvertibility property in our code examples, including in the next section.

Uses of pointer arithmetic within an object

Pointer arithmetic within an object is also allowed in C++, although one should be careful about how this is handled (using the appropriate casts, which we will explore in *Chapter 3*, and ensuring that one performs pointer arithmetic appropriately).

For example, the following code is correct, albeit not something one should seek to do (it makes no sense, and it does things in unnecessarily complicated ways, but it's legal and does no harm):

```
struct A {
    int a;
    short s;
};
short * f(A &a) {
    // pointer interconvertibility in action!
    int *p = reinterpret_cast<int*>(&a);
    p++;
    return reinterpret_cast<short*>(p); // Ok, within the
                                        // same object
}
int main() {
    A a;
    short *p = f(a);
    *p = 3; // fine, technically
}
```

We will not abuse this aspect of the C++ language in this book, but we do need to be aware of it in order to write correct, low-level code.

> **About the difference between pointer and address**
>
> In order to strengthen hardware and software security, there has been work on hardware architectures that can provide a form of "pointer tagging", which allows the hardware tracking of pointer provenance, among other things. Two well-known examples are the CHERI architecture (`https://packt.link/cJeLo`) and **Memory Tagging Extensions (MTEs)** (Linux: `https://packt.link/KXeRn` | Android: `https://packt.link/JDfEo`, and `https://packt.link/fQM2T`| Windows: `https://packt.link/DgSaH`).
>
> To benefit from such hardware, the language needs to distinguish between the low-level idea of addresses and the high-level idea of pointers, as the latter could take into account the fact that a pointer is more than just a memory location. If your code absolutely needs to compare unrelated pointers for ordering, one thing you can do is cast the pointers to `std::intprt_t` or to `std::uintptr_t` and compare the (numeric) results instead of comparing the actual pointers. Note that compiler support for those two types is optional, although all major compiler vendors offer it.

The null pointer

The idea of a null pointer as a recognizable value for pointers that lead to nowhere valid can be traced back to C.A.R. Hoare (`https://packt.link/ByfeX`). In the C language, through the `NULL` macro, it has been represented first as a `char*` of value 0, then as a `void*` of value 0, then in C++ as value 0 simply since such things as `int *p = NULL;` with a typed `NULL` were legal C but not legal C++. This is because the type system is stricter in C++. Note that a pointer with value 0 does not mean "point to address zero" as this address is in itself perfectly valid and is used as such on many platforms.

In C++, the preferred way of expressing a null pointer is `nullptr`, an object of the `std::nullptr_t` type that converts to pointers of any type and behaves as expected. This solves some longstanding issues with literal 0 in C++, such as the following:

```
int f(int); //#0
int f(char*); // #1
int main() {
    int n = 3;
    char c;
    f(n); // calls #0
    f(&c); // calls #1
    f(0); // ambiguous before C++11, calls #0 since
    f(nullptr); // only since C++11; unambiguously calls #1
}
```

Note that `nullptr` is not a pointer; it's an object that implicitly converts to a pointer. For that reason, the `std::is_pointer_v<nullptr>` trait is false, and C++ offers a distinct trait named `std::is_null_pointer<T>` to statically test whether T is a `std::nullptr_t` or not (taking `const` and `volatile` into account).

Dereferencing a null pointer is UB, just as dereferencing an uninitialized pointer is. The point of using `nullptr` in your code is to make that state recognizable: `nullptr` is a distinguishable value, whereas an uninitialized pointer could be anything.

In C++ (contrary to C), arithmetic on a null pointer is well-defined... as long as you add zero to the null pointer. Or, to put it differently: if you add zero to a null pointer, the code remains well-defined, but if you add anything else, you're on your own. There's an explicit provision to that effect in `wg21.link/c++draft/expr.add#4.1`. This means that the following is correct as in the case of an empty `Array`, `begin()` yields `nullptr` and `size()` yields zero, so `end()` effectively computes `nullptr+0`, which respects the rules:

```
template <class T> class Array {
    T *elems = nullptr; // pointer to the beginning
    std::size_t nelems = 0; // number of elements
public:
    Array() = default; // =empty array
    // ...
    auto size() const noexcept { return nelems; }
    // note: could return nullptr
    auto begin() noexcept { return elems; }
    auto end() noexcept { return begin() + size(); }
};
```

We will return to this `Array` example in more detail in *Chapters 12, 13*, and *14*; it will help us discuss several important aspects of efficient memory management techniques. For now, let's look at another source of risky programming maneuvers.

Type punning

Another area where a C++ programmer can get into trouble is **type punning**. By type punning, we mean techniques that subvert the language's type system somewhat. The consecrated tool to perform type conversions is casts, as they are explicit in source code text and (apart from C-style casts) express the intent for the conversion, but that topic deserves its own chapter (*Chapter 3*, if you're wondering).

In this section, we will examine other ways to achieve type punning, including both recommendable ones and others that you should seek to avoid.

Type punning through members of a union

A union is a type for which the members are all at the same address. The size of a union is the size of its largest member, and the alignment of a union is the strictest alignment of its members.

Consider the following example:

```
struct X {
    char c[5]; short s;
} x;
// one byte of padding between x.c and x.s
static_assert(sizeof x.s == 2 && sizeof x == 8);
static_assert(alignof(x) == alignof(short));
union U {
    int n; X x;
} u;
static_assert(sizeof u == sizeof u.x);
static_assert(alignof(u) == alignof(u.n));
int main() {}
```

It's tempting to think that one can use a union to implicitly convert such things as a four-byte floating point number into a four-byte integral number, and in the C language (not C++), that is indeed possible.

Even though there is a widespread belief that this practice is legal in C++, the reality is that it is not (with one special caveat, which we will explore shortly). Indeed, in C++, the last member of a union one has written to is called the union's **active member**, and that member is the only one your code is allowed to read from. Thus, the following code is illegal since reading from a non-active member of a union is UB, and UB is not allowed in a constexpr function:

```
union U {
    float f;
    int n;
};
constexpr int f() {
    U u{ 1.5f };
    return u.n; // UB (u.f is the active member)
}
int main() {
    // constexpr auto r0 = f(); // would not compile
    auto r1 = f(); // compiles, as not a constexpr
                   // context, but still UB
}
```

As you might know, a constexpr function such as f() in the preceding example cannot contain code that is UB if it is called in a constexpr context. This sometimes makes it an interesting tool to make a point.

There is a caveat with respect to conversions between union members, and that caveat is associated with the common initial sequence.

Common initial sequence

As explained at wg21.link/class.mem.general#23, the **common initial sequence** of two structs is made of the initial members of these two structs that have corresponding layout-compatible types. For example, the common initial sequence of A and B is made of their first two members (int is layout-compatible with const int and float is layout-compatible with volatile float):

```
struct A { int n; float f; char c; };
struct B{ const int b0; volatile float x; };
```

With a union, it is possible to read from a non-active member if the value read is part of both the common initial sequence of that member and of the active member. Here's an example:

```
struct A { int n0; char c0; };
struct B { int n1; char c1; float x; };
union U {
    A a;
    B b;
};
int f() {
    U u{ { 1, '2' } }; // initializes u.a
    return u.b.n1; // not UB
}
int main() {
    return f(); // Ok
}
```

Note that such type punning should be kept to a minimum, as it can make it harder to reason about source code, but it can be quite useful. For example, it can be used to implement some interesting underlying representations for classes that can have two distinct representations (classes such as optional or string), making it easier to switch from one to the other. Some useful optimizations can be built on this.

The intptr_t and uintptr_t types

As mentioned earlier in this chapter, one cannot directly compare pointers to arbitrary locations in memory in a well-defined manner in C++. One can, however, compare the integral values associated with pointers in a well-defined manner, such as here:

```
#include <iostream>
#include <cstdint>
int main() {
    using namespace std;
    int m,
```

```
        n;
    // simply comparing &m with &n is not allowed
    if(reinterpret_cast<intptr_t>(&m) <
        reinterpret_cast<intptr_t>(&n))
        cout << "m precedes n in address order\n";
    else
        cout << "n precedes m in address order\n";
}
```

The std::intptr_t and std::uintptr_t types are aliases for integral types that are large enough to hold an address. Use the signed type, intptr_t, for operations that could lead to negative values (for example, subtraction).

The std::memcpy() function

For historical (and C compatibility) reasons, std::memcpy() is *special* as it can start the lifetime of an object if used appropriately. An incorrect use of std::memcpy() for type punning would be as follows:

```
// suppose this holds for this example
static_assert(sizeof(int) == sizeof(float));
#include <cassert>
#include <cstdlib>
#include <cstring>
int main() {
    float f = 1.5f;
    void *p = malloc(sizeof f);
    assert(p);
    int *q = std::memcpy(p, &f, sizeof f);
    int value = *q; // UB
    //
}
```

The reason why this is illegal is that the call to std::memcpy() copies a float object into the storage pointed to by p, effectively starting the lifetime of a float object in that storage. Since q is an int*, dereferencing it is UB.

On the other hand, the following is legal and shows how std::memcpy() can be used for type punning:

```
// suppose this holds for this example
static_assert(sizeof(int) == sizeof(float));
#include <cassert>
#include <cstring>
int main() {
```

```
    float f = 1.5f;
    int value;
    std::memcpy(&value, &f, sizeof f); // Ok
    // ...
}
```

Indeed, in this second example, using `std::memcpy()` to copy the bits from `f` to `value` starts the lifetime of `value`. That object can be used as any other `int` from that point on.

The special cases of char*, unsigned char*, and std::byte*

The `char*`, `unsigned char*` (not `signed char*`), and `std::byte*` types have special status in C++ as they can literally point anywhere and alias anything (`wg21.link/basic.lval#11`). For that reason, if you need to access the underlying bytes of the value representation of an object, these types are an important tool in your toolbox.

We will, later in this book, occasionally resort to these types to perform low-level byte manipulation. Note that such maneuvers are inherently fragile and non-portable, as such details as the order of bytes in an integer can vary from platform to platform. Use such low-level facilities with care.

The std::start_lifetime_as<T>() function

One last set of facilities for this chapter is `std::start_lifetime_as<T>()` and `std::start_lifetime_as_array<T>()`. These functions have been discussed for years but came into their own with C++23. Their role is to take as arguments something such as a buffer of raw memory bytes and return a pointer to some `T` (pointing to that buffer) whose lifetime has started, such that the pointee can be used as such from that point on:

```
static_assert(sizeof(short) == 2);
#include <memory>
int main() {
    char buf[]{ 0x00, 0x01, 0x02, 0x03 };
    short* p = std::start_lifetime_as<short>(buf);
    // use *p as a short
}
```

This is, again, a low-level feature to be used with care. The intent here is to be able to implement such things as low-level file I/O and networking code (for example, receiving a UDP packet and treating its value representation as if it were an existing object) in pure C++ without falling into a UB trap. We will discuss these functions in more detail in *Chapter 15*.

Summary

This chapter explored some low-level and sometimes unpleasant facilities that we will sometimes use, in order to put up the proper "warning signs" and remind us that we have to be responsible and write sensible and correct code even though our language of choice gives significant freedom.

When writing advanced memory management facilities in the later chapters of this book, these dangerous facilities will sometimes be useful to us. Inspired by the contents of this chapter on things to be careful with, we will resort to these facilities sparingly, carefully, and in ways that make them hard to misuse.

In our next chapter, we will examine the key C++ casts put at our disposal; the intent is to make us aware of what each cast does, as well as when (and to what end) it should be used, such that we can thereafter build the powerful memory management abstractions we want to use.

3

Casts and cv-qualifications

We are progressing. In *Chapter 1*, we looked at what memory, objects, and pointers are, as we know we will need to understand these basic ideas if we are to take control of memory management mechanisms. Then, in *Chapter 2*, we looked at some low-level constructs that could get us in trouble if misused are essential to understand in certain situations to take control of how our programs manage memory. That's a somewhat dry way to start, but that also means the fun parts of our work are still to come. I hope that's encouraging!

At the end of *Chapter 2*, we examined approaches to type punning, a way to subvert the type system, including some that are believed to work by some but actually do not. C++ offers a number of controlled and explicit ways to interact with the type system, informing the compiler that it should see the type of an expression as something different than what it can otherwise infer from the source code. These tools, the **type casts** (or simply *casts*), are the subject of this chapter.

We will first examine what casts are in the general sense, distinguishing the various fundamental reasons to perform casts and showing why C-style casts are mostly inappropriate (except for some specific cases) in a C++ program. Then, we will take a quick look at a safety-related aspect of the C++ system, **cv-qualifications**, and discuss the role of cv-qualifiers in the hygiene and overall quality of C++ code. After that, we will examine the six C++ casts at our disposal. Finally, we will return to the C casts to show the limited situations in which they might still be appropriate.

In this chapter, we will learn the following:

- What casts are and what they mean in a program
- What cv-qualifications are and how they interact with casts
- What C++ casts are, including the C cast, and when they should be used

Technical requirements

You can find the code files for this chapter in the book's GitHub repository here: https://github.com/PacktPublishing/C-Plus-Plus-Memory-Management/tree/main/chapter3.

What is a cast?

You will use a cast to adjust the compiler's view on the type of an expression. The thing is, the compiler sees our source code and understands what we wrote and what other people's code expresses. Most of the time (hopefully), this code will make sense, and the compiler will translate your sources into proper binaries without complaining.

Sometimes, of course, there will be (hopefully temporary) discrepancies between programmer intent and code, as expressed through the sources seen by the compiler. Most of the time, the compiler will be right, and the programmer will rewrite the source code, at least in part, in order to better express the intent, inspired by the error or warning messages that revealed (in their own poetic way) a problem. Sometimes, of course, the source code matches the programmer's intent, but there are still disagreements with the compiler and adjustments required to attain some agreement with it. For example, suppose a programmer wants to allocate a buffer large enough to store `lots` of integers (`lots` being a value that's either too large to reasonably use the stack or one that's not known at compile time); one (low-level and error-prone but legal nonetheless) way to achieve this would be to call the `std::malloc()` function:

```
// ...
int *p = std::malloc(lots * sizeof(int)); // <-- HERE
if(p) {
    // use p as an array of int objects
    std::free(p);
}
// ...
```

This code excerpt, as you might know, is not valid C++ – `std::malloc()` returns `void*` (a pointer to a chunk of raw memory of at least the requested size, or `nullptr` if the allocation failed), and `void*` is not implicitly convertible to `int*` in C++ (the reverse is, of course, true – `int*` is indeed implicitly convertible to `void*`).

Note that we could have replaced `std::malloc(lots*sizeof(int))` with `new int[lots]` in this (oversimplified) case, but things are not always so simple, and sometimes, we need to lie to the type system, if only for a moment. And that's where casts come in.

So, what are casts? Casts are a controlled way to guide the compiler's type system in understanding programmer intent. Casts also provide information in source code about the reasons behind such temporary lies; they document what the programmer intended to do at the very moment when a lie was required. The C++ casts are very clear in the intent they are conveying and very precise in their effect; the C-style cast (also seen in other languages) is much more vague in matters of intent, as we will see later in this chapter, and can perform inappropriate transformations in a language with such a rich type system as C++.

Safety in the type system – cv-qualifications

C++ provides two safety-related qualifiers in its type system. These are named `const` and `volatile`, and they are related in many ways.

The `const` qualifier means the object thus qualified is considered immutable in the current scope, such as the following:

```
const int N = 3; // global constant
class X {
    int n; // note: not const
public:
    X(int n) : n{ n } {
    }
    int g() { // note: not const
      return n += N; // thus, n's state can be mutated
    }
    int f() const { // const applies to this, and
                    // transitively to its members
      // return g(); // illegal as g() is not const
      return n + 1;
    }
};
int f(const int &n) { // f() will not mutate argument n
    return X{ n }.f() + 1; // X::X(int) takes its argument
                           // by value so n remains intact
}
int main() {
    int a = 4;
    a = f(a); // a is not const in main()
}
```

Marking an object as `const` means that in the context where it is marked as such, it cannot be mutated. In the case of class members, the `const` guarantee is maintained transitively through `const` member functions, in the sense that a `const` member function cannot modify the members of `*this`, and nor can it call a non-`const` member function of the same object. In the preceding example, `X::f` is `const`, and as such, it could not call `X::g`, which does not offer that guarantee; allowing `X::f` to call `X::g` would effectively break the `const` guarantee, as `X::g` can mutate `*this` but `X::f` cannot.

The `const` qualifier is well-known and well-documented in C++. Being "const-correct" is generally seen as good code hygiene and is something you should strive to do in practice; using `const` wherever it makes sense is one of the strongest assets of the C++ language, and many languages claiming to be "type-safe" lack this essential feature, without which, correctness is so much harder to achieve.

The volatile keyword is the counterpart to const; hence, the term *cv-qualifier* refers to both these terms. Woefully underdefined in the standard, volatile has a few meanings.

When applied to a fundamental type (for example, volatile int), it means that the object it qualifies could be accessed through ways unknown to the compiler and not necessarily visible from the source code. As such, this term is mostly useful when writing device drivers where some action external to the program itself (such as the physical pressure of a key) could change the memory associated with the object, or when some hardware or software component external to the source code could observe changes in that object's state.

Informally, if the source code states, *"Please read the value of that volatile object,"* the code that will be generated should read that value even if the program does not seem to modify it in any way; likewise, if the source code states *"Please write to that volatile object,"* then a write to that memory location should occur, even if nothing in the program seems to read from that memory location subsequently. Thus, volatile can be seen as something that prevents optimizations that the compiler would otherwise be allowed to perform.

In C++'s abstract machine, accessing a volatile-qualified object is the moral equivalent of an I/O operation – it can change the state of the program. On an object of some class type, volatile can be applied to a member function just as const can. Indeed, a non-static member function can be qualified const, volatile, const volatile, or none of these (among other things).

The meaning of applying the const qualifier on a member function was described earlier with the X::f member function – *this is const; its non-mutable, non-static data members are const in that function, and the only non-static member functions that can be called through *this are those that are const-qualified. A non-static member function qualified as volatile is, likewise, quite similar – *this is volatile during that function's execution, and so are all of its members, which impacts what operations you can perform with these objects. For example, taking the address of volatile int yields volatile int*, which is not implicitly convertible to int*, since the conversion would drop some security guarantees. This is one of the reasons why we have casts.

The C++ casts

Traditionally, C++ has supported four ways to perform those explicit type conversions we call casts – static_cast, dynamic_cast, const_cast, and reinterpret_cast. C++11 has added a fifth one, duration_cast, which is tangentially related to this book but will sometimes show up in examples, particularly when we measure the execution time of a function. Finally, C++20 introduced a sixth case, bit_cast, which is of interest to our work in this book.

The following sections give a brief overview of each C++ cast, along with a few examples of how and when they can be useful.

Your best friend (most of the time) – static_cast

The best, most efficient tool in our type-casting toolset is static_cast. It's mostly safe, costs essentially nothing in most cases, and can be used in a constexpr context, which makes it amenable to compile-time maneuvers.

You can use static_cast in situations involving potential risks, such as converting an int to a float or vice versa. In the latter case, it explicitly acknowledges the loss of the decimal part. You can also use static_cast to cast a pointer or a reference from a derived class to one of its direct or indirect bases (as long as there's no ambiguity), which is totally safe and could be done implicitly, as well as from a base to one of its derived classes. Casting from a base class to a derived class using static_cast is highly efficient but extremely risky if the cast is incorrect, as it does not perform runtime checks.

Here are some examples:

```
struct B { virtual ~B() = default; /* ... */ };
struct D0 : B { /* ... */ };
struct D1 : B { /* ... */ };
class X {
public:
    X(int, double);
};
void f(D0&);
void f(D1*);
int main() {
    const float x = 3.14159f;
    int n = static_cast<int>(x); // Ok, no warning
    X x0{ 3, 3.5 }; // Ok
    // compiles, probably warns (narrowing conversion)
    X x1(3.5,0);
    // does not compile, narrowing not allowed with braces
    // X x2{ 3.5, 0 };
    X x3{ static_cast<int>(x), 3 }; // Ok
    D0 d0;
    // illegal, no base-derived relationship with D0 and D1
    // D1* d1 = static_cast<D1*>(&d0);
    // Ok, static_cast could be omitted
    B *b = static_cast<B*>(&d0);
    // f(*b); // illegal
    f(*static_cast<D0*>(b)); // Ok
    f(static_cast<D1*>(b)); // compiles but very dangerous!
}
```

Pay special attention to the last use of static_cast of the preceding example – converting from a base class to one of its derived classes is appropriately done with static_cast. However, you must ensure that the conversion leads to an object of the chosen type, as there is no runtime verification made of the validity of that conversion; as the name implies, only compile-time checks are done with this cast. If you're not sure of what you're doing with a downcast, this is not the tool for you.

static_cast does not only change the perspective of the compiler to the type of an expression; it also can adjust the memory address being accessed to take into account the types involved in the conversion. For example, when a D class has at least two non-empty base classes, B0 and B1, these two parts of the derived class are not at the same address within a D object (if they were, they would overlap!), so static_cast from D* to one of its bases might yield a different address than that of D* itself. We will return to this when discussing reinterpret_cast, for which the behavior is different (and more dangerous).

A sign something's wrong – dynamic_cast

There will be cases where you have a pointer or a reference to an object of some class type, and that type happens to be different from (but related to) the type needed. This often happens – for example, in game engines where most classes derive from some Component base and functions tend to take Component* arguments but need to access members from an object of the derived class they expect.

The main problem here is, typically, that the function's interface is wrong – it accepts arguments of types that are insufficiently precise. Still, we all have software to deliver, and sometimes, we need to make things work even though we made some choices along the way that we will probably want to revisit later on.

The safe way to do such casts is dynamic_cast. This cast lets you convert a pointer or a reference from one type to another, related type in a way that lets you test whether the conversion worked or not; with pointers, an incorrect conversion yields nullptr, whereas with references, an incorrect conversion throws std::bad_cast. The relatedness of types with dynamic_cast is not limited to base-derived relationships and includes casting from one base to another base in a multiple inheritance design. However, note that, in most cases, dynamic_cast requires that the expression that is cast to another type is of the polymorphic type, in the sense that it must have at least one virtual member function.

Here are some examples:

```
struct B0 {
    virtual int f() const = 0;
    virtual ~B0() = default;
};
struct B1 {
    virtual int g() const = 0;
    virtual ~B1() = default;
```

```cpp
};
class D0 : public B0 {
    public: int f() const override { return 3; }
};
class D1 : public B1 {
    public: int g() const override { return 4; }
};
class D : public D0, public D1 {};
int f(D *p) {
    return p? p->f() + p->g() : -1; // Ok
}
// g has the wrong interface: it accepts a D0& but
// tries to use it as a D1&, which makes sense if
// the referred object is publicly D0 and D1 (for
// example, class D
int g(D0 &d0) {
    D1 &d1 = dynamic_cast<D1&>(d0); // throws if wrong
    return d1.g();
}
#include <iostream>
int main() {
    D d;
    f(&d); // Ok
    g(d); // Ok, a D is a D0
    D0 d0;
    // calls f(nullptr) as &d0 does not point to a D
    std::cout << f(dynamic_cast<D*>(&d0)) << '\n'; // -1
    try {
      g(d0); // compiles but will throw bad_cast
    } catch(std::bad_cast&) {
        std::cerr << "Nice try\n";
    }
}
```

Note that even though this example displays a message when `std::bad_cast` is thrown, this is in no way what we could call exception handling; we did not solve the "problem," and code execution continues in a potentially corrupt state, which could make things worse in more serious code. In a toy example such as this, just letting code fail and stop executing would also have been a reasonable choice.

In practice, the use of `dynamic_cast` should be rare, as it tends to be a sign that we chose our function interfaces in a perfectible manner. Note that `dynamic_cast` requires binaries to be compiled with **runtime type information** (**RTTI**) included, leading to larger binaries. Unsurprisingly, due to these costs, some application domains will tend to avoid this cast, and so will we.

Playing tricks with safety – const_cast

Neither `static_cast` nor `dynamic_cast` (nor `reinterpret_cast`, for that matter) can change the cv-qualifiers of an expression; to do this, you need `const_cast`. With `const_cast`, you can add or remove the `const` or `volatile` qualifiers from an expression. As you might have guessed, this only makes sense on a pointer or on a reference.

Why would you do something such as remove `const`-ness from an expression? Surprisingly, there are many situations where this comes in handy, but a common one is allowing the use of a `const`-correct type in a setting where `const`-ness was not used appropriately – for example, legacy code that did not use `const`, such as the following:

```
#include <vector>
struct ResourceHandle { /* ... */ };
// this function observes a resource without modifying it,
// but the type system is not aware of that fact (the
// argument is not const)
void observe_resource(ResourceHandle*);
class ResourceManager {
    std::vector<ResourceHandle *> resources;
    // ...
public:
    // note: const member function
    void observe_resources() const {
      // we want to observe each resource, for example
      // to collect data
      for(const ResourceHandle * h : resources) {
       // does not compile, h is const
       // observe_resource(h);
       // temporarily dismiss constness
          observe_resource(const_cast<ResourceHandle*>(h));
      }
    }
    // ...
};
```

`const_cast` is a tool to play with the security of the type system; it should be used in specific, controlled situations and not to do unreasonable things such as changing the value of a mathematical constant, such as pi. If try something like that, you'll incur **Undefined Behavior (UB)** – and rightfully so.

"Believe me, compiler" – reinterpret_cast

Sometimes, you just have to make the compiler believe you. For example, knowing sizeof(int)==4 on your platform, you might want to treat int as char[4] to interoperate with an existing API that expects that type. Note that you should ensure that this property holds (maybe through static_ assert), rather than relying on the belief that this property holds on all platforms (it does not).

That's what reinterpret_cast gives you – the ability to cast a pointer of some type to a pointer of an unrelated type. This can be used in situations where you seek to benefit from pointer-interconvertibility, as we saw in *Chapter 2*, just as this can be used to lie to the type system in several rather dangerous and non-portable ways.

Take the aforementioned conversion from an integer to an array of four bytes – if the aim is to facilitate addressing individual bytes, you have to be aware that the endianness of integers depends on the platform, as well as that the code written will probably be non-portable unless some careful measures are taken.

Also, note that reinterpret_cast only changes the type associated with an expression – for example, it does not perform the slight address adjustments that static_cast would make when converting from a derived class to a base class in multiple inheritance situations.

The following example shows the difference between these two casts:

```
struct B0 { int n = 3; };
struct B1 { float f = 3.5f; };
// B0 is the first base subobject of D
class D : public B0, public B1 { };
int main() {
    D d;
    // b0 and &d point to the same address
    // b1 and &d do not point to the same address
    B0 *b0 = static_cast<B0*>(&d);
    B1 *b1 = static_cast<B1*>(&d);
    int n0 = b0->n; // Ok
    float f0 = b1->f; // Ok
    // r0 and &d point to the same address
    // r1 and &d also point to the same address... oops!
    B0 *r0 = reinterpret_cast<B0*>(&d); // fragile
    B1 *r1 = reinterpret_cast<B1*>(&d); // bad idea
    int nr0 = r0->n; // Ok but fragile
    float fr0 = r1->f; // UB
}
```

Use `reinterpret_cast` sparingly. Relatively safe uses include converting a pointer to an integral representation when given a sufficiently wide integral type (and vice versa), converting between null pointers of different types, and converting between function pointer types – although in that case, the results of calling the function through the resulting pointer are undefined. The complete list of conversions that can be performed with this cast can be found at `wg21.link/expr.reinterpret.cast` if you want to know more.

I know the bits are right – bit_cast

C++20 introduced `bit_cast`, a new cast that can be used to copy bits from one object to another of the same width, starting the lifetime of the destination object (and the objects enclosed therein, if any) along the way, as long as both the source and destination types are trivially copyable. This somewhat magical library function can be found in the `<bit>` header and is `constexpr`.

Here's an example:

```
#include <bit>
struct A { int a; double b; };
struct B { unsigned int c; double d; };
int main() {
    constexpr A a{ 3, 3.5 }; // ok
    constexpr B b = std::bit_cast<B>(a); // Ok
    static_assert(a.a == b.c && a.b == b.d); // Ok
    static_assert((void*)&a != (void*)&b); // Ok
}
```

As can be seen in this example, both A and B are constructed at compile time and are bitwise identical to one another, but their addresses are different, as they are entirely different objects. Their data members are partially of different types but are of the same sizes, in the same order, and are all trivially copyable.

Also, note the use of a C-style cast on the last line of this example. As we will soon discuss, this is one of the few reasonable uses of C-style casts (we could have used `static_cast` here too and it would have been just as efficient).

Somewhat unrelated, but still – duration_cast

We won't dwell too long on `duration_cast`, as it is only tangentially related to our topic of interest, but since it will be part of our toolset for micro-benchmarking in this book, it at least deserves a mention.

The `duration_cast` library function can be found in the `<chrono>` header and is part of the `std::chrono` namespace. It is `constexpr` and can be used to convert between expressions of different measurement units.

For example, suppose that we want to measure the time it took to execute some function, f(), using the system_clock provided by our library vendor. We can read that clock using its now() static member function before and after calling f(), which gives us two time_point objects for that clock (two moments in time), and then compute the difference between them to get a duration for that clock. We do not know what measurement unit was used to represent that duration, but if we want to use it expressed as, say, microseconds, we use duration_cast to perform than conversion:

```
#include <chrono>
#include <iostream>
int f() { /* ... */ }
int main() {
    using std::cout;
    using namespace std::chrono;
    auto pre = system_clock::now();
    int res = f();
    auto post = system_clock::now();
    cout << "Computed " << res << " in "
        << duration_cast<microseconds>(post - pre);
}
```

We will systematize our benchmarking practices later in this book, showing a more formal way to measure the execution time of functions or code blocks, but duration_cast will be our tool of choice to ensure that the format in which we present the results is appropriate for our needs.

The reviled one – the C cast

You might be tempted to use C-style casts when type conversions are needed, as the C syntax appears in other languages and tends to be short to express – (T)expr treats expression, expr, as being of type T. That terseness is actually a downside, not an upside, as we will see. Limit C-style casts to a minimum in C++ code:

- The C-style casts are harder to find when performing an automated search through source code text, since they look like arguments in a function call. Since casts are ways through which we lie to the type system, revisiting the decision to use them from time to time is worthwhile, so being able to find them is valuable. In comparison, the C++ casts are keywords, which makes them easier to find.

- A C-style cast does not convey information about why a conversion occurred. When writing (T)expr, we are not saying whether we want to change cv-qualifiers, navigate a class hierarchy, simply change to type of a pointer, and so on. In particular, when converting between pointers to different types, a C-style cast will generally behave as reinterpret_cast, which, as we have seen, can lead to disastrous results in some circumstances.

You will sometimes see C-style casts in C++ code, mostly for situations where the intent is absolutely clear. We saw an example at the end of our `bit_cast` section. Another example would be to silence compiler warnings – for example, when calling a function that's `[[nodiscard]]` but still really wanting to discard the results nonetheless for some reason.

In yet another example, consider the following generic function:

```
template <class ItA, class ItB>
    bool all_equal(ItA bA, ItA eA, ItB bB, ItB eB) {
        for(; bA != eA && bB != eB; ++bA, (void) ++bB)
            if (*bA != bB)
                return false;
        return true;
    }
```

This function iterates through two sequences that are delimited, respectively, by `[bA,eA)` and `[bB,eB)` (making sure to stop as soon as the shortest sequence has been processed), compares the elements at the "same position" in these two sequences, and yields `true` only if all comparisons between elements of those two sequences are equal.

Note that the cast to `void` uses a C-style cast between the increments of `bA` and `bB` in this code, which cast the result of `++bB` to `void`. This may look strange, but this is code that can be used in many situations by pretty much anyone, including hostile (or distracted) users. Suppose someone with a twisted mind had decided to overload the comma operator (yes, you can do that) between the types of `operator++(ItA)` and `operator++(ItB)`. That person could then essentially hijack our function to run unexpected code. By casting one of the arguments to `void`, we ensure that this is not possible.

Summary

That concludes our quick overview of casts and cv-qualifications in C++. Now that we've seen some ways to trick the type system and get in trouble, as well as know why we should do these things carefully (if at all), we can start building beautiful things with C++ and work toward safe, efficient abstractions in our endeavor to write correct programs that control how we manage memory.

In the next chapter, we will start by using one of the language's defining features, the destructor, to automate the way our code handles resources, with an eye in particular on the way memory is handled.

Part 2:
Implicit Memory
Management Techniques

In this part, we will examine some well-known approaches to implicit resource management (including memory management) in C++. These are all techniques you can use in your daily programming practices that will lead to simpler and safer programs than what you would get if you wanted to manage memory explicitly. You could say that the chapters in this part concern what people call "modern" or "contemporary" C++.

This part has the following chapters:

- *Chapter 4, Using Destructors*
- *Chapter 5, Using Standard Smart Pointers*
- *Chapter 6, Writing Smart Pointers*

4

Using Destructors

Our journey to a better and deeper understanding of memory management in C++ now emerges into the world of clean code and contemporary practices. In previous chapters we have explored fundamental concepts of in-memory representation (what are objects, references, pointers, and so on), what pitfalls await us if we stray from sound programming practices in inappropriate ways, and how we can lie to the type system in a controlled and disciplined manner, all of which will be helpful in the rest of this book. We will now discuss fundamental aspects of resource management in our language; memory being a special kind of resource, the ideas and techniques found in this chapter will help us write clean and robust code, including code that performs memory management tasks.

C++ is a programming language that supports (among other paradigms) object-oriented programming, but with actual objects. This sounds like a jest of sorts, but it's actually a true statement: many languages only provide indirect access to objects (through pointers or references), which means that in these languages the semantics of assignment are usually sharing the referred object (*the pointee*). There are upsides to this, of course: for example, copying a reference typically cannot fail whereas copying an object can fail if the copy constructor or copy assignment (depending on the situation) throws an exception.

In C++, by default, programs use objects, copy objects, assign to objects, and so on, and indirect access is opt-in, requiring additional syntax both for pointers and references. This requires C++ programmers to think about object lifetimes, what it means to copy an object, what it means to move from an object... These can be deep topics depending on the types involved.

> **Note**
>
> See *Chapter 1* for more information on objects and object lifetime, including the role of constructors and destructors.

Even if having actual objects in your source code requires adjusting your mindset when programming, it also provides a significant advantage: automatic objects are destroyed when they reach the end of the scope in which they were declared (when they reach the closing brace of that scope) and when an object gets destroyed a special function, the type's **destructor**, gets called. This special moment allows us to execute arbitrary code at definite moments and is a part of a key C++ idiom named **RAII**, an acronym we will explain in the *The RAII idiom* section later in this chapter. This has led some luminaries to claim that the most beautiful instruction in C++ is }, the closing brace.

In this chapter, we will look at what destructors do, what they should not do, when they should be written (and when we should stick to what the compiler does by default), as well as how our code can use destructors effectively to manage resources in general… and memory more specifically. Then, we will take a quick look at some key types from the standard library that use destructors to our advantage.

In more detail, in his chapter, we will:

- Provide a general overview of how resources can be managed safely in C++;
- Take a close look at the RAII idiom, a well-known idiomatic practice that uses an object's lifetime to ensure that resources managed by that object are properly released;
- Examine some pitfalls associated with automated resource management;
- Give a quick overview of some automated resource management tools provided by the standard library.

By the end of this chapter, we will understand the most common ideas and practices one associates with resource management in C++. This will allow us to build more powerful abstractions throughout the remainder of the book.

Technical requirements

You can find the code files for this chapter in the book's GitHub repository here: https://github. com/PacktPublishing/C-Plus-Plus-Memory-Management/tree/main/chapter4.

On destructors: a short recap

This chapter aims to discuss the use of destructors to manage resources, in particular memory, but since we discussed destructors a while ago (in *Chapter 1*) we will allow ourselves a quick recap of the basic idea behind this powerful idea:

- When an object reaches the end of its lifetime, a special member function called the destructor is called. For some class X, that member function is named X::~X(). This function is an occasion for type X to perform a few "last-minute" actions before concluding its lifetime. As we will discuss in this chapter, one idiomatic use of the destructor is to release resources held by the object being destroyed;
- In a class hierarchy, when an object reaches the end of its lifetime, what happens is (a) the destructor for that object gets called, then the same goes for (b) the destructor of each of its non-static data member in order of declaration followed by (c) the destructor of each of its base class sub-objects (its "parents", informally) in order of declaration;

- When explicitly destroying an object through the application of operator delete on a pointer, the resulting process involves the destruction of the pointee followed by the deallocation of the memory block where the object was located. Unsurprisingly, there are caveats to this as we will see *Chapter 7*;

- In some situations, notably when some class X exposes at least one virtual member function, this sends the message that an X* might in practice point to an object of a class Y directly or indirectly derived from X. To ensure that the destructor of Y is actually called, not the destructor of X, it is customary to also qualify X::~X() as virtual. Not doing so risks not calling the correct destructor, leading to resource leaks.

For a small example, consider the following:

```cpp
#include <iostream>
struct Base {
    ~Base() { std::cout << "~Base()\n"; }
};
struct DerivedA : Base {
    ~DerivedA() { std::cout << "~DerivedA()\n"; }
};
struct VirtBase {
    virtual ~VirtBase() {
        std::cout << "~VirtBase()\n";
    }
};
struct DerivedB : VirtBase {
    ~DerivedB() {
        std::cout << "~DerivedB()\n";
    }
};
int main() {
    {
        Base base;
    }
    {
        DerivedA derivedA;
    }
    std::cout << "----\n";
    Base *pBase = new DerivedA;
    delete pBase; // bad
    VirtBase *pVirtBase = new DerivedB;
    delete pVirtBase; // Ok
}
```

If you run that code, you will see one destructor called for base and two called for derivedA: the derived class' destructor followed by the base class' destructor. This is as expected, and this part of the code is correct.

The problematic case is pBase, a pointer of type Base* which points to an object of a class derived from Base, as the destructor of Base is not virtual which indicates that trying to delete the derived object through a pointer to the base class is probably a breach of intent: delete pBase only calls Base::~Base(), never calling DerivedA::~DerivedA(). With pVirtBase this problem is avoided as VirtBase::~VirtBase() is virtual.

Of course, in C++, we have options because there are always surprising use-cases that come up, and we will see one in *Chapter 7* where we will delete a pointer-to-derived from a pointer-to-base without the mediation of a virtual destructor for good (if specialized) reasons.

Note that virtual member functions are useful, but they have costs: a typical implementation will make a table of function pointers per type with at least one virtual member function and store a pointer to that table in each such object, which makes objects slightly bigger. As such, use virtual destructors when you expect to use a pointer to a derived object from a pointer to one of its bases, particularly when you expect the destructor to be called through a pointer to said base class.

With that being said, let's examine how all this relates to resource management.

Managing resources

Suppose you are writing a function that opens a file, reads from it, and closes it afterward. You are developing on a procedural platform (like most operating system APIs are) offering a set of functions to perform these tasks. Note that all "operating system" functions in this example are deliberately fictional but resemble their real-world counterparts. The functions interesting to us in that API are:

```
// opens the file called "name", returns a pointer
// to a file descriptor for that file (nullptr on failure)
FILE *open_file(const char *name);
// returns the number of bytes read from the file into
// buf. Preconditions: file is non-null and valid, buf
// points to a buffer of at least capacity bytes, and
// capacity >= 0
int read_from(FILE *file, char *buf, int capacity);
// closes file. Precondition: file is non-null and valid,
void close_file(FILE *file);
```

Suppose your code needs to process the data read from the file, but that this processing can throw an exception. The reason for that exception is unimportant here: it can be corrupt data, failure to allocate memory, calling some auxiliary function that throws, and so on. The key point is that there is a risk that the function will throw.

If we try to write code for that function naïvely, it might look like this:

```
void f(const char *name) {
    FILE *file = open_file(name);
    if(!file) return false; // failure
    vector<char> v;
    char buf[N]; // N is a positive integral constant
    for(int n = read_from(file, buf, N); n != 0;
        n = read_from(file, buf, N))
        v.insert(end(v), buf + 0, buf + n);
    process(v); // our processing function
    close_file(file);
}
```

💡 **Quick tip**: Enhance your coding experience with the **AI Code Explainer** and **Quick Copy** features. Open this book in the next-gen Packt Reader. Click the **Copy** button (**1**) to quickly copy code into your coding environment, or click the **Explain** button (**2**) to get the AI assistant to explain a block of code to you.

```
                                              Copy      Explain
function calculate(a, b) {
  return {sum: a + b};                          1          2
};
```

📱 **The next-gen Packt Reader** is included for free with the purchase of this book. Unlock it by scanning the QR code below or visiting https://www.packtpub.com/unlock/9781805129806.

That code works, and in the absence of exceptions does pretty much what we want. Now, suppose process(v) throws an exception… What happens?

In this case, function f() exits, failing to meet its postconditions. The call to process(v) never concludes… and close_file(file); never gets called. We have a leak. Not necessarily a *memory* leak, but a leak nonetheless as file never gets closed, since an exception thrown from process() but not caught in calling code f() will conclude f() and let the exception flow through to f()'s caller (and so on, until caught or until the program crashes, whichever comes first).

There are ways around this situation. One is to proceed "manually" and add a `try ... catch` block around the code that could throw:

```cpp
void f(const char *name) {
    FILE *file = open_file(name);
    if(!file) return; // failure
    vector<char> v;
    char buf[N]; // N is a positive integral constant
    try {
        for(int n = read_from(file, buf, N); n != 0;
            n = read_from(file, buf, N))
            v.insert(end(v), buf + 0, buf + n);
        process(v); // our processing function
        close_file(file);
    } catch(...) { // catch anything
        close_file(file);
        throw; // re-throw what we caught
    }
}
```

I agree this is a bit "clunky", with two occurrences of `close_file(file)`, one at the end of the `try` block to close the file under normal occurrences, and another at the end of the `catch` block to avoid leaking the file's resources.

The manual approach can be made to work, but that is a brittle approach to the problem: in C++, any function that is neither `noexcept` nor `noexcept(true)` could throw; this means that in practice, almost any expression could throw.

> **Catching anything**
>
> In C++, there's no single, mandated base class for all exception types as one could see in some other languages. Indeed, `throw 3;` is totally legal C++ code. On top of this, C++ has extremely powerful generic programming mechanisms which makes generic code prevalent in our language. Consequently, we often find ourselves calling functions that could throw but for which we cannot really know what could be thrown. Know that `catch(...)` will catch any C++ object used to represent an exception: you will not know *what* you caught, but you *will* have caught it.
>
> In such cases, we will typically want to intercept exceptions, probably to do some cleanup, then let that exception continue on its way unchanged in order to let client code deal with it as needed. The cleanup part is because we want our function to be **exception-safe** (no leaks, no corrupted state, and so on.) as well as **exception-neutral** (do not hide the nature of the problem from those who will want to handle it). To rethrow whatever exception object you have caught, even from a `catch(...)` block, simply use `throw;` which is said to be the "re-throw".

Exception handling... or not?

This leads to another question: in a function such as `f()` where we only aim to consume data and process it for our purposes, should we really seek to handle exceptions? Think about it: the requirements for throwing an exception are significantly different from those for *handling* an exception.

Indeed, we throw an exception from a function to signal that our function cannot achieve its postconditions (it cannot do the task it was meant to do): maybe memory is insufficient, maybe the file to read from does not exist, maybe performing that integral division you asked for would lead to dividing by zero, therefore destroying the universe (and we don't want that to happen), maybe one of the functions called by our function cannot satisfy its own postconditions in ways we did not foresee or did not want to handle... There are plenty of reasons for a function to fail. Many are the situations where a function might find itself in a position where to proceed further would lead to severe problems, and in some cases (constructors and overloaded operators come to mind) exceptions really are the only sensible way to signal a problem to client code.

Handling an exception per se is a much rarer occurrence: to throw an exception, one has to recognize a problem, but to handle an exception one needs an understanding of context. Indeed, the actions one would perform in reaction to an exception in an interactive console application are different from those performed for an audio application when people are moving on the dance floor, or from those required when facing a nuclear code meltdown.

Most functions need to be exception-safe to some extent (there are flavors to this) more than they need to handle the problem. In our example, the difficulties stem from the manual closing of `file` in the advent of an exception. The easiest way to avoid this manual resource handling is to automate it, and what happens at the end of a function whether that function completes normally (reaching the function's closing brace, hitting a `return` statement, seeing an exception "fly by") is better modelled by a destructor. This practice has become so well ingrained in C++ programmers' practices that it is considered idiomatic and has been given a name: the *RAII idiom*.

The RAII idiom

C++ programmers tend to use destructors to automate the releasing of resources, and this can truly be said to be an idiomatic programming technique in our language, so much that we have given it a name. Probably not the best of names, but a well-known name nonetheless: **RAII**, which stands for **Resource acquisition is initialization** (some have also suggested **Responsibility acquisition is initialization**, which also works and carries a similar meaning). The general idea is that objects tend to acquire resources at construction time (or later), but (and more importantly!) that releasing resources held by an object is something that usually should be done at the end of that object's lifetime. Thus, RAII has more to do with destructors than with constructors, but as I said, we tend to be bad with names and acronyms.

Revisiting our file reading and processing example from the Managing resources section, earlier in this chapter, we can build an RAII resource handler to facilitate file closing regardless of how the function concludes:

```cpp
class FileCloser { // perfectible, as we will see
    FILE * file;
public:
    FileCloser(FILE *file) : file{ file } {
    }
    ~FileCloser() {
        close_file(file);
    }
};
void f(const char *name) {
    FILE *file = open_file(name);
    if(!file) return; // failure
    FileCloser fc{ file }; // <-- fc manages file now
    vector<char> v;
    char buf[N]; // N is a positive integral constant
    for(int n = read_from(file, buf, N); n != 0;
        n = read_from(file, buf, N))
        v.insert(end(v), buf + 0, buf + n);
    process(v); // our processing function
} // implicit close_file(file)
```

The details and granularity of what `FileCloser` does will vary with our perception of its role: does this class just manage the closing of the file or does it actually represent the file with all of its services? I went for the former in this case but both options are reasonable: it all depends on the semantics you are seeking to implement. The key point is that by using a `FileCloser` object, we are relieving client code of a responsibility, instead delegating the responsibility of closing a file to an object that automates this task, simplifying our own code and reducing the risks of inadvertently leaving it open.

This `FileCloser` object is very specific to our task. We could generalize it in many ways, for example through a generic object that performs a user-supplied set of actions when destroyed:

```cpp
template <class F> class scoped_finalizer { // simplified
    F f;
public:
    scoped_finalizer(F f) : f{ f } {
    }
    ~scoped_finalizer() {
        f();
    }
};
```

```
void f(const char *name) {
   FILE *file = open_file(name);
   if(!file) return; // failure
   auto sf = scoped_finalizer{ [&file] {
      close_file(file);
   } }; // <-- sf manages file now
   vector<char> v;
   char buf[N]; // N is a positive integral constant
   for(int n = read_from(file, buf, N); n != 0;
       n = read_from(file, buf, N))
      v.insert(end(v), buf + 0, buf + n);
   process(v); // our processing function
} // implicit close_file(file) through sf's destructor
```

The RAII idiom is pretty much everywhere in C++; one could say it's the language's most pervasive idiom, and one of its most recognizable and defining programming practice. Many languages offer similar features today: C# has `using` blocks, Java has `try`-with blocks, Go has a `defer` keyword, etc., but in C++ the possibility to use scope in order to automate actions, often related to resource management, flows directly from the type system and makes objects, not user code, the ones that idiomatically manage resources.

RAII and C++'s special member functions

Chapter 1 described the six special member functions (default constructor, destructor, copy constructor, copy assignment, move constructor, and move assignment). When one implements these functions in a class, it usually means that class is responsible for some resource. As mentioned in *Chapter 1*, when a class does not explicitly manage resources, we can often leave those functions to the compiler and the resulting default behavior will usually lead to simpler and more efficient code.

Consider now that the RAII idiom is mostly about resource management, as we associate the moment of destruction for an object with the act of releasing previously acquired resources. Numerous RAII objects (including classes `FileCloser` and `scoped_finalizer` in the preceding examples) can be said to be responsible for the resources we provide them with, which means that copying these objects could induce bugs (who would be responsible for the resources, the original or the copy?). Thus, consider deleting the copy operations for your RAII types unless you have a good reason to implement them explicitly:

```
template <class F> class scoped_finalizer {
   F f;
public:
   scoped_finalizer(const scoped_finalizer&) = delete;
   scoped_finalizer& operator=
      (const scoped_finalizer&) = delete;
   scoped_finalizer(F f) : f{ f } {
```

```
    }
    ~scoped_finalizer() {
        f();
    }
};
```

Like most idioms, RAII is a generally accepted good programming practice, but it's not a panacea and the same goes for the use of destructors in general. We will look at some risks involved with destructors, and how we can avoid getting in such trouble.

Some pitfalls

Destructors are wonderful. They allow us to automate tasks, they simplify code and they make it safer in general. Still, there are some caveats, some aspects of using destructors that require particular attention.

Destructors should not throw

The title of this section says it quite simply: destructors should not throw. They *can* throw, but it's a bad idea to do so.

That might seem surprising at first. After all, constructors can (and do!) throw exceptions. When a constructor throws, it means that the constructor cannot satisfy its postconditions: the object under construction was not constructed (the constructor did not complete!) so that object does not exist. That's a simple, working model.

If a destructor throws... well, it's probably the end of your program. Indeed, destructors are implicitly noexcept, which means that throwing from a destructor will call std::terminate() and that will be the end of your program.

Well, you might think, what if I explicitly mark my destructor as noexcept(false) then, thus overriding the default behavior? Well, this can work, but be careful as if a destructor throws during stack unwinding, such as what happens when an exception is already in flight, then this still calls std::terminate() and since you've been bad and have broken the rules, the compiler can optimize some of your code away. For example, in the following program it's quite possible that neither "A\n" nor "B\n" will be printed even though the destructor of Evil has not been called at that point:

```
#include <iostream>
class Darn {};
void f() { throw 3; }
struct Evil {
    Evil() { std::cout << "Evil::Evil()\n"; }
    ~Evil() noexcept(false) {
        std::cout << "Evil::~Evil()\n";
        throw Darn {};
```

```
        }
    };
    void g() {
        std::cout << "A\n";
        Evil e;
        std::cout << "B\n";
        f();
        std::cout << "C\n";
    }
    int main() {
        try {
            g();
        } catch(int) {
            std::cerr << "catch(int)\n";
        } catch(Darn) {
            std::cerr << "darn...\n";
        }
    }
```

A probable result from this code can simply be that the program will display nothing at all, and some information to the effect that throwing Darn has led to calling std::terminate() will be output. Why is some of the code (notably the messages we tried to output) visibly removed by the compiler? The answer is that an exception thrown but never caught enters implementation-defined behavior, and the throwing of Darn in this case cannot be caught (it directly calls std::terminate() as it happens during stack unwinding) which lets the compiler optimize our code significantly.

Summarizing: don't throw from a destructor unless you really know what you're doing, control the context where it will be called, and have discussed it with others to make sure it's reasonable even though all evidence points to the contrary. Even then, it's probably better to look for alternative approaches.

Know thy destruction order

The title of this section might seem like a funny admonition. Why is it important to know about the order in which our objects will be destroyed? After all, the basic rule is simple: construction and destruction of objects are symmetrical, thus objects are destroyed in reverse order of construction… right?

Well, that is the case for local, automatic objects. If you write the following:

```
    void f() {
        A a; // a's ctor
        B b; // b's ctor
        {
            C c; // c's ctor
        } // c's dtor
```

```
    D d; // d's ctor
} // d's dtor, b's dtor, a's dtor (in that order)
```

... then the order of construction and destruction will be as noted in the comments: automatic objects in scope are destroyed in reverse order of construction, and nested scopes behave as expected.

The situation gets more complex if you add non-automatic objects to the mix. C++ lets one have `static` objects declared within a function: these are constructed when the function is called for the first time and stay alive from that point on until the end of the program's execution. C++ lets one have global variables (there are many nuances here with linkage specifications such as `static` or `extern`) C++ lets one have `static` data members in a class: these are essentially global variables too. I won't even get to `thread_local` variables here as they are out of scope for this book but if you use them, know that they can be lazily initialized which adds to the complexity of the overall picture. Global objects are destroyed in reverse order of construction, but that order of construction is not always trivial to predict from our human perspective.

Consider the following example, which uses `Verbose` objects that inform us of their moment of construction as well as of their moment of destruction:

```cpp
#include <iostream>
#include <format>
struct Verbose {
    int n;
    Verbose(int n) : n{ n } {
        std::cout << std::format(«Verbose({})\n», n);
    }
    ~Verbose(){
        std::cout << std::format(«~Verbose({})\n», n);
    }
};
class X {
    static inline Verbose v0 { 0 };
    Verbose v1{ 1 };
};
Verbose v2{ 2 };
static void f() {
    static Verbose v3 { 3 };
    Verbose v4{ 4 };
}
static void g() { // note : never called
    static Verbose v5 { 5 };
}
int main() {
    Verbose v6{ 6 };
```

```
    {
        Verbose v7{ 7 };
        f();
        X x;
    }
    f();
    X x;
}
```

Take a moment to let this example sink in and try to figure out what will be displayed. We have a global object, a `static` and `inline` data member in a class, two `static` objects local to functions as well as some local automatic objects.

So, what will be displayed if we run this program? If you try it, you should see:

```
Verbose(0)
Verbose(2)
Verbose(6)
Verbose(7)
Verbose(3)
Verbose(4)
~Verbose(4)
Verbose(1)
~Verbose(1)
~Verbose(7)
Verbose(4)
~Verbose(4)
Verbose(1)
~Verbose(1)
~Verbose(6)
~Verbose(3)
~Verbose(2)
~Verbose(0)
```

The first one to be constructed (and the last one to be destroyed) is v0, the `static inline` data member. It also happens to be our first global object, followed by v2 (our second global object). We then enter `main()` and create v6 which will be destroyed at the end of `main()`.

Now, if you look at the output for that program, you'll see that symmetry breaks down at this point since after the construction of v6, we construct v7 (in an inner, narrower scope; v7 will be destructed soon after) and then call `f()` for the first time which constructs v3, but v3 is a global object and will for that reason be destroyed *after* v6 and v7.

The overall process is mechanical and deterministic, but understanding it requires some thought and analysis. If we use our objects' destructors to release resources, failure to understand what happens and when it happens can lead to our code trying to use resources that have already been freed.

For a concrete example involving a mix of automated and manual resource management, let's look at something the C++ standard knows nothing about: dynamically linked libraries (.dll files). I'm not going to get into details here, so know that if you are on a Linux machine (using shared objects, .so files) or on a Mac (.dylib files), the general idea's the same but the function names will differ.

Our program will (a) load a dynamically linked library, (b) get the address of a function, (c) call this function and (d) unload the library. Suppose the library is named Lib and the function we want to call is named factory which returns a X* from which we want to call member function f():

```
#include "Lib.h"
#include <Windows.h> // LoadLibrary, GetProcAddress
int main() {
    using namespace std;
    HMODULE hMod = LoadLibrary(L"Lib.dll");
    // suppose the signature of factory is in Lib.h
    auto factory_ptr = reinterpret_cast<
        decltype(&factory)
    >(GetProcAddress(hMod, "factory"));
    X *p = factory_ptr();
    p->f();
    delete p;
    FreeLibrary(hMod);
}
```

You might have noticed the manual memory management in there: we acquire a resource (a X* pointing to something that's at least an X) calling factory() through factory_ptr, then we use (call f() on) and manually dispose of the *pointee*.

At this point, you're probably telling yourself that manual resource management's not the best of ideas (here: what happens to the resource if p->f() throws?), so you look through the standard and find that an object of type std::unique_ptr will take responsibility over the *pointee* and destroy it when its destructor is reached. Beautiful, isn't it? And indeed it probably is, but consider the following excerpt, rewritten to use a std::unique_ptr and automate the resource management process:

```
#include "Lib.h"
#include <memory> // std::unique_ptr
#include <Windows.h> // LoadLibrary, GetProcAddress
int main() {
    using namespace std;
    HMODULE hMod = LoadLibrary(L"Lib.dll");
    // suppose the signature of factory is in Lib.h
```

```
   auto factory_ptr = reinterpret_cast<
      decltype(&factory)
   >(GetProcAddress(hMod, "factory"));
   std::unique_ptr<X> p { factory_ptr() };
   p->f();
   // delete p; // not needed anymore
   FreeLibrary(hMod);
} // p is destroyed here... but is this good?
```

At first glance, this new version seems safer since p is now an RAII object responsible for the destruction of the *pointee*. Being destroyed at the closing brace of our main() function, we know that the destructor of the *pointee* will be called even if p->f() throws, so we consider ourselves more exception-safe than before...

... except that this code crashes on that closing brace! If you investigate the source of the crash, you will probably end up realizing that the crash happens at the point where the destructor of p calls operator delete on the X* it has stored internally. Reading further, you will notice that the reason why this crash happens is that the library the object came from has been freed (call to FreeLibrary()) before the destructor ran.

Does that mean we cannot use an automated memory management tool here? Of course not, but we need to be more careful with the way in which we put object lifetime to contribution. In this example, we want to make sure that p is destroyed before the call to FreeLibrary() happens; this can be achieved through the simple introduction of a scope in our function:

```
#include "Lib.h"
#include <memory> // std::unique_ptr
#include <Windows.h> // LoadLibrary, GetProcAddress
int main() {
   using namespace std;
   HMODULE hMod = LoadLibrary(L"Lib.dll");
   // suppose the signature of factory is in Lib.h
   auto factory_ptr = reinterpret_cast<
      decltype(&factory)
   >(GetProcAddress(hMod, "factory"));
   {
      std::unique_ptr<X> p { factory_ptr() };
      p->f();
   } // p is destroyed here
   FreeLibrary(hMod);
}
```

In this specific example, we could find a simple solution; in other cases we might have to move some declarations around to make sure the scopes in which our objects find themselves don't alter the intended semantics of our function. Understanding the order in which objects are destroyed is essential to properly using this precious resource management facility that is the destructor.

Standard resource management automation tools

The standard library offers a significant number of classes that manage memory efficiently. One needs only consider the standard containers to see shining examples of the sort. In this section, we will take a quick look at a few examples of types useful for resource management. Far from providing an exhaustive list, we'll try to show different ways to benefit from the RAII idiom.

As mentioned before, when expressing a type that provides automated resource management, the key aspects of that type's behavior are expressed through its six special member functions. For that reason, with each of the following types, we will take a brief look at what the semantics of these functions are.

unique_ptr<T> and shared_ptr<T>

This short section aims to provide a brief overview of the two main standard smart pointers types in the C++ standard library: `std::unique_ptr<T>` and `std::shared_ptr<T>`. It is meant to provide a broad overview of each type's role; a more detailed examination of how these types can be used appears in *Chapter 5*, and we will implement simplified versions of both types (as well as of a few other smart pointer types) in *Chapter 6*.

We have seen an example using `std::unique_ptr<T>` earlier in this chapter. An object of this type implements "single ownership of the resource" semantics: an object of type `std::unique_ptr<T>` is uncopiable, and when provided with a `T*` to manage, it destroys the *pointee* at the end of its lifetime. By default, this type will call `delete` on the pointer it manages, but it can be made to use some other means of disposal if needed.

A default `std::unique_ptr<T>` represents an empty object and mostly behaves like a null pointer. Since this type expresses exclusive ownership of a resource, it is uncopiable. Moving from a `std::unique_ptr<T>` transfers ownership of the resource, leaving the moved-from object into an empty state conceptually analogous to a null pointer. The destructor of this type destroys the resource managed by the object, if any.

Type `std::shared_ptr<T>` implements "shared ownership of the resource" semantics. With this type, each `std::shared_ptr<T>` object that co-owns a given pointer shares responsibilities with respect to the pointee's lifetime and the last co-owner of the resource is responsible for freeing it; as is the case with most smart pointers, this responsibility falls on the object's destructor. This type is surprisingly complicated to write, even in a somewhat naïve implementation like the one we will write in *Chapter 6*, and is less frequently useful than some people think, as the main use case (expressing ownership in the type system for cases where the last owner of the pointee is a priori unknown, something most frequently seen in multithreaded code) is more specialized than many would believe, but when one needs to fill this niche, it's the kind of type that's immensely useful.

A default `std::shared_ptr<T>` also represents an empty object and mostly behaves like a null pointer. Since this type expresses shared ownership of a resource, it is copyable but copying an object means sharing the *pointee*; copy assignment releases the resource held by the object on the left hand of the assignment and then shares the resource held by the object on the right side of the assignment between both objects. Moving from a `std::unique_ptr<T>` transfers ownership of the resource, leaving the moved-from object into an empty state. The destructor of this type releases ownership of the shared resource, destroying the resource managed by the object if that object was the last owner thereof.

What does the "shared" in shared_ptr mean?

There can be confusion with respect to what the word "shared" in the name of the `std::shared_ptr` type actually means. For example, should we use that type whenever we want to share a pointer between caller and callee? Should we use it when whenever client code makes a copy of a pointer with the intent of sharing the pointee, such as when passing a pointer by value to a function or sharing resources stored in a global manager object?

The short answer is that this is the wrong way to approach smart pointers. Sharing a dynamically allocated resource does not mean co-owning that resource: only the latter is what `std::shared_ptr` models, whereas the former can be done with much more lightweight types. We will examine this idea in detail in *Chapter 5* from a usage perspective, then reexamine it in *Chapter 6* with our implementer eyes, hopefully building a more comprehensive understanding of these deep and subtle issues.

---

lock_guard and scoped_lock

Owning a resource is not limited to owning memory. Indeed, consider the following code excerpt and suppose that `string_mutator` is a class used to perform arbitrary transformations to characters in a `string`, but is expected to be used in a multithreaded context in the sense that one needs to synchronize accesses to that `string` object:

```
#include <thread>
#include <mutex>
#include <string>
#include <algorithm>
#include <string_view>
class string_mutator {
    std::string text;
    mutable std::mutex m;
public:
    // note: m in uncopiable so string_mutator
    // also is uncopiable
```

```
    string_mutator(std::string_view src)
        : text{ src.begin(), src.end() } {
    }
    template <class F> void operator()(F f) {
        m.lock();
        std::transform(text.begin(), text.end(),
                       text.begin(), f);
        m.unlock();
    }
    std::string grab_snapshot() const {
        m.lock();
        std::string s = text;
        m.unlock();
        return s;
    }
};
```

In this example, a `string_mutator` object's function call operator accepts an arbitrary function f applicable to a char and that returns something that can be converted to a char, then applies f to each char in the sequence. For example, the following call would display `"I LOVE MY INSTRUCTOR"`:

```
// ...
string_mutator sm{ "I love my instructor" };
sm([](char c) {
    return static_cast<char>(std::toupper(c));
});
std::cout << sm.grab_snaphot();
// ...
```

Now, since `string_mutator::operator()(F)` accepts any function of the appropriate signature as argument, it could among other things accept a function that could throw an exception. Looking at the implementation of that operator, you will notice that with the current (naïve) implementation, this would lock m but never unlock it, a bad situation indeed.

There are languages that offer specialized language constructs to solve this problem. In C++, there's no need for such specialized support as robust code just flows from the fact that one could write an object that locks a mutex at construction time and unlocks it when destroyed... and that's pretty much all we need. In C++, the simplest such type is `std::lock_guard<M>`, where a simple implementation could look like:

```
template <class M>
    class lock_guard { // simplified version
        M &m;
    public:
```

```
        lock_guard(M &m) : m { m } { m.lock(); }
        ~lock_guard() { m.unlock(); }
        lock_guard(const lock_guard&) = delete;
        lock_guard& operator=(const lock_guard&) = delete;
    };
```

The simplest types are often the best. Indeed, applying this type to our `string_mutator` example, we end up with a simpler, yet much more robust implementation:

```
#include <thread>
#include <mutex>
#include <string>
#include <algorithm>
#include <string_view>
class string_mutator {
    std::string text;
    mutable std::mutex m;
public:
    // note: m in uncopiable so string_mutator
    // also is uncopiable
    string_mutator(std::string_view src)
        : text{ src.begin(), src.end() } {
    }
    template <class F> void operator()(F f) {
        std::lock_guard lck{ m };
        std::transform(text.begin(), text.end(),
                        text.begin(), f);
    } // implicit m.unlock
    std::string grab_snapshot() const {
        std::lock_guard lck{ m };
        return text;
    } // implicit m.unlock
};
```

Clearly, using destructors to automate unlocking our mutex is advantageous for cases such as this: it simplifies code and helps make it exception-safe.

stream objects

In C++, stream objects are also resource owners. Consider the following code example where we copy each byte from file `in.txt` to the standard output stream:

```
#include <fstream>
#include <iostream>
```

```
int main() {
    std::ifstream in{ "in.txt" };
    for(char c; in.get(c); )
        std::cout << c;
}
```

You might notice a few interesting details in this code: we never call `close()`, there's no `try` block where we would be preparing ourselves for exception management, there's no call to `open()` in order to open the file, there's no explicit check for some end-of-file state… yet, this code works correctly, does what it's supposed to do, and does not leak resources.

How can such a simple program do all that? Through "the magic of destructors", or (more precisely) the magic of a good API. Think about it:

- The constructor's role is to put the object in a correct initial state. Thus, we use it to open the file as it would be both pointless and inefficient to default-construct the stream, then open it later.

- Errors when reading from a stream are not exceptional at all… Think about it, how often do we face errors when reading from a stream? In C++, reading from a stream (here: calling `in.get(c)`) returns a reference to the stream after reading from it, and that stream behaves like a `false` Boolean value if the stream is in an error state.

- Finally, the destructor of a stream object closes whatever representation of a stream it is responsible for. Calling `close()` on a stream in C++ is unnecessary most of the time; just using the stream object in a limited scope generally suffices.

Destructors (and constructors!), when used appropriately, lead to more robust and simpler code.

vector<T> and other containers

We will not write a full-blown comparison of containers with raw arrays or other low-level constructs such as linked lists with manually managed nodes or dynamic arrays maintained explicitly through client code. We will however examine how one can write containers such as `std::vector` or `std::list` in later chapters of this book (*Chapters 12*, *13*, and *14*) when we know a bit more on memory management techniques.

Please note, still, that using `std::vector<T>` (for example) is not only significantly simpler and safer than managing a dynamically allocated array of T: in practice, it's most probably significantly *faster*, at least if used knowledgeably. As we will come to see, there's no way users can invest the care and attention that goes into memory management and object creation, destruction and copying or movement that goes in a standard container when writing day-to-day code. The destructor of these types, coupled with the way their other special member functions are implemented, make them almost as easy to use as `int` objects, a worthy goal if there ever was one!

Summary

In this chapter, we have discussed some safety-related issues, with a focus on those involving exceptions. We have seen that some standard library types offer specialized semantics with respect to resource management, where "resource" includes but is not limited to memory. In *Chapter 5*, we will spend some time examining how to use and benefit from standard smart pointer; then, in *Chapter 6*, we will go further and look at some of the challenges behind writing your own versions of these smart pointers, as well as some other smart pointer-inspired types with other semantics. Then, we will delve into deeper memory management-related concerns.

5

Using Standard Smart Pointers

C++ emphasizes programming with values. By default, your code uses objects, not indirections (references and pointers) to objects. Indirect access to objects is, of course, allowed, and rare is the program that never uses such semantics, but it is an opt-in and requires additional syntax. *Chapter 4* explored the association of resource management with object lifetime through destructors and the RAII idiom, demonstrating one of C++'s main strengths in that essentially all resources (including memory) can be handled implicitly through the very mechanics of the language.

C++ allows the use of raw pointers in code but does not actively encourage it. Quite the contrary, in fact – raw pointers are a low-level facility, extremely efficient but easy to misuse, and for which it is not easy to infer responsibility about the *pointee* directly from the source code. Starting with the (now-removed) `auto_ptr<T>` facility of decades past, there has been an effort in the C++ community to define abstractions around lower-level facilities, such as raw pointers, through types that provide clear, well-defined semantics and reduce the risk of programming errors. This effort has met with significant success, in large part due to the expressiveness of the C++ language and its ability to create powerful and efficient abstractions, without losing speed or using more memory at runtime. For this reason, in contemporary C++, raw pointers are usually encapsulated underneath harder-to-misuse abstractions, examples of which include standard containers and smart pointers, such as the ones we will explore in this chapter; raw pointers that are not encapsulated are mostly used to mean "*Here's a resource you can use but do not own.*"

This chapter will look at how to use the standard smart pointer types of C++. We will first look at what they are, and then delve into ways to use the main smart pointer types efficiently. Finally, we will look at those moments where we need to "get our hands dirty" (so to speak) and use raw pointers, ideally (but not only) through the mediation of smart pointers. This should lead us to learn how to choose standard smart pointers for a given use case, how to use them appropriately, and how to handle resources that have to be freed through custom mechanisms. Throughout this journey, we will keep in mind and explain the costs of the choices we make.

In this chapter, we will do the following:

- Take a quick look at the general idea of standard smart pointers to develop an idea of their reason for being

- Look more closely at std::unique_ptr, including how it can be used to handle scalars, arrays, and release resources that are allocated in atypical ways

- Look at std::shared_ptr and the use cases for this essential but more costly type, in order to grasp when alternatives should be preferred

- Take a quick look at std::weak_ptr, a companion to std::shared_ptr that is useful when there is a need to model temporary shared ownership

- Look at cases where raw pointers should be used, as they still have their place in the C++ ecosystem

Ready? Let's dive in!

Technical requirements

You can find the code files for this chapter in the book's GitHub repository here: https://github.com/PacktPublishing/C-Plus-Plus-Memory-Management/tree/main/chapter5.

The standard smart pointers

C++ has a relatively small *zoo* of smart pointers. Before looking at the set of options provided by the standard, let's take a moment to show the problem we are trying to solve. Consider the following (deliberately incomplete) program. Do you see anything wrong with it?

```
class X {
    // ...
};
X *f();
void g(X *p);
void h() {
    X *p = f();
    g(p);
    delete p;
}
```

This is code that is legal but not something you want to see in a contemporary program. There's just so much that can go wrong here, such as the following from a non-exhaustive list of potential problems:

- We don't know whether g() will call delete p, leading to a second delete (on a destroyed object!) in h() afterward

- We don't know whether g() might throw, in which case the delete p; instruction in h() will never be reached

- We don't know whether h() should be assumed to own p, in the sense that we do not know whether it should be responsible for calling operator delete() on p (maybe it's meant to be the responsibility of g(), or some other function)

- We do not know whether what p points to has been allocated with new, new[], or something else (malloc(), some facility from another language, some custom utility in your code base, etc.)

- We don't even know whether what p points to has been dynamically allocated at all; p could point to a global or a static variable declared in f(), for example (a bad idea, but some people do that – for example, when implementing the singleton design pattern in a non-idiomatic way for C++)

Compare, for example, two possible implementations of f() (there are many, many more we could consider, but these will suffice for now):

```
X *f() { // here's one possibility
    return new X;
}
X *f() { // here's another
    static X x;
    return &x;
}
```

In the first case, it *might* make sense to call delete on the returned pointer, but in the second case, it would be disastrous to do so. Nothing in the function's signature clearly informs the client code whether we are facing one situation or the other, or even something else entirely.

As a "bonus" of sorts, what happens if someone calls f() without using the returned value? If f() is implemented as return new X; or something similar, then the code will leak – an unpleasant perspective indeed. Note that since C++17, you can mitigate this specific problem by annotating the return type of f() with the [[nodiscard]] attribute, but it's still something you should be aware of. Returning raw pointers from a function is something we mostly try to avoid, even though we sometimes have to do so.

There are other possible pitfalls here, and they all have a common theme – using raw pointers, we traditionally cannot tell from the source code what the semantics are. More specifically, we cannot say for sure who is responsible for both the pointer and what it points to. The fact that raw pointers do not provide clear ownership information has been a recurring source of bugs in C++ over the years.

Now, for a different situation, consider the following code excerpt:

```
// ...
void f() {
    X *p = new X;
    thread th0{ [p] { /* use *p */ };
    thread th1{ [p] { /* use *p */ };
    th0.detach();
    th1.detach();
}
```

In this case, `f()` allocates an X object pointed to by p, after which two threads, th0 and th1, copy p (thus sharing the X object that p points to). Finally, th0 and th1 are detached, meaning that the threads will run until completion, even after `f()` is done. If we do not know in what order th0 and th1 will conclude, we cannot clearly state which one should be responsible for calling `operator delete()` on p. This is yet another issue of unclear responsibility over the *pointee* but of a different kind than our first example, and as such, it needs a different solution.

For the cases where there is a clearly identified last owner of a pointed-to object, regardless of whether the *pointee* is shared or not between pointers, you probably want to use `std::unique_ptr`. In the (more niche, but very real and quite subtle) case where the pointed-to object is shared by at least two "co-owners" and the order in which these owners will be destroyed is a priori unknown, `std::shared_ptr` is the tool of choice. The following sections go into the roles and meaning of these types in more detail, hopefully helping you make an informed choice when choosing a smart pointer type for a given use case.

On the exposition of intent through function signatures

Even though we have not looked in detail at the standard smart pointers yet, it might be appropriate to offer a few words on what they mean, in particular for `std::unique_ptr` and `std::shared_ptr`. These two types convey *ownership semantics* – `std::unique_ptr` represents *sole ownership* of the pointee, and `std::shared_ptr` represents *co-ownership* (or *shared ownership*) of the pointee.

It's important to understand the difference between *owning* (in particular, *co-owning*) a pointee and *sharing* a pointee. Consider the following example, which uses `std::unique_ptr` (even though we have not covered it yet, but we're getting there) and raw pointers *together* in order to inscribe ownership semantics in the type system:

```
#include <memory>
#include <iostream>
```

```
// print_pointee() shares a pointer with the caller
// but does not take ownership
template <class T> void print_pointee(T *p) {
    if (p) std::cout << *p << '\n';
}
std::unique_ptr<T> make_one(const T &arg) {
    return std::make_unique<T>(arg);
}
int main() {
    auto p = make_one(3); // p is a std::unique_ptr<int>
    print_pointee(p.get()); // caller and callee share the
                            // pointer during this call
}
```

As mentioned when introducing this example, we used a `std::unique_ptr` object to model ownership – `make_one()` constructs `std::unique_ptr<T>` and transfers ownership to the caller; then, that caller keeps ownership of that object and shares the underlying pointer with others (here, `print_pointee()`) but does not relinquish ownership of the pointee. Using yet not owning is modeled by a raw pointer. This shows us in a highly simplified setting that there is a difference between owning and sharing a resource – p in `main()` owns the resource, yet it shares it with the non-owner, p, in `print_pointee()`. This is all safe and idiomatic C++ code.

Knowing that the standard smart pointer types model represents ownership, we know that as long as there is a single, clear last user of a resource, `std::unique_ptr` tends to be the type of choice; it is much more lightweight than `std::shared_ptr` (as we will see), and it provides the appropriate ownership semantics.

There are, of course, use cases where `std::unique_ptr` is not a good choice. Consider this simplified, not thread-safe, and incomplete code excerpt:

```
class entity {
    bool taken{ false };
public:
    void take() { taken = true; }
    void release() { taken = false; }
    bool taken() const { return taken; }
    // ...
};
constexpr int N = ...;
// entities is where the entity objects live. We did
// not allocate them dynamically, but if we had we would
// have used unique_ptr<entity> as this will be the
// single last point of use for these objects
array<entity,N> entities;
```

```
class nothing_left{};
// this function returns a non-owning pointer (Chapter 6
// will cover more ergonomic options than a raw pointer)
entity * borrow_one() {
    if(auto p = find_if(begin(entities), end(entities),
                [](auto && e) { return !e.taken(); };
        p != end(entities)) {
        p->take();
        return &(*p); // non-owning pointer
    }
    throw nothing_left{};
}
```

Note that `borrow_one()` shares a pointer with the calling code but does not share *ownership* of that pointer – the provider of the `entity` objects remains solely responsible for the lifetime of these objects in this case. This would neither be a case for `std::unique_ptr` (the sole owner of the resource) nor `std::shared_ptr` (the co-owner of the resource). There are alternatives to using raw pointers to express a non-owning pointer, as we will see in *Chapter 6*.

The important point here is that *function signatures convey meaning*, and it's important to use the types that convey our intent. To do so, we have to understand that intent. Let's keep that in mind as we explore how to use the standard smart pointers to our advantage in the following sections.

Type unique_ptr

As its name suggests, a `unique_ptr<T>` object represents sole (unique) ownership of a pointed-to object. That happens to be a common case – maybe even the most common case – of ownership semantics when dealing with dynamically allocated memory.

Consider our first (still deliberately incomplete) example in this chapter, where ownership of the *pointee* was not something we could determine from the source code, and let's rewrite it with `unique_ptr` objects instead of raw pointers:

```
#include <memory>
class X {
    // ...
};
std::unique_ptr<X> f();
void g(std::unique_ptr<X>&);
void h() {
    // we could write std::unique_ptr<X> instead of auto
    auto p = f();
    g(p);
} // p implicitly releases the pointed-to X object here
```

With this code, it's clear that the object returned by f() is responsible for the lifetime of the X object it points to, and it's also clear that g() uses the enclosed X* without becoming responsible for the pointed-to X object. Add to this the fact that p is an object and, as such, will be destroyed if g() throws or if f() is called in such a way that the calling code forgets to use the return value, and you get an exception-safe program – one that's shorter and simpler than the original one!

> ### Murphy and Machiavelli
>
> You might be thinking, "*But I'm sure I could steal the pointer managed by the* std::unique_ptr *in* g()," and you would be correct. Not only is it possible but also easy, as unique_ptr gives you direct access to the underlying pointer in more than one way. However, the type system is designed to protect us from accidents and make reasonable well-written code work well. It will protect you from Murphy, the accidents that happen, not from Machiavelli, the deliberately hostile code.
>
> If you write deliberately broken code, you will end up with a deliberately broken program. It's pretty much what you would expect.

In terms of semantics, you could tell a story just with function signatures, using std::unique_ptr objects. Note that in the following example, the functions have been left deliberately incomplete to make it clear that we are concerned with their signatures only:

```
// ...
// dynamically create an X or something derived from
// X and return it without risk of a leak
unique_ptr<X> factory(args);
// pass-by-value which means in practice pass-by-movement
// since unique_ptr is uncopiable
unique_ptr<X> borrowing(unique_ptr<X>);
// pass-by-reference to allow mutating the pointee. In
// practice, X* would be a better choice here
void possible_mutation(unique_ptr<X>&);
// pass by reference-to-const to consult the pointee but
// not mutate it. In practice, prefer const X* here
void consult(const unique_ptr<X>&);
// sink() consumes the object passed as argument : gets
// in, never gets out. This could use pass-by-value but
// intent is probably clearer with a rvalue-reference
void sink(unique_ptr<X> &&);
// ...
```

As we can see, function signatures talk to us. It's better if we pay attention.

Handling objects

The `unique_ptr` type is a remarkable tool, one you should strive to get acquainted with if you have not done so already. Here are some interesting facts about that type and how it can be used to manage pointers to objects.

A `unique_ptr<T>` object is non-copyable, as its copy constructor and copy assignment member functions are marked as deleted. That's why `g()` in the first example of the *Type unique_ptr* section takes its argument by reference – `g()` shares the pointee with the caller but does not take ownership of it. We could also have expressed `g()` as taking `X*` as an argument, with the contemporary acceptance that function arguments that are raw pointers are meant to model using a pointer but without owning it:

```
#include <memory>
class X {
    // ...
};
std::unique_ptr<X> f();
void g(X*);
void h() {
    // we could write std::unique_ptr<X> instead of auto
    auto p = f();
    g(p.get());
} // p implicitly releases the pointed-to X object here
```

`unique_ptr<T>` is also movable – a moved-from `unique_ptr<T>` behaves like a null pointer, as the movement for this type semantically implements a transfer of ownership. This makes it simpler to implement various types that need to manage resources indirectly.

Consider, for example, the following `solar_system` class, which supposes a hypothetical `Planet` type as well as a hypothetical implementation for `create_planet()`:

```
#include "planet.h"
#include <memory>
#include <string>
#include <vector>
std::unique_ptr<Planet>
    create_planet(std::string_view name);
class solar_system {
    std::vector<std::unique_ptr<Planet>> planets {
        create_planet("mercury.data"),
        create_planet("venus.data"), // etc.
    };
public:
    // solar_system is uncopyable by default
    // solar_system is movable by default
```

```
    // no need to write ~solar_system as planets
    // manages its resources implicitly
};
```

If we had decided to implement `solar_system` with `vector<Planet*>` or as `Planet*` instead, then the memory management of our type would have to be performed by `solar_system` itself, adding to the complexity of that type. Since we used a `vector<unique_ptr<Planet>>`, everything is implicitly correct by default. Of course, depending on what we are doing, `vector<Planet>` might be even better, but let's suppose we need pointers for the sake of the example.

A `unique_ptr<T>` offers most of the same operations as `T*`, including `operator*()` and `operator->()`, as well as the ability to compare them with `==` or `!=` to see whether two `unique_ptr<T>` objects point to the same `T` object. The latter two might seem strange, as the type represents sole ownership of the *pointee*, but you could use references to `unique_ptr<T>`, in which case these functions make sense:

```
#include <memory>
template <class T>
    bool point_to_same(const std::unique_ptr<T> &p0,
                       const std::unique_ptr<T> &p1) {
        return p0 == p1;
    }
template <class T>
    bool have_same_value(const std::unique_ptr<T> &p0,
                        const std::unique_ptr<T> &p1) {
        return p0 && p1 && *p0 == *p1;
    }
#include <cassert>
int main() {
    // two distinct pointers to objects with same value
    std::unique_ptr<int> a{ new int { 3 } };
    std::unique_ptr<int> b{ new int { 3 } };
    assert(point_to_same(a, a) && have_same_value(a, a));
    assert(!point_to_same(a, b) && have_same_value(a, b));
}
```

For good reasons, you cannot do pointer arithmetic on `unique_ptr<T>`. If you need to do pointer arithmetic (and we sometimes will – for example, when we write our own containers in *Chapter 13*), it's always possible to get to the raw pointer owned by a `unique_pointer<T>` through its `get()` member function. This is often useful when interfacing with C libraries, making system calls, or calling functions that use a raw pointer without taking ownership of it.

Oh, and here's a fun fact – `sizeof(unique_ptr<T>)==sizeof(T*)` with a few exceptions that will be discussed later in this chapter. This means that there's generally no cost in terms of memory space to using a smart pointer instead of a raw pointer. In other words, by default, the only state found in a `unique_ptr<T>` object is `T*`.

Handling arrays

A nice aspect of `unique_ptr` is that it offers a specialization to handle arrays. Consider the following:

```
void f(int n) {
    // p points to an int of value 3
    std::unique_ptr<int> p{ new int{ 3 } };
    // q points to an array of n int objects
    // initialized to zero
    std::unique_ptr<int[]> q{ new int[n] {} };
    // example usage
    std::cout << *p << '\n'; // displays 3
    for(int i = 0; i != n; ++i) {
        // operator[] supported for unique_ptr<T[]>
        q[i] = i + 1;
    }
    // ...
} // the destructor of q calls delete [] on its pointee
    // the destructor of p calls delete on its pointee
```

What, you might think, is the use case for this? Well, it all depends on your needs. For example, if you require a variable-sized array of T that grows as needed, use `vector<T>`. It's a wonderful tool and extremely efficient if used well.

If you want a fixed-sized array that's small enough to fit on your execution stack where the number of elements, N, is known at compile time, use a raw array of T or an object of type `std::array<T,N>`.

If you want a fixed-sized array that's either not small enough to fit on your execution stack or where the number of elements, n, is known at runtime, you can use `vector<T>`, but you'll pay for facilities you might not require (`vector<T>` remains an awesome choice, that being said), or you could use `unique_ptr<T[]>`. Note that if you go for this latter option, you will end up having to track the size yourself, separately from the actual array, since `unique_ptr` does no such tracking. Alternatively, of course, you can wrap it in your own abstraction, such as `fixed_size_array<T>`, as follows:

```
#include <cstddef>
#include <memory>
template <class T>
    class fixed_size_array {
```

```
    std::size_t nelems{};
    std::unique_ptr<T[]> elems {};
public:
    fixed_size_array() = default;
    auto size() const { return nelems; }
    bool empty() const { return size() == 0; }
    fixed_size_array(std::size_t n)
        : nelems { n }, elems{ new T[n] {} } {
    }
    T& operator[](int n) { return elems[n]; }
    const T& operator[](int n) const { return elems[n]; }
    // etc.
};
```

This is a naïve implementation that brings together knowledge of the number of elements with implicit ownership of the resource. Note that we don't have to write the copy operations (unless we want to implement them!), the move operations, or the destructor, as they all implicitly do something reasonable. Also, this type will be relatively efficient if type T is trivially constructible but will (really) not be as efficient as vector<T> for numerous use cases. Why is that? Well, it so happens that vector does significantly better memory management than we do... but we'll get there.

Note that, as with scalar types, the fact that sizeof(unique_ptr<T[]>) is equal to sizeof(T*) is also true, which I'm sure we can all appreciate.

Custom deleters

You might think, "*Well, in my code base, we don't use* delete *to deallocate objects because [insert your favorite reason here], so I cannot use* unique_ptr." There are indeed many situations where applying operator delete on a pointer to destroy the pointed-to object is not an option:

- Sometimes, T::~T() is private or protected, making it inaccessible to other classes such as unique_ptr<T>.

- Sometimes, the finalization semantics require doing something else than calling delete – for example, calling a destroy() or release() member function

- Sometimes, the expectation is to call a free function that will perform auxiliary work in addition to freeing a resource.

No matter what the reasons are for freeing a resource in an unconventional manner, `unique_ptr<T>` can take a **custom deleter** that will perform those custom resource deallocation tasks. A custom deleter can be a functor or a function that will be applied to the `T*` stored within `unique_ptr<T>` when the destructor of that smart pointer is called. Indeed, the actual signature of the `unique_ptr` template is as follows:

```
template<class T, class D = std::default_delete<T>>
    class unique_ptr {
        // ...
    };
```

Here, `default_delete<T>` itself is essentially the following:

```
template<class T> struct default_delete {
    constexpr default_delete() noexcept = default;
    // ...
    constexpr void operator()(T *p) const { delete p; }
};
```

The presence of a default type for D is what usually allows us to write code that ignores that parameter. The D parameter in the `unique_ptr<T, D>` signature is expected to be stateless, as it's not stored within the `unique_ptr` object but instantiated as needed, and then it's used as a function that takes the pointer and does whatever is required to finalize the *pointee*.

As such, imagine the following class with a `private` destructor, a common technique if you seek to prevent instantiation through other means than dynamic allocation (you cannot use an automatic or a static object of that type, since it cannot be implicitly destroyed):

```
#include <memory>
class requires_dynamic_alloc {
    ~requires_dynamic_alloc() = default; // private
    // ...
    friend struct cleaner;
};
// ...
struct cleaner {
    template <class T>
        void operator()(T *p) const { delete p; }
};
int main() {
    using namespace std;
    // requires_dynamic_alloc r0; // no
    //auto p0 = unique_ptr<requires_dynamic_alloc>{
    //    new requires_dynamic_alloc
```

```
    //}; // no, as delete not available to default deleter
    auto p1 = unique_ptr<requires_dynamic_alloc, cleaner>{
        new requires_dynamic_alloc
    }; // ok, will use cleaner::operator() to delete pointee
}
```

Note that by making the `cleaner` functor its friend, the `requires_dynamic_alloc` class lets `cleaner` specifically access both its `protected` and `private` members, which includes access to its `private` destructor.

Imagine now that we are using an object through an interface that hides from client code information on whether we are the sole owner of the pointed-to resource, or whether we share that resource with others. Also, imagine that the potential sharing of that resource is done through intrusive means, as is done on many platforms, such that the way to signal that we are disconnecting from that resource is to call its `release()` member function, which will, in turn, either take into account that we have disconnected or free the resource if we were its last users. To simplify client code, our code base has a `release()` free function that calls the `release()` member function on such a pointer if it is non-null.

We can still use `unique_ptr` for this, but note the syntax, which is slightly different, as we will need to pass the function pointer as an argument to the constructor, since that pointer will be stored within. Thus, this specialization of `unique_ptr` with a function pointer as a *deleter* leads to a slight size increase:

```
#include <memory>
struct releasable {
    void release() {
        // overly simplified for the sake of this example
        delete this;
    }
protected:
    ~releasable() = default;
};
class important_resource : public releasable {
    // ...
};
void release(releasable *p) {
    if(p) p->release();
}
int main() {
    using namespace std;
    auto p = unique_ptr<important_resource,
                        void(*)(releasable*)>{
```

```
        new important_resource, release
    }; // ok, will use release() to delete pointee
}
```

If the extra cost of a function pointer's size (plus alignment) in the size of unique_ptr is unacceptable (for example, because you are on a resource-constrained platform or because you have a container with many unique_ptr objects, which makes the costs increase significantly faster), there's a neat trick you can play by pushing the runtime use of the deleter function into the wonderful world of the type system:

```
#include <memory>
struct releasable {
    void release() {
        // overly simplified for the sake of this example
        delete this;
    }
protected:
    ~releasable() = default;
};
class important_resource : public releasable {
    // ...
};
void release(releasable *p) {
    if(p) p->release();
}
int main() {
    using namespace std;
    auto p = unique_ptr<important_resource,
                      void(*)(releasable*)>{
        new important_resource, release
    }; // ok, will use release() to delete pointee
    static_assert(sizeof(p) > sizeof(void*));
    auto q = unique_ptr<
        important_resource,
        decltype([](auto p) { release(p); })>{
        new important_resource
    };
    static_assert(sizeof(q) == sizeof(void*));
}
```

As you can see, in the case of p, we used a function pointer as a deleter, which requires storing the address of the function, whereas with q, we replaced the function pointer with the *type of a hypothetical lambda*, which will, when instantiated, call that function, passing the pointer as an argument. It's simple and can save space if used judiciously!

make_unique

Since C++14, unique_ptr<T> has been accompanied by a factory function that perfectly forwards its arguments to a constructor of T, allocates and constructs the T as well as unique_ptr<T> to hold it, and returns the resulting object. That function is std::make_unique<T>(args...), and a naïve implementation would be as follows:

```
template <class T, class ... Args>
   std::unique_ptr<T> make_unique(Args &&... args) {
      return std::unique_ptr<T>{
         new T(std::forward<Args>(args)...);
      }
   }
```

There are also variants to create a T[], of course. You might wonder what the point of such a function is, and indeed, that function was not shipped along with unique_ptr initially (unique_ptr is a C++11 type), but consider the following (contrived) example:

```
template <class T>
   class pair_with_alloc {
      T *p0, *p1;
   public:
      pair_with_alloc(const T &val0, const T &val1)
         : p0{ new T(val0) }, p1{ new T(val1) } {
      }
      ~pair_with_alloc() {
         delete p1; delete p0;
      }
      // copy and move operations left to your imagination
   };
```

We can suppose from this example that this class is used when, for some reason, client code prefers to dynamically allocate the T objects (in practice, using objects rather than pointers to objects makes your life simpler). Knowing that subobjects in a C++ object are constructed in order of declaration, we know that p0 will be constructed before p1:

```
// ...
      T *p0, *p1; // p0 declared before p1
   public:
// below:
// - new T(val0) will occur before construction of p0
// - new T(val1) will occur before construction of p1
// - construction of p0 will precede construction of p1
      pair_with_alloc(const T &val0, const T &val1)
         : p0{ new T(val0) }, p1{ new T(val1) } {
```

```
        }
// ...
```

However, suppose that the order of operations is new T(val0), the construction of p0, new T(val1), and the construction of p1. What happens then if new T(val1) throws an exception, either because new fails to allocate sufficient memory or because the constructor of T fails? You might be tempted to think that the destructor of pair_with_alloc will clean up, but that will not be the case – for a destructor to be called, the corresponding constructor must have completed first; otherwise, there is no object to destroy!

There are ways around this ,of course. One of them might be to use unique_ptr<T> instead of T*, which would be wonderful, given that this is what we're currently discussing! Let's rewrite pair_with_alloc that way:

```cpp
#include <memory>
template <class T>
   class pair_with_alloc {
      std::unique_ptr<T> p0, p1;
   public:
      pair_with_alloc(const T &val0, const T &val1)
         : p0{ new T(val0) }, p1{ new T(val1) } {
      }
      // destructor implicitly correct
      // copy and move operations implicitly work
      // or are left to your imagination
   };
```

With this version, if the order of operations is new T(val0), the construction of p0, new T(val1), the construction of p1, then if new T(val1) throws an exception, the pair_with_alloc object will still not be destroyed (it has not been constructed). However, p0 itself *has* been constructed by that point, and as such, it will be destroyed. Our code has suddenly become simpler and safer!

What then has that to do with make_unique<T>()? Well, there's a hidden trap here. Let's look closer at the order of operations in our constructor:

```cpp
// ...
      std::unique_ptr<T> p0, p1; // p0 declared before p1
   public:
// below, suppose we identify the operations as follows:
// A: new T(val0)
// B: construction of p0
// C: new T(val1)
// D: construction of p1
// We know that:
// - A precedes B
```

```
// - C precedes D
// - B precedes D
    pair_with_alloc(const T &val0, const T &val1)
        : p0{ new T(val0) }, p1{ new T(val1) } {
    }
// ...
```

If you look at the rules laid out in the comments, you will see that we could have the operations in the following order, A→B→C→D, but we could also have them ordered as A→C→B→D or C→A→B→D, in which case the two calls to new T(...) would occur, followed by the two unique_ptr<T> constructors. If this happens, then an exception thrown by the second call to new or the associated constructor of T would still lead to a resource leak.

Now, that's a shame. But that's also the point of make_unique<T>() – with a factory function, client code never finds itself with "floating results from calls to new"; it either has a complete unique_ptr<T> object or not:

```
#include <memory>
template <class T>
    class pair_with_alloc {
        std::unique_ptr<T> p0, p1;
    public:
        pair_with_alloc(const T &val0, const T &val1)
            : p0{ std::make_unique<T>(val0) },
              p1{ std::make_unique<T>(val1) } {
        }
        // destructor implicitly correct
        // copy and move operations implicitly work
        // or are left to your imagination
    };
#include <string>
#include <random>
#include <iostream>
class risky {
    std::mt19937 prng{ std::random_device{}() };
    std::uniform_int_distribution<int> penny{ 0,1 };
public:
    risky() = default;
    risky(const risky &) {
        if(penny(prng)) throw 3; // throws 50% of the time
    }
    ~risky() {
        std::cout << "~risky()\n";
    }
```

```
};
int main() {
    // the following objects do not leak even if
    // an exception is thrown
    if(std::string s0, s1; std::cin >> s0 >> s1)
        try {
            pair_with_alloc a{ s0, s1 };
            pair_with_alloc b{ risky{}, risky{} };
        } catch(...) {
            std::cerr << "Something was thrown...\n";
        }
}
```

As you can see, make_unique<T>() is a security feature, mostly useful to avoid exposing ownerless resources in client code. As a bonus, make_unique<T>() allows us to limit how we repeat ourselves in source code. Check the following:

```
unique_ptr<some_type> p0 { new some_type{ args } };
auto p1 = unique_ptr<some_type> { new some_type{ args } };
auto p2 = make_unique<some_type>(args);
```

As you can see, p0 and p1 require you to spell the name of the pointed-to type twice whereas p2 only requires you to write it once. That's always nice.

Types shared_ptr and weak_ptr

In most cases, unique_ptr<T> will be your smart pointer of choice. It's small, fast, and does what most code requires. There are some specialized but important use cases where unique_ptr<T> is not what you need, and these have in common the following:

- The semantics being conveyed is the *shared ownership* of the resource

- The last owner of the resource is not known a priori (which mostly happens in concurrent code)

Note that if the execution is not concurrent, you will, in general, know who the last owner of the resource is – it's the last object to observe the resource that will be destroyed in the program. This is an important point – you can have concurrent code that shares resources and still uses unique_ptr to manage the resource. Non-owning users of the resource, such as raw pointers, can access it without taking ownership (more on that later in this chapter), and this approach is sufficient.

You can, of course, have non-concurrent code where the last owner of a resource is not known a priori. An example might involve a protocol where the provider of the resource still holds on to it after returning it to the client, but they might be asked to release it at a later point while client code retains it, making the client the last owner from that point on, or they might never be asked to release it, in which case the provider might be the last owner of the resource. Such situations are highly specific, obviously, but they show that there might be reasons to use shared ownership semantics as expressed through `std::shared_ptr`, even in non-concurrent code.

Since concurrent code remains the posterchild for situations where the last owner of a shared resource is not known a priori, we will use this as a basis for our investigation. Remember this example from the beginning of this chapter:

```
// ...
void f() {
    X *p = new X;
    thread th0{ [p] { /* use *p */ };
    thread th1{ [p] { /* use *p */ };
    th0.detach();
    th1.detach();
}
```

Here, p in f() does not own the X it points to, being a raw pointer, and both th0 and th1 copy that raw pointer, so neither is responsible for the pointee (at least on the basis of the rules enforced by the type system; you could envision acrobatics to make this work, but it's involved, tricky, and bug-prone).

This example can be amended to have clear ownership semantics by shifting p from X* to `shared_ptr<X>`. Indeed, let's consider the following:

```
// ...
void f() {
    std::shared_ptr<X> p { new X };
    thread th0{ [p] { /* use *p */ };
    thread th1{ [p] { /* use *p */ };
    th0.detach();
    th1.detach();
}
```

In f(), the p object is initially the sole owner of the X it points to. When p is copied, as it is in the capture blocks of the lambdas executed by th0 and th1, the mechanics of `shared_ptr` ensure that p and its two copies share both X* and an integral counter, used to determine how many shared owners there are for the resource.

The key functions of `shared_ptr` are its copy constructor (shares the resource and increments the counter), copy assignment (disconnects from the original resource, decrementing its counter, and then connects to the new resource, incrementing its counter), and the destructor (decrements the counter and destroys the resource if there's no owner left). Each of these functions is subtle to implement; to help understand what the stakes are, we will provide simplified implementation examples in *Chapter 6*. Move semantics, unsurprisingly, implement transfer of ownership semantics for `shared_ptr`.

Note that `shared_ptr<T>` implements extrusive (non-intrusive) shared ownership semantics. Type T could be a fundamental type and does not need to implement a particular interface for this type to work. This differs from the intrusive shared semantics that were mentioned earlier in this chapter, with the `releasable` type an example.

Usefulness and costs

There are intrinsic costs to the `shared_ptr<T>` model. The most obvious one is that `sizeof(shared_ptr<T>)>sizeof(unique_ptr<T>)` for any type T, since `shared_ptr<T>` needs to handle both a pointer to the shared resource and a pointer to the shared counter.

Another cost is that copying a `shared_ptr<T>` is not a cheap operation. Remember that `shared_ptr<T>` makes sense mostly in concurrent code, where you do not know a priori the last owner of a resource. For that reason, the increments and decrements of the shared counter require synchronization, meaning that the counter is typically an `atomic` integer, and mutating an `atomic<int>` object (for example) costs more than mutating an `int`.

Another non-negligible cost is the following:

```
shared_ptr<X> p{ new X };
```

An instruction such as this one will lead to *two* allocations, not one – there will be one for the X object and another one (performed internally by the `shared_ptr`) for the counter. Since these two allocations will be done separately, one by the client code and one by the constructor itself, the two allocated objects might find themselves in distinct cache lines, potentially leading to a loss of efficiency when accessing the `shared_ptr` object.

make_shared()

There is a way to alleviate the latter cost, and that is to make the same entity perform both allocations, instead of letting the client code do one and the constructor do the other. The standard tool to achieve this is the `std::make_shared<T>()` factory function.

Compare the following two instructions:

```
shared_ptr<X> p{ new X(args) };
auto q = make_shared<X>(args);
```

When constructing p, `shared_ptr<X>` is provided an existing `X*` to manage, so it has no choice but to perform a second, separate allocation for the shared counter. Conversely, the call expressed as `make_shared<X>(args)` specifies the type X to construct along with the arguments `args` to forward directly to the constructor. It falls upon that function to create `shared_ptr<X>`, X, and the shared counter, which lets us put both X and the counter in the same contiguous space (the **control block**), using mechanisms such as a *union* or the *placement new* mechanism, which will be explored in *Chapter 7*.

Clearly, given the same arguments used for construction, the preceding p and q will be equivalent shared_ptr<X> objects, but in general, q will perform better than p, as its two key components will be organized in a more cache-friendly manner.

What about weak_ptr?

If shared_ptr<T> is a type with a narrower (yet essential) niche than unique_ptr<T>, weak_ptr<T> occupies an even narrower (but still essential) niche. The role of weak_ptr<T> is to model the *temporary* ownership of T. Type weak_ptr<T> is meant to interact with shared_ptr<T> in a way that makes the continued existence of the *pointee* testable from client code.

A good example of weak_ptr usage, inspired by the excellent cppreference website (https://en.cppreference.com/w/cpp/memory/weak_ptr), is as follows:

```cpp
// inspired from a cppreference example
#include <iostream>
#include <memory>
#include <format>
void observe(std::weak_ptr<int> w) {
   if (std::shared_ptr<int> sh = w.lock())
      std::cout << std::format("*sh == {}\n", *sh);
   else
      std::cout << "w is expired\n";
}
int main() {
   std::weak_ptr<int> w;
   {
      auto sh = std::make_shared<int>(3);
      w = sh; // weak_ptr made from shared_ptr
      // w points to a live shared_ptr<int> here
      observe(w);
   }
   // w points to an expired shared_ptr<int> here
   observe(w);
}
```

As this example shows, you can make weak_ptr<T> from shared_ptr<T>, but weak_ptr does not own the resource until you call lock() on it, yielding shared_ptr<T>, from which you can safely use the resource after having verified that it does not model an empty pointer.

Another use case for `std::weak_ptr` and `std::shared_ptr` would be a cache of resources such that the following occurs:

- The data in a `Resource` object is sufficiently big or costly to duplicate that it's preferable to share it than to copy it

- A `Cache` object shares the objects it stores, but it needs to invalidate them before replacing them when its capacity is reached

In such a situation, a `Cache` object could hold `std::shared_ptr<Resource>` objects but provide its client code, `std::weak_ptr<Resource>`, on demand, such that the `Resource` objects can be disposed of when the `Cache` needs to do so, but the client code needs to be able to verify that the objects it points to have not yet been invalidated.

A full (simplified) example would be the following (see the GitHub repository for this book to get the full example):

```cpp
// ...
template <auto Cap>
   class Cache {
      using clock = std::chrono::system_clock;
      // a cache of capacity Cap that keeps the
      // most recently used Resource objects
      std::vector<std::pair<
         decltype(clock::now()),
         std::shared_ptr<Resource>
      >> resources;
      bool full() const { return resources.size() == Cap; }
      // precondition: !resources.empty()
      void expunge_one() {
         auto p = std::min_element(
            std::begin(resources), std::end(resources),
            [](auto && a, auto && b) {
               return a.first < b.first;
            }
         );
         assert(p != std::end(resources));
         p->second.reset(); // relinquish ownership
         resources.erase(p);
      }
   public:
      void add(Resource *p) {
         const auto t = clock::now();
         if(full()) {
            expunge_one();
```

```
        }
        resources.emplace_back(
            t, std::shared_ptr<Resource>{ p }
        );
    }
    std::weak_ptr<Resource> obtain(Resource::id_type id){
        const auto t = clock::now();
        auto p = std::find_if(
            std::begin(resources),
            std::end(resources),
            [id](auto && p) {
                return p.second->id() == id;
            }
        );
        if(p == std::end(resources))
            return {};
        p->first = t;
        return p->second; // make weak_ptr from shared_ptr
    }
};

int main() {
    Cache<5> cache;
    for(int i = 0; i != 5; ++i)
        cache.add(new Resource{ i + 1 });
    // let's take a pointer to resource 3
    auto p = cache.obtain(3);
    if(auto q = p.lock(); q)
        std::cout << "Using resource " << q->id() << '\n';
    // things happen, resources get added, used, etc.
    for(int i = 6; i != 15; ++i)
        cache.add(new Resource{ i + 1 });
    if(auto q = p.lock(); q)
        std::cout << "Using resource " << q->id() << '\n';
    else
        std::cout << "Resource not available ...\n";
}
```

After a sufficient number of additions to the cache, the object pointed to by p in main() becomes invalidated and erased from the set of resources, one of our requirements for this example (without that requirement, we could have simply used std::shared_ptr objects in this case). Yet, main() can test for the validity of the object pointed to by p through the construction of std::shared_ptr from the std::weak_ptr it holds.

In practice, `weak_ptr` is sometimes used to break cycles when `shared_ptr` objects refer to each other in some way. If you have two types whose objects mutually refer to one another (say, X and Y) and do not know which one will be destroyed first, then consider making one of them the owner (`shared_ptr`) and the other one the non-owner in a verifiable manner (`weak_ptr`), which will ensure that they will not keep each other alive forever. For example, this will conclude, but the X and Y destructors will never be called:

```cpp
#include <memory>
#include <iostream>
struct Y;
struct X {
  std::shared_ptr<Y> p;
  ~X() { std::cout << "~X()\n"; }
};
struct Y {
  std::shared_ptr<X> p;
  ~Y() { std::cout << "~Y()\n"; }
};
void oops() {
  auto x = std::make_shared<X>();
  auto y = std::make_shared<Y>();
  x->p = y;
  y->p = x;
}
int main() {
  oops();
  std::cout << "Done\n";
}
```

If you change either `X::p` or `Y::p` to `weak_ptr`, you will see both the X and Y destructors being called:

```cpp
#include <memory>
#include <iostream>
struct Y;
struct X {
  std::weak_ptr<Y> p;
  ~X() { std::cout << "~X()\n"; }
};
struct Y {
  std::shared_ptr<X> p;
  ~Y() { std::cout << "~Y()\n"; }
};
void oops() {
  auto x = std::make_shared<X>();
```

```
    auto y = std::make_shared<Y>();
    x->p = y;
    y->p = x;
}
int main() {
    oops();
    std::cout << "Done\n";
}
```

Of course, the easiest way not to get to the point where you face a cycle of shared_ptr<T> objects is to not build such a cycle, but when faced with external libraries and third-party tools, that's sometimes easier said than done.

When to use raw pointers

We have seen that smart pointer types such as unique_ptr<T> and shared_ptr<T> shine when there is a need to describe ownership of a type T resource through the type system. Does that mean that T* has become useless?

No, of course not. The trick is to use it in controlled situations. The first is that for a function, being passed a T* as an argument should mean the function is *an observer, not an owner*, of that T. If your code base used raw pointers in that sense, you will most probably not run into trouble.

Secondly, you can use a raw pointer inside a class that implements your preferred ownership semantics. It's fine to implement a container that manipulates objects through raw pointers (for example, a tree-like structure meant for various traversal orders), as long as that container implements clear copy and move semantics. What you don't want to do is expose pointers to the internal nodes of your container to external code. Pay attention to the container's interface.

Indeed, consider this single-linked list of (excerpt):

```
template <class T>
    class single_linked_list {
        struct node {
            T value;
            node *next = nullptr;
            node(const T &val) : value { val } {
        };
        node *head = nullptr;
        // ...
    public:
        // ...
        ~single_linked_list() {
            for(auto p = head; p;) {
                auto q = p->next;
```

```
            delete p;
            p = q;
        }
    }
};
```

We will explore this example in greater detail in *Chapter 13*. The destructor works fine and (supposing the rest of the class is reasonably well-written) the class is usable and useful. Now, suppose we decide to use `unique_ptr<node>` instead of `node*` as the head data member for `single_linked_list`, and as a replacement for the `next` member of the node. This seems like a good idea, except when you consider the consequences:

```
template <class T>
    class single_linked_list {
        struct node {
            T value;
            unique_ptr<node> next; // good idea?
            node(const T &val) : value { val } {
        };
        unique_ptr<node> head; // good idea?
        // ...
    public:
        // ...
        ~single_linked_list() = default;
    };
```

This seems like a good idea on the surface, but it does not convey the proper semantics – it's *not* true that a node *owns* and *is responsible for* the next node. We don't want to make the removal of a node destroy the node that follows (and so on, recursively) and if that looks like a simplification in the destructor of `single_linked_list`, think about the consequences – this strategy leads to as many destructors recursively called as there are nodes in the list, which is a very good way to achieve a stack overflow!

Use a smart pointer when the use case matches the semantics it models. Of course, when the relationship modeled by your pointers is neither unique ownership nor shared ownership, you probably do not want smart pointer types that provide these semantics, resorting instead to either nonstandard and non-owning smart pointers or, simply, raw pointers.

Finally, you often need raw pointers to use lower-level interfaces – for example, when performing system calls. That does not disqualify higher-level abstractions, such as vector<T> or unique_ptr<T>, when writing system-level code – you can get access to the underlying array of vector<T> through its data() member function, just as you can get access to the underlying raw pointer of unique_ptr<T> through its get() member function. As long as it makes sense, see the called code as borrowing the pointer from the caller code for the duration of the call.

And if you have no other choice, use raw pointers. They exist, after all, and they work. Simply remember to use higher-level abstractions wherever possible – it will make your code simpler, safer, and (more often than you would think) faster. If you cannot define the higher-level semantics, maybe it's still a bit early to write that part of the code, and you'll get better results if you spend more time thinking about these semantics.

Summary

In this chapter, we saw how to use standard smart pointers. We discussed the ownership semantics they implement (sole ownership, shared co-ownership, and temporary co-ownership), saw examples of how they can be used, and discussed some ways in which they can be used while acknowledging that other, more appropriate options exist.

In the next chapter, we'll take this a step further and write our own (usable, if naïve) versions of unique_ptr<T> and shared_ptr<T>, in order to get an intuitive grasp of what this entails, and we will write some nonstandard but useful smart pointers too. This will help us build a nicer, more interesting resource management toolset.

6
Writing Smart Pointers

In *Chapter 5*, we examined the standard smart pointers at our disposal, with emphasis on the most important ones: `unique_ptr<T>` and `shared_ptr<T>`. These types are precious and important tools in every contemporary C++ programmer's toolbox, and using them when appropriate leads to programs that are smaller, faster, and simpler than they would be with most handwritten alternatives.

This book aims to discuss how to manage memory in a C++ program. For that reason, in this chapter, we will write simple versions of both `unique_ptr<T>` and `shared_ptr<T>` to show ways in which one could write naïve-yet-workable versions of these types if needed. We *strongly* recommend that you use the standard versions in practice, not those in this book (at least in production code): standard versions have been thoroughly tested, optimized, and used by a multitude of programmers to good effect. The reason we write "homemade" flavors here is simply to develop an intuition as to how one could write such as type: there still exist companies using pre-C++11 compilers, sometimes for reasonable reasons, and there might be reasons in some settings to write a smart pointer inspired by the standard ones yet slightly different.

We will then examine some niches not covered by the standard smart pointers, either because they are deemed simple enough that users can roll out their own, they are deemed specialized enough that they should be covered through third-party libraries, or there is no clear path to standardizing them yet.

To summarize, in this chapter, we will do the following:

- Take a brief look at ownership semantics, those of the standard smart pointers as well as others that we could – and sometimes will – implement ourselves.

- Implement our own naïve-yet-usable version of `std::unique_ptr` in order to grasp some of the techniques this might entail.

- Implement our own naïve-yet-usable version of `std::shared_ptr`. Note that by "usable" here we mean usable in simple contexts, as a full implementation of something such as `std::shared_ptr` is significantly more complex than what a book such as this one can reasonably cover.

- Implement a non-standard smart pointer with single ownership and duplication semantics, showing different techniques to achieve this objective.

- Implement two distinct non-owning "smart" pointers that are very lightweight types yet help write better and safer code.

After reading this chapter, we should have a better grasp of the techniques involved in writing types that syntactically behave as pointers but provide (or simply clarify) ownership semantics. The techniques used should be in large part reusable to other types of problems, memory-management related or not.

Does that sound like a plan? Let's get to it then!

Technical requirements

You can find the code files for this chapter in the book's GitHub repository here: https://github.com/PacktPublishing/C-Plus-Plus-Memory-Management/tree/main/chapter6.

Ownership semantics

Smart pointers are all about clarifying ownership over indirectly accessed resources. If we restrict ourselves to the standard facilities, smart or not-so-smart, what we have is the following:

Type	Niche
unique_ptr<T>	**Ownership semantics**: Single ownership. **Notable special member functions**: Non-copyable. The destructor is responsible for destroying the pointee.
shared_ptr<T>	**Ownership semantics**: Shared ownership. **Notable special member functions**: Copying, assigning, and destroying update a shared use count. The destructor of the last co-owner is responsible for destroying both the pointee and the use count.
T*	**Ownership semantics**: No ownership is defined in the type system (ownership rules have to be inscribed in user code). **Notable special member functions**: Not applicable (this is a fundamental type).

Table 6.1 – Usage category per pointer type

It's a small zoo, all things considered. What are the other kinds of semantics we could envision in order to fill this table? Well, there could be the following:

- An observer_ptr<T> type that behaves like T* but makes it more difficult to accidentally claim ownership with such operations as applying delete on the pointer (accidents happen indeed)

- A non_null_ptr<T> type that behaves like T* but for which a null pointer never occurs, simplifying client code

- A remote_ptr<T> type that behaves like a proxy to remote pointees

- A dup_ptr<T> type that implements single ownership of the pointee, as unique_ptr<T> does, but is copyable and duplicates the pointee when dup_ptr<T> is copied, and so on

We will not implement all of these (the remote_ptr<T> case in particular, interesting as it is, falls outside the scope of this book, and there are numerous other exotic semantics we could entertain that you are welcome to implement based on the ideas you will find in this chapter), but we will write a few. The important aspect in each case is to define clearly what the intended semantics are, ensure they are not already covered by an existing type, and make sure we implement them appropriately.

Let's start with a simple implementation of what is perhaps the best-known standard smart pointer: unique_ptr.

Writing your own (naïve) unique_ptr

We will first try a simple, homegrown version of std::unique_ptr<T>. As mentioned at the beginning of this chapter, our goal is to develop an intuition for the kind of code required to write such a type and not to encourage you to try to replace the standard facilities: they exist, they work, they are tested, use them. Oh, and they use many cool tricks we cannot explore in this book as we want to keep the book's size under control!

Type signature

As mentioned in *Chapter 5*, unique_ptr<T> does not really exist as the type is, in fact, unique_ptr<T, D>, where D defaults to default_deleter<T>.

We will cover both forms (scalar and array) of unique_ptr. The reason for these two specializations is that for T[], we will want unique_ptr to expose operator[] but we will not want to expose this for a scalar T type.

Let's start with the basic deleter types we will offer. Note that users can supply other deleter types if needed as long as they use the same signature for `operator()`:

```cpp
namespace managing_memory_book {
    // basic deleter types
    template <class T>
    struct deleter_pointer_wrapper {
        void (*pf)(T*);
        deleter_pointer_wrapper(void (*pf)(T*)) : pf{ pf } {
        }
        void operator()(T* p) const { pf(p); }
    };
    template <class T>
    struct default_deleter {
        void operator()(T* p) const { delete p; }
    };
    template <class T>
    struct default_deleter<T[]> {
        void operator()(T* p) const { delete[] p; }
    };
    // ...
}
```

What we have so far are three deleter types that are callable in the same way and that are all class types (the reason for this will become evident soon but know that there's sometimes value in uniformity). The odd one is `deleter_pointer_wrapper<T>`, which wraps a copyable state (a function pointer) but otherwise behaves like the other two: when called on `T*`, it applies some (user-supplied) function to that pointer.

The next step will be to choose the form of `unique_ptr<T,D>`. We will expect most deleters to be stateless and use **empty base optimization** (**EBO**) to our advantage by deriving from our deleter type. The one exception will be when the deleter is a function pointer, as we cannot use such a type as a base class; in that case, we will instead derive from `deleter_pointer_wrapper<T>`. To choose between these two options, we will need to detect whether D is a function pointer or not, which we will achieve using our own `is_deleter_function_candidate<T>` trait.

The part of our implementation that detects deleter function candidates is the following:

```cpp
#include <type_traits>
namespace managing_memory_book {
    // ...
    template <class T>
    struct is_deleter_function_candidate
        : std::false_type {};
    template <class T>
```

```
    struct is_deleter_function_candidate<void (*)(T*)>
        : std::true_type {};
    template <class T>
    constexpr auto is_deleter_function_candidate_v =
        is_deleter_function_candidate<T>::value;
    // ...
}
```

This bit is probably self-explanatory, but the idea is that most types are not candidates to be deleter functions, but functions of the void(*)(T*) type are.

We then get to the general unique_ptr<T> type, used for scalars. We will use our deleter function detection trait to conditionally choose between D types and deleter_pointer_wrapper<T> as the base class for our type, and cast this to a pointer to that base in order to release the resource in our destructor:

```
namespace managing_memory_book {
    // ...
    // unique_ptr general template
    template <class T, class D = default_deleter<T>>
    class unique_ptr : std::conditional_t <
        is_deleter_function_candidate_v<D>,
        deleter_pointer_wrapper<T>, D
    > {
        using deleter_type = std::conditional_t <
            is_deleter_function_candidate_v<D>,
            deleter_pointer_wrapper<T>,
            D
        >;
        T* p = nullptr;
    public:
        unique_ptr() = default;
        unique_ptr(T* p) : p{ p } {
        }
        unique_ptr(T* p, void (*pf)(T*))
            : deleter_type{ pf }, p{ p } {
        }
        ~unique_ptr() {
            (*static_cast<deleter_type*>(this))(p);
        }
    };
    // ...
}
```

The same approach, essentially, is taken for the T[] specialization of our type:

```cpp
namespace managing_memory_book {
    // ...
    // unique_ptr specialization for arrays
    template <class T, class D>
    class unique_ptr<T[], D> : std::conditional_t <
        is_deleter_function_candidate_v<D>,
        deleter_pointer_wrapper<T>,
        D
    > {
        using deleter_type = std::conditional_t <
            is_deleter_function_candidate_v<D>,
            deleter_pointer_wrapper<T>,
            D
        >;
        T* p = nullptr;
    public:
        unique_ptr() = default;
        unique_ptr(T* p) : p{ p } {
        }
        unique_ptr(T* p, void (*pf)(T*))
            : deleter_type{ pf }, p{ p } {
        }
        ~unique_ptr() {
            (*static_cast<deleter_type*>(this))(p);
        }
    };
}
```

Notice that a default `unique_ptr` will behave conceptually like a `null` pointer, something that should be unsurprising to most. Now that we have the basic idea in place, let's explore the semantics specific to `unique_ptr`.

Special member functions

The code for the special member functions will be the same for both the scalar and the array forms of `unique_ptr`. We have already looked at the destructor and the default constructor in the previous section, so let's look at the other four, in pairs:

- We want the type to be non-copyable, as it represents sole ownership of the pointee (if it was copyable, would ownership of the pointee belong to the original or the copy?)

- We want move operations to implement the transfer of ownership

The code for both the general case and its array specialization will be as follows (note that the code uses `std::exchange()` and `std::swap()`, both found in the `<utility>` header):

```cpp
// ...
    unique_ptr(const unique_ptr&) = delete;
    unique_ptr& operator=(const unique_ptr&) = delete;
    void swap(unique_ptr &other) noexcept {
        using std::swap;
        swap(p, other.p);
    }
    unique_ptr(unique_ptr &&other) noexcept
        : p{ std::exchange(other.p, nullptr) } {
    }
    unique_ptr& operator=(unique_ptr &&other) noexcept {
        unique_ptr{ std::move(other) }.swap(*this);
        return *this;
    }
// ...
```

Most of this should be self-evident by this point. You might notice the use of `std::exchange()`, which has the effect of copying `other.p` to `this->p` and then copying `nullptr` to `other.p`, implementing the transfer of ownership as expected. Note that move operations for our type are trivial and never throw, both of which are highly desirable properties.

There are some operations that will be implemented in both the general case and the array case, namely, `operator bool` (`true` only if the object does not model a `null` pointer), `empty()` (`true` only if the object does model a `null` pointer), as well as `operator==()` and `operator!=()`. These are essentially trivial to implement. The other member function we will want to expose is `get()` in both its `const` and non-`const` versions in order to expose the underlying pointer for client code that needs to interact with lower-level functions such as system calls:

```cpp
// ...
    bool empty() const noexcept { return !p; }
    operator bool() const noexcept { return !empty(); }
    bool operator==(const unique_ptr &other)
        const noexcept {
        return p == other.p;
    }
    // inferred from operator==() since C++20
    bool operator!=(const unique_ptr &other)
        const noexcept {
        return !(*this == other);
    }
```

```
        T *get() noexcept { return p; }
        const T *get() const noexcept { return p; }
// ...
```

As mentioned in the comments in the preceding code excerpt, one does not need to explicitly implement operator!=() since C++20 as long as operator==() offers the expected signature. The compiler will synthesize operator!=() from operator==(), quite simply.

Now, let's take a look at how the operator*(), operator->(), and operator[]() pointer-like functions are implemented.

Pointer-like functions

The pointer-like functions are different for the scalar case and the array case. For pointer-to-scalar, we will want to implement operator*() and operator->():

```
// ...
        T& operator*() noexcept { return *p; }
        const T& operator*() const noexcept { return *p; }
        T* operator->() noexcept { return p; }
        const T* operator->() const noexcept { return p; }
// ...
```

The operator->() member function is a strange beast: when used on an object, it will be reinvoked on the returned object (and again on that returned object, and so on) until something returns a raw pointer, at which point the compiler will know what to do. It's a very powerful mechanism.

For pointer-to-array (the unique_ptr<T[]> specialization), we will want to implement operator[], which will make more sense than either operator*() or operator->():

```
// ...
        T& operator[](std::size_t n) noexcept {
            return p[n];
        }
        const T& operator[](std::size_t n) const noexcept {
            return p[n];
        }
// ...
```

You might notice the apparent duplication of these member functions as each one is exposed in both a const and non-const form, a "trend" started by the get() member function a bit earlier. This is a *syntactic* resemblance as they are *semantically* different: in particular, only the const form is available through a const unique_ptr<T> object.

If you have a C++23 compiler, you can make it so the compiler will synthesize the forms you use in practice given a properly written set of template member functions:

```
// the following is for both the array and non-array cases
template <class U>
    decltype(auto) get(this U && self) noexcept {
        return self.p;
    }
// the following two are only for the non-array case
template <class U>
    decltype(auto) operator*(this U && self) noexcept {
        return *(self.p);
    }
template <class U>
    decltype(auto) operator->(this U && self) noexcept {
        return self.p;
    }
// the following is only for the array case
template <class U>
    decltype(auto) operator[](this U && self,
                              std::size_t n) noexcept {
    return self.p[n];
}
```

This reduces the number of member functions we have to write by half. How does this work? Well, C++23 introduces the "deduced this" mechanism that allows one to explicitly mark the first argument of a member function with the this keyword. Doing so and combining it with a forwarding reference (the U&& type) lets the compiler deduce the const-ness (or lack thereof) of this, in effect, expressing both the const and non-const versions in a single function. Note the decltype(auto) return types that accompany these functions, which infer both the **cv-qualifications** (discussed in *Chapter 3*) and reference-ness of the return type based on the type of the expression evaluated in the return statement.

And that's it! We now have a simple, yet functional unique_ptr<T> implementation that works for most use cases.

Of course, as nice as it is, unique_ptr<T> is not a panacea and there are other needs to be covered in real programs. Let's move on to a simplified implementation of shared_ptr<T> to see how we could implement shared ownership semantics.

A simple program that uses our homemade `unique_ptr<T>` with a default deleter would be as follows:

```
// ... (our own unique_ptr<T> goes here...)
struct X {};
int main() {
   unique_ptr<X> p{ new X };
} // X::~X() called here
```

Another that uses a custom deleter would be as follows:

```
// ... (our own unique_ptr<T> goes here...)
class X {
   ~X(){}
public:
   static void destroy(X *p) { delete p; }
};
int main() {
   unique_ptr<X, &X::destroy> p{ new X };
} // X::destroy(p.get()) called here
```

Writing your own (naïve) shared_ptr

A `shared_ptr<T>` type is a difficult beast to implement and a harder beast yet to optimize. The invitation to use the standard version of existing smart pointers is stronger in this case than it was for `unique_ptr<T>`: this type is hard to get right, and the standard version benefits from years of experience and testing. Only use the naïve version in this section for experimentation (it works and does the job for simple cases, but writing an industrial-strength implementation is major-league work).

The main difficulty when writing a `shared_ptr` is that it's a type with two responsibilities: it co-owns both the pointee and the usage counter, requiring some measure of care, especially with respect to exception safety. The single responsibility principle of classical object-oriented programming is a sound principle: a type with a single responsibility is exceedingly simpler to get right than a type with two or more responsibilities.

To keep our proposition simple, we will eschew many details of the standard `shared_ptr` contract, limiting ourselves to managing a scalar T. Let's take this type step by step:

```
#include <atomic>
#include <utility>
namespace managing_memory_book {
   // naïve shared_ptr
   template <class T>
   class shared_ptr {
```

```
    T* p = nullptr;
    std::atomic<long long> *ctr = nullptr;
    // ...
```

As mentioned previously, `shared_ptr<T>` is responsible for `T*` and a pointer to a client counter, both of which need to be managed and shared between co-owners. Note that our shared counter is a pointer to an atomic integral since `shared_ptr<T>` is particularly relevant in multithreaded cases where one does not know which of the threads will be the last user of the object. For that reason, operations such as incrementing and decrementing the counter require synchronization to avoid incurring a *data race*.

> ### Avoiding data races
>
> If a program meets a situation where a given object is (a) accessed concurrently by at least two threads, (b) at least one of these accesses is a write, and (c) there is no synchronization, then that program has what we call a **data race** and we essentially lose the capacity to reason about it from the source code. This is a really bad situation.
>
> In our case, operations on the shared counter will most probably be done concurrently and, as such, they have to be synchronized. This explains our use of the low-level synchronization objects that are atomic integrals as counters.

Constructing a `shared_ptr<T>` object can be tricky:

- By default, we will define `shared_ptr<T>` to be empty, thus conceptually equivalent to a `null` pointer.

- The constructor of `shared_ptr<T>` that takes `T*` as an argument represents the act of *taking ownership* of the pointee. For that reason, if an exception is thrown when allocating the counter, that pointee is destroyed.

- The copy constructor will represent *sharing ownership* of the pointee, making sure to consider the case where the source object models a `null` pointer.

- The move constructor models the *transfer of ownership*. As is often the case for move operations, it's very fast and it shows highly predictable behavior.

As can be seen from the following code excerpt, with a type that has more than one responsibility, even construction is a delicate endeavor. In the constructor that takes `T*`, we might need to allocate the shared counter, which might throw, a situation we need to manage. In the copy constructor, we need to take into account that the argument might model an empty `shared_ptr<T>`, in which case the shared counter would be `null`:

```
    // ...
  public:
    shared_ptr() = default;
```

```
    shared_ptr(T* p) : p{ p } {
       if(p) try {
          ctr = new std::atomic<long long>{ 1LL };
       } catch(...) {
          delete p;
          throw;
       }
    }
    shared_ptr(const shared_ptr &other)
       : p{ other.p }, ctr{ other.ctr } {
       if(ctr) ++(*ctr);
    }
    shared_ptr(shared_ptr &&other) noexcept
       : p{ std::exchange(other.p, nullptr) },
         ctr{ std::exchange(other.ctr, nullptr) } {
    }
    bool empty() const noexcept { return !p; }
    operator bool() const noexcept { return !empty(); }
// ...
```

The `empty()` and `operator bool()` member functions have been included in that excerpt since these functions directly tie into the way the default constructor (the empty state of this type) is expressed.

The assignment operator is unsurprising: copy assignment models the act of releasing control of the currently held resource and sharing the resource of its argument, whereas move assignment models the act of releasing control of the currently held resource and transferring control of the resource held by the argument to the assigned-to object:

```
    // ...
    void swap(shared_ptr &other) noexcept {
       using std::swap;
       swap(p, other.p);
       swap(ctr, other.ctr);
    }
    shared_ptr& operator=(const shared_ptr &other) {
       shared_ptr{ other }.swap(*this);
       return *this;
    }
    shared_ptr& operator=(shared_ptr &&other) noexcept {
       shared_ptr{ std::move(other) }.swap(*this);
       return *this;
    }
    // ...
```

Destruction is probably the trickiest aspect of this type. We want to make sure that the last owner of the pointee destroys it, to avoid immortal objects. The key point is that shared_ptr<T> should only destroy the pointed-to T object if it was the last user of that object.

There are at least two "self-evident" naïve algorithms that do not work. One is *If ctr is not null, then if *ctr==1, delete p and delete ctr.* This algorithm allows the case where two threads enter the destructor concurrently with *ctr==2. In that case, it is possible that neither thread sees *ctr==1, and the pointees are never destroyed:

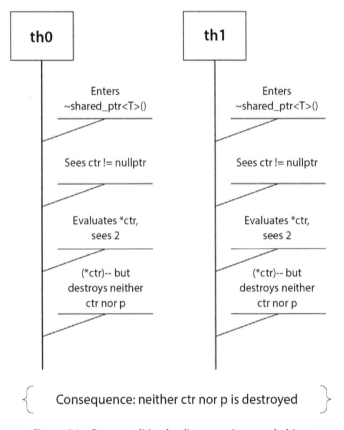

Figure 6.1 – Race condition leading to an immortal object

The other is *If ctr is not null, then decrement *ctr. If *ctr==0, delete p and delete ctr.* This algorithm allows the case where two threads enter the destructor concurrently with *ctr==2, and then both concurrently decrement *ctr leading to the possibility of both seeing *ctr==0, resulting in a double deletion of the pointees:

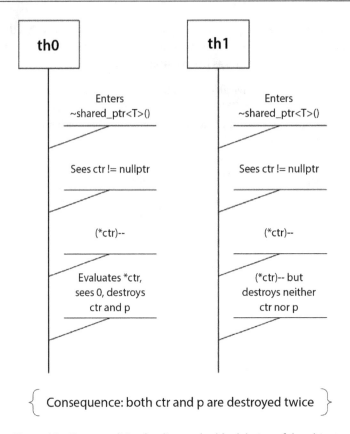

Figure 6.2 – Race condition leading to double deletion of the object

Both cases are bad, albeit for different reasons, so we need to do better. The difficult part of the process is ensuring that the executing thread can be made aware that it is the one that made it so *ctr became zero. The general solution to such a problem requires enclosing two steps (changing the value of a variable only if it had a known-beforehand value and being informed that this write did or did not happen) in a single operation, something that must be supported by at least one hardware operation on a multicore machine.

C++ offers abstractions over these essential hardware operations through atomics. One such atomic operation is named compare_exchange_weak(), which takes the expected value (what is believed to be in the variable) and the desired value (what one seeks to write to that variable, but only if it holds expected), and returns true only if the *write* actually happened. For convenience, expected is taken by reference and updated with the value actually held by the object at that time, since this function is usually called in a loop until a successful write of desired actually occurs, which involves re-reading expected every time to update the function's view of the variable's current state.

A dance with pictures

This `expected` and `desired` dance can be seen as taking pictures. A thread wants to decrement `*ctr`, but `*ctr` holds a mutable state and is accessed concurrently, which means its value can change at any time. Thus, we take a picture (`expected`) in a local variable under our control. We base the value we want to write (`desired`) on that local picture that we know did not change. Then, we try to act based on that (potentially obsolete) knowledge and see whether our assumption (that `*ctr` holds `expected`) is held. This lets us know that we were the ones to write `desired` in `*ctr`.

With this knowledge, a possible implementation of the destructor would be the following:

```
// ...
~shared_ptr() {
    if(ctr) {
        auto expected = ctr->load();
        auto desired = expected - 1;
        while(ctr->compare_exchange_weak(expected,
                                         desired))
            desired = expected - 1;
        if(desired == 0) { // I was the last user of *p
            delete p;
            delete ctr;
        }
    }
}
// ...
```

After the loop, we know that we wrote `desired` when `*ctr` held `expected`, thus if `desired` was 0 (implying `expected` was 1), we know we were the last user of that pointee. Yes, it's subtle. And this is only a toy version of `shared_ptr<T>`. We could optimize it in many ways, but that goes beyond the scope of this book.

A simpler solution

The solution shown here with `compare_exchange_weak()` is one of many options at our disposal. It was preferred for this book because it's an interesting approach for a general solution to the concurrent update problem and opens up optimization opportunities if you are comfortable with memory order constraints (which we will not go into here). In this specific case, we could have replaced the loop with something like `if((*ctr)-- == 1)`, as if one decrements `*ctr` atomically and the value previously held was 1, then we know for a fact that `*ctr` is now 0.

The other important member functions of our `shared_ptr<T>` implementation involve comparison (`operator==` and `operator!=`), the `get()` member functions that let one obtain the underlying, raw `T*` for code that needs it, and the indirection operators that are `operator*()` and `operator->()`:

```
        // ...
        bool operator==(const shared_ptr &other)
           const noexcept { return p == other.p; }
        // inferred from operator==() since C++20
        bool operator!=(const shared_ptr &other)
           const noexcept { return !(*this == other); }
        T *get() noexcept { return p; }
        const T *get() const noexcept { return p; }
        T& operator*() noexcept { return *p; }
        const T& operator*() const noexcept { return *p; }
        T* operator->() noexcept { return p; }
        const T* operator->() const noexcept { return p; }
    };
}
```

If you want to, feel free to apply the "deduced `this`" C++23 feature shown in the `unique_ptr` section earlier to simplify this code. Also remember that in C++20, `operator!=()` will be inferred from `operator==()` and does not need to be written explicitly in the source code.

A very simple example of client code for this smart pointer would be the following:

```
#include <thread>
#include <chrono>
#include <random>
#include <iostream>
using namespace std::literals;
struct X {
    int n;
    X(int n) : n{ n } {}
    ~X() { std::cout << "X::~X()\n"; }
};
int main() {
    using managing_memory_book::shared_ptr;
    std::mt19937 prng{ std::random_device{}() };
    std::uniform_int_distribution<int> die{ 200, 300 };
    shared_ptr<X> p{ new X{ 3 } };
    using std::chrono::milliseconds; // shortcut
    std::thread th0{ [p, dt = die(prng)] {
        std::this_thread::sleep_for(milliseconds{dt});
        std::cout << "end of th0, p->n : " << p->n << '\n';
```

```
    } };
    std::thread th1{ [p, dt = die(prng)] {
        std::this_thread::sleep_for(milliseconds{dt});
        std::cout << "end of th1, p->n : " << p->n << '\n';
    } };
    th1.detach();
    th0.detach();
    std::this_thread::sleep_for(350ms);
    std::cout << "end main()\n";
}
```

In this example, th0 and th1 both sleep for a pseudorandom number of milliseconds, then display something and conclude execution, so we cannot know in advance which of th0 and th1 will conclude first; both threads are detached, which means there is no later point at which we will call join() on them, so we cannot suppose that main() is the last user of the shared resource.

The example is contrived to keep it simple, and it bears repeating that as shared_ptr<T> is significantly more costly to use than unique_ptr<T> would be, one will generally prefer the latter over the former when there is a clear last owner of the resource.

A few words on make_shared()

It is possible that when reading about C++ in general and shared_ptr<T> in particular, you might have read that, whenever possible, it is recommended practice to replace this:

```
  std::shared_ptr<X> p{ new X { /* ... args ... */ } };
```

Replace it with the following:

```
  auto p= std::make_shared<X>( /* ... args ... */ );
```

If that is the case, you might be wondering (a) why this is recommended practice, and (b) why we have not addressed it yet. The answer to (a) we can provide now, but the answer to (b) is that we will need to wait until we reach *Chapter 7* to have the tools and knowledge required to implement such a facility.

To understand why we recommend preferring the make_shared<T>() factory function to a direct call to the shared_ptr<T> constructor, the key idea is that with the shared_ptr<T> constructor, the T object is allocated by client code, and given to shared_ptr<T> under construction, which takes ownership of that pointer and allocates a shared counter *separately*. We then end up with two allocations (the T object and the counter), probably on separate cache lines.

Now, if we go through make_shared<T>(), this factory function is responsible for allocating both the T object *and* the counter, perfectly forwarding the arguments received by the function to the T constructor. Since the same function performs both allocations, it can fuse them in a single allocation of a memory block that contains both the T object and the counter, *putting them both on* *the same cache line*. This can lead to enhanced performance characteristics if a single thread tends to read from both pointers (T* and the counter) in a short time span, but (as can sometimes be the case) can be hurtful if another thread observes frequent changes to the counter's value. As is often the case in optimization-related situations, measure and make sure what works well in general is also good for your own, specific use cases.

Clearly, to achieve this optimization, we need to be able to create such a block (conceptually, a struct containing T and an atomic integral) and make sure that shared_ptr<T> can contain either representation (two separate pointers or a pointer to a block with two objects) while remaining usable and efficient. Controlled use of the tricks seen in *Chapter 2* and *Chapter 3* will be helpful when we get there.

Writing a policy-based duplicating pointer

Let's leave aside the standard smart pointers for a moment. Suppose we seek to write a smart pointer type whose semantics fit neither the sole ownership mold of std::unique_ptr<T> nor the shared ownership mold of std::shared_ptr<T>. For the sake of this example, suppose more specifically that we want single ownership semantics but, unlike std::unique_ptr<T>, which is movable but non-copyable, we want duplication of the pointer to lead to duplication of the pointee. What can we do?

Well, this is C++, so we can of course write our own. Let's call this new smart pointer type of ours dup_ptr<T> (for "duplicating pointer", or "pointer that duplicates the pointee"). Since we examined how one could implement sole ownership through our homemade unique_ptr<T> earlier in this chapter, this section will mostly focus on the question of duplicating the pointee.

What do we mean by duplication? Well, there are two expected cases: copying an object of a non-polymorphic type and copying an object of a polymorphic type, with polymorphic meaning "with at least one virtual member function" for the sake of this example. Of course, programmers, being highly inventive creatures, know that someone will end up with more exotic situations so we will try to take care of the aforementioned "expected cases" and leave a door open for those with unusual applications.

Why is there a difference between polymorphic and non-polymorphic types? Consider the following program:

```
struct X { int n; };
struct B {
    int n;
    B(int n) : n{ n } {}
    virtual ~B() = default;
};
struct D0 : B {
    D0(int n) : B{ n } { /* ... */ }
```

```cpp
   // ...
};
struct D1 : B {
   D1(int n) : B{ n } { /* ... */ }
   // ...
};
// precondition: p != nullptr (to keep things simple)
X* duplicate(X *p) {
   return new X{ *p }; // Ok
}
// precondition: p != nullptr (to keep things simple)
B* duplicate(B *p) {
   return new B{ *p }; // Bad idea!
}
#include <memory>
int main() {
   using std::unique_ptr;
   X x{ 3 };
   unique_ptr<X> px { duplicate(&x) };
   D0 d0{ 4 };
   unique_ptr<B> pb{ duplicate(&d0) }; // trouble ahead
}
```

We can suppose that the `duplicate(X*)` function can safely create an object of the X type since X has no `virtual` member function and, as such, is probably not meant to serve as a public base class. However, there is a high probability that `duplicate(B*)` does the wrong thing by calling the constructor of B, as B* passed as an argument could be B or a pointer to an object of any class derived from B (here, D0*). Hence, calling `new B{ *p };` only constructs the base part, slicing away any state from the pointed-to object and resulting in a probably incorrect program.

As is well known in object-oriented programming circles, the customary way to duplicate an object of a polymorphic type is through *subjective duplication*, otherwise known as **cloning**. Expressed informally, when one holds a pointer to an object with at least one `virtual` member function, the only entity that can really claim to know the type of the pointee is… the pointee itself.

What `dup_ptr<T>` will do, then, is to pick a *duplication policy* based on the characteristics of T: by default, if T is polymorphic, then we will duplicate through cloning; otherwise, we will duplicate through copying. Of course, we will let the client code specify a custom duplication mechanism if needed.

We will explore three approaches to this selection of a default duplication policy: an intrusive approach based on interfaces, a non-intrusive approach based on traits and compile-time detection of a cloning member function using C++17 features, and another non-intrusive approach based on C++20 concepts.

Detection through interfaces

One thing we could do in user code is impose that cloneable types implement a specific interface, as in this example:

```
struct cloneable {
    virtual cloneable * clone() const = 0;
    virtual ~cloneable() = default;
};
```

Such a solution is probably not standardization-worthy: it is intrusive, imposes some overhead (we are assuming that cloneable types will be polymorphic types, something that is likely but not mandatory), and so on. It can be a solution for your own code base, of course. Applying this idea to a revisitation of the example that mishandled duplication of a polymorphic type, earlier, we end up with the following:

```
// ... type cloneable
struct X { int n; };
struct B : cloneable { // every B is cloneable
    int n;
    B(int n) : n{ n } {}
    virtual ~B() = default;
    B * clone()
protected: // cloneable types are meaningfully copied
           // in a subjective manner
    B(const B&) = default;
};
struct D0 : B {
    D0(int n) : B{ n } { /* ... */ }
    D0* clone() const override { return new D0{ *this }; }
    // ...
};
struct D1 : B {
    D1(int n) : B{ n } { /* ... */ }
    D1* clone() const override { return new D1{ *this }; }
    // ...
};
```

Now, suppose we want to develop a skeleton of dup_ptr<T> that copies types that are not derived from cloneable and clones types that are. To that effect, we can use the std::conditional type trait and choose between two function object types, a Copier type that copies and a Cloner type that clones:

```
// ... type cloneable
struct Copier {
    template <class T> T* operator()(const T *p) const {
```

```
        return new T{ *p };
    }
};
struct Cloner {
    template <class T> T* operator()(const T *p) const {
        return p->clone();
    }
};
#include <type_traits>
template <class T,
          class Dup = std::conditional_t<
              std::is_base_of_v<cloneable, T>,
              Cloner, Copier
          >>
class dup_ptr {
    T *p{};
    // use an object of type Dup when duplication is
    // required: copy constructor and copy assignment
    // ...
public:
    dup_ptr(const dup_ptr &other)
        : p{ other.empty()? nullptr : Dup{}(other.p) } {
    }
    // ...
};
```

This implementation supposes a stateless (no member variables) Dup type, which is highly probable but should be documented in practice (if we accept stateful Dup types, we need to instantiate a Dup object and write code to copy and move that object, leading to a much more involved implementation). With this implementation, any type that derives from `cloneable` will be cloned and other types will be copied, unless the user code supplies an exotic implementation of the Dup type.

Detection through traits

If we do not want to impose a base class to our `cloneable` types, we can use type traits to detect the presence of a `const`-qualified `clone()` member function and suppose this is a reasonable claim that cloning is a better choice than copying. Note that this non-intrusiveness supposes an unspoken agreement on the meaning of `clone()`.

We can achieve this in many ways, but the cleanest and most general one probably uses Dr. Walter Brown's `std::void_t` type, found in `<type_traits>` since C++17:

```
// types Cloner and Copier (see above)
template <class, class = void>
```

```
      struct has_clone : std::false_type { };
   template <class T>
      struct has_clone <T, std::void_t<
         decltype(std::declval<const T*>()->clone())
      >> : std::true_type { };
   template <class T>
      constexpr bool has_clone_v = has_clone<T>::value;
   template <class T, class Dup = std::conditional_t<
               has_clone_v<T>, Cloner, Copier
   >> class dup_ptr {
      T *p{};
   public:
      // ...
      dup_ptr(const dup_ptr &other)
         : p{ other.empty()? nullptr : Dup{}(other.p) } {
      }
      // ...
   };
```

The `std::void_t` type is a brilliant piece of work that lets knowledgeable people simulate, in a limited manner but for general expressions, what `requires` has allowed since C++20. The way to read this example is as follows:

- In general, `has_clone<T>::value` is `false`

- For any T type for which `p->clone()` for some `const T*` object p, `has_clone<T>::value` is `true`

Once the Dup type has been chosen, normal operations continue. The advantage of this implementation over the previous one is that this one checks for the existence of a suitably written `clone()` member function, whereas the previous one checks for the existence of a specific base class. Implementing a function is a lighter contract than deriving from a specific base class.

A word on std::void_t

The `std::void_t` type is a brilliant piece of work. Using it relies on **substitution failure is not an error (SFINAE)** to choose between a basic, general implementation that says "no" and a specialized version that says "yes" when some expression is well-formed. In our case, `has_clone<T>` is `false` for most types but is `true` when expression `p->clone()` is valid for some `const T*` object p. That we can easily test the validity of any expression even before concepts came into their own is just beautiful, and we owe Dr. Walter Brown much for this gem (among many other gems).

Detection through concepts

Since C++20, tricks such as std::void_t are less useful than they were since concepts are now part of the language's type system. Through concepts, we can define a cloneable type, T, to be something for which a call to clone() is well-formed on const T* and yields something that is convertible to T*.

With this, we have the following:

```cpp
template <class T>
   concept cloneable = requires(const T *p) {
      { p->clone() } -> std::convertible_to<T*>;
   };
template <class T, class Dup = std::conditional_t<
            cloneable<T>, Cloner, Copier
>> class dup_ptr {
   T *p{};
public:
   // ...
   dup_ptr(const dup_ptr &other)
      : p{ other.empty()? nullptr : Dup{}(other.p) } {
   }
   // ...
};
```

Concepts, like traits, are a non-intrusive solution to this problem. Where traits are a programming technique, however, they are ingrained in the type system and we can (for example) write code that's specialized for cloneable<T> and code that is not. In our case, the fact that we want to leave the door open for types that use neither the copy constructor nor a clone() member function suggests that the current setup, which lets client code supply other duplication mechanisms, is probably preferable.

C++26

C++26 will contain two standard types named std::indirect and std::polymorphic that will cover a niche close to the one described by this dup_ptr. It was voted in on February 15 2025.

Some not-so-smart yet useful smart pointers

So we have standard smart pointers, such as `unique_ptr<T>` (single ownership) and `shared_ptr<T>` (shared ownership), and we can write our own for more exotic situations (we examined `dup_ptr<T>` where we have single ownership but duplication of the pointee when the pointer is duplicated). Are there other common semantics we might want to ensconce in the type system of our program?

Well, there are at least two "easy" ones one could think of: implementing a "never null" semantic and implementing an "only observing" semantic.

A non_null_ptr type

Let's go back to an earlier example where we wrote the following:

```
// ...
// precondition: p != nullptr (to keep things simple)
X* duplicate(X *p) {
    return new X{ *p }; // Ok
}
// ...
```

Note the comment, which puts the burden of not supplying a null pointer on user code. We could have approached this constraint in many other ways, including the following:

- Asserting !p

- Calling std::abort() if !p

- Calling std::terminate() if !p

- Throwing if !p, and so on

The important thing is that if we care about pointers being non-null, and if we inject if (!p) tests in our runtime code, we are probably doing something wrong as this could (or should?) be part of the type system: *this function only accepts non-null pointers*. Code speaks louder than comments.

This idea appears in some commercial libraries (for example, `gsl::non_null<T>` from the guideline support library offered by some major compiler vendors) and is easy to implement as long as one has a clear way of signaling errors. For the sake of the example, we will suppose that this clear way is throwing an exception:

```
class invalid_pointer {};
template <class T>
    class non_null_ptr {
        T *p;
    public:
```

```
    non_null_ptr(T *p) : p{ p } {
        if (!p) throw invalid_pointer{};
    }
    T* get() const { return p; }
    constexpr operator bool() const noexcept {
        return true;
    }
// ...
```

Using this type, any function that accepts a `non_null_ptr<T>` argument knows that the `T*` pointer therein will be non-null, relieving client code from the burden of validation. This makes `non_null_ptr<T>` a beautiful type for the interface of functions that expect a non-null `T*`.

The rest of this class is mostly trivial to write at this point. The key peculiarity is that `non_null_ptr<T>` will not expose a default constructor, as that constructor would have to initialize the `p` data member to some default value (probably `nullptr`) but the `non_null_ptr<T>` type models a non-null pointer, which would lead to nonsensical code.

In terms of usage, take a look at this:

```
struct X { int n; };
class invalid {};
int extract_value(const X *p) {
    if(!p) throw invalid{};
    return p->n;
}
#include <iostream>
int main() try {
    X x{ 3 };
    std::cout << extract_value(&x) << '\n'
              << extract_value(nullptr) << '\n';
} catch(invalid) {
    std::cerr << "oops\n";
}
```

Now, compare it with this, supposing that `non_null_ptr<T>` throws when constructed with a null pointer:

```
// definition of the non_null_ptr type (omitted)
struct X { int n; };
int extract_value(const non_null_ptr<X> &p) {
    return p->n; // no need for validation as it stems
                 // from the type system itself
}
```

```
#include <iostream>
int main() try {
    X x{ 3 };
    std::cout << extract_value(&x) << '\n'
              << extract_value(nullptr) << '\n';
} catch(...) {
    std::cerr << "oops\n";
}
```

The two main advantages of non_null_ptr<T> over T* in this case are that the type system documents the intent better with non_null_ptr<T> (with T*, a null pointer might be fine, but with non_null_ptr<T>, it is clearly not) and that the called functions can proceed without validating, the validation being (again) ingrained in the type system. Using a richer type than T* makes both caller code and called code better.

What if the called function needs T*? This can happen, for example, in the case where it needs to call a C function. Well, then, use the non_null_ptr<T> object's get() member function. C++ is nothing if not pragmatic.

An observer_ptr type

How about having a very dumb smart pointer type named observer_ptr<T> that solely cares about expressing the idea that that "smart" pointer is, indeed, *not* a pointer, in the sense that operations that would apply to a raw pointer are restricted on that type. The canonical issue is that applying delete on T* would work but applying delete on observer_ptr<T> would not since observer_ptr<T> is... not a pointer. Indeed, consider the following:

```
class X { /* ... */ };
void f(X *p) {
    // use *p
    // we passed a raw pointer to f(), so f() should
    // observe it, not own it
    delete p; // wait! You're not supposed to do that!
}
```

You might say, as the comment states, "But that function's not supposed to do that! It does not own *p!" but, well, mistakes happen, as do misunderstandings. In this case, the impact of misunderstandings is made worse by the fact that nothing in the argument's type states that applying operator delete to p is incorrect!

Now, let's change the signature slightly:

```
class X { /* ... */ };
void f(observer_ptr<X> p) {
    // use *p
```

```
    // delete p; // nope, does not compile
}
```

The "use `*p`" comment remains the same in both versions. The `observer_ptr<T>` type offers almost trivial versions of all reasonable operators and member functions (`get()`, `operator*()`, `operator->()`, `empty()`, and so on) so usage of `T*` and of `observer_ptr<T>` should be mostly equivalent in user code; the only difference is in misguided uses such as applying `delete` or performing pointer arithmetic.

Sometimes, just clarifying intent in a function interface makes code better.

Summary

In *Chapter 5*, we spent some time on the proper usage of standard smart pointers. In the current chapter, we "dirtied our hands," so to speak, and we wrote homemade (and simplified) versions of `unique_ptr<T>` and `shared_ptr<T>`. As mentioned more than once, this is meant as an educational exploration, as your library vendor assuredly provides significantly better (more complete, more performant, better tested, etc.) implementations in both cases.

In this chapter, we also explored the possibility of providing homemade smart pointer types, with a policy-based `dup_ptr<T>` based on three distinct approaches to the selection of a duplication algorithm. The intent was to show that it can be done, how it can be done, and how we can provide reasonable, usable defaults without blocking user code with more exotic requirements.

Toward the end of this chapter, we examined some relatively simple (but useful) smart (well, lightly smart) pointers that can be used at the edges of functions (typically, as argument types) to make semantic requirements implicit through the type system instead of forcing user code to enforce these requirements explicitly… and sometimes fail to do so.

Unsurprisingly, memory management is not limited to smart pointers. In the next chapter, we will explore how the `new`, `new[]`, `delete`, and `delete[]` operators work, how we can implement them ourselves, and why we sometimes want to do so.

Part 3: Taking Control (of Memory Management Mechanisms)

In this part, we will delve somewhat deeper and examine ways in which you can take over some of the core memory allocation mechanisms in the C++ language and customize them to your needs. We will see how you can control what operators such as new and delete do, how to use specialized knowledge to obtain specific execution properties, and how these operators can be used in innovative ways. We will also use this knowledge for a few real-life applications and to achieve fast, sometimes extremely fast, memory management operations.

This part has the following chapters:

- *Chapter 7, Overloading Memory Allocation Operators*
- *Chapter 8, Writing a Naïve Leak Detector*
- *Chapter 9, Atypical Allocation Mechanisms*
- *Chapter 10, Arena-Based Memory Management and Other Optimizations*
- *Chapter 11, Deferred Reclamation*

7

Overloading Memory Allocation Operators

Enjoying yourself so far? I hope you are! We are at the point where we hold all the keys and can start to do what this book advertises and look in more detail at how memory management works in C++. It's not a simple topic, nor is it something trivial, so we needed to make sure we were ready... but we are now, so let's do it!

Chapter 5 and *Chapter 6* examined the standard tools one can use to ensconce responsibility over dynamically allocated resources into the C++ type system through smart pointers, the ones provided by the standard as well as those we could write to fill other niches. Using smart pointers instead of raw pointers as data members and function return types tends to simplify (and clarify) a significant proportion of memory management tasks in C++ programs.

Sometimes, we want to work at a lower level than this and take control over what happens when someone writes new X. The reasons for wanting such control are numerous, and we will explore a few in this book, but in this chapter, we will focus on the basics of memory management functions and how to take control of these mechanisms in C++.

After these basics are covered, we will do the following:

- See how our knowledge of the memory allocation mechanisms of C++ lets us write a simple (yet working) leak detector in *Chapter 8*

- Examine how one can manage atypical (persistent, shared, and so on) memory in C++ in *Chapter 9*

- Write arena-based memory allocation in *Chapter 10* to ensure deterministic time allocation and deallocation, leading to blazingly fast implementations of new and delete when context allows it

Later chapters will use the knowledge acquired in this chapter and the ones that follow to write efficient containers and deferred reclamation mechanisms that resemble a garbage collector. Past that point, we will examine how containers can use these facilities, with and without allocators.

Why would one overload allocation functions?

Before we start discussing how to overload memory allocation mechanisms, let's take a step back and examine why one would want to do this. Indeed, most programmers (even experienced ones) never end up doing anything of the sort, and we could wager that a majority of programmers never thought they had a reason to do so. Yet, we will allocate (!) a few chapters to that very topic. There has to be a reason…

The thing about memory allocation is that there's no perfect solution to the problem in general; there are many good solutions on average, and there are very good solutions to more specialized versions of the problem. What constitutes a good solution for a given use case in programming language A might be inappropriate for another use case or in programming language B.

Take, for example, languages where is it idiomatic to allocate dynamically large numbers of small objects, something customary of Java or C#. In such a language, one could expect the allocation strategies to be optimized for that usage pattern. In a language such as C, where one would tend to allocate when faced with objects too large to put on the stack or when using node-based data structures for example, the best dynamic memory allocation strategy could be quite different. In *Chapter 10*, we will see an example where the allocation process benefits from the fact that the allocated objects are all of the same size and alignment, another interesting use case.

C++ emphasizes control and provides sophisticated and versatile tools to programmers. When facing a situation where we know the context in which allocations will be performed, we can sometimes use these tools to do better (even *much* better, as we will see in *Chapter 11*!) than a default implementation would, and for numerous metrics: better execution time, more deterministic execution time, reduced memory fragmentation, and so on.

Brief overview of the C language allocation functions

Before we get to the memory allocation mechanisms of C++, let's first take a brief look at the C family of memory allocation functions through its most distinguished representatives: `malloc()` and `free()`. There are, of course, many other memory-allocation-related functions such as `calloc()`, `realloc()`, and `aligned_alloc()`, not counting operating-system-specific services that perform similar tasks for specialized use cases, but these will serve our discussion well.

Note that since this is a book on memory management with C++, I will use the C++ version of these functions (from `<cstdlib>` instead of `<stdlib.h>`), which really changes nothing to the code we will write except for the fact that in C++, these functions are located in the `std` namespace.

The signatures for these two functions are as follows:

```
void* malloc(size_t n);
void free(void *p);
```

💡 **Quick tip**: Enhance your coding experience with the **AI Code Explainer** and **Quick Copy** features. Open this book in the next-gen Packt Reader. Click the **Copy** button (**1**) to quickly copy code into your coding environment, or click the **Explain** button (**2**) to get the AI assistant to explain a block of code to you.

```
                                          Copy      Explain
function calculate(a, b) {
   return {sum: a + b};                     1           2
};
```

📖 **The next-gen Packt Reader** is included for free with the purchase of this book. Unlock it by scanning the QR code below or visiting `https://www.packtpub.com/unlock/9781805129806`.

The role of `malloc(n)` is to find a location where there are at least n consecutive bytes available, potentially marking that location as "taken" and returning an abstract pointer (a `void*`) to the beginning of that block of memory. Note that the pointer returned has to be aligned for the worst possible natural case in a given machine, which means that it has to suit the alignment requirements of `std::max_align_t`. On most machines, this type is an alias for `double`.

Interestingly, it is legal to call `malloc()` with `n==0`, but the results of such a call are implementation-defined: a call to `malloc(0)` could return `nullptr` but it could also return a non-null pointer. Note that the pointer returned by `malloc(0)` should not be dereferenced, regardless of whether it is null or not.

If `malloc()` fails to allocate memory, it returns `nullptr` since the C language does not support exceptions in the C++ sense. In contemporary C (since C11), a `malloc()` implementation has to be thread-safe and has to synchronize appropriately with other C allocation functions if they are called concurrently, including with `free()`.

The role of `free(p)` is to ensure that the memory pointed to by p becomes available for further allocation requests, as long as p points to a block that has been allocated through a memory allocation function such as `malloc()` and has not yet been freed. It is **undefined behavior** (**UB**) to try to `free()` an address that has not been allocated through such an allocation function... Don't do that! Also, know that once the memory has been freed, it is no longer considered allocated, so code such as the following leads to UB:

```
#include <cstdlib>
int main() {
    using std::malloc, std::free;
    int *p = static_cast<int*>(malloc(sizeof(int)));
    free(p); // fine since it comes from malloc()
    free(p); // NOOOOOO unless (stroke of luck?) p is null
}
```

As mentioned in the preceding example, `free(nullptr)` does nothing, and has been defined as doing nothing for decades as of this writing. If there is code in your code base that verifies p!=nullptr before calling `free()` – for example, `if(p) free(p)` – you can safely get rid of that test.

We will sometimes (not always) use these C functions to implement our homemade C++ allocation functions. They work, they are well understood, and they are low-level abstractions we can use to our advantage when building higher-level ones.

Overview of the C++ allocation operators

In C++, there are many (infinitely many!) flavors of memory allocation operators, but there are rules to follow when writing your own. The current chapter is mostly about those rules; the chapters that follow will explore ways to benefit from this freedom C++ gives us:

- C++ lets us overload the **global versions** of the memory allocation operators. If we do so, then even things such as `new int` will use our homemade versions. One has to be careful here since small mistakes can have a significant impact on code execution: if your implementation of `operator new()` is slow, you will slow down most memory allocations in your program! We will use this approach when writing a simple-yet-working leak detector in *Chapter 8*.

- C++ lets us overload **member function versions** of the memory allocation operators. If we do, then the global versions (overloaded or not) apply in general, but the member function versions apply for specific types. This can be useful when we have knowledge specific to the usage pattern of some types but not to others. We will use that to our advantage in *Chapter 10*.

- C++ lets us overload **versions with additional arguments** of the memory allocation operators. In the current chapter, we will examine some standard versions of these operators such as the `nothrow` version and the (extremely important) **placement new**-related versions. We can also use this feature to benefit from "exotic" memory such as shared memory or persistent memory, as we will see in *Chapter 9*.

In each case, memory allocation functions come in groups of four: `operator new()`, `operator new[]()`, `operator delete()`, and `operator delete[]()`. There are some exceptions to this rule, as we will see, but the rule generally holds. If we overload at least one of these functions, it's important that we overload all four to keep the behavior of our program consistent. When playing with low-level facilities like this, mistakes tend to bite harder than they would otherwise, which explains why we took so much care in *Chapter 2* and *Chapter 3* explaining ways we could get in trouble… and how to play by the rules at the same time.

Memory allocation interacts closely with the object model (see *Chapter 1* for the basics) and with exception safety (a topic that's pervasive throughout this book), so make sure to grasp these interactions in the pages and chapters that follow. They will help you make the best of what you will read here.

A word on Heap Allocation Optimization (HALO)

It's important to know that there are benefits to *not* overloading memory allocation operators. One of them is that your library vendor provides very good ones by default; another is that if you do not overload the memory allocation operators, the compiler can assume that the number of allocations you make is not observable. This means that it is allowed to replace *n* calls to new with a single call that allocates everything at once, and then manages the results as if you had performed many allocations. That can lead to some spectacular optimizations in practice, including the removal of calls to new and delete altogether from the generated code even when they appear in the source code! If in doubt, please make sure that your optimizations provide measurable benefits before committing them and using them in production code.

Note that for the allocation operator overloads we will see in this chapter, you will want to include the `<new>` header as this is where `std::bad_alloc` is declared, among other things, and this is the type that allocation functions typically use to report failure to allocate.

Global allocation operators

Suppose we want to take control of the global versions of the allocation operators in C++. For the sake of exposing how this can work, we will simply use them to delegate to `malloc()` and `free()` for now, and show a more elaborate example in *Chapter 8*.

If we stick to the basic forms of these operators, we will want to overload… well, four functions before C++11 or six functions since then. Of course, this book supposes that we're over a decade past C++14, so we will proceed accordingly.

The signatures we want to overload are the following:

```
void *operator new(std::size_t);
void *operator new[](std::size_t);
void operator delete(void *) noexcept;
void operator delete[](void *) noexcept;
```

```
// since C++14
void operator delete(void *, std::size_t) noexcept;
void operator delete[](void *, std::size_t) noexcept;
```

That's a lot, I agree, but taking control of memory management facilities is specialized work. As soon as you write one of these functions, you officially replace the ones provided by your standard library for that program and that function becomes responsible for the allocation (or deallocation) requests that come through that channel. Replacing an allocation function requires you to use the exact same signature as the original.

The reason why it is important that you overload the whole set of functions if you overload at least one of them is that these functions form a consistent whole. For example, if you change the way new behaves but neglect to change the way the standard library-provided delete performs its task, it's essentially impossible to predict how much damage your program will incur. As a well-known popular comic book hero stated many times, *"with great power comes great responsibility."* Be careful, be rigorous, and follow the rules.

Pay attention to the signatures of these functions as they provide interesting information...

On operators new and new[]

Functions operator new() and operator new[]() both take a single std::size_t object as an argument and both return void*. The argument is, in both cases, the minimal number of contiguous bytes to allocate. As such, their signatures resemble that of std::malloc(). That often surprises people; how can the new X expression create an X object if new is not a template and does not know what to create?

That's the thing: new does *not* create objects. What new does is find the location where an object will be constructed. It's the constructor that turns the raw memory found by new into an object. In practice, you could write something such as the following:

```
X *p = new X{ /* ... args ... */ };
```

What you have written is a two-step operation:

```
// allocate enough space to put an X object
void * buf = operator new(sizeof(X));
// construct an X object at that location
X *p = ... // apply X::X( /* ... args ... */ ) on buf
```

This means the constructor is like a coat of paint applied to a block of memory, turning that memory into an object. This also means that an expression such as new X can fail either on operator new(), if the allocation request could not succeed, or on X::X(), because the constructor failed somehow. Only if both steps succeed does client code become responsible for the pointed-to object.

A note on calling these operators

You might have noticed in the preceding example that we sometimes write new X and we sometimes write operator new(sizeof(X)). The first form – the *operator form* – will do the two-step process of allocation followed by construction, whereas the second form – the *function form* – directly calls the allocation function without invoking a constructor. This distinction also applies to operator delete().

The situation is similar with operator new[]: the number of bytes passed as argument to the function is the total number of bytes for the array, so the allocation function itself knows neither the type of object that will be created nor the number of elements or the individual size of the objects. A call to new X[N] will, in practice, call operator new[](N*sizeof(X)) to find a place to put the array that will be constructed, then call X::X() on each of the N blocks of size sizeof(X) in that array. Only when the entire sequence completes successfully does client code become responsible for the resulting array.

Failure to allocate a scalar through operator new should result in something that matches std::bad_alloc being thrown. With operator new[](), one can also throw std::bad_array_new_length (derived from std::bad_alloc) if the requested size is problematic, typically because it exceeds implementation-defined limits.

On operators delete and delete[]

Like the C language's free() function, operators delete() and delete[]() both take a void* as argument. This means that they cannot destroy your object... When they are called, the object has already been destroyed! Indeed, you could write the following:

```
delete p; // suppose that p is of type X*
```

This is, in practice, a two-step operation that is equivalent to the following:

```
p->~X(); // destroy the pointed-to object
operator delete(p); // free the associated memory
```

In C++, neither your destructors nor operator delete() should throw exceptions. If they do, the program is pretty much terminated, for reasons that will become self-evident in *Chapter 12*.

The size-aware versions of operator delete() and operator delete[]() have been introduced with C++14 and it is customary to implement them today, in addition to the classical versions of these functions. The idea is that operator new() was informed of the size of the blocks to allocate but operator delete() was not, which required unneeded acrobatics on the part of implementations that sought to do size-related tasks, such as filling the block of memory with some value in order to try to obscure what was stored at that location. Contemporary implementations of these functions require us to write a version that accepts the size of the pointed-to objects in addition to the classical version; if one's implementation does not need that size, one can simply call the classical version from the size-aware one and be done with it.

> **A note on sized operator delete[]() overloads**
>
> If you trace the execution of your overloads, you might be surprised to see that the sized version of `operator delete[]()` is not necessarily called for some types. Indeed, if you have an array `arr` of objects of trivially destructible types, the standard leaves it unspecified as to which one of the sized and the unsized versions of `operator delete[]()` will be used when you write `delete [] arr`. It's not a bug, rest assured.

A full, yet naïve implementation of these functions that essentially delegate work to the C allocation functions could be as follows:

```cpp
#include <iostream>
#include <cstdlib>
#include <new>
void *operator new(std::size_t n) {
    std::cout << "operator new(" << n << ")\n";
    auto p = std::malloc(n);
    if(!p) throw std::bad_alloc{};
    return p;
}
void operator delete(void *p) noexcept {
    std::cout << "operator delete(...)\n";
    std::free(p);
}
void operator delete(void *p, std::size_t n) noexcept {
    std::cout << "operator delete(..., " << n << ")\n";
    ::operator delete(p);
}
void *operator new[](std::size_t n) {
    std::cout << "operator new[](" << n << ")\n";
    auto p = std::malloc(n);
    if(!p) throw std::bad_alloc{};
    return p;
}
void operator delete[](void *p) noexcept {
    std::cout << "operator delete[](...)\n";
    std::free(p);
}
void operator delete[](void *p, std::size_t n) noexcept {
    std::cout << "operator delete[](..., " << n << ")\n";
    ::operator delete[](p);
```

```
}
int main() {
    auto p = new int{ 3 };
    delete p;
    p = new int[10];
    delete []p;
}
```

As is probably clear by now, the default behavior when `operator new()` and `operator new[]``()` fail to achieve their postconditions and actually allocate the requested amount of memory is to throw `std::bad_alloc` or, when appropriate, `std::bad_array_new_length`. Since allocation is followed by construction, client code might also face any exception thrown by the constructor. We will look at ways to handle these situations when writing custom containers in *Chapter 12*.

There are application domains where exceptions are not an option. This can be due to memory constraints; most exception handlers make programs slightly bigger, which can be unacceptable in domains such as embedded systems. It can also be due to speed constraints; the code in `try` blocks is usually fast as these blocks represent the "normal" execution paths, but code in `catch` blocks is usually seen as the rare ("exceptional") path and can be significantly slower to execute. Of course, some will simply avoid exception usage for philosophical reasons, which is fine too.

Luckily, there is a way to perform dynamic memory allocation without resorting to exceptions to signal failure.

Non-throwing versions of the allocation operators

There are also versions of the allocation operators that do not throw upon failure to allocate. The signatures for these functions are as follows:

```
void *operator new(std::size_t, const std::nothrow_t&);
void *operator new[](std::size_t, const std::nothrow_t&);
void operator delete(void *, const std::nothrow_t&)
    noexcept;
void operator delete[](void *, const std::nothrow_t&)
    noexcept;
// since C++14
void operator delete
    (void *, std::size_t, const std::nothrow_t&) noexcept;
void operator delete[]
    (void *, std::size_t, const std::nothrow_t&) noexcept;
```

You might be wondering why someone would want to explicitly request that failure to allocate returns a null pointer instead of throwing an exception. It's certainly more annoying to litter one's code with tests for `nullptr` than to just write it as if no failure occurred! The fact is that there are costs to using exceptions in one's programs: it can make binaries slightly bigger, and it can slow down code execution, particularly when exceptions are caught (there are also issues of style involved; some people would not use exceptions even if they led to faster code, and that's just part of life). For that reason, application domains such as games or embedded systems often shun exceptions and go to some lengths to write code that does not depend on them. The non-throwing versions of the allocation functions target these domains.

Type `std::nothrow_t` is what is called a **tag type**: an empty class whose instances (here, the global `std::nothrow` object) can be used to guide the compiler when generating code. Note that these function signatures require the `std::nothrow_t` arguments to be passed by `const` reference, not by value, so make sure you respect this signature if you seek to replace them.

An example usage of these functions would be as follows:

```
X *p = new (nothrow) X{ /* ... args ... */ };
if (p) {
    // ... use *p
    // note: this is not the nothrow version of delete
    delete p; // would be Ok even if !p
}
```

You might be surprised about the position of `nothrow` in the new expression, but if you think about it, it's essentially the only syntactic space for additional arguments passed to `operator new()`; the first argument passed to the function is the number of contiguous bytes to allocate (here: `sizeof(X)`), and in expression `new X { ...args... }`, what follows the type of object to construct is the list of arguments passed to its constructor. Thus, the place to specify the additional arguments to `operator new()` itself is between new and the type of the object to construct, between parentheses.

A word on the position of additional arguments to operator new()

To illustrate this better with an artificially crafted example, one could write the following `operator new()` overload:

```
void* operator new(std::size_t, int, double);
```

Then, a possible call to that hypothetical operator would be as follows:

```
X *p = new (3, 1.5) X{ /* ... */ };
```

Here, we can see how two additional arguments, an `int` argument and a `double` argument, are passed by client code.

Returning to the `nothrow` version of `operator new()` and `operator new[]()`, one thing that is subtle and needs to be understood is why one needs to write overloads of `operator delete()` and `operator delete[]()`. After all, even with client code that uses the `nothrow` version of new, as was the case in our example, it's highly probable that the "normal" version of `operator delete()` will be used to end the life of that object. Why, then, write a `nothrow` version of `operator delete()`?

The reason is **exception safety**. But why worry about exceptions, you're surely thinking, when writing a non-throwing version of `operator new()`? Well, remember that memory allocation through `operator new()` is a two-step operation: find the location to place the object, then construct the object at that location. Thus, even if `operator new()` does not throw, we do not know whether the constructor that will be called will throw. Our code will obtain the pointer only after both the allocation *and* the construction that follows have successfully completed execution; as such, client code cannot manage exceptions that occur after allocation succeeded but during the construction of the object, at least not in such a way as to deallocate the memory... It's difficult to deallocate a pointer your code has not yet seen!

For that reason, it falls on the C++ runtime to perform the deallocation if an exception is thrown by the constructor, and this is true for all versions of `operator new()`, not just the `nothrow` ones. The algorithm (informally) is as follows:

```
// step 1, try to perform the allocation for some T object
p = operator new(n, ... maybe additional arguments ...)
// the following line is only for a nothrow new
if(!p) return p
try {
   // step 2, construct the object at address p
   apply the constructor of T at address p // might throw
} catch(...) { // construction threw an exception
   deallocate p // this is what concerns us here
   re-throw the exception, whatever it was
}
return p // p points to a fully constructed object
         // only after this point does client code see p
```

As this algorithm shows, the C++ runtime has to deallocate the memory for us when the constructor throws an exception. But how does it do so? Well, it will use the `operator delete()` (or `operator delete[]()`) whose signature matches that of the version of new or new[] that was used to perform the allocation. For example, if we use `operator new(size_t, int, double)` to allocate and the constructor fails, it will use `operator delete(void*, int, double)` to perform the implicit deallocation.

That is the reason why, if we overload the nothrow versions of new and new [], we have to overload the nothrow versions of delete and delete [] (they will be used for deallocation if a constructor throws), and why we also have to overload the "normal" throwing versions of new, new [], delete, and delete []. Expressed informally, code that uses X *p = new (nothrow) X; will usually call delete p; to end the life of the pointee, and as such, the nothrow and throwing versions of the allocation functions have to be coherent with one another.

Here is a full, yet naïve implementation where the throwing versions delegate to the non-throwing ones to reduce repetition:

```cpp
#include <iostream>
#include <cstdlib>
#include <new>
void* operator new(std::size_t n, const std::nothrow_t&) noexcept {
    return std::malloc(n);
}
void* operator new(std::size_t n) {
    auto p = operator new(n, std::nothrow);
    if (!p) throw std::bad_alloc{};
    return p;
}
void operator delete(void* p, const std::nothrow_t&)
    noexcept {
        std::free(p);
    }
void operator delete(void* p) noexcept {
    operator delete(p, std::nothrow);
}
void operator delete(void* p, std::size_t) noexcept {
    operator delete (p, std::nothrow);
}
void* operator new[](std::size_t n,
                     const std::nothrow_t&) noexcept {
    return std::malloc(n);
}
void* operator new[](std::size_t n) {
    auto p = operator new[](n, std::nothrow);
    if (!p) throw std::bad_alloc{};
    return p;
}
void operator delete[](void* p, const std::nothrow_t&)
    noexcept {
    std::free(p);
}
```

```
void operator delete[](void* p) noexcept {
   operator delete[](p, std::nothrow);
}
void operator delete[](void* p, std::size_t) noexcept {
   operator delete[](p, std::nothrow);
}
int main() {
   using std::nothrow;
   auto p = new (nothrow) int{ 3 };
   delete p;
   p = new (nothrow) int[10];
   delete[]p;
}
```

As you can see, there are quite a few functions to write to get a full, cohesive set of allocation operators if we want to cover both the throwing and the non-throwing versions of this mechanism.

We still have a lot to cover. For example, we mentioned a few times already the idea of placing an object at a specific memory location, in particular at the second of the two-step process modeled by calls to new. Let's see how this is done.

The most important operator new: placement new

The most important version of `operator new()` and friends is not one you can replace, but even if you could… well, let's just state that it would be difficult to achieve something more efficient:

```
// note: these exist, you can use them but you cannot
// replace them
void *operator new(std::size_t, void *p) { return p; }
void *operator new[](std::size_t, void *p) { return p; }
void operator delete(void*, void*) noexcept { }
void operator delete[](void*, void*) noexcept { }
```

We call these the placement allocation functions, mostly known as **placement new** by the programming community.

What is the purpose of these functions? You might remember, at the beginning of our discussion of the global versions of the allocation operators, that we stated: "What new does is find the location where an object will be constructed." This does not necessarily mean that new will allocate memory, and indeed, placement new does not allocate; it simply yields back the address it has been given as argument. *This allows us to place an object wherever we want in memory…* as long as we have the right to write the memory at that location.

Placement new serves many purposes:

- If we have sufficient rights, it can let us map an object onto a piece of memory-mapped hardware, giving us an *extremely* thin layer of abstraction over that device.

- It enables us to decouple allocation from construction, leading to significant speed improvements when writing containers.

- It opens up options to implement important facilities such as types optional<T> (that might or might not store a T object) and variant<T0,T1,...,Tn> (that stores an object of one of types T0,T1,...,Tn), or even **small object optimization** (**SOO**)-enabled types such as std::string and std::function that sometimes allocate external memory, but sometimes use their internal data structures and avoid allocation altogether. Placement new is not the only way to do this, but it is one of the options in our toolbox.

One important benefit of placement new is most probably in the implementation of containers and the interaction between containers and allocators, themes we will explore from *Chapter 12* to *Chapter 14* of this book. For now, we will limit ourselves to a simple, artificial example that's meant as an illustration of how placement new works its magic, not as an example of something you should do (indeed, you should *not* do what the following example does!).

Suppose that you want to compute the length of a null-delimited character string and cannot remember the name of the C function that efficiently computes its length (better known as std::strlen()). One way to achieve similar results but *much* less efficiently would be to write the following:

```
auto string_length(const char *p) {
    return std::string{ p }.size(); // augh! But it works...
}
```

That's inefficient because the std::string constructor might allocate memory. We just wanted to count the characters until the first occurrence of a zero in the sequence, but it works (note: if you do the same maneuver with a std::string_view instead of with a std::string, its performance will actually be quite reasonable!). Now, suppose you want to show off to your friends the fact that you can place an object where you want in memory, and then use that object's data members to do what you set out to do. You can (but should not) write the following:

```
auto string_length(const char *p) {
    using std::string;
    // A) make a local buffer of the right size and
    // alignment for a string object
    alignas(string) char buf[sizeof(string)];
    // B) "paint" a string object in that buffer
    // (note: that object might allocate its
    // own data externally, but that's not
    // our concern here)
```

```
    string *s = new (static_cast<void*>(buf)) string{ p };
    // C) use that object to compute the size
    const auto sz = s->size();
    // D) destroy the object without releasing the memory
    // for the buffer (it's not dynamically allocated,
    // it's just local storage)
    s->~string(); // yes, you can do this
    return sz;
}
```

What are the benefits of the complicated version in comparison to the simple one? None whatsoever, but it shows the intricacies of doing this sort of low-level memory management maneuver. From the comments in the code example, the steps work as follows:

- Step A) makes sure that the location where the object will be constructed is of the right size and shape: it's a buffer of bytes (type char), aligned in memory as a std::string object should be, and of sufficient size to hold a std::string object.

- Step B) paints a std::string object in that buffer. That's what a constructor does, really: it (conceptually) transforms raw memory into an object and initializes the state of that object. If the std::string constructor throws an exception, then the object has never been constructed and our string_length() function concludes without satisfying its postconditions. There is no memory allocation involved here unless the constructor itself allocates, but that's fair (the object does what it has to do).

- Step C) uses the newly constructed object; in our case, it's just a matter of querying the size of that character string, but we could do whatever we want here. Do note, however, that (a) the object's lifetime is tied to the buffer in which it is located, and (b) since we explicitly called the constructor, we will need to explicitly destroy it, which means that if an exception is thrown when we use the object, we will need to make sure the object's destructor is called somehow.

- Step D) destroys the object before we leave the function, as not doing so would lead to a possible leak of resources. If the buffer's lifetime ends at a point where the object is not yet destroyed, things will be very wrong: either the destructor of the object we put in that buffer will never be called and code will leak, or someone might try to use the object even though the storage for that object is not ours anymore, leading to UB. Note the syntax, s->~string(), which calls the destructor but does not deallocate the storage for *s.

This is a bad example of placement new usage, but it is explicit and (hopefully) instructive. We will use this feature in much more reasonable ways in order to gain significant speed advantages when we write containers with explicit memory management in *Chapter 12*.

A note on make_shared<T>(args...)

We mentioned in *Chapter 6* that `make_shared<T>(args...)` usually leads to a better memory layout than `shared_ptr<T>{ new T(args...) }` would, at least with respect to cache usage. We can start to see why that is so.

Calling `shared_ptr<T>::shared_ptr(T*)` makes the object responsible for a preexisting pointee, the one whose address is passed as argument. Since that object has been constructed, the `shared_ptr<T>` object has to allocate a reference counter separately, ending up with two separate allocations, probably on different cache lines. In most programs, this worsened locality may induce slowdowns at runtime.

On the other hand, calling `make_shared<T>(args...)` makes this factory function responsible for creating a block of memory whose layout accommodates the T object and the reference counter, respecting the size and alignment constraints of both. There's more than one way to do this, of course, including (a) resorting to a `union` where "coexist" a pair of pointers and a single pointer to a block that contains a counter and a T object, and (b) resorting to a byte buffer of appropriate size and alignment, then performing placement new for both objects in the appropriate locations within that buffer. In the latter case, we end up with a single allocation for a contiguous block of memory able to host both objects and two placement new calls.

Member versions of the allocation operators

Sometimes, we have special knowledge of the needs and requirements of specific types with respect to dynamic memory allocation. A full example that goes into detail about a real-life (but simplified) use case of such type-specific knowledge is given in *Chapter 10*, where we discuss arena-based allocation.

For now, we will limit ourselves to covering the syntax and the effect of a member function overload of the allocation operators. In the example that follows, we suppose class X would somehow benefit from a per-class specialization of these mechanisms, and show that client code will call these specializations when we call `new X` but not when we call `new int`:

```
#include <iostream>
#include <new>
class X {
    // ...
public:
    X() { std::cout << "X::X()\n"; }
    ~X() { std::cout << "X::~X()\n"; }
    void *operator new(std::size_t);
    void *operator new[](std::size_t);
    void operator delete(void*);
    void operator delete[](void*);
    // ...
};
```

```
// ...
void* X::operator new(std::size_t n) {
    std::cout << "Some X::operator new() magic\n";
    return ::operator new(n);
}
void* X::operator new[](std::size_t n) {
    std::cout << "Some X::operator new[]() magic\n";
    return ::operator new[](n);
}
void X::operator delete(void *p) {
    std::cout << "Some X::operator delete() magic\n";
    return ::operator delete(p);
}
void X::operator delete[](void *p) {
    std::cout << "Some X::operator delete[]() magic\n";
    return ::operator delete[](p);
}
int main() {
    std::cout << "p = new int{3}\n";
    int *p = new int{ 3 }; // global operator new
    std::cout << "q = new X\n";
    X *q = new X; // X::operator new
    std::cout << "delete p\n";
    delete p; // global operator delete
    std::cout << "delete q\n";
    delete q; // X::operator delete
}
```

One important detail to mention is that these overloaded operators will be inherited by derived classes, which means that if the implementation of these operators somehow depends on details specific to that class – for example, its size of alignment or anything else that might be invalidated in derived classes through such seemingly inconspicuous details as adding a data member – consider marking the class that overloads these operators as final.

Alignment-aware versions of the allocation operators

When designing C++17, a fundamental problem with the memory allocation process was fixed with respect to what we call **overaligned types**. The idea is that there are types for which we will want alignment constraints that are stricter than the alignment of the strictest natural alignment on a machine as modeled by type std::max_align_t.

There are many reasons for this, but a simple example would be when communicating with specialized hardware with requirements that differ from the ones on our computer. Suppose the following `Float4` type is such a type. Its size is `4*sizeof(float)`, and we require a `Float4` to be aligned on a 16-byte boundary:

```
struct alignas(16) Float4 { float vals[4]; };
```

In this example, if we remove `alignas(16)` from the type declaration, the natural alignment of type `Float4` would be `alignof(float)`, which is probably 4 on most platforms.

The problem with such types before C++17 is that variables generated by the compiler would respect our alignment requirements, but those located in dynamically allocated storage would, by default, end up with an alignment of `std::max_align_t`, which would be incorrect. That makes sense, of course; functions such as `malloc()` and `operator new()` will, by default, cover the "worst-case scenario" of the platform, not knowing what will be constructed in the allocated storage, but they cannot be assumed to implicitly cover even worse scenarios than this.

Since C++17, we can specify **overaligned type requirements** when calling either `operator new()` or `operator new[]()` by passing an additional argument of type `std::align_val_t`, an integral type. This has to be done explicitly at the call site, as the following example shows:

```cpp
#include <iostream>
#include <new>
#include <cstdlib>
#include <type_traits>
void* operator new(std::size_t n, std::align_val_t al) {
   std::cout << "new(" << n << ", align: "
             << static_cast<std::underlying_type_t<
                   std::align_val_t
                >>(al) << ")\n";
   return std::aligned_alloc(
      static_cast<std::size_t>(al), n
   );
}
// (others omitted for brevity)
struct alignas(16) Float4 { float vals[4]; };
int main() {
   auto p = new Float4; // calls operator new(size_t)
   // calls operator new(size_t, align_val_t)
   auto q = new(std::align_val_t{ 16 }) Float4;
   // leaks, of course, but that's beside the point
}
```

The memory block allocated for p in this example will be aligned on a boundary of std::max_ align_t, whereas the memory block allocated for q will be aligned on a 16-byte boundary. The former might satisfy the requirements of our type if we're lucky and cause chaos otherwise; the latter will respect our constraints if the allocation operator overload is implemented correctly.

Destroying delete

C++20 brings a novel and highly specialized feature called destroying delete. The use case targeted here is a member function overload that benefits from specific knowledge of the type of object being destroyed in order to better perform the destruction process. When that member function is defined for some type T, it is preferred over other options when delete is invoked on a T*, even if T exposes another overload of operator delete(). To use destroying delete for some type X, one must implement the following member function:

```
class X {
    // ...
public:
    void operator delete(X*, std::destroying_delete_t);
    // ...
};
```

Here, std::destroying_delete_t is a tag type like std::nothrow_t, which we saw earlier in this chapter. Note that the first argument of the destroying delete for class X is an X*, not a void*, as the destroying delete has the double role of destroying the object and deallocating memory... hence its name!

How does that work, and why is that useful? Let's look at a concrete example with the following Wrapper class. In this example, an object of type Wrapper hides one of two implementations, modeled by Wrapper::ImplA and Wrapper::ImplB. The implementation is selected at construction time based on an enumerated value of type Wrapper::Kind. The intent is to remove the need for virtual functions from this class, replacing them with if statements based on the kind of implementation that was chosen. Of course, in this (admittedly) small example, there's still only one virtual function (Impl::f()) as we aim to minimize the example's complexity. There is also a wish to keep the destructor of class Wrapper trivial, a property that can be useful on occasion.

We will look at this example step by step as it is a bit more elaborate than the previous ones. First, let's examine the basic structure of Wrapper including Wrapper::Kind, Wrapper::Impl, and its derived classes:

```
#include <new>
#include <iostream>
class Wrapper {
public:
    enum class Kind { A, B };
```

```
private:
    struct Impl {
        virtual int f() const = 0;
    };
    struct ImplA final : Impl {
        int f() const override { return 3; }
        ~ImplA() { std::cout << "Kind A\n"; }
    };
    struct ImplB final : Impl {
        int f() const override { return 4; }
        ~ImplB() { std::cout << "Kind B\n"; }
    };
    Impl *p;
    Kind kind;
    // ...
```

Visibly, `Wrapper::Impl` does not have a `virtual` destructor, yet `Wrapper` keeps as a data member an `Impl*` named p, which means that simply calling `delete p` might not call the appropriate destructor for the pointed-to object.

The `Wrapper` class exposes a constructor that takes a `Kind` as argument, then calls `Wrapper::create()` to construct the appropriate implementation, modeled by a type derived from `Impl`:

```
    // ...
    static Impl *create(Kind kind) {
        switch(kind) {
        using enum Kind;
        case A: return new ImplA;
        case B: return new ImplB;
        }
        throw 0;
    }
public:
    Wrapper(Kind kind)
        : p{ create(kind) }, kind{ kind } {
    }
    // ...
```

Now comes the destroying `delete`. Since we know by construction that the only possible implementations would be `ImplA` and `ImplB`, we test `p->kind` to know which one was chosen for `p`, then directly call the appropriate destructor. Once that is done, the `Wrapper` object itself is finalized and memory is freed through a direct call to `operator delete()`:

```
// ...
void operator delete(Wrapper *p,
                     std::destroying_delete_t) {
   if(p->kind == Kind::A) {
      delete static_cast<ImplA*>(p->p);
   } else {
      delete static_cast<ImplB*>(p->p);
   }
   p->~Wrapper();
   ::operator delete(p);
}
int f() const { return p->f(); }
};
```

For client code, the fact that we decided to use a destroying `delete` is completely transparent:

```
int main() {
   using namespace std;
   auto p = new Wrapper{ Wrapper::Kind::A };
   cout << p->f() << endl;
   delete p;
   p = new Wrapper{ Wrapper::Kind::B };
   cout << p->f() << endl;
   delete p;
}
```

The destroying `delete` is a recent C++ facility as of this writing, but it is a tool that can let us get more control over the destruction process of our objects. Most of your types probably do not need this feature, but it's good to know it exists for those cases where you need that extra bit of control over execution speed and program size. As always, measure the results of your efforts to ensure that they bring the desired benefits.

Summary

Whew, that was quite the ride! Now that we have the basics of memory allocation operator overloading handy, we will start to use them to our advantage. Our first application will be a leak detector (*Chapter 8*) using the global forms of these operators, followed by simplified examples of exotic memory management (*Chapter 9*) using specialized, custom forms of the global operators, and arena-based memory management (*Chapter 10*) with member versions of the operators that will perform very satisfying optimizations.

Unlock this book's exclusive benefits now

This book comes with additional benefits designed to elevate your learning experience.

https://www.packtpub.com/
unlock/9781805129806

Note: Have your purchase invoice ready before you begin.

8

Writing a Naïve Leak Detector

In *Chapter 7*, we examined various ways to overload the memory allocation operators, which are new, new[], delete, and delete[], in order to grasp the syntax involved in writing these operators as well as how they can be used in client code. We discussed how these operators interact with exceptions (even in the case of the nothrow versions) and saw why they should, in most cases, be written in groups of four or multiples thereof. For example, code that calls the nothrow version of operator new() to obtain some pointer, pV and later on calls delete p will quickly get in trouble if one overloads the nothrow version but not the "regular" one, as both might then end up not being compatible with one another.

What we have not really discussed is how our code could benefit from taking control of these operators. There are indeed multiple uses for this: tracing how or where memory is allocated, measuring memory fragmentation in a process, implementing a specialized strategy to control performance characteristics of the allocation or deallocation process, and so on. Since this book has a finite size, we cannot hope to cover examples of all possible options so we will pick one, hoping that this example is sufficiently inspirational to let you explore other avenues on your own.

The example we will explore in this chapter is a simple yet functional memory leak detector. In more detail, we will do the following:

1. We will first detail the plan, giving an overview of how our leak detector will work and what tricks we will use to meet our objectives.

2. Then, we will implement the first version of our tool, and that version will seem to work, at least on the surface. We will walk through a call to operator new() and the corresponding operator delete() to understand what happens in memory throughout this process.

3. At this point, we will use the knowledge acquired in previous chapters to identify the flaws in our first solution as well as ways in which we can fix them.

4. Finally, we will revisit our initial implementation and end up with something that is simple yet usable in real code.

Since this will be a very concrete chapter, you can expect to develop (or refine) some useful skills as we go:

- The first one is to plan before coding. We will be writing very low-level code in this chapter, which makes it particularly important for us to have a clear direction in mind. After all, when coding "close to the machine" and playing with raw memory, the compiler-provided safety net that is the type system tends to be a bit thinner and it's easier to make mistakes (costly ones at that) if we're not careful.

- The second one is to safely use shared mutable resources. Our leak detector will use the global versions of the memory allocation operators in order to cover allocation requests for all types, at least unless users decide to use specialized versions of these operators, and as such, we will need to manage the state that will be global to our program. In addition, we know that user code might be multithreaded so our accounting of the allocated memory will require a form of synchronization to avoid data races.

- The third one will be to acknowledge the impact of alignment when bypassing the type system. As we will handle raw memory for the a priori unknown needs of client code, we will learn to make choices that work for all "natural" (in the sense of "non-overaligned") memory allocation use cases.

- Finally, we will examine how to debug our code based on the contents of raw memory. Since we aim to keep this book tooling-agnostic, we will apply a schematical approach to this problem, but in practice, you should adapt what we do in this chapter to the metaphors of your favorite debugging utility. All reasonable debuggers will let you examine the contents of a specific memory address, something you will assuredly want to do on occasion.

Let's dive in!

Technical requirements

You can find the code files for this chapter in the book's GitHub repository here: `https://github.com/PacktPublishing/C-Plus-Plus-Memory-Management/tree/main/chapter8`.

The plan

We are planning to write a memory leak detector, a task that might seem strange and abstract at first. How do we start? Well, one way to clarify what we need to do is to write a small test program, showing at once how we expect our tool to be used and highlighting the key aspects of our tool from the perspective of user code:

```
#include <iostream>
// this is incomplete (for now)
int main() {
    auto pre = // current amount of allocated memory
```

```
{ // BEGIN
  int *p = new int{ 3 };
  int *q = new int[10]{ }; // initialized to zero
  delete p;
  // oops! Forgot to delete[] q
} // END
auto post = // current amount of allocated memory
// with this code, supposing sizeof(int)==4, we
// expect to see "Leaked 40 bytes" printed
if(post != pre)
  std::cout << "Leaked " << (post - pre) << " bytes\n";
}
```

As you can see, this "deliberately leaky" program performs two allocations but only a single deallocation, "forgetting" (conveniently for our purposes) to deallocate an array of ten int objects. Supposing sizeof(int)==4, our leak detector should allow the program to report a leak of 40 bytes.

This program does not tell us how we will (portably) obtain the amount of dynamically allocated memory at a given time (we will write this service in this chapter, after all), but it does show the allocations and deallocations being located between a pair of braces (see BEGIN and END in the comments of that example program). In C++, as you know, matching braces delimit a scope, and scope ensures the destruction of automatic variables defined therein. The idea here is that we want to detect leaks even in the presence of RAII objects (see *Chapter 4*) as they too could have bugs, so we want to make sure they are destroyed before we try to issue a diagnostic.

As mentioned in this chapter's introduction, we will implement our leak detector through the overloading of the *global* forms of memory allocation operators. As you might have already guessed, these operators will need to share some state: at the very least, they will need shared knowledge of the amount of memory allocated at a given moment since the new and new[] operators will increment that amount and the delete and delete[] operators will decrement it.

Note that for our leak detector, the array and non-array forms of these operators will be identical but that is *not* always the case: one could envision different strategies to allocate scalars and arrays, for example, just as one could want to track what these two forms do separately in a program. For simplicity, in this chapter, we will often simply mention new to describe both new and new[] and will use the same approach for delete.

Since these are free functions, not member functions of some object, we will need to resort to a *global variable* for this state. I know global variables are often frowned upon, mostly for good reasons, but they exist for cases such as this.

> **Global variables, oh my!**
>
> Reasons to dislike global variables abound: they make local reasoning difficult (who knows where and when they are being accessed?), they tend to be bottlenecks for cache access and slow programs down, they tend to require synchronization in contemporary (potentially multithreaded) programs, and so on. We are resorting to this mechanism here because we need to: C++ provides us with a wide variety of tools because it is a language that is used to solve a wide variety of problems, so there's no shame in using these tools when they are the right tools for the task at hand. Just ensure you make informed choices that you can justify!

To reduce (ever so slightly) the feeling of apparent revulsion that global variables provide to so many of us, we will encapsulate that state in an object, but of course, this object will also be global.

We will apply the **singleton** design pattern (also reviled by programmers at large, I know) to that end, a singleton being a class of which there is only one instance in a program. The benefit of this approach will be that we will control the ways in which the global state will be accessed; hopefully, it will also help clarify what we are doing. We will name our singleton class `Accountant` since its responsibilities will be to help the memory allocation operators keep track of the number of bytes allocated and deallocated during program execution.

> **Singletons, oh my!**
>
> As far as design patterns go, the singleton is probably one of the least liked ones, for reasons similar to those behind the dislike of global variables: difficult to test or mock, requires synchronization, tends to become a performance bottleneck, and so on. The real culprit here to be honest is **shared mutable state**, made worse by the fact that this state is globally accessible throughout the program. As you might have guessed by now, since the shared mutable state is exactly what we need to keep track of the amount of memory allocated at a given time, well… this is what we will use!

Now, for the actual implementation, we will need to develop a strategy to track the number of bytes allocated and deallocated. The overall idea is that `operator new()` will tell the `Accountant` object that bytes have been allocated, and that `operator delete()` will tell the `Accountant` object that bytes have been deallocated. Now, for the purpose of this activity, we will use the traditional (up to and including C++11) form of these operators. As you might remember from *Chapter 7*, their signatures are as follows:

```
void *operator new(std::size_t n);
void *operator new[](std::size_t n);
void operator delete(void*p) noexcept;
void operator delete[](void*p) noexcept;
```

Since you are reading this book, you are assuredly a most astute reader, so you might have already noticed a problem here: our allocation functions know from their argument the number of bytes to allocate, but our deallocation functions do not have that privilege, being only provided the address where the block to deallocate begins. This means that we need a way to make the connection between the address returned by `operator new()` and the size of the associated memory block.

That seems like an easy enough problem to solve: just allocate the moral equivalent of something like `std::vector<std::pair<void*,std::size_t>>` or `std::map<void*,std::size_t>` to make it easy to retrieve the `std::size_t` associated with a given address, but such containers need to allocate memory, and that would mean allocating memory in order to implement the way in which we allocate memory. This could get problematic, to say the least, so we need another solution.

We will do what any sane programmer would do under similar circumstances: we will lie. Yes, we will! Why do you think we took the time to look at tricky and dangerous code in those first chapters?

How will lying help us solve the problem, you say? Well, remember that writing the following code leads to calling `operator new()` with `sizeof(X)` as an argument:

```
X *p = new X{ /* ... */ };
```

Let us name this argument n. This means that if the allocation and the ensuing construction both succeed, from the perspective of client code, the situation will be as follows:

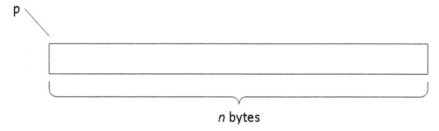

Figure 8.1 – Allocated block of memory from the perspective of client code

In order for `operator delete()` to be able to find the value of n based on p, one strategy (and the one we will adopt for this example) will be to hide the value of n just before p. The actual layout in memory from our own code's perspective would then be as follows:

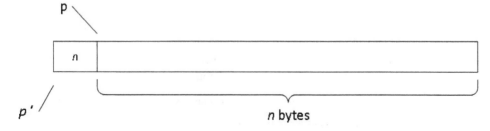

Figure 8.2 – Allocated block of memory from the perspective of the allocation operators.

Here, p would be the address as seen from the client code, but p' would be where the actually allocated block of memory starts. Clearly, *this is a lie*: the address returned by the allocation function will be a valid address where an object can be constructed, but it will not be the start of the memory block we have actually allocated. As long as the space between p and p' is known to both `operator new()` and `operator delete()`, this can be made to work.

For obvious reasons, overloading `operator new()` to do this trickery means that we have to overload `operator delete()` to do the reverse gymnastics: given some pointer p, go backward in memory where p' was, find the value of n that was hidden there, and inform the `Accountant` object of the fact that n bytes were released.

Now, let's see how we will do this.

A first implementation (that almost works)

We now have a plan, so we are ready to start implementing the initial version of our leak detector. This implementation will be slightly naïve but will help us understand the general idea; we will examine the more delicate aspects of the implementation once the basic infrastructure is in place. *Do not use this first version in production code* as it will be (slightly yet dangerously) incorrect. We will provide a correct version later in this chapter, of course.

As a suggestion, try to see if you can identify the "rough edges" of our implementation by yourself before we cover them later in this chapter. There will be clues left here and there for you, and if you read the chapters that preceded this one, you might already have an idea of what you should be looking for.

The Accountant singleton class

Our `Accountant` class will be a reification of the singleton design pattern whose role will be to allow the global overloads of the memory allocation operators to keep track of the number of bytes of dynamically allocated memory in a program. As previously mentioned, a singleton is an idea: a class for which there is only one instance in a program. This idea can be reified in various languages (at least those supporting some variant of the object-oriented paradigm) in ways that respect the particularities of each language.

One key particularity of C++ is the presence of actual objects, not just references to objects, in user code. This means that a C++ singleton will usually have the following characteristics:

- A `private` default constructor, since if that constructor was `public`, it could be called more than once which would make the class a non-singleton.

- Deleted copy operations, as allowing copies of our object would make it a non-singleton.

- A way to ensure the singleton can be created and, of course, accessed. That mechanism has to be such that it cannot be abused to create more than one object. Since our default constructor will be `private`, this mechanism will either be a `static` member function (this will be our choice) or a `friend` function.

- Finally, the state used for the object's representation and the services offered by the singleton, if any.

An object of our Accountant class will expose three services: one to let the new and new[] operators inform the Accountant object that memory has been taken, one to inform it that memory has been given back, and one to let client code know how much memory is used at a given time.

An incomplete view of the Accountant class given what we have discussed so far would be as follows:

```
#ifndef LEAK_DETECTOR_H
#define LEAK_DETECTOR_H
#include <cstddef>
#include <new>
class Accountant {
   Accountant(); // note: private
   //...
public:
   // deleted copy operations
   Accountant(const Accountant&) = delete;
   Accountant& operator=(const Accountant&) = delete;
   // to access the singleton object
   static Accountant& get();
   // services offered by the object
   // n bytes were allocated
   void take(std::size_t n);
   // n bytes were deallocated
   void give_back(std::size_t n);
   // number of bytes currently allocated
   std::size_t how_much() const;
};
// allocation operators (free functions)
void *operator new(std::size_t);
void *operator new[](std::size_t);
void operator delete(void*) noexcept;
void operator delete[](void*) noexcept;
#endif
```

With this, we can already complete the skeleton of our test program as presented earlier in this chapter:

```
#include "leak_detector.h"
#include <iostream>
int main() {
   auto pre = Accountant::get().how_much();
   { // BEGIN
      int *p = new int{ 3 };
```

```
      int *q = new int[10]{ }; // initialized to zero
      delete p;
      // oops! Forgot to delete[] q
    } // END
  auto post = Accountant::get().how_much();
  // with this code, supposing sizeof(int)==4, we
  // expect to see "Leaked 40 bytes" printed
  if(post != pre)
      std::cout << "Leaked " << (post - pre) << " bytes\n";
}
```

Now, we need to examine the implementation of the Accountant class. The first thing we need to decide is how and where the actual object will be created. It happens that there are surprisingly many ways to do this, but in our case (where we are not concerned by execution speed), the simplest way to correctly instantiate the object is what is called a **Meyers Singleton**, in honor of the now-retired but always respected **Scott Meyers**, who suggested that technique as part of *item 47* in his well-known book, *Effective C++: Specific Ways to Improve Your Programs and Designs (3rd Edition), Addison-Wesley Professional*.

The Meyers Singleton technique

The Meyers Singleton technique aims to avoid something colloquially called the **static initialization order fiasco**, an informal name given to the fact that in a C++ program made of multiple translation units, one cannot know from the source code in which order the global objects will be constructed (the problem also exists for the order of destruction, although the Meyers technique is not helpful for this).

The trick is to declare the singleton object as a static local variable in the static member function that provides access to the object (here, the get() function): doing so ensures the object will be created only once, the first time the function is called, and will keep its state throughout the execution of the program. There is a slight but measurable cost to doing so as there is a form of low-level implicit synchronization surrounding the object's construction to avoid the object being created more than once even in a multithreaded program.

This technique ensures all such singletons are created in the correct order (meaning that, if the constructor of singleton A needs a service from singleton B, this will lead to singleton B being constructed "just in time") even if they are technically "global" variables, as long as there is no cycle in the calls that create them of course.

In terms of state, since take() and give_back() both accept an argument of type std::size_t, it would be tempting to represent the current amount of memory also as std::size_t, but allow me to recommend something else. Indeed, std::size_t is an alias for an *unsigned* integral type, which means that this representation would make it difficult to detect a case where there have been more bytes *deallocated* than allocated, an unpleasant situation we would surely like to handle. For that reason, we will use a (large) signed integral instead.

Fine, you might think: we can use a `long long` representation then! However, remember that memory allocation and deallocation mechanisms need to be thread-safe, so we need to ensure that all accesses to that integral representation will be synchronized. There are many ways to do this, but the simplest one is probably to use an atomic type, in our case, `std::atomic<long long>`. Note that atomic objects are uncopiable so our singleton would implicitly be uncopiable, but there's no harm in stating that fact explicitly as we did when deleting the copy operations.

A complete implementation of the `Accountant` class would be as follows:

```cpp
#ifndef LEAK_DETECTOR_H
#define LEAK_DETECTOR_H
#include <cstddef>
#include <atomic>
#include <new>
class Accountant {
   std::atomic<long long> cur;
   Accountant() : cur{ 0LL } { // note: private
   }
public:
   // deleted copy operations
   Accountant(const Accountant&) = delete;
   Accountant& operator=(const Accountant&) = delete;
   // to access the singleton object
   static auto& get() { // auto used for simplicity
      static Accountant singleton; // here it is
      return singleton;
   }
   // services offered by the object
   // n bytes were allocated
   void take(std::size_t n) { cur += n; }
   // n bytes were deallocated
   void give_back(std::size_t n) { cur -= n; }
   // number of bytes currently allocated
   std::size_t how_much() const { return cur.load(); }
};
// allocation operators (free functions)
void *operator new(std::size_t);
void *operator new[](std::size_t);
void operator delete(void*) noexcept;
void operator delete[](void*) noexcept;
#endif
```

The services are probably trivial to understand for the most part. Since `cur` is an atomic object, operations such as `+=` or `-=` modify `cur` in a synchronized manner, avoiding data races. Two subtle aspects of `how_much()` deserve a short discussion:

- The first is that we are returning `cur.load()`, not `cur`, since we care about the value represented by the `atomic` object, not the atomic object itself (which is a synchronization mechanism, not an integral value, and is uncopiable as previously mentioned). It's like taking a picture of that value at a specific point in time, really.

- The second, a consequence of the first, is that by the time the client code gets the value returned by that function, the actual value might have changed, so this function is inherently "racy" if used in a multithreaded situation. It's not a problem for our test code, of course, but it's something to be aware of.

Now that we have put in place a scaffolding for keeping track of the number of bytes allocated, we can start to write the actual allocation and deallocation functions.

Implementing the new and new[] operators

If you remember our plan, what we will do in our memory allocation operators is take the number of bytes, n, requested by client code, then allocate slightly more because we will hide n just before the beginning of the block of n bytes we will end up returning to our client. Minimally, we will need to allocate `n + sizeof n` bytes to achieve this. In this example, we will use `std::malloc()` and `std::free()` to perform the low-level allocation operations.

We will signal failure to allocate by throwing `std::bad_alloc` as is customary in C++. If the allocation succeeds, we will then inform the `Accountant` object that n bytes have been allocated, even though we will have allocated a bit more. The fact that our strategy leads us to allocate more than requested is an artifact that does not concern client code, and that might even be confusing when trying to diagnose problems: a program that allocates a single byte and is informed that it leaked much more than this would be somewhat awkward.

A complete but naïve (and slightly incorrect, as announced) implementation would be as follows:

```
#include <cstdlib>
void *operator new(std::size_t n) {
    // allocate n bytes plus enough space to hide n
    void *p = std::malloc(n + sizeof n); // to revisit
    // signal failure to meet postconditions if needed
    if(!p) throw std::bad_alloc{};
    // hide n at the beginning of the allocated block
    auto q = static_cast<std::size_t*>(p);
    *q = n; // to revisit
    // inform the Accountant of the allocation
    Accountant::get().take(n);
```

```
    // return the beginning of the requested block memory
    return q + 1; // to revisit
}
void *operator new[](std::size_t n) {
    // exactly the same as operator new above
}
```

Remember that even though `operator new()` and `operator new[]()` are identical in this example, there is no obligation to make them the same in all situations. Also, note that some of the lines in this excerpt have a comment stating "to revisit" as we will want to take a closer look at these later in this chapter.

Implementing the delete and delete[] operators

Our deallocation operators will collaborate in the elaborate lie prepared by the allocation operators: we know that the new and new[] operators return pointers to a block of n bytes, but that block is not what has really been allocated, it's "just" the place where an object lived for a while. For that reason, it's important that the `delete` and `delete[]` operators do the required address adjustment before performing the actual deallocation.

The rules for a correct implementation of `operator delete` are as follows:

- Applying `operator delete()` or `operator delete[]()` on a null pointer is a no-op
- Deallocation functions should not throw
- The deallocation code should be coherent with the associated allocation function

> **Not all null pointers are the same**
>
> While it's true that given some `T*` object named p, writing `delete p` or `delete[] p` will be a no-op if p==nullptr. However, writing `delete nullptr` will fail to compile as `nullptr` is an object of type `std::nullptr_t`, not a pointer.

Given the implementation of our allocation operators in the previous section, this means a mostly adequate deallocation operator could be as follows:

```
void operator delete(void *p) noexcept {
    // delete on a null pointer is a no-op
    if (!p) return;
    // find the beginning of the block that was allocated
    auto q = static_cast<std::size_t*>(p) - 1; // to revisit
    // inform the Accountant of the deallocation
    Accountant::get().give_back(*q);
    // free the memory
```

```
    std::free(q);
  }
void operator delete[](void *p) noexcept {
    // exactly the same as operator delete above
  }
```

That completes the lie, or so to say, and it completes the leak detector, at least for this first (and imperfect) implementation. If you run the test program with our implementation on a compiler where `sizeof(int)==4`, you can expect it to display that its execution leaked 40 bytes as expected.

Visualizing it all

When enjoying low-level programming such as this (taking over the memory allocation functions of your program, manipulating raw memory blocks, hiding information, and playing tricks with addresses), it can be hard to visualize what one is doing, and what the consequences are.

If your favorite debugger allows you to do so, you might want to try to go through the test program's execution step by step. Please make sure you work in so-called "debug" (unoptimized) mode to fully benefit from the experience, as optimized code is often sufficiently transformed by the compiler to make the association between source code and generated code difficult to make.

Let's walk through a call to `operator new()` step by step. The first thing we do is ask `Accountant` for the amount of dynamically allocated memory at the beginning of the `main()` function:

```
int main() {
    auto pre = Accountant::get().how_much();
    { // BEGIN
        int *p = new int{ 3 };
        int *q = new int[10]{ }; // initialized to zero
        delete p;
        // oops! Forgot to delete[] q
    } // END
    auto post = Accountant::get().how_much();
    if(post != pre)
        std::cout << "Leaked " << (post - pre) << " bytes\n";
}
```

One can expect `pre==0` at this point but there are situations, such as a global object calling new in its constructor, that could lead to `pre` having other values. This is fine, as what we are monitoring with this approach is whether there is a leak in between the braces marked with BEGIN and END, and this should hold regardless of whether the amount of bytes allocated outside of those braces is zero or not.

The next step is calling `operator new()` and requesting a memory block big enough to store an `int` object:

```cpp
int main() {
    auto pre = Accountant::get().how_much();
    { // BEGIN
        int *p = new int{ 3 };
        int *q = new int[10]{ }; // initialized to zero
        delete p;
        // oops! Forgot to delete[] q
    } // END
    auto post = Accountant::get().how_much();
    if(post != pre)
        std::cout << "Leaked " << (post - pre) << " bytes\n";
}
```

This leads us to our implementation of `operator new()` where `n==sizeof(int)`. Supposing `sizeof(int)==4` and `sizeof(std::size_t)==8` for the sake of this example, our call to `std::malloc()` will request a block of at least 12 bytes:

```cpp
void *operator new(std::size_t n) {
    void *p = std::malloc(n + sizeof n);
    if(!p) throw std::bad_alloc{};
    auto q = static_cast<std::size_t*>(p);
    *q = n;
    Accountant::get().take(n);
    return q + 1;
}
```

If you look at the memory pointed to by p with your debugger once the call to `std::malloc()` completes, you might see something like the following (all numbers are expressed in hexadecimal form):

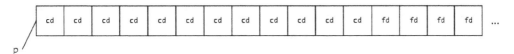

Figure 8.3 – Possible initial state for the allocated block

Note that there is no guarantee that you will see these specific values as C++ does not impose any requirement on the initialization of the memory block returned by `std::malloc()`. These `0xcd` hexadecimal values (or similar recognizable patterns) are however probable when using a "debug build" as libraries compiled for debugging will often place recognizable bit patterns in uninitialized memory to help detect programming errors.

You might also notice the trailing four bytes (each containing 0xfd), which are also suspiciously recognizable, suggesting that the implementation of std::malloc() I used allocated more than what I requested and stored a marker just after the block my code requested, probably to help detect buffer overruns. Our library has the same implementation freedom as we do, after all!

The first lie we did was the overallocation of memory with respect to the actual request we got. We now commit a second lie about the very nature of the memory we are pointing to:

```cpp
void *operator new(std::size_t n) {
    void *p = std::malloc(n + sizeof n);
    if(!p) throw std::bad_alloc{};
    auto q = static_cast<std::size_t*>(p);
    *q = n;
    Accountant::get().take(n);
    return q + 1;
}
```

Converting a pointer from or to void* can be done efficiently with static_cast, as explained in *Chapter 3*. We now have two perspectives on the same memory block with p claiming that the block holds raw memory and q claiming (erroneously) that it holds at least one std::size_t:

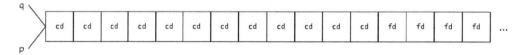

Figure 8.4 – Two perspectives on the same memory block

Through q, we hide the value of n at the beginning of the allocated memory block. Remember that this is not what we will be returning to our caller, so this is done without the client code's knowledge:

```cpp
void *operator new(std::size_t n) {
    void *p = std::malloc(n + sizeof n);
    if(!p) throw std::bad_alloc{};
    auto q = static_cast<std::size_t*>(p);
    *q = n;
    Accountant::get().take(n);
    return q + 1;
}
```

One possible view of the memory pointed to by both p and q would now be as follows:

Figure 8.5 – Possible state of the memory block after hiding the value of n

Again, your view might differ from this one: we wrote an eight-byte integral value, which explains the number of consecutive bytes affected by this write, but the order of bytes in an integer depends on the underlying hardware architecture: some architectures are **big-endian** and store the *most* significant byte of an integer at its lowest memory address; others are **little-endian** and store the *least* significant byte at the highest memory address. Within a program, you typically will not notice this unless you serialize data to persistent storage or on a network. As such, on another machine, you could see the value 4 closer to the right and of that eight-byte write instead of being on the left as it is in this example.

After informing Accountant that we allocated 4 bytes (not 12, remember), we reach the point where we return to our caller the beginning of the 4-byte block that was actually requested:

```
void *operator new(std::size_t n) {
    void *p = std::malloc(n + sizeof n);
    if(!p) throw std::bad_alloc{};
    auto q = static_cast<std::size_t*>(p);
    *q = n;
    Accountant::get().take(n);
    return q + 1;
}
```

Looking at our memory block, the situation is now as follows:

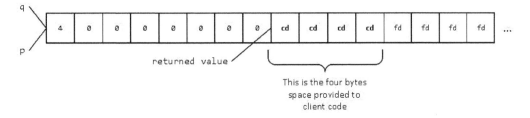

Figure 8.6 – State of the memory block at the point of return

Returning to the caller, the constructor of the `int` object is applied to the block returned by `operator new()`:

```cpp
int main() {
   auto pre = Accountant::get().how_much();
   { // BEGIN
      int *p = new int{ 3 };
      int *q = new int[10]{ }; // initialized to zero
      delete p;
      // oops! Forgot to delete[] q
   } // END
   auto post = Accountant::get().how_much();
   if(post != pre)
      std::cout << "Leaked " << (post - pre) << " bytes\n";
}
```

After having applied the constructor on the memory pointed to by p in `main()`, our memory block looks like the following:

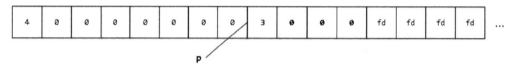

Figure 8.7 – Possible state of the memory block after constructing *p

Voilà! The beauty of all this is that client code (the `main()` function) has no idea that we played those tricks and performed those lies, just as we really have no idea what other tricks `std::malloc()` did for us (unless we can look at its source code, of course). Program execution continues normally and *p can be used like any other `int` until we reach the point where we decide to deallocate it:

```cpp
int main() {
   auto pre = Accountant::get().how_much();
   { // BEGIN
      int *p = new int{ 3 };
      int *q = new int[10]{ }; // initialized to zero
      delete p;
      // oops! Forgot to delete[] q
   } // END
   auto post = Accountant::get().how_much();
   if(post != pre)
      std::cout << "Leaked " << (post - pre) << " bytes\n";
}
```

When entering `operator delete()`, you might notice that the memory pointed to by the `p` argument begins with value 3 (the value of the `int`), not value 4. This makes sense as `p` points to the memory block that was given to the client code, not to the beginning of the block we actually allocated:

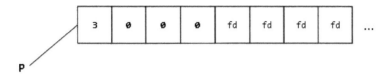

Figure 8.8 – State of the memory block prior to destruction (caller's perspective)

Before continuing, it's important to understand here that the reason why you probably see 3 here is that `int` is a trivially destructible type so its destructor was essentially a no-op. Normally, at the point where `operator delete()` begins its execution, the destructor for the pointed-to object has already run and the memory block could contain pretty much anything.

Within `operator delete()`, our first task is to retrieve the location where we hid the value of `n` during the corresponding call to `operator new()`:

```
void operator delete(void *p) noexcept {
    if(!p) return;
    auto q = static_cast<std::size_t*>(p) - 1;
    Accountant::get().give_back(*q);
    std::free(q);
}
```

At this point, `q` is the location where the value of `n` was stored as well at the beginning of the memory block that was allocated. We inform `Accountant` of the fact that `n` bytes were deallocated, and call `std::free()` to perform the actual deallocation.

If you are observing the memory pointed to by `q` when calling `std::free()`, it is possible (but not guaranteed) that you will see that memory being written to. It is also possible (but also not guaranteed) that you will see memory written to *before* `q` as well as *after* the end of the bytes memory block you had allocated. Remember that `std::free()`, like `std::malloc()`, can do whatever bookkeeping tasks it requires just as it can overwrite memory blocks that have been freed, particularly in builds meant for debugging; or, it can just leave the memory as it was, which is more probable with optimized builds.

That was fun, wasn't it? It seems to work indeed, at least on some machines. Yet, as stated earlier, this version of our leak detector has bugs, and these bugs can really hurt us. As a hint, know that if we compile this leak detector on a compiler where `std::size_t` is four bytes wide and try to call `new double`, we might get into *very* serious trouble. It is now time to take a closer look at our implementation to grasp why this is so and fix the problems we caused.

Identifying (and fixing) the problems

Our initial implementation has in fact one real problem, as well as something that works but could be cleaner and deserves discussion.

The real problem is that we express our lies in dangerous ways and that we are not giving proper consideration to alignment requirements. Indeed, look at our initial implementation of `operator new()`:

```
void *operator new(std::size_t n) {
    // allocate n bytes plus enough space to hide n
    void *p = std::malloc(n + sizeof n); // to revisit
    // signal failure to meet postconditions if needed
    if(!p) throw std::bad_alloc{};
    // hide n at the beginning of the allocated block
    auto q = static_cast<std::size_t*>(p);
    *q = n; // to revisit
    // inform the Accountant of the allocation
    Accountant::get().take(n);
    // return the beginning of the requested block memory
    return q + 1; // to revisit
}
```

We know for a fact that the memory returned by `std::malloc()` has to be aligned appropriately for the strictest (meaning *worst*) natural alignment of our machine: indeed, since that function does not know what object will be constructed once the allocation has completed, it has to make sure that the memory block allocated will be properly aligned in all "natural" cases. C++ compilers offer `std::max_align_t` as an alias for the type with the strictest natural alignment in a machine, which is often, but not necessarily, type `double` in practice.

Now, we allocate a bit more than was requested, `sizeof(std::size_t)` more bytes to be precise. That's fine up to a point: we can assuredly store `std::size_t` at the beginning of the block returned by `std::malloc()` since that block is well aligned even in the worst case.

Then, we "jump over" `std::size_t` and return an address that is `sizeof(std::size_t)` bytes more than the one we allocated. This can be fine if it still yields a correctly aligned address even in the worst case, but that is only the case if `std::size_t` and `std::max_align_t` are of the same size, something that is *not* guaranteed (in practice, their sizes are often different).

What happens if these types are of different sizes and, consequently, the address returned by `operator new()` does not match the alignment requirements of `std::max_align_t`? Well, it depends:

- It can work if we get "lucky" and the address returned is aligned correctly for the type we want to construct. For example, suppose that `alignof(int)==4` and `alignof(std::max_align_t)==8`, then calling `new int` will work even if `operator new` returns an address that is a multiple of four but not of eight. However, it's probable that calling new double will only lead to pain. This sort of "luck" can be a curse, hiding a latent, damaging bug for a while and making for unpleasant surprises later.

- You can end up with slow and dangerous code, as some hardware will support access to misaligned objects. You don't want to do that, however, as for the machine to achieve this, it needs to perform acrobatics and transform a seemingly simple operation such as loading double in a register into a sequence of operations (load the "low" bytes, load the "high" bytes, and make a double out of these two parts through bitwise manipulations). This leads to code that is significantly slower to execute, obviously, but also dangerous if you have a multithreaded program as one thread could read a partially formed object (this is called a **torn read**) or write to a partially formed object (a **torn write**). You really do not want to debug code where this happens.

- Your code can simply crash, as will be the case on many embedded platforms (including quite a few game consoles). It's arguably the most reasonable outcome in such a situation.

To fix this problem, we need to ensure that the address returned from our overloaded operator new() is properly aligned for std::max_align_t, and that operator delete() is adjusted accordingly. One way to do this would be to ensure that the size of the "hiding spot" for n is such that jumping over that additional memory block still results in an address that is properly aligned for a std::max_align_t object:

```
void *operator new(std::size_t n) {
    // allocate n bytes plus enough space to hide n,
    // taking worst case natural alignment into account
    void *p = std::malloc(sizeof(std::max_align_t) + n);
    // signal failure to meet postconditions if needed
    if(!p) throw std::bad_alloc{};
    // hide n at the beginning of the allocated block
    *static_cast<std::size_t*>(p) = n; // to revisit
    // inform the Accountant of the allocation
    Accountant::get().take(n);
    // return the beginning of the requested block memory
    return static_cast<std::max_align_t*>(p) + 1;
}
```

As you can see, this implementation allocates space for std::max_align_t in addition to the requested n bytes, then "jumps over" that additional storage to yield an address that is still properly aligned for the worst case. This might mean wasting more space than in the initial (incorrect) implementation if sizeof(std::size_t) happens to be less than sizeof(std::max_align_t), but at least we know that client code will be able to construct its object there.

The corresponding `operator delete()` will do the same pointer gymnastics but in reverse, going back `sizeof(std::max_align_t)` bytes in memory:

```
void operator delete(void *p) noexcept {
    // delete on a null pointer is a no-op
    if(!p) return;
    // find the beginning of the block that was allocated
    p = static_cast<std::max_align_t*>(p) - 1;
    // inform the Accountant of the deallocation
    Accountant::get().give_back(
        *static_cast<std::size_t*>(p)
    );
    // free the memory
    std::free(p);
}
```

Note that this implementation assigns `std::max_align_t*` to `void*` (pointer p), something that is perfectly legal and does not require a cast.

The other issue we should discuss is not technically a problem in this implementation but is a problem in general. Look at this excerpt from `operator new()`:

```
void *operator new(std::size_t n) {
    void *p = std::malloc(n + sizeof(std::max_align_t));
    if(!p) throw std::bad_alloc{};
    // hide n at the beginning of the allocated block
    *static_cast<std::size_t*>(p) = n; // to revisit
    Accountant::get().take(n);
    return static_cast<std::max_align_t*>(p) + 1;
}
```

Do you notice something strange? The highlighted line of code performs an assignment where p points, but the assignment only makes sense on an existing object. Is there an object at location `*p` at that moment?

The answer is… strange. To create an object, one has to call its constructor, but we never called the constructor of `std::size_t` at location p in this code. This might make you wonder why our code seems to work. It happens that the following is the case:

- Some types in C++ are said to be **implicit lifetime types**. These types include scalars (pointers, pointer to members, arithmetic types, enumerations, `std::nullptr_t` including their cv-qualified counterparts) and implicit lifetime classes (aggregates with no user-provided destructor, at least one eligible trivial constructor as well as a non-deleted trivial destructor). You will notice that `std::size_t`, being an alias for an unsigned integral type, falls under the umbrella of implicit lifetime types. If you have a C++23 compiler, you can programmatically test if some type T qualifies as an implicit lifetime type through the `std::is_implicit_lifetime<T>` trait.

- Some standard library functions implicitly start the lifetime of objects of implicit lifetime types. These include some C functions, such as `std::memcpy()`, `std::memmove()`, and `std::malloc()`, but also `std::bit_cast`, some functions in allocators (see *Chapter 14*) as well as two functions from C++23 respectively named `std::start_lifetime_as()` and `std::start_lifetime_as_array()`.

What makes this assignment operation work in this specific case is that we are writing to an object of an implicit lifetime type in a block of memory that is properly aligned and has been allocated with one of these special functions that have the property of implicitly starting the lifetime of objects. If we had decided to store something more elaborate than an object of some implicit lifetime type, our assignment would either fail at compile-time (if our compiler is nice enough to notice our mistake) or risk causing damage at runtime.

A better, and in general, safer approach to the act of hiding the value of n in some uninitialized storage is to use `placement new`, as seen in *Chapter 7*. The following implementation of `operator new()` is thus preferable in general as it avoids an (often misguided) assignment to a non-object:

```
void *operator new(std::size_t n) {
    void *p = std::malloc(n + sizeof(std::max_align_t));
    if(!p) throw std::bad_alloc{};
    // hide n at the beginning of the allocated block
    new (p) std::size_t{ n };
    Accountant::get().take(n);
    return static_cast<std::max_align_t*>(p) + 1;
}
```

Note that since `std::size_t` has a trivial destructor, there is no need to call its destructor in `operator delete()`; simply freeing its underlying storage is sufficient to end its lifetime. We now have a correct, working leak detector!

Revisiting our implementation (and lessons learned)

We just overloaded memory allocation operators, blatantly lied our way through the protections of the type system, performed potentially dangerous operations that risked leading to misaligned objects, and saw how to avoid this pitfall. That was an interesting adventure indeed, but the astute reader that you are is probably wondering about the cost of this trick, particularly in terms of how much memory it consumes.

With our "allocate more than requested and hide n at the beginning" approach, each allocation consumes `sizeof(std::max_align_t)` bytes more than needed by client code. If our code allocates large objects, that cost might be minor, but if we allocate smaller objects, this overhead can be unreasonable and dominate the memory consumption of our entire program.

Remember from *Chapter 7* that C++14 made it possible to provide an overload of `operator delete()` that accepts the size of the just-destroyed object as an argument. This makes the act of hiding n during `operator new()` redundant, as we did so precisely in order to retrieve n in `operator delete()`, something we no longer need to do.

Since we do not need to hide n, we can both simplify our implementation and significantly reduce our memory consumption:

```
void *operator new(std::size_t n) {
    // allocate n bytes (no need for more!)
    void *p = std::malloc(n);
    // signal failure to meet postconditions if needed
    if(!p) throw std::bad_alloc{};
    // inform the Accountant of the allocation
    Accountant::get().take(n);
    // return the beginning of the requested block memory
    return p;
}
void *operator new[](std::size_t n) {
    // exactly the same as operator new above
}
void operator delete(void *p, std::size_t n) noexcept {
    // delete on a null pointer is a no-op
    if(!p) return;
    // inform the Accountant of the deallocation
    Accountant::get().give_back(n);
    // free the memory
    std::free(p);
}
void operator delete[](void *p, std::size_t n) noexcept {
    // exactly the same as operator delete above
}
```

This leak detector still works and represents a strict upgrade when compared with the more naïve version that preceded it.

Summary

That was fun, wasn't it? You can take this very simple tool and make it more interesting: for example, you could use it to check for overflow and underflow of the allocated memory blocks by injecting sentinel values before and after each block, or you could use it to make a sort of map of the way your memory is being used.

This concludes our first foray into applications that benefit from taking charge of the memory allocation facilities at our disposal. Our next step, and next chapter, will lead us to examine how a C++ program can interact with atypical memory or deal with atypical allocation situations.

Of course, no programming language (even one as versatile and wide-ranging as C++) can profess to cover all possible types of memory that an operating system could provide services for, nor should that be the language's role. Still, as we will see, C++ provides us with the kind of "syntactic glue" required to build bridges between atypical needs and the rest of the program.

9

Atypical Allocation Mechanisms

We are progressing in our exploration of memory management with C++. In *Chapter 7*, we explored the various syntactic ways in which one can overload `operator new()` and `operator delete()` (as well as their array counterparts), and in *Chapter 8*, we wrote an actual, real-life example (a memory leak detector) relying on the capacity to write such overloads. It's a nice start, showing concretely that this knowledge has practical uses, but you might (rightfully) wonder what else we can do when controlling memory management facilities.

This chapter will be slightly different from the others. What we will do here is present a non-exhaustive set of ways in which one can benefit from taking control of the memory allocation functions of C++. More precisely, we will show the following:

- How placement `new` can let us drive memory-mapped hardware efficiently

- How one can simplify usage of error management with the `nothrow` version of `operator new()`

- How one can install and use `std::new_handler` to make it easier to react to out-of-memory situations

- How one can handle "exotic" memories such as shared memory or persistent memory through the mediation of standard C++

At the end of this chapter, we will have a broader view of what opportunities the basic memory allocation facilities of C++ provide us with. Later chapters will return to more focused topics such as arena-based allocation (*Chapter 10*), deferred reclamation (*Chapter 11*), and, in later chapters, how to control memory allocation with containers and allocators.

Technical requirements

You can find the code files for this chapter in the book's GitHub repository here: https://github. com/PacktPublishing/C-Plus-Plus-Memory-Management/tree/main/chapter9.

Placement new and memory-mapped hardware

There are many uses for placement new (an important feature discussed in *Chapter 7*, as you might remember) but one use that is particularly interesting is that it allows us to map software objects to memory-mapped hardware, effectively allowing us to drive hardware as if it was software.

A working example of this feature would be tricky to write as we would find ourselves in "non-portable code land," using operating-system-specific features to get the address of a particular device and discussing ways to get read and write privileges to memory locations normally accessed by software drivers. For that reason, we will craft an artificial yet illustrative example and ask you, esteemed reader, to imagine that the missing parts of this example exist.

First, suppose that we are developing a driver for a new video card, one that is so wonderful that its codename is super_video_card. For the sake of this illustration, we will model this through the following class:

```cpp
#include <cstdint>
class super_video_card {
  // ...
public:
  // super duper registers
  volatile std::uint32_t r0{}, r1{}, r2{}, r3{};
  static_assert(sizeof(float) == 4); // sanity check
  volatile float f0{}, f1{}, f2{}, f3{};
  // etc.
  // initialize the video card's state
  super_video_card() = default;
  super_video_card(const super_video_card&) = delete;
  super_video_card&
    operator=(const super_video_card&) = delete;
  // could be used to reset the video card's state
  ~super_video_card() = default;
  // various services (omitted for brevity)
};
// ...
```

The important aspects of this class for our purpose are the following:

- It is an uncopiable type, as it is meant to map to a specific zone of memory. Copying an object of this type would be counterproductive, to say the least.

- It has been designed in such a way that its state can conceptually be superimposed on its hardware equivalent. For example, given the preceding class declaration, starting at the beginning of the hardware's memory layout, we expect four 32-bit integral registers followed by four 32-bit floating point registers. We used <cstdint> to get the aliases for fixed-width integral types on our compiler.

- As should be the case under such circumstances, we express our expectations through static_ assert whenever possible. Also, since the state of the hardware registers can change through other actions than that of our program, we qualified the register-equivalents as volatile such that accesses to these member variables will be equivalent to I/O operations for the purpose of C++'s abstract machine.

> **Why do we use volatile variables in this example?**
>
> If you are not used to volatile variables, you might be wondering why we used this qualification on the data members of our memory-mapped hardware-representing class. The reason why this is important is that we want to avoid our compiler optimizing code based on the (wrong, in this case) assumption that if our code does not touch these variables, then they do not change state or that if our writes to these variables are not followed by reads in our code, then that can be assumed to have no effect. Through volatile-qualified variables, we are effectively telling the compiler "*There are things you do not know happening on these objects, so please do not assume too much.*"

For simplicity, we used a constructor that zeros out the data members and a trivial destructor, but in practice, we could have used constructors (default or otherwise) to initialize the state of the memory-mapped device to match our needs and the destructor to reset the state of that device to some acceptable state.

Normally, for a program to access the memory-mapped hardware, we would probably communicate with the operating system with services that accept as argument the required information to identify the device whose address we seek. In our case, we will simply make it look like we can access a zone of memory of the right size and alignment to which we can read and write. The memory address is exposed as raw memory (of type void*), which is what we can realistically expect from an operating system function under similar circumstances:

```
// somewhere in memory where we have read / write
// access privileges is a memory-mapped hardware
// that corresponds to the actual device
alignas(super_video_card) char
  mem_mapped_device[sizeof(super_video_card)];
void* get_super_card_address() {
  return mem_mapped_device;
}
// ...
```

We then arrive at how one can use placement new to map an object to some memory-mapped hardware location. Note that we need to include the `<new>` header as this is where placement new is defined. The steps to meet our objective are as follows:

1. First, obtain the address where we want to map our carefully crafted `super_video_card` object.

2. Then, through placement new at that address, construct a `super_video_card` object such that the data members of that object correspond to the address of the registers they represent.

3. For the duration of that object's lifetime, use the object through the corresponding pointer (the `the_card` variable in the following code excerpt).

4. When we are done, the one thing we do not want to do is apply `operator delete()` on `the_card` as we never allocated the associated memory in the first place. We do want to finalize the object through `~super_video_card()`, however, to make sure the cleanup or reset code (if any) for that object is run.

We thus end up with the following:

```cpp
// ...
#include <new>
int main() {
   // map our object to the hardware
   void* p = get_super_card_address();
   auto the_card =
      new(p) super_video_card{ /* args */ };
   // through pointer the_card, use the actual memory-
   // mapped hardware
   // ...
   the_card->~super_video_card();
}
```

If the explicit destructor call is a problem, such as in code where exceptions could be thrown along the way, we can use a `std::unique_ptr` object with a custom deleter (see *Chapter 5*) to finalize the `super_video_card` object:

```cpp
// ...
#include <new>
#include <memory>
int main() {
   // map our object to the hardware
   void* p = get_super_card_address();
   std::unique_ptr<
      super_video_card,
```

```
        decltype([](super_video_card *p) {
          p->~super_video_card(); // do not call delete p!
        })
    > the_card {
        new(p) super_video_card{ /* args */ }
    };
    // through pointer the_card, use the actual memory-
    // mapped hardware
    // ...
    // implicit call to the_card->~super_video_card()
}
```

In this case, the `std::unique_ptr` object finalizes the pointee (the `super_video_card` object) but does not free its memory storage, leading to more robust code in the presence of exceptions during the lifetime of the `the_card` variable.

Simplifying nothrow new usage

As mentioned in *Chapter 7*, the default behavior of `operator new()` when unable to perform an allocation request is to throw an exception. This can result from such situations as running out of memory or otherwise being unable to service the allocation request, in which case, one usually throws `std::bad_alloc`; from an incorrect array length (for example, a negative length of one exceeding implementation-defined limits), usually leading to `std::bad_array_new_length` being thrown; or from failure to complete the subsequent construction of the object following the completion of `operator new()`, in which case, the exception that will be thrown will be whatever was thrown from the failing constructor.

Exceptions are the "normal" way for a C++ function to signal failure to meet the function's postconditions. In some cases, such as a constructor or an overloaded operator, it's the only real, workable way to do so: a constructor has no return value, and the signature of functions that overload operators generally does not leave room for additional arguments or error-reporting return values, although one could make a case for some types such as `std::optional` or `std::expected` as allowing an alternative for some overloaded operator use cases.

Of course, some domains typically do not use exceptions: a significant number of video games are compiled without exception support, for example, and the same goes for a lot of programs written for embedded systems. Reasons invoked go from the technical (fear of overhead considered undesirable in terms of memory space consumption, execution speed, or both) to the more philosophical (dislike for what is seen as hidden control paths), but no matter what the reasons are, the fact is that C++ code compiled without exception support exists and the `nothrow` version of `operator new()` is a reality.

This does mean, of course, that even seemingly simple code such as the following can lead to **undefined behavior (UB)**:

```
#include <new>
#include <iostream>
struct X {
   int n;
   X(int n) : n { n } { }
};
int main() {
   auto p = new (std::nothrow) X{ 3 };
   std::cout << p->n; // <-- HERE
   delete p;
}
```

The reason for this potential UB is that if the nothrow version of operator new() fails (unlikely but not impossible, especially in memory-constrained situations), then p will be null, and accessing the n data member through p will be... a very bad idea.

Of course, the solution is simple, and being the astute reader that you are, you have probably noticed it already: just test the pointer before using it! This works, of course, as shown here:

```
#include <new>
#include <iostream>
struct X {
   int n;
   X(int n) : n { n } { }
};
int main() {
   auto p = new (std::nothrow) X{ 3 };
   if(p) {
       std::cout << p->n; // ...use *p as needed...
   }
   delete p; // fine even in p is null
}
```

The problem with this approach is that code quickly becomes littered with tests, as there is rarely only one pointer in a program, reminding us that the beauty of code using exceptions is that one does not need to worry about those tests. With exceptions, either operator new() and the subsequent construction both succeeded and one can use the resulting pointer confidently, or one of these steps failed and code execution did not reach the point where one could get into trouble:

```
#include <new>
#include <iostream>
struct X {
```

```
  int n;
  X(int n) : n { n } { }
};
int main() {
  auto p = new X{ 3 }; // throws if operator new() or
                       //  X::X(int) fails
  std::cout << p->n; // ...use *p as needed...
  delete p;
}
```

Of course, one can get in trouble even with exceptions, for example, if there is an execution path that lets p remain null or uninitialized and others where that cannot happen (you can usually avoid this by initializing your objects on declaration, but that is not always possible); let us leave these code hygiene considerations aside for now as they would deviate from our topic of interest.

An important consideration when facing a failure-to-allocate situation is what to do when it happens. Whether our code base uses exceptions or not, we most probably do not want to let the execution of our program continue and therefore incur UB through such things as the improper use of a null pointer.

A common way to stop execution at the point of failure-to-allocate is to wrap the tentative allocation and construction operation, the subsequent test on the resulting pointer, and the action to take if the pointer is null in some code construct. The code we want to wrap will be something like the following, supposing we want to allocate-then-construct an `int` object:

```
// ...
int *p = new int{ 3 };
if(!p) std::abort(); // for example
return p;
// ...
```

This code used `std::abort()` as a mechanism to end program execution; exceptions would provide us with potentially recoverable errors, but without exceptions, most standard mechanisms at our disposal will lead to program termination, and `std::abort()` is a reasonable choice in this case.

Ways to conclude program execution

A C++ program can conclude in many different ways: reaching the end of the `main()` function is the most obvious one, but other examples exist. For example, `std::exit()` is used for normal program termination accompanied by cleanup steps; `std::quick_exit()` is used for program termination without cleanup steps. One can use `std::atexit()` and `std::at_quick_exit()` to register some functions to be called before exiting, and `std::abort()` is used to signal abnormal program termination without cleanup steps. The `std::terminate()` function is used when some unpleasantness in a documented list of situations occurs (this list includes such things as an exception being thrown from the constructor of a `static` variable or from the body of a `noexcept` function). In our case, the only mechanism that really fit was `std::abort()`.

One possible approach to solve this problem is to use a macro and an **immediately-invoked function expression (IIFE)**, which is the name given to an expression made from an anonymous lambda that is at once created, executed, and discarded. To make our solution general, we need to be able to do the following:

- Specify the type of object to create

- Make the macro variadic, as we need to be able to pass any number of arguments of any type to the object's constructor

A possible implementation of such a macro would be TRY_NEW as follows:

```
#include <new>
#include <cstdlib>
#define TRY_NEW(T,...) [&] { \
  auto p = new (std::nothrow) T(__VA_ARGS__); \
  if(!p) std::abort(); \
  return p; \
}()
struct dies_when_newed {
  void* operator new(std::size_t, std::nothrow_t) {
      return {};
  }
};
int main() {
  // p0 is int*, points to an int{ 0 }
  auto p0 = TRY_NEW(int);
  // p1 is int*, points to an int{ 3 }
  auto p1 = TRY_NEW(int, 3);
  auto q = TRY_NEW(dies_when_newed); // calls abort()
}
```

Not everyone is familiar with variadic macros, so let's take it step by step:

- The "signature" of our macro is TRY_NEW(T, ...), meaning T is mandatory and ... could be any number of tokens (including none at all) separated by commas. Unsurprisingly, we will use T for the type to construct and ... for the arguments to pass to the constructor that will be invoked.

- Since we wrote the macro on more than one line (for readability), each line but the last terminates with a space followed by a backslash to inform the preprocessor that it should continue parsing on the next line.

- The symbols on ... are relayed through the special macro named __VA_ARGS__, which expands to what ... contained and can be empty if ... itself is empty. This works in both C and C++. Note that we use parentheses, not braces, in the constructor call as we want to avoid unwittingly building an initializer list if all elements of __VA_ARGS__ are of the same type.

- We test the p pointer resulting from the call to a `std::nothrow` version of `operator new()` and call `std::abort()` if p is null.

- This entire sequence of operations is, as announced, wrapped in an IIFE and the newly allocated pointer is returned. Note that we could also have returned a `std::unique_ptr<T>` object from that lambda if we had wanted to do so. Also, note that this lambda expression uses a `[&]` capture block to ensure the availability of tokens in `__VA_ARGS__` within the scope of the lambda.

> **A small but interesting side effect**
>
> Note that since we used parentheses (the same would hold for braces), an empty `__VAR_ARGS__` will lead this macro to zero-initialize fundamental types such as `int` instead of leaving them uninitialized. You can compare: as of C++23, `new int;` yields a pointer to an uninitialized `int` object, but `new int();` and `new int{};` both initialize the allocated block with a value of zero. There is an upside to this, as with this macro, we will not end up with a pointer to an uninitialized object, even for trivial types. However, there is also a downside as we will be paying for an initialization even in cases where it might not have been necessary.

Another approach would be to use a variadic function template, which might lead to a better debugging experience in practice. It has slightly different-looking client code but is otherwise similar in usage and effect:

```
#include <new>
#include <cstdlib>
#include <utility>
template <class T, class ... Args>
  auto try_new(Args &&... args) {
      auto p =
        new (std::nothrow) T(std::forward<Args>(args)...);
      if(!p) std::abort();
      return p;
  }
struct dies_when_newed {
  void* operator new(std::size_t, std::nothrow_t) {
      return {};
  }
};
int main() {
  // p0 is int*, points to an int{ 0 }
  auto p0 = try_new<int>();
  // p1 is int*, points to an int{ 3 }
  auto p1 = try_new<int>(3);
  auto q = try_new<dies_when_newed>(); // calls abort()
}
```

The call syntax for the variadic function version looks like a cast, and arguments passed to `try_new()` are perfectly forwarded to the constructor of `T` to ensure that the expected constructor is called in the end. As was the case with the macro, we could have chosen to return a `std::unique_ptr<T>` object instead of a `T*` object with this function.

Out-of-memory situations and new_handler

So far in this book, including this chapter, we have stated that `operator new()` and `operator new[]()` typically throw `std::bad_alloc` when failing to allocate memory. It's true to a wide extent, but there is a subtlety we have avoided so far and to which we will now give some time and attention.

Imagine a situation where user code has specialized the memory allocation functions to fetch memory blocks from a pre-allocated data structure with interesting performance characteristics. Suppose that this data structure initially allocates space for a small number of blocks and then goes on to allocate more space once the user code exhausts the blocks from the initial allocation. Expressed otherwise: in this situation, we have an initial, fast setting (let's call that the "optimistic" state) and a secondary setting (let's call that the "second chance" state) that lets user code continue allocating once the "optimistic" state's resources have been consumed.

For a scenario such as this to be seamless, with a transparent change of allocation strategy achievable without the explicit intervention of user code, explicitly throwing `std::bad_alloc` would be insufficient. Throwing would complete the execution of `operator new()` and client code could catch the exception and take action, of course, but in this (reasonable) scenario, we would like failure to allocate to lead to some action being taken and `operator new()` to try again with the updated state of things, if any.

In C++, scenarios such as this are handled through a `std::new_handler`, which is an alias for a function pointer of type `void(*)()`. What one needs to know is the following:

- There is a global `std::new_handler` in a program, and by default, its value is `nullptr`.

- One can set the active `std::new_handler` through the `std::set_new_handler()` function, and one can get the active `std::new_handler` through the `std::get_new_handler()` function. Note that as a convenience, `std::set_new_handler()` returns the `std::new_handler` that is being replaced.

- When an allocation function such as `operator new()` fails, what it should do is first get the active `std::new_handler`. If that pointer is null, then the allocation function should throw `std::bad_alloc` as we have done so far; otherwise, it should call that `std::new_handler` and try again under the new conditions that this call installed.

As could be expected, your standard library should already implement this algorithm, but our own overloads of `operator new()` and `operator new[]()` have not done so, at least so far. To show how to benefit from a `std::new_handler`, we will now implement an artificial version of the aforementioned two-step scenario.

This toy implementation will use the member version of the allocation operators for some X type and behave as if we initially had enough memory for limit objects of that type (normally, we would actually manage that memory, and you can see an example of such management in *Chapter 10* where we will provide a more realistic example). We will install a std::new_handler that, when called, changes limit to a higher number, and then resets the active handler to nullptr such that subsequent failures to allocate X objects will lead to throwing std::bad_alloc:

```cpp
#include <new>
#include <vector>
#include <iostream>
struct X {
  // toy example, not thread-safe
  static inline int limit = 5;
  void* operator new(std::size_t n) {
      std::cout << "X::operator new() called with "
                << limit << " blocks left\n";
      while (limit <= 0) {
        if (auto hdl = std::get_new_handler(); hdl)
            hdl();
        else
            throw std::bad_alloc{};
      }
      --limit;
      return ::operator new(n);
  }
  void operator delete(void* p) {
      std::cout << "X::operator delete()\n";
      ::operator delete(p);
  }
  // same for the array versions
};
int main() {
  std::set_new_handler([] () noexcept {
      std::cout << "allocation failure, "
                   "fetching more memory\n";
      X::limit = 10;
      std::set_new_handler(nullptr); // as per default
  });
  std::vector<X*> v;
  v.reserve(100);
  try {
      for (int i = 0; i != 10; ++i)
          v.emplace_back(new X);
  } catch(...) {
```

```
    // this will never be reached with this program
    std::cerr << "out of memory\n";
}
for (auto p : v) delete p;
}
```

Note the way that `X::operator new()` handles failure: if it notices that it will not be able to meet its postconditions, it gets the active `std::new_handler`, and if it's non-null, calls it before trying again. This means that the `std::new_handler`, when called, has to either change the situation in such a way that a subsequent tentative allocation could succeed or change the `std::new_handler` to `nullptr` such that failure will lead to an exception being thrown. Failure to respect these rules could lead to an infinite loop and much sadness would ensue.

The handler installed in `main()` for this toy example does this: when called, it changes the conditions under which the allocations will be performed (it raises the value of `X::limit`). It then calls `std::set_new_handler()` with `nullptr` as we have not planned for another approach after the "optimistic" and "second chance" situations, so if we exhaust the second chance resources, we (as they say) are toast.

> **A lambda as new_handler?**
>
> You might have noticed that we described the `std::new_handler` type as being an alias for a function pointer of the `void(*)()` type, yet in our toy example, we installed a lambda. Why does that work? Well, it happens that a stateless lambda—a lambda expression with an empty capture block—is implicitly convertible to a function pointer with the same calling signature. It's a useful thing to know under many circumstances, such as when writing C++ code that interfaces with C code or operating system APIs.

We are now about to enter a strange and quite technical part of this chapter, where we will see how to leverage C++ to handle atypical memory.

Standard C++ and exotic memory

Our last example in this slightly strange chapter with examples of unusual memory management usage is concerned with the ways in which we can write standard C++ programs that deal with "exotic" memory. By "exotic," we mean memory that requires explicit actions to "touch" (allocate, read from, write to, deallocate, and so on) and that differs from a "normal" memory block under the control of our program, such as the one used in the illustrative example of memory-mapped usage with placement `new` earlier in this chapter. Examples of such memory include persistent (non-volatile) memory or shared memory, but anything *out of the ordinary* will do, really.

Since we have to pick an example, we will write an example using a (fictional) shared memory block.

A little white lie…

It's important to understand that we are describing a mechanism for memory that would normally be shared between *processes*, but inter-process communication is the domain of the operating system. Standard C++ only describes the rules for sharing data between *threads* in a process; for that reason, we will tell a little white lie and write a multithreaded system, not a multiple-process one, using that memory to share data. Our focus is on memory management facilities, not inter-process communication, so that should not pose a problem.

Following the same approach as we did in previous sections of this chapter, we will craft a portable illustration of how to proceed in code that seeks to manage atypical memory, and let you map the details to the services of your chosen platform. Our example code will take the following shape:

- A shared memory block will be allocated. We will make it look like this memory is special in the sense that one needs special operating system functions to create it, allocate it, or deallocate it, but we will deliberately avoid using actual operating system functions. This means that if you want to use the code in this section for a real application, you will need to adapt it to your chosen platform's API.

- We will craft a "handmade" version of a toy program that uses this fictional API for shared memory in order to illustrate what user code would look like under these circumstances.

- Then, we will show how understanding the memory management facilities of C++ can help us write more pleasant and "normal looking" user code that does the same thing as the "handmade" one… or even better.

Fictional realism?

This entire section on C++ and exotic memory, which we cover next, will hopefully be interesting, and the code we will write will strive to be realistic with respect to memory management. As mentioned previously, since the C++ standard is mostly silent on the idea of multi-process systems, we will try to make multithreaded code look kind of like multi-process code. I hope you, astute reader, will accept this proposition.

Please note that there will be a small amount of low-level synchronization in user code for this section, including some through atomic variables. I tried to keep it minimal yet reasonably realistic and hope you will be able to accept it even though I will not explain it all in detail, with this book's focus being on memory management rather than on concurrent computing (another fine topic, of course). Feel free to use your favorite concurrent programming resource if you want to know more about such things as waiting on atomics or using thread fences.

Ready? Let's do this!

A fictional shared memory API

We will write an API that is fictional but inspired by what one finds in most operating systems, except that we will report errors through exceptions to simplify user code. Operating systems mostly report errors through error codes expressed from return values, but this leads to user code that is more involved. I hope this seems like an acceptable compromise to you, dear reader.

As most operating systems do, we will abstract the actual resource through a form of handle, or key; creating a "shared memory" segment of some size will yield a key (an integral identifier), after which, accessing that memory will require that key, and so will destroying that memory. As can be expected with a facility meant to be used to share data between processes, destroying the memory will not finalize the objects therein, so user code will need to ensure that objects in the shared memory are destroyed before releasing the shared memory segment.

The signatures and types for our API will be as follows:

```
// ...
#include <cstddef> // std::size_t
#include <new> // std::bad_alloc
#include <utility> // std::pair
class invalid_shared_mem_key {};
enum shared_mem_id : std::size_t;
shared_mem_id create_shared_mem(std::size_t size);
std::pair<void*, std::size_t>
  get_shared_mem(shared_mem_id);
void destroy_shared_mem(shared_mem_id);
// ...
```

You might notice that we are using an enum type for shared_mem_id. The reason for this is that enum types are distinct types in C++, not just aliases as one would get from using or typedef. Having distinct types can be useful when overloading functions based on the types of their arguments. It's a useful trick to know: if we write two functions with the same name (one that takes an argument of the shared_mem_id type and another that takes an argument of the std::size_t type), these will be distinct functions, even though the underlying type of shared_mem_id is std::size_t.

Since we are building an artificial implementation of "shared memory" to show how memory allocation functions can simplify user code, the implementation for the functions of our API will be written to be simple, but let us write client code that behaves as if it were using shared memory. We will define a shared memory segment as a shared_mem_block modeled by a pair made from an array of bytes and a size in bytes. We will keep a std::vector object of that type, using the indices in that array as shared_mem_id. This means that when a shared_mem_block object is destroyed, we will not reuse its index in the std::vector (the container will eventually have "holes," so to speak).

Our implementation is as follows. Note that it is not thread-safe, but that does not impact our memory management-related discourse:

```cpp
// ...
#include <vector>
#include <memory>
#include <utility>
struct shared_mem_block {
  std::unique_ptr<char[]> mem;
  std::size_t size;
};
std::vector<shared_mem_block> shared_mems;
std::pair<void*, std::size_t>
  get_shared_mem(shared_mem_id id) {
  if (id < std::size(shared_mems))
      return { shared_mems[id].mem.get(),
               shared_mems[id].size };
  return { nullptr, 0 };
}
shared_mem_id create_shared_mem(std::size_t size) {
  auto p = std::make_unique<char[]>(size);
  shared_mems.emplace_back(std::move(p), size);
  // note the parentheses
  return shared_mem_id(std::size(shared_mems) - 1);
}
// function for internal purposes only
bool is_valid_shared_mem_key(shared_mem_id id) {
  return id < std::size(shared_mems) &&
         shared_mems[id].mem;
}
void destroy_shared_mem(shared_mem_id id) {
  if (!is_valid_shared_mem_key(id))
      throw invalid_shared_mem_key{};
  shared_mems[id].mem.reset();
}
```

If you want to experiment, you can replace the implementation of these functions with equivalent implementations that call the functions of your chosen operating system, adjusting the API if needed.

Equipped with this implementation, we can now compare a "handmade" example of shared memory-using code with one that benefits from the facilities of C++. We will do this comparison with code where one allocates some chunk of data from a shared memory segment and then launches two threads (a writer and a reader). The writer will write to that shared data, and then (with minimal synchronization) the reader will read from it. As mentioned previously, our code will use *intra*-process synchronization

(C++ atomic variables), but in real code, you should use *inter*-process synchronization mechanisms provided by the operating system.

A note on lifetime

You might remember from *Chapter 1* that each object has an associated lifetime, and that the compiler keeps track of this fact in your programs. Our fictional multiple-process example is really a single-process, multithreaded example, so the usual C++ lifetime rules apply.

If you want to take the code in this section and write a real multi-process system to run some tests, you might want to consider using `std::start_lifetime_as()` from C++23 in those processes that did not explicitly create the `data` object, and avoid detrimental optimizations from happening based on the compiler's reasoning that, in these processes, the objects have never been constructed. In earlier compilers, one trick that generally works is calling `std::memcpy()` of the not-officially-constructed object onto itself, effectively starting its lifetime.

In both our "handmade" and our standard-looking implementations, we will be using a `data` object made of an `int` value and a Boolean `ready` flag:

```
struct data {
   bool ready;
   int value;
};
```

In a single-process implementation, a better choice for the completion flag would be an `atomic<bool>` object as we want to make sure the write to the `ready` flag happens before the write to the value, but since we want this example to look like we are using inter-process shared memory, we will limit ourselves to a simple `bool` and ensure this synchronization through other means.

A word on synchronization

In a contemporary program, optimizing compilers will often reorder operations that seem independent to generate better code, and processors will do the same once the code has been generated in order to maximize usage of the processor's internal pipeline. Concurrent code sometimes contains dependencies that are neither visible to the compiler nor to the processor. In our examples, we will want the `ready` completion flag to become `true` only after the write to `value` has been performed; this order is only important because the writes are performed in one thread but *another* thread will look at `ready` to know whether `value` can be read.

Not enforcing the `value`-then-`ready` sequence of writes through some form of synchronization would let either the compiler or the processor reorder these (seemingly independent) writes and break our assumptions on the meaning of `ready`.

A handmade user code example

We can, of course, write user code that uses our fictional API without resorting to specialized memory management facilities of C++, simply relying on placement new usage as seen in *Chapter 7*. It might be tempting to think of placement new as a specialized facility since you might have learned of it from this book, but if that is your perspective, you are invited to reconsider: the placement new mechanism is a fundamental memory management tool used in almost every program, whether user code is aware of it or not.

As a reminder, our example program will do the following:

- Create a shared memory segment of some size (we will allocate much more than we need in this case).

- Construct a data object at the beginning of that segment, obviously through placement new.

- Start a thread that will wait for a signal on the go variable of type atomic<bool>, then obtain access to the shared memory segment, write to the value data member and then only signal that the write has occurred through the ready data member.

- Start another thread that will obtain access to the shared memory segment, get a pointer to the shared data object therein, and then do some (very inefficient) busy waiting on the ready flag to change state, after which value will be read and used. Once this has been done, completion will be signaled through the done flag of type atomic<bool>.

- Our program will then read a key from the keyboard, signal the threads (the writer thread, really) that it's time to start working, and wait until they are done before freeing the shared memory segment and concluding its work.

We thus end up with the following:

```
// ...
#include <thread>
#include <atomic>
#include <iostream>
int main() {
  // we need a N-bytes shared memory block
  constexpr std::size_t N = 1'000'000;
  auto key = create_shared_mem(N);
  // map a data object in the shared memory block
  auto [p, sz] = get_shared_mem(key);
  if (!p) return -1;
  // start the lifetime of a non-ready data object
  auto p_data = new (p) data{ false };
  std::atomic<bool> go{ false };
  std::atomic<bool> done{ false };
```

```cpp
std::jthread writer{ [key, &go] {
    go.wait(false);
    auto [p, sz] = get_shared_mem(key);
    if (p) {
        auto p_data = static_cast<data*>(p);
        p_data->value = 3;
        std::atomic_thread_fence(
            std::memory_order_release
        );
        p_data->ready = true;
    }
} };
std::jthread reader{ [key, &done] {
    auto [p, sz] = get_shared_mem(key);
    if (p) {
        auto p_data = static_cast<data*>(p);
        while (!p_data->ready)
            ; // busy waiting, not cool
        std::cout << "read value "
                  << p_data->value << '\n';
    }
    done = true;
    done.notify_all();
} };
if (char c; !std::cin.get(c)) exit(-1);
go = true;
go.notify_all();
// writer and reader run to completion, then complete
done.wait(false);
p_data->~data();
destroy_shared_mem(key);
}
```

We made this work: we have an infrastructure of sorts to manage shared memory segments, we can use these memory blocks to share data, and we can write code that reads from that shared data as well as writes to it. Note that we captured the key in each thread in a key variable and then obtained the memory block within each lambda through that key, but it would also be reasonable to simply capture the p_data pointer and use it.

Notice, however, that we did not really manage that block: we created it and used a small chunk of size sizeof(data) at the beginning. Now, what if we had wanted to create multiple objects in that zone? And what if we had wanted to write code that both creates and destroys objects, introducing the need to manage what parts of that block are in use at a given time? With what we just wrote, that would mean doing it all in user code, a somewhat burdensome endeavor.

Keeping that in mind, we will now solve the same problem but with a different approach.

A standard-looking user code equivalent

So, what mechanism does C++ offer us if we want to use "exotic" memory in a more idiomatic manner? Well, one way to do so is as follows:

- To write a manager class for the "exotic" memory, encapsulating the non-portable interface to the operating system and exposing services that are closer to what C++ user code would expect

- To write overloads of the memory allocation operators (operator new(), operator delete(), and so on) that take a reference to such a manager object as an additional argument

- To make these overloaded memory allocation operators bridge the gap between portable and non-portable code through delegation on the memory manager object

This way, user code can be written essentially as "normal looking" code that calls new and delete operators, except that these calls will use the same kind of extended notation seen in *Chapter 7* for such things as the nothrow or placement versions of operator new().

Our shared_mem_mgr class will use the fictional operating system API described earlier in this section but, normally, one would write a class that encapsulates whatever operating system services are required to access the atypical memory one aims to use in a program.

Being an example made for simplicity, mostly to show how the feature works and can be used, the astute reader that you are will hopefully see much room for improvement and optimization… Indeed, this manager is really slow and memory consuming, keeping a std::vector<bool> object where each bool value indicates whether a byte in the memory block is taken or not and performing a naïve linear search through that container whenever an allocation request is made (also, it's not thread-safe, which is bad!). We will examine some quality of implementation considerations in *Chapter 10*, but nothing stops you from taking shared_mem_mgr and making it significantly better in the meantime.

You will notice that shared_mem_mgr has been expressed as an RAII type: its constructor creates a shared memory segment, its destructor frees that memory segment, and the shared_mem_mgr type has been made uncopiable as is often the case for RAII types. The key member functions to look at in the following code excerpt are allocate() and deallocate(); the former tries to allocate a block from the shared memory segment and notes that this has been done, whereas the latter frees the memory associated with an address within the block:

```
#include <algorithm>
#include <iterator>
#include <new>
class shared_mem_mgr {
  shared_mem_id key;
  std::vector<bool> taken;
  void *mem;
```

```
  auto find_first_free(std::size_t from = 0) {
      using namespace std;
      auto p = find(begin(taken) + from, end(taken),
                    false);
      return distance(begin(taken), p);
  }
  bool at_least_free_from(std::size_t from, int n) {
      using namespace std;
      return from + n < size(taken) &&
             count(begin(taken) + from,
                   begin(taken) + from + n,
                   false) == n;
  }
  void take(std::size_t from, std::size_t to) {
      using namespace std;
      fill(begin(taken) + from, begin(taken) + to,
           begin(taken) + from, true);
  }
  void free(std::size_t from, std::size_t to) {
      using namespace std;
      fill(begin(taken) + from, begin(taken) + to,
           begin(taken) + from, false);
  }
public:
  // create shared memory block
  shared_mem_mgr(std::size_t size)
      : key{ create_shared_mem(size) }, taken(size) {
      auto [p, sz] = get_shared_mem(key);
      if (!p) throw invalid_shared_mem_key{};
      mem = p;
  }
  shared_mem_mgr(const shared_mem_mgr&) = delete;
  shared_mem_mgr&
      operator=(const shared_mem_mgr&) = delete;
  void* allocate(std::size_t n) {
      using namespace std;
      std::size_t i = find_first_free();
      // insanely inefficient
      while (!at_least_free_from(i, n) && i != size(taken))
        i = find_first_free(i + 1);
      if (i == size(taken)) throw bad_alloc{};
      take(i, i + n);
      return static_cast<char*>(mem) + i;
```

```
    }
    void deallocate(void *p, std::size_t n) {
        using namespace std;
        auto i = distance(
            static_cast<char*>(mem), static_cast<char*>(p)
        );
        take(i, i + n);
    }
    ~shared_mem_mgr() {
        destroy_shared_mem(key);
    }
};
```

As you can see, shared_mem_mgr really is a class that manages a chunk of memory, and there is no magic involved. Should someone want to improve the memory management algorithms, one could do so without touching the interface of this class, benefiting from the low coupling that stems from encapsulation.

If you want to play…

One interesting way to refine shared_mem_mgr would be to first make this class responsible for allocating and freeing the shared memory, as it already does, then write a different class to manage the memory within that shared memory block, and finally, make them work together. This way, one could use shared_mem_mgr with different memory management algorithms and pick management strategies based on the needs of individual programs, or sections thereof. Something to try if you want to have fun!

The next step is to implement the allocation operator overloads that take an argument of type shared_mem_mgr&. This is essentially trivial since all these overloads need to do is delegate the work to the manager:

```
void* operator new(std::size_t n, shared_mem_mgr& mgr) {
    return mgr.allocate(n);
}
void* operator new[](std::size_t n, shared_mem_mgr& mgr) {
    return mgr.allocate(n);
}
void operator delete(void *p, std::size_t n,
                     shared_mem_mgr& mgr) {
    mgr.deallocate(p, n);
}
void operator delete[](void *p, std::size_t n,
                       shared_mem_mgr& mgr) {
    mgr.deallocate(p, n);
}
```

Equipped with our manager and these overloads, we can write our test program that performs the same task as the "handmade" one from the previous section. In this case, however, there are some differences:

- We do not need to manage the shared memory segment's creation and destruction. These tasks are handled by the shared_mem_mgr object as part of its implementation of the RAII idiom.

- We do not need to manage the shared memory block at all, as this task is assigned to the shared_mem_mgr object. Finding a location in the block to put an object, tracking how the block is being used for objects, ensuring that it's possible to distinguish used areas from unused ones, and so on are all part of that class's responsibilities.

- As a corollary, in the "handmade" version, we constructed an object at the beginning of the shared memory block and stated that it would be a burden on user code to construct more objects or manage the shared memory segment to take into account numerous calls to the new and delete operators, but in this implementation, we can freely call new and delete as much as we want since this memory management becomes transparent to client code.

The construction aspect of objects in atypical memory is rather easy: just pass the additional argument in the call to the new and new[] operators. The finalization part of objects managed through a manager such as this is slightly more complex though: we cannot write the equivalent of delete p on our pointers as this would try to finalize the object *and* deallocate the memory through "normal" means. Instead, we need to manually finalize the objects, and then manually call the appropriate version of the operator delete() function in order to do the exotic memory cleanup tasks. Of course, given what we have written in *Chapter 6*, you could encapsulate these tasks in a smart pointer of your own to get simpler and safer user code.

We end up with the following example program:

```cpp
int main() {
   // we need a N-bytes shared memory block
   constexpr std::size_t N = 1'000'000;
   // HERE
   shared_mem_mgr mgr{ N };
   // start the lifetime of a non-ready data object
   auto p_data = new (mgr) data{ false };
   std::atomic<bool> go{ false };
   std::atomic<bool> done{ false };
   std::jthread writer{ [p_data, &go] {
       go.wait(false);
       p_data->value = 3;
       std::atomic_thread_fence(std::memory_order_release);
       p_data->ready = true;
   } };
   std::jthread reader{ [p_data, &done] {
       while (!p_data->ready)
         ; // busy waiting, not cool
```

```
          std::cout << "read value " << p_data->value << '\n';
          done = true;
          done.notify_all();
     } };
     if (char c; !std::cin.get(c)) exit(-1);
     go = true;
     go.notify_all();
     // writer and reader run to completion, then complete
     done.wait(false);
     p_data->~data();
     operator delete(p_data, sizeof(data), mgr);
}
```

This is still not a trivial example, but the memory management aspect is clearly simpler than in the "handmade" version, and the compartmentalization of tasks makes it easier to optimize the way in which memory is managed.

And... we're done. Whew! That was quite the ride, once more!

Summary

This chapter explored various ways in which one can use the C++ memory management facilities in unusual ways: mapping objects onto memory-mapped hardware, integrating basic forms of error handling with the nothrow version of operator new(), reacting to out-of-memory situations with a std::exception_handler, and accessing atypical memory with non-portable services through a specialization of the "normal" allocation operator and a manager object. This gives us a broader overview of memory management facilities in C++ and how one can use them to one's advantage.

One thing we have mentioned but not yet discussed is optimization: how to make memory allocation and memory allocation fast, blazingly fast even, and deterministic in terms of execution speed when some conditions are met. This is what we will do in *Chapter 10* when explaining how to write arena-based allocation code.

Oh, and as a bonus, we will kill Orcs.

> **Orcs? What are you talking about?**
>
> Orcs are fictional creatures found in numerous works of fictional fantasy, usually mean beasts used as foes and that have an unhealthy relation to Elves, another kind of fictional creature that often has a better reputation. As your friendly author has worked a lot with game programmers over the last few decades, Orcs tend to appear in his examples and will be central to the code we write in *Chapter 10*.

Sounds good? Then, on to the next chapter!

Unlock this book's exclusive benefits now

This book comes with additional benefits designed to elevate your learning experience.

Note: Have your purchase invoice ready before you begin.

https://www.packtpub.com/
unlock/9781805129806

10

Arena-Based Memory Management and Other Optimizations

Our memory-management toolbox is growing with every chapter. We now know how to overload memory allocation operators (*Chapter 7*) and how to put this skill to work in ways that solve a variety of concrete problems (*Chapter 8* and *Chapter 9* both give a few illustrative, real-world examples).

One important reason why one would want to take control of memory allocation mechanisms is *performance*. Now, it would be presumptuous (and plain wrong!) to state that it's trivial to beat the implementation of these functions as provided by your library vendor, as these are good, often *very* good, for the average case. The key element of the previous phrase, of course, is "for the average case." When one's use case has specificities that are known of beforehand, it is sometimes possible to benefit from that information and carve an implementation that outperforms, maybe by a wide margin, anything that could have been designed for excellent *average* performance.

This chapter is about using knowledge of the memory management problem we want to solve and building a solution that excels for us. This can mean a solution that's faster on average, that's fast enough even in the worst case, that shows deterministic execution times, that reduces memory fragmentation, and so on. There are many different needs and constraints in real-world programs after all, and we often have to make choices.

Once this chapter is over, our toolbox will be expanded to let us do the following:

- Write arena-based allocation strategy algorithms optimized to face a priori known constraints
- Write per-memory block-size allocation strategies
- Understand the benefits as well as the risks associated with such techniques

The techniques covered in this chapter will lead us to explore use cases very close to those for which memory allocation operators are overloaded in some specialized application domains. Thus, we will initially apply them to a "real life" problem: the fight between Orcs and Elves in a medieval fantasy game.

> **On the (sometimes diminishing) returns of optimization**
>
> Since we will be discussing optimization techniques (among other things) in this chapter, some words of warning are in order: *optimization is a tricky thing*, a moving target, and what makes code better one day could pessimize it another day. Similarly, what can seem like a good idea in theory can lead to slowdowns in practice once implemented and tested, and one can sometimes spend a lot of time optimizing a piece of code that is rarely taken, effectively wasting time and money.
>
> Before trying to optimize parts of your program, it's generally wise to measure, ideally with a profiling tool, and identify the parts that might benefit from your efforts. Then, keep a simple (but correct) version of your code close by and use it as a baseline. Whenever you try an optimization, compare the results with the baseline code and run these tests regularly, particularly when changing hardware, library, compiler, or version thereof. Sometimes, something such as a compiler upgrade might induce a new optimization that "sees through" the simple baseline code and makes it faster than your finely crafted alternative. Be humble, be reasonable, measure early, and measure often.

Technical requirements

You can find the code files for this chapter in the book's GitHub repository here: `https://github.com/PacktPublishing/C-Plus-Plus-Memory-Management/tree/main/chapter10`.

Arena-based memory management

The idea behind arena-based memory management is to allocate a chunk of memory at a known moment in the program and manage it as a "small, personalized heap" based on a strategy that benefits from knowledge of the situation or of the problem domain.

There are many variants on this general theme, including the following:

- In a game, allocate and manage the memory by scene or by level, deallocating it as a single chunk at the end of said scene or level. This can help reduce memory fragmentation in the program.

- When the conditions in which allocations and deallocations are known to follow a given pattern or have bounded memory requirements, specialize allocation functions to benefit from this information.

- Express a form of ownership for a group of similar objects in such as way as to destroy them all at a later point in the program instead of doing so one object at a time.

The best way to explain how arena-based allocation works is probably to write an example program that uses it and shows both what it does and what benefits this provides. We will write code in such a way as to use the same test code with either the standard library-provided allocation functions or our own specialized implementation, depending on the presence of a macro, and, of course, we will measure the allocation and deallocation code to see whether there is a benefit to our efforts.

Specific example – size-based implementation

Suppose we are working on a video game where the action converges toward a stupendous finale where Orcs and Elves meet in a grandiose battle. No one really remembers why these two groups hate each other, but there is a suspicion that one day, one of the Elves said to one of the Orcs "You know, you don't smell all that bad today!" and this Orc was so insulted that it started a feud that still goes on today. It's a rumor, anyway.

It so happens that, in this game, some things are known about the behavior of Orc-using code, specifically, the following:

- There will never be more than a certain number of dynamically allocated Orc objects overall, so we have an upper bound to the space required to store these beasties.

- The Orcs that die will not come back to life in that game, as there are no shamans to resurrect them. Expressed otherwise, there is no need to implement a strategy that reuses the storage of an Orc object once it has been destroyed.

These two properties open algorithmic options for us:

- If we have enough memory available, we could allocate upfront a single memory block large enough to put all the Orc objects in the game as we know what the worst-case scenario is

- Since we know that we will not need to reuse the memory associated with individual Orc objects, we can implement a simple (and very fast) strategy for allocation that does almost no bookkeeping and, as we will see, lets us achieve deterministic, constant-time allocation *for this type*

For the sake of this example, the Orc class will be represented by three data members, name (a char[4] as these beasties have a limited vocabulary), strength (of type int), and smell (of the double type as these things have… a reputation), as follows:

```
class Orc {
  char name[4]{ 'U', 'R', 'G' };
  int strength = 100;
  double smell = 1000.0;
public:
  static constexpr int NB_MAX = 1'000'000;
  // ...
};
```

We will use arbitrary default values for our `Orc` objects as we are only concerned about allocation and deallocation for this example. You can write more elaborate test code that uses non-default values if you feel like it, of course, but that would not impact our discussion so we will target simplicity.

Since we are discussing the memory allocation of a large block upfront through our size-based arena, we need to look at memory size consumption for `Orc` objects. Supposing `sizeof(int)==4` and `sizeof(double)==8` and supposing that, being fundamental types, their alignment requirements match their respective sizes, we can assume that `sizeof(Orc)==16` in this case. If we aim to allocate enough space for all `Orc` objects at once, ensuring `sizeof(Orc)` remains reasonable for the resources at our disposal is important. For example, defining the maximum number of `Orc` objects in a program as `Orc::NB_MAX` and the maximal amount of memory we can allocate at once for `Orc` objects as some hypothetical constant named `THRESHOLD`, we could leave a `static_assert` such as the following in our source code as a form of *constraints-respected check*:

```
static_assert(Orc::NB_MAX*sizeof(Orc) <= THRESHOLD);
```

💡 **Quick tip**: Enhance your coding experience with the **AI Code Explainer** and **Quick Copy** features. Open this book in the next-gen Packt Reader. Click the **Copy** button (**1**) to quickly copy code into your coding environment, or click the **Explain** button (**2**) to get the AI assistant to explain a block of code to you.

```
                                                Copy      Explain
function calculate(a, b) {                       (1)        (2)
    return {sum: a + b};
};
```

📕 **The next-gen Packt Reader** is included for free with the purchase of this book. Unlock it by scanning the QR code below or visiting `https://www.packtpub.com/unlock/9781805129806`.

This way, if we end up evolving the `Orc` class to the point where resources become an issue, the code will stop compiling and we will be able to reevaluate the situation. In our case, with a memory consumption of approximately 16 MB, we will suppose we are within budget and that we can proceed with our arena.

We will want to compare our arena-based implementation with a baseline implementation, which, in this case, will be the standard library-provided implementation of the memory allocation functions. It's important to note upfront that each standard library implementation provides its own version of these functions, so you might want to run the code we will be writing here on more than one implementation to get a better perspective on the impact of our techniques.

To write code that allows us to do a proper comparison, we will need two distinct executables as we will be in an either/or situation (we either get the standard version or the "homemade" one we are writing), so this is a good use case for macro-based conditional compilation. We will thus write a single set of source files that will conditionally replace the standard library-provided versions of the allocation operators with ours but will otherwise be essentially identical.

We will work from three files: `Orc.h`, which declares the `Orc` class and the conditionally defined allocation operator overloads; `Orc.cpp`, which provides the implementation for these overloads as well as the arena implementation itself; and a test program that allocates `Orc::NB_MAX` objects of type `Orc` then later destroys them and measures the time it takes to do these two operations. Of course, as with most microbenchmarks, take these measurements with a grain of salt: the numbers will not be the same in a real program where allocations are interspersed with other code, but at least we will apply the same tests to both implementations of the allocation operators so the comparison should be reasonably fair.

Declaring the Orc class

First, let us examine `Orc.h`, which we have already seen in part when showing the data member layout of the `Orc` class earlier:

```
#ifndef ORC_H
#define ORC_H
// #define HOMEMADE_VERSION
#include <cstddef>
#include <new>
class Orc {
  char name[4]{ 'U', 'R', 'G' };
  int strength = 100;
  double smell = 1000.0;
public:
  static constexpr int NB_MAX = 1'000'000;
#ifdef HOMEMADE_VERSION
  void * operator new(std::size_t);
  void * operator new[](std::size_t);
  void operator delete(void *) noexcept;
  void operator delete[](void *) noexcept;
#endif
};
#endif
```

The HOMEMADE_VERSION macro can be uncommented to use our version of the allocation functions. As can be expected, since we are applying a special strategy for the Orc class and its expected usage patterns, we are using member-function overloads for the allocation operators. (We would not want to treat int objects or – imagine! – Elves the same way we will treat Orcs, would we? I thought not.)

Defining the Orc class and implementing an arena

The essence of the memory management-related code will be in Orc.cpp. We will go through it in two steps, the arena implementation and the allocation operator overloads, and analyze the different important parts separately. The whole implementation found in this file will be conditionally compiled based on the HOMEMADE_VERSION macro.

We will name our arena class Tribe, and it will be a singleton. Yes, that reviled design pattern we used in *Chapter 8* again, but we really do want a single Tribe object in our program so that conveys the intent well. The important parts of our implementation are as follows:

- The default (and only) constructor of the Tribe class allocates a single block of Orc::NB_MAX*sizeof(Orc) bytes. It is important to note right away that there are no Orc objects in that chunk: this memory block is just the right size and shape to put all the Orc objects we will need. A key idea for arena-based allocation is that, at least for this implementation, *the arena manages raw memory, not objects*: object construction and destruction are the province of user code, and any object not properly destroyed at the end of the program is user code's fault, not the fault of the arena.

- We validate at once that the allocation succeeded. I used an assert() in this case, as the rest of the code depends on this success, but throwing std::bad_alloc or calling std::abort() would also have been reasonable options. A Tribe object keeps two pointers, p and cur, both initially pointing at the beginning of the block. We will use p as the *beginning of block* marker, and cur as the *pointer to the next block to return*; as such, p will remain stable throughout program execution and cur will move forward by sizeof(Orc) bytes with each allocation.

> **Using char* or Orc***
>
> This Tribe implementation uses char* for the p and cur pointers but Orc* would have been a correct choice also. One simply needs to remember that, as far as the Tribe object is concerned, there are no Orc objects in the arena and the use of type Orc* is simply a convenient lie to simplify pointer arithmetic. The changes this would entail would be replacing static_cast<char*> with static_cast<Orc*> in the constructor, and replacing cur+=sizeof(Orc) with ++cur in the implementation of the allocate() member function. It's mostly a matter of style and personal preference.

- The destructor frees the entire block of memory managed by the Tribe object. This is a very efficient procedure: it's quicker than separately freeing smaller blocks, and it leads to very little memory fragmentation.

- This first implementation uses the Meyers singleton technique seen in *Chapter 8*, but we will use a different approach later in this chapter to compare the performance impacts of two implementation strategies for the same design pattern… because there are such impacts, as we will see.

The way our size-based arena implementation will benefit from our a priori knowledge of the expected usage pattern is as follows:

- Each allocation will return a sequentially "allocated" Orc-sized block, meaning that there is no need to search for an appropriately sized block – we always know where it is.

- There is no work to do when deallocating as we are not reusing the blocks once they have been used. Note that, per standard rules, the allocation and deallocation functions have to be thread-safe, which explains our use of std::mutex in this implementation.

The code follows:

```
#include "Orc.h"
#ifdef HOMEMADE_VERSION
#include <cassert>
#include <cstdlib>
#include <mutex>
class Tribe {
  std::mutex m;
  char *p, *cur;
  Tribe() : p{ static_cast<char*>(
      std::malloc(Orc::NB_MAX * sizeof(Orc))
  ) } {
      assert(p);
      cur = p;
  }
  Tribe(const Tribe&) = delete;
  Tribe& operator=(const Tribe&) = delete;
public:
  ~Tribe() {
      std::free(p);
  }
  static auto &get() {
      static Tribe singleton;
      return singleton;
  }
  void * allocate() {
      std::lock_guard _ { m };
      auto q = cur;
      cur += sizeof(Orc);
```

```
        return q;
    }
    void deallocate(void *) noexcept {
    }
};
// ...
```

As you might have guessed already, these allocation conditions are close to optimal, but they happen more often than we would think in practice. A similarly efficient usage pattern would model a stack (the last block allocated is the next block freed), and we write code that uses local variables every day without necessarily realizing that we are using what is often an optimal usage pattern for the underlying memory.

We then come to the overloaded allocation operators. To keep this implementation simple, we will suppose there will be no array of Orc objects to allocate, but you can refine the implementation to take arrays into account (it's not a difficult task; it's just more complicated to write relevant test code). The role played by these functions is to delegate the work to the underlying arena, and they will only be used for the Orc class (there is a caveat to this, which will be discussed in the *When parameters change* section later in this chapter). As such, they are almost trivial:

```
// ...
void * Orc::operator new(std::size_t) {
    return Tribe::get().allocate();
}
void * Orc::operator new[](std::size_t) {
    assert(false);
}
void Orc::operator delete(void *p) noexcept {
    Tribe::get().deallocate(p);
}
void Orc::operator delete[](void *) noexcept {
    assert(false);
}
#endif // HOMEMADE_VERSION
```

Testing our implementation

We then come to the test code implementation we will be using. This program will be made of a microbenchmark function named test() and of a main() function. We will examine both separately.

The test () function will take a non-void function, f (), a variadic pack of arguments, args, and call f (args...) making sure to use perfect forwarding for the arguments in that call to make sure the arguments are passed with the semantic intended in the original call. It reads a clock before and after the call to f () and returns a pair made of the result of executing f (args...) and the time elapsed during this call. I used high_resolution_clock in my code but there are valid reasons to use either system_clock or steady_clock in this situation:

```cpp
#include <chrono>
#include <utility>
template <class F, class ... Args>
  auto test(F f, Args &&... args) {
      using namespace std;
      using namespace std::chrono;
      auto pre = high_resolution_clock::now();
      auto res = f(std::forward<Args>(args)...);
      auto post = high_resolution_clock::now();
      return pair{ res, post - pre };
  }
// ...
```

You might wonder why we are requiring non-void functions and returning the result of calling f (args...) even if, in some cases, the return value might be a little artificial. The idea here is to ensure that the compiler thinks the result of f (args...) is useful and does not optimize it away. Compilers are clever beasts indeed and can remove code that seems useless under what is colloquially known as the "as-if rule" (simply put, if there is no visible effect to calling a function, just get rid of it!).

For the test program itself, pay attention to the following aspects:

- First, we will use std::vector<Orc*>, not std::vector<Orc>. This might seem strange at first, but since we are testing the speed of Orc::operator new() and Orc::operator delete(), we will want to actually call these operators! If we were using a container of Orc objects, there would be no call to our operators whatsoever.

- We call reserve() on that std::vector object before running our tests, to allocate the space to put the pointers to the Orc objects we will be constructing. That is an important aspect of our measurements: calls to push_back() and similar insertion functions in a std::vector object will need to reallocate if we try to add an element to a full container, and this reallocation will add noise to our benchmarks, so ensuring the container will not need to reallocate during the tests helps us focus on what we want to measure.

- What we measure with our test() function (used many times already in this book) is a sequence of Orc::NB_MAX calls to Orc::operator new(), eventually followed by the same number of calls to Orc::operator delete(). We suppose a carnage of sorts in the time between the constructions and the destructions, but we are not showing this violence out of respect for you, dear reader.

- Once we reach the end, we print out the results of our measurements, using microseconds as the measurement unit – our computers today are fast enough that milliseconds would probably not be granular enough.

The code follows:

```
// ...
#include "Orc.h"
#include <print>
#include <vector>
int main() {
  using namespace std;
  using namespace std::chrono;
#ifdef HOMEMADE_VERSION
  print("HOMEMADE VERSION\n");
#else
  print("STANDARD LIBRARY VERSION\n");
#endif
  vector<Orc*> orcs;
  auto [r0, dt0] = test([&orcs] {
      for(int i = 0; i != Orc::NB_MAX; ++i)
        orcs.push_back(new Orc);
      return size(orcs);
  });
  // ...
  // CARNAGE (CENSORED)
  // ...
  auto [r1, dt1] = test([&orcs] {
      for(auto p : orcs)
        delete p;
      return size(orcs);
  });
  print("Construction: {} orcs in {}\n",
      size(orcs), duration_cast<microseconds>(dt0));
  print("Destruction:  {} orcs in {}\n",
      size(orcs), duration_cast<microseconds>(dt1));
}
```

At this point, you might wonder whether this is all worth the effort. After all, our standard libraries are probably very efficient (and indeed, they are, on average, excellent!). The only way to know whether the results will make us happy is to run the test code and see for ourselves.

Looking at the numbers

Using an online gcc 15 compiler with the -O2 optimization level and running this code twice (once with the standard library version and once with the homemade version using a Meyers singleton), I get the following numbers for calls to the new and delete operators on Orc::NB_MAX (here, 10^6) objects:

N=10^6	Standard library	Homemade Meyers singleton
operator new()	23433μs	17906μs
operator delete()	7943μs	638μs

Table 10.1 – Speed comparison with Meyers singleton implementation

Actual numbers will vary depending on a variety of factors, of course, but the interesting aspect of the comparison is the ratio: our homemade operator new() only took 76.4% of the time consumed by the standard library-provided version and our homemade operator delete() took… 8.03% of the time required by our baseline.

Those are quite pleasant results, but they should not really surprise us: we perform constant-time allocation and essentially "no time" deallocation. We do take the time to lock and unlock a std::mutex object on every allocation, but most standard libraries implement mutexes that expect low contention and are very fast under those circumstances, and it so happens that our program does single-threaded allocations and deallocations that lead to code that is clearly devoid of contention.

Now, your acute reasoning skills might lead you to be surprised that deallocation is not actually faster than what we just measured. It's an empty function we are calling, after all, so what's consuming this CPU time?

The answer is… our singleton, or more precisely, access to the static local variable used for the Meyers implementation. Remember from *Chapter 8* that this technique aims to ensure that a singleton is created when needed, and static local variables are constructed the first time their enclosing function is called.

C++ implements "magic statics" where the call to the static local object's constructor is guarded by synchronization mechanisms that ensure the object is constructed only once. As we can see, this synchronization, efficient as it is, is not free. In our case, if we can guarantee that no other global object will need to call Tribe::get() before main() is called, we can replace the Meyers approach with a more classical approach where the singleton is simply a static data member of the Tribe class, declared within the scope of that class and defined at global scope:

```
// ...
// "global" singleton implementation (the rest of
// the code remains unchanged)
class Tribe {
```

```
   std::mutex m;
   char *p, *cur;
   Tribe() : p{ static_cast<char*>(
       std::malloc(Orc::NB_MAX * sizeof(Orc))
   ) } {
       assert(p);
       cur = p;
   }
   Tribe(const Tribe&) = delete;
   Tribe& operator=(const Tribe&) = delete;
   static Tribe singleton;
public:
   ~Tribe() {
       std::free(p);
   }
   static auto &get() {
       return singleton;
   }
   void * allocate() {
       std::lock_guard _ { m };
       auto q = cur;
       cur += sizeof(Orc);
       return q;
   }
   void deallocate(void *) noexcept {
   }
};
// in a .cpp file somewhere, within a block surrounded
// with #ifdef HOMEMADE_VERSION and #endif
Tribe Tribe::singleton;
// ...
```

Moving the definition of the singleton object away from within the function – placing it at global scope – removes the need for synchronization around the call to its constructor. We can now compare this implementation with our previous results to evaluate the costs involved, and the gains to be made (if any).

With the same test setup as used previously, adding the "global" singleton to the set of implementations under comparison, we get the following:

N=10^6	Standard library	Homemade	
		Meyers singleton	Global singleton
Operator new()	23433µs	17906µs	17573µs
Operator delete()	7943µs	638µs	0µs

Table 10.2 – Speed comparison with Meyers and "global" singleton implementations

Now, this is more like it! The calls to `operator new()` are slightly faster than they were 74.99% (of the time it took with the standard library version, and 98.14% of the time it took with the Meyers singleton), but the calls to `operator delete()` have become no-ops. It's hard to do better than this!

So, is it worth the effort? It depends on your needs, of course. Speed is a factor; in some programs, the speed gain can be a necessity, but in others, it can be a non-factor or almost so. The reduction in memory fragmentation can make a big difference in some programs too, and some will use arenas precisely for that reason. The point is this: if you need to do this, now you know how.

Generalizing to SizeBasedArena<T,N>

The `Tribe` class as written seems specific to the `Orc` class but, in practice, it really is specific to `Orc`-*sized* objects as it never calls any function of the `Orc` class; it never constructs an `Orc` object, nor does it ever destroy one. This means that we could turn that class into a generic class and reuse it for other types that are expected to be used under similar constraints.

To achieve this, we would decouple the arena code from the `Orc` class and put it in a separate file, maybe called `SizeBasedArena.h`, for example:

```
#ifndef SIZE_BASED_ARENA_H
#define SIZE_BASED_ARENA_H
#include <cassert>
#include <cstdlib>
#include <mutex>
template <class T, std::size_t N>
class SizeBasedArena {
  std::mutex m;
  char *p, *cur;
  SizeBasedArena() : p{ static_cast<char*>(
      std::malloc(N * sizeof(T))
  ) } {
      assert(p);
      cur = p;
```

```
    }
    SizeBasedArena(const SizeBasedArena&) = delete;
    SizeBasedArena&
        operator=(const SizeBasedArena&) = delete;
public:
    ~SizeBasedArena() {
        std::free(p);
    }
    static auto &get() {
        static SizeBasedArena singleton;
        return singleton;
    }
    void * allocate_one() {
        std::lock_guard _ { m };
        auto q = cur;
        cur += sizeof(T);
        return q;
    }
    void * allocate_n(std::size_t n) {
        std::lock_guard _ { m };
        auto q = cur;
        cur += n * sizeof(T);
        return q;
    }
    void deallocate_one(void *) noexcept {
    }
    void deallocate_n(void *) noexcept {
    }
};
#endif
```

It might be surprising that we used T and N as template parameters. Why type T instead of an integer initialized with sizeof(T) if we do not use T in the arena? Well, if the Elf class (for example) used a size-based arena too, and if we were unlucky enough that sizeof(Orc)==sizeof(Elf), then basing ourselves on the sizes of the types rather than on the types themselves might, if the values for their respective N parameters are the same, lead Orc and Elf to use the same arena… and we do not want that (nor do they!).

To simplify the initialization of the singleton in this generic example, we went back to the Meyers technique. It's more difficult to guarantee the absence of interdependence at construction time for global objects when writing generic code than it was writing the Orc-specific equivalent, as the move to generic code just enlarged the potential user base significantly.

The implementation in `Orc.cpp` would now be as follows:

```cpp
#include "Orc.h"
#ifdef HOMEMADE_VERSION
#include "SizeBasedArena.h"
using Tribe = SizeBasedArena<Orc, Orc::NB_MAX>;
void * Orc::operator new(std::size_t) {
  return Tribe::get().allocate_one();
}
void * Orc::operator new[](std::size_t n) {
  return Tribe::get().allocate_n(n / sizeof(Orc));
}
void Orc::operator delete(void *p) noexcept {
  Tribe::get().deallocate_one(p);
}
void Orc::operator delete[](void *p) noexcept {
  Tribe::get().deallocate_n(p);
}
#endif
```

You might have noted that since `SizeBasedArena<T,N>` implements allocation functions for a single object or an array of n objects, we have extended the `Orc` class's member function allocation operator overloads to cover `operator new[]()` and `operator delete[]()`. There's really no reason not to do so at this point.

When parameters change

Our size-based arena implementation is very specific: it supposes the possibility of sequential allocations and the ability to dismiss the (generally important) question of reusing memory after it has been freed.

An important caveat to any size-based implementation is, obviously, that we are counting on a specific size. Know, thus, that with this constraint, our current implementation is slightly dangerous. Indeed, consider the following evolution of our program, where we envision tougher, meaner `Orc` subclasses such as the following:

```cpp
class MeanOrc : public Orc {
  float attackBonus; // oops!
  // ...
};
```

It might not be apparent at first, but we just might have broken something important with this new class, as *the member function allocation operators are inherited by derived classes.* This means that the `Tribe` class, also known under the somewhat noisier name of `SizeBasedArena<Orc,Orc::NB_MAX>`, would implement a strategy meant for blocks of `sizeof(Orc)` bytes but be used (accidentally) also for objects of size `MeanOrc`. This can only lead to pain.

We can protect ourselves from this disastrous situation in two ways. For the `Orc` class, we could disallow derived classes altogether by marking the class as `final`:

```
class Orc final {
  // ...
};
```

This removes the possibility of writing `MeanOrc` as a derived class of `Orc`; we can still write `MeanOrc`, but through composition or other techniques, which would sidestep the inherited operators problem.

From the perspective of `SizeBasedArena<T,N>` itself, we can also decide to restrict our implementation to `final` types, as in this example:

```
// ...
#include <type_traits>
template <class T, std::size_t N>
class SizeBasedArena {
  static_assert(std::is_final_v<T>);
  // ...
};
```

This last part might not be for everyone, however. There are lots of types (fundamental types, for example) that are not `final` and that could reasonably be used in a size-based arena, so it's up to you to see whether this is a good idea or not for the kind of code you write. If it's not good for you, then these constraints could be expressed as prose rather than as code.

Size-based arenas are far from the only use case for memory arenas. We could envision many variations on both the size-based theme and the allocation strategy.

For example, suppose we introduce shamans in our game and the need to reuse memory becomes a reality. We could have a situation where there are, at most, `Orc::NB_MAX` objects of the `Orc` type in the program *at once*, but there might be more than that number *overall* during the entire program's execution. In such a situation, we need to consider the following things:

- If we allow arrays, we will have to deal with *internal* fragmentation within the arena, so we might want to consider an implementation that allocates more than $N*sizeof(T)$ bytes per arena, but how much more?

- We will need a strategy to reuse memory. There are many approaches at our disposal, including maintaining an ordered list of `begin, end` pairs to delimit the free blocks (and fuse them more easily to reduce fragmentation) or keeping a stack (maybe a set of stacks based on block size) of recently freed blocks to make it easier to reuse freed blocks quickly.

Answers to such questions as "*What is the best approach for our code base?*" are in part technical and in part political: what makes allocation fast may slow down deallocation, what makes allocation speed deterministic may cost more in memory space overhead, and so on. The question is to determine what trade-offs work best in our situation and measure to ensure we reap the desired benefits. If we cannot manage to do better than the standard library already does, then by all means, use the standard library!

Chunked pools

Our size-based arena example was optimized for a single block size and specific usage patterns, but there are many other reasons to want to apply a specialized allocation strategy. In this section, we will explore the idea of a "chunked pool," or a pool of pre-allocated raw memory of selected block sizes. This is meant as an academic example to build upon more than as something to use in production; the code that follows will be reasonably fast and can be made to become very fast, but in this book, we will focus on the general approach and leave you, dear reader, to enjoy optimizing it to your liking.

The idea in this example is that user code plans to allocate objects of similar (but not necessarily identical) sizes and of various types and supposes an upper bound on the maximal number of objects. This gives us additional knowledge; using that knowledge, we will write a `ChunkSizedAllocator<N,Sz...>` type where N will be the number of objects of each "size category" and each integral value in `Sz...` will be a distinct size category.

To give a clarifying example, a `ChunkSizedAllocator<10,20,40,80,160>` object would pre-allocate sufficient raw memory to hold 10 objects of size 20 bytes, 40 bytes, 80 bytes, and 160 bytes each for a total of at least 3,000 bytes (the sum of the minimal size required for each size category being *200 + 400 + 800 + 1600*). We say "at least" in this case because to be useful, our class will need to consider alignment and will generally need more than the minimal amount of memory if we are to avoid allocating misaligned objects.

To understand what we are going to do, here are some pointers (pun intended):

- In the variadic sequence of integral values `Sz...` we will require the values to be sorted in ascending order, as this will make further lookup faster (linear complexity rather than quadratic complexity). Since these values are known at compile time, being part of the template parameters of our type, this has no runtime costs and is more of a constraint imposed on the user. We will, of course, validate this at compile time to avoid unpleasant mishaps.

- In C++, variadic packs can be empty, but in our case, an empty set of size categories would make no sense so we will ensure that does not happen (at compile time, of course). Obviously, N has to be more than zero for this class to be useful so we will validate this also.

- What might not be self-evident is that values in `Sz...` have to be at least `sizeof(std::max_align_t)` (we could have tested for `alignof` too but, for fundamental types, this is redundant) and that, in practice, we will need to make the effective size categories powers of two to make sure arbitrary types can be allocated. This latter part will be handled internally, as it's trickier to impose on user code.

Looking at the code, we can see these constraints expressed explicitly. Note that to make the "code narrative" easier to follow, the code that follows is presented step by step, so make sure to look at the complete example if you want to experiment with it:

```cpp
#include <algorithm>
#include <vector>
#include <utility>
#include <memory>
#include <cassert>
#include <concepts>
#include <limits>
#include <array>
#include <iterator>
#include <mutex>
// ... helper functions (shown below)...
template <int N, auto ... Sz>
  class ChunkSizedAllocator {
      static_assert(is_sorted(make_array(Sz...)));
      static_assert(sizeof...(Sz) > 0);
      static_assert(
        ((Sz >= sizeof(std::max_align_t)) && ...)
      );
      static_assert(N > 0);
      static constexpr unsigned long long sizes[] {
        next_power_of_two(Sz)...
      };
      using raw_ptr = void*;
      raw_ptr blocks[sizeof...(Sz)];
      int cur[sizeof...(Sz)] {}; // initialized to zero
      // ...
```

Note that we have two data members – namely, `blocks`, which will contain a pointer to a block of raw memory for each size category, and `cur`, which will contain the index of the next allocation within a block for each size category (initialized to zero by default, as we will start from the beginning in each case).

The code for this class continues shortly. For now, you might notice some unexplained helper functions:

- We use `make_array(Sz...)`, a `constexpr` function that constructs an object of type `std::array<T,N>` from the values of `Sz...`, expecting all values to be of the same type (the type of the first value of `Sz...`). We know N for the resulting `std::array<T,N>` to be a compile-time constant as it is computed from the number of values in `Sz...`.

- We use the is_sorted() predicate on that std::array<T,N> object to ensure, at compile time, that the values are sorted in ascending order, as we expect them to be. Unsurprisingly, this will simply call the std::is_sorted() algorithm, which is constexpr and thus usable in this context.

- The non-static member array named sizes will contain the next power of two for each value in Sz..., including that value, of course: if the value is already a power of two, wonderful! Thus, if Sz... is 10,20,32, then sizes will contain 16,32,32.

Why powers of two?

In practice, blocks that are not powers of two will lead to misaligned objects after the first allocation if we allocate them contiguously, and managing padding to avoid this is possible but would complicate our implementation significantly. To make allocations quicker, we compute the next power to two for each element of Sz... at compile time and store them in the sizes array. This means we could have two size categories that end up being of the same size (for example, 40 and 60 would both lead to 64 bytes blocks) but that's a minor issue (as code would still work) considering that this is a specialized facility designed for knowledgeable users.

The code for these helper functions, in practice, defined before the declaration of the ChunkSizedAllocator<N,Sz...> class is as follows:

```
// ...
template <class T, std::same_as<T> ... Ts>
  constexpr std::array<T, sizeof...(Ts)+1>
      make_array(T n, Ts ... ns) {
        return { n, ns... };
      }
constexpr bool is_power_of_two(std::integral auto n) {
  return n && ((n & (n - 1)) == 0);
}
class integral_value_too_big {};
constexpr auto next_power_of_two(std::integral auto n) {
  constexpr auto upper_limit =
      std::numeric_limits<decltype(n)>::max();
  for(; n != upper_limit && !is_power_of_two(n); ++n)
      ;
  if(!is_power_of_two(n)) throw integral_value_too_big{};
  return n;
}
template <class T>
  constexpr bool is_sorted(const T &c) {
      return std::is_sorted(std::begin(c), std::end(c));
  }
// ...
```

Note that make_array() uses concepts to constrain that all values are of the same type, and that is_power_of_two(n) ensures that the proper bits of n are tested to make this test quick (it also tests n to ensure we do not report 0 as being a power of two). The next_power_of_two() function could probably be made much faster but that's of little consequence here as it is only used at compile time (we could enforce this by making it consteval instead of constexpr, but there might be users that want to choose between run time and compile time usage so we'll give them that choice).

Returning to our ChunkSizedAllocator<N, Sz...> implementation after this short digression on helper functions, we have a member function named within_block(p, i) that returns true only if pointer p is within blocks[i], which is the i-th pre-allocated block of memory of our object. The logic for that function seems deceptively simple: one might simply want to test something that looks like blocks[i]<=p&&p<blocks[i]+N but with the proper casts applied, as the blocks[i] variable is of type void*, which precludes pointer arithmetic, but that happens to be incorrect in C++ (remember our discussion of the intricacies of pointer arithmetic in *Chapter 2*). It probably works in practice for compatibility with C code, but it's not something you want to rely on.

As of this writing, there are ongoing discussions to add a standard library function to test whether a pointer is between two others, but until this happens, we can at least use the standard library-provided std::less functor to make the comparisons somewhat legal. This is unsatisfactory, I know, but it will probably work on all compilers today... and by making this test local to a specialized function, we will simplify source code updates once we have a real standard solution to this problem:

```
// ...
bool within_block(void *p, int i) {
  void* b = blocks[i];
  void* e = static_cast<char*>(b) + N * sizes[i];
  return p == b ||
         (std::less{}(b, p) && std::less{}(p, e));
}
// ...
```

There's no reason to make objects of ChunkSizedAllocator<N, Sz...> globally available: this is a tool that could be instantiated many times in a program and used to solve various problems. We do not want that type to be copyable, however (we could, but that would really complicate the design for limited returns).

Through std::malloc(), our constructor allocates the raw memory blocks for the various sizes in Sz..., or at least the next power of two for each of these sizes, as explained earlier in this section, ensuring afterward that all of the allocations succeeded. We used assert() for this, but one could also throw std::bad_alloc on failure as long as one carefully called std::free() on the memory blocks that were successfully allocated before doing so.

Our destructor, unsurprisingly, calls `std::free()` on each memory block: as with the arena implementation earlier in this chapter, a `ChunkSizedAllocator<N,Sz...>` object is responsible for memory, not the objects put there by client code, so we have to suppose that client code destroyed all objects stored within the memory blocks of a `ChunkSizedAllocator` object before that object's destructor is called.

Note the presence of a `std::mutex` data member, as we will need this (or some other synchronization tool) to ensure allocations and deallocations are thread-safe later:

```
// ...
    std::mutex m;
public:
    ChunkSizedAllocator(const ChunkSizedAllocator&)
        = delete;
    ChunkSizedAllocator&
      operator=(const ChunkSizedAllocator&) = delete;
    ChunkSizedAllocator() {
        int i = 0;
        for(auto sz : sizes)
            blocks[i++] = std::malloc(N * sz);
        assert(std::none_of(
            std::begin(blocks), std::end(blocks),
            [](auto p) { return !p; }
        ));
    }
    ~ChunkSizedAllocator() {
        for(auto p : blocks)
            std::free(p);
    }
    // ...
```

Finally, we reach the crux of our effort with the `allocate()` and `deallocate()` member functions. In `allocate(n)`, we search for the smallest element, `sizes[i]`, for which the allocated block size is sufficiently big to hold n bytes. Once one such block is found, we lock our `std::mutex` object to avoid race conditions and then look to see whether there is still at least one available block in `blocks[i]`; this implementation takes them sequentially and does not reuse them, to keep the discussion simple. If there is one, we take it, update `cur[i]`, and return the appropriate address to the user code.

Note that when we do not find a free block in our pre-allocated blocks, or when n is too large for the blocks we allocated upfront, we delegate the allocation responsibility to `::operator new()` such that the allocation request might still succeed. We could also have thrown `std::bad_alloc` in this case, depending on what the intent is: if it's important to us that the allocation is made within our blocks and nowhere else, throwing or otherwise failing is a better choice.

> ### How could failing be a good thing?
>
> Some applications, particularly in embedded systems of low-latency or real-time system domains, are such that software that delivers the right answer or produces the right computation but not in due time is as bad as software that produces a wrong answer. Think, for example, of a system that controls the brakes of a car: a car that stops after colliding is of limited usefulness indeed. Such systems are rigorously tested to catch failures before being released and will count on specific runtime behavior; for that reason, when under development, they might prefer failing (in a way that will be caught during their testing phase) rather than defaulting to a strategy that might sometimes not meet their timing requirements. Of course, please do not ship critical systems that stop working when used in real life: test them well and make sure users are kept safe! But maybe you are developing a system where, if something bad happens, you will prefer to print "Sorry, we messed up" somewhere and just restart the program, and that's perfectly fine too sometimes.

The `deallocate(p)` deallocation function goes through each memory block to see whether p is within that block. Remember that our `within_block()` function would benefit from a pointer comparison test that the standard does not yet provide as of this writing, so if you use this code in practice, make sure you leave yourself a note to apply this new function as soon as it becomes available. If p is in none of our blocks, then it was probably allocated through `::operator new()` so we make sure to free it through `::operator delete()` as we should.

As stated previously, our implementation does not reuse memory once it has been freed, but the location where that reuse should happen has been left in comments (along with code that locks the mutex for that section) so feel free to implement memory block reuse logic there if you want to:

```cpp
// ...
auto allocate(std::size_t n) {
  using std::size;
  // use smallest block available
  for(std::size_t i = 0; i != size(sizes); ++i) {
      if(n < sizes[i]) {
        std::lock_guard _ { m };
        if(cur[i] < N) {
            void *p = static_cast<char*>(blocks[i]) +
                      cur[i] * sizes[i];
            ++cur[i];
            return p;
        }
      }
  }
  // either no block fits or no block left
  return ::operator new(n);
}
```

```
        void deallocate (void *p) {
          using std::size;
          for(std::size_t i = 0; i != size(sizes); ++i) {
              if(within_block(p, i)) {
                  //std::lock_guard _ { m };
                  // if you want to reuse the memory,
                  // it's in blocks[i]
                  return;
              }
          }
          // p is not in our blocks
          ::operator delete(p);
      }
  };
  // ...
```

Since this is a specialized form of allocation to be used by client code as needed, we will use specialized overloads of the allocation operators. As can be expected, these overloads will be templates based on the parameters of the ChunkSizedAllocator object to be used:

```
template <int N, auto ... Sz>
  void *operator new(std::size_t n, ChunkSizedAllocator<
      N, Sz...
  > &chunks) {
      return chunks.allocate(n);
  }
template <int N, auto ... Sz>
  void operator delete (void *p, ChunkSizedAllocator<
      N, Sz...
  > &chunks) {
      return chunks.deallocate(p);
  }
// new[] and delete[] left as an exercise ;)
```

Now, we wrote these allocation facilities, but we need to test them, as we need to see whether there are benefits to this approach.

Testing ChunkSizedAllocator

We will now write a simple test program that uses a `ChunkSizedAllocator` object with an appropriate set of size categories, then allocate and deallocate objects with sizes that fit within these categories in ways that should benefit our class. In so doing, we are supposing that users of this class do so seeking to benefit from a priori known size categories. Other tests could be conducted to verify the code's behavior with inappropriate size requests or in the presence of throwing constructors, for example, so feel free to write a more elaborate test harness than the one we will be providing for the sake of our execution speed-related discussion.

The `test()` function used to test our size-based arena earlier in this chapter will be used here again. See that section for an explanation of its workings.

It's not trivial to write a good test program to validate the behavior of a program that allocates and deallocates objects of various sizes. What we will do is use a dummy<N> type whose objects will each occupy a space of N bytes in memory (as we will use `char [N]` data members to get this result, we know that `alignof (dummy<N>) ==1` for all valid values of N).

We will also write two distinct `test_dummy<N>()` functions. Each of these functions will allocate and then construct the dummy<N> object and set up the associated destroy-then-deallocate code, but one will use the standard library implementation of the allocation operators and the other will use our overloads.

You will note that both of our `test_dummy<N>()` functions return a pair of values: one will be a pointer to the allocated object and the other will be the code to destroy and deallocate that object. Since we will store this information in client code, we need these pairs to be abstractions that share a common type, which explains our use of `void*` for the address and `std::function<void(void*)>` for the destruction code. We need `std::function` or something similar here: a function pointer would not suffice as the destruction code can be stateful (we sometimes need to remember what object was used to manage the allocation).

The code for these tools follows:

```
#include <chrono>
#include <utility>
#include <functional>
template <class F, class ... Args>
  auto test(F f, Args &&... args) {
      using namespace std;
      using namespace std::chrono;
      auto pre = high_resolution_clock::now();
      auto res = f(std::forward<Args>(args)...);
      auto post = high_resolution_clock::now();
      return pair{ res, post - pre };
  }
```

```
template <int N> struct dummy { char _[N] {}; };
template <int N> auto test_dummy() {
  return std::pair<void *, std::function<void(void*)>> {
      new dummy<N>{},
      [](void *p) { delete static_cast<dummy<N>*>(p); }
  };
}
template <int N, class T> auto test_dummy(T &alloc) {
  return std::pair<void *, std::function<void(void*)>> {
      new (alloc) dummy<N>{},
    [&alloc](void *p) { ::operator delete(p, alloc); }
  };
}
// ...
```

Finally, we have to write the test program. We will discuss this program step by step to make sure we grasp all the subtleties involved in the process.

Our program first decides on a value of N for the ChunkSizedAllocator object as well as on size categories Sz... for that memory manager to use (the value I picked for N is arbitrary). I deliberately used one *non-power-of-two* size category to show that the values are "rounded up" to the next power of two appropriately: the size request of 62 is translated into 64 when constructing the sizes data member of our type. We then construct that object and name it chunks because... well, why not?

```
// ...
#include <print>
#include <vector>
int main() {
  using namespace std;
  using namespace std::chrono;
  constexpr int N = 100'000;
  using Alloc = ChunkSizedAllocator<
      N, 32, 62 /* 64 */, 128
  >;
  Alloc chunks; // construct the ChunkSizedAllocator
  // ...
```

The tests that follow take the same form for the standard library and for our specialized facility. Let's look at them in detail:

1. We create a `std::vector` object of pairs named `ptrs` filled with default values (null pointers and non-callable functions) for N objects in three size categories (because `sizeof...(Sz)==3` in our example). This ensures that the allocation for the space used by the `std::vector` object is performed prior to our measurements (prior to the execution of the lambda expression passed to `test()`) and does not interfere with them later. Note that each tested lambda is mutable as it needs to modify the captured `ptrs` object.

2. For each of the three size categories, we then allocate N objects of sizes that fit in that category and remember through the returned `pair` both that object's address and the code that will correctly finalize it later.

3. Then, to end each test, we use the finalization code on each object and destroy and then deallocate it.

It sounds worse than it is, happily for us. Once the tests have run to completion, we print out the execution time of each test expressed as microseconds:

```
// ...
auto [r0, dt0] = test([ptrs = std::vector<
    std::pair<
        void*, std::function<void(void*)>
    >>(N * 3)]() mutable {
    // allocation
    for(int i = 0; i != N * 3; i += 3) {
        ptrs[i] = test_dummy<30>();
        ptrs[i + 1] = test_dummy<60>();
        ptrs[i + 2] = test_dummy<100>();
    }
    // cleanup
    for(auto & p : ptrs)
        p.second(p.first);
    return std::size(ptrs);
});
auto [r1, dt1] = test([&chunks, ptrs = std::vector<
    std::pair<
        void*, std::function<void(void*)>
    >>(N * 3)]() mutable {
    // allocation
    for(int i = 0; i != N * 3; i += 3) {
        ptrs[i] = test_dummy<30>(chunks);
        ptrs[i + 1] = test_dummy<60>(chunks);
        ptrs[i + 2] = test_dummy<100>(chunks);
```

```
      }
      // cleanup
      for(auto & p : ptrs)
          p.second(p.first);
      return std::size(ptrs);
   });
    std::print("Standard version : {}\n",
              duration_cast<microseconds>(dt0));
    std::print("Chunked version  : {}\n",
              duration_cast<microseconds>(dt1));
  }
```

Okay, so that was slightly intricate but hopefully instructive. Is it worth the trouble? Well, it depends on your needs.

When I ran this code on the same online gcc 15 compiler with the -O2 optimization level as with the size-based arena, the standard library version reported an execution time of 13,360, whereas the time reported for the "chunked" version was 12,032, effectively 90.05% of the standard version's execution time. This kind of speedup can be lovely as long as we remember that the initial allocation done in the constructor of our `chunks` object was not measured: the idea here is to show we can save time when it's important and choose to pay for it when we are not in a hurry.

It's important to remember that this implementation does not reuse memory, but the standard version does so, which means our speedup might be counterbalanced by a loss of functionality (if it's a functionality you need, of course). In the tests I ran, locking the `std::mutex` object or not doing so had a significant impact on speedup, so (a) depending on your platform, there might be a better choice of synchronization mechanism at your disposal, and (b) this implementation is probably too naïve to bring benefits as is if the `deallocate()` member function also needs to lock the `std::mutex` object.

Of course, one could optimize this (quite academic) version quite a bit, and I invite you dear readers to do so (and test the results every step of the way!). The point of this section was more to show (a) that chunk size-based allocation can be done, (b) how it can be done from an architectural standpoint, and (c) point out some risks and potential pitfalls along the way.

That was fun, wasn't it?

Summary

As a reminder, in this chapter, we examined arena-based allocation with a concrete example (a size-based arena with a particular usage pattern) and saw we could get significant results from it, and then saw another use case with pre-allocated memory blocks from which we picked chunks where we placed objects, again seeing some benefits. These techniques showed new ways to control memory management, but in no way are they meant to represent an exhaustive discussion on the subject. To be honest, this entire book cannot be an exhaustive treatise on the subject, but it can hopefully give us ideas!

The next step in our journey will be to expand the techniques seen in this chapter and write something that is not really a garbage collector but is in some ways weaker and in some ways better: deferred reclamation memory zones. This will be our last step before we start discussing memory management in containers.

11

Deferred Reclamation

In *Chapter 9*, we showed some examples of unusual memory allocation mechanisms and how they can be used, including how to react to errors to give our programs a form of "second chance" to continue, as well as how to use atypical or exotic memory through the mediation of the C++ language facilities. Then, in *Chapter 10*, we examined arena-based allocation and some variants thereof with an eye on issues of speed, determinism, and control over resource consumption.

What we will do in the current chapter is something that is not often done in C++ but that is common practice in programs written in many other languages, particularly those with integrated garbage collectors: we will write mechanisms that delay the destruction of dynamically allocated objects at selected moments in the execution of a program.

We will *not* write a proper garbage collector, as that would involve deeper involvement in the inner workings of the compiler and impact the programming model that makes C++ such a wonderful tool. However, we will put together mechanisms for **deferred reclamation**, in the sense that selected objects will deliberately be destroyed and see their underlying storage freed together at chosen moments, but without necessarily guaranteeing a destruction order. We will, of course, not provide an exhaustive overview of techniques to achieve this objective, but we will hopefully give you, dear reader, enough "food for thought" to build your own deferred reclamation mechanisms should you need to.

The techniques in this chapter can be coupled with those seen in *Chapter 10* to make programs faster and reduce memory fragmentation, but we will cover deferred reclamation as a standalone topic to make our discourse clearer. After reading this chapter, you will be able to do the following:

- Understand the trade-offs associated with deferred reclamation, as there are gains to be made but there are also costs involved (this is not a panacea!)

- Implement an almost transparent external wrapper to track the memory that needs to be collected

- Implement an almost transparent external wrapper to help finalize the objects that are subjected to deferred reclamation

- Implement a counting pointer akin to the reference counter of a `std::shared_ptr` object in order to identify objects that can be reclaimed at the end of a chosen scope

The first step we need to take is to try to understand some problem domains where deferred reclamation can be helpful, including its relation to the (different but not entirely dissimilar) problem of garbage collection.

> **Finalization? Reclamation?**
>
> You will notice that, in this chapter, we will often use the word *finalization* instead of the word *destruction*, as we seek to emphasize the fact that the code executed at the end of an object's lifetime (its destructor) is distinct from the code that frees its underlying storage. As a bonus, **finalization** is also more common in garbage-collected languages, and garbage collection is a cousin of the techniques discussed in the sections that follow. Consider finalization (without reclamation) as the equivalent of calling the destructor of an object (without deallocating the underlying storage).
>
> As stated earlier in this chapter, we will name **reclamation** the act of freeing the memory for one or many objects at selected moments, for example, at the end of a scope or when reaching the end of a program's execution. Again, this term is more common in garbage-collected languages than it is in C++, but the topic of this chapter is in some ways closer to what these languages do so, hopefully, using similar terms will help develop a common understanding of the ideas and techniques involved.

Technical requirements

You can find the code files for this chapter in the book's GitHub repository here: `https://github.com/PacktPublishing/C-Plus-Plus-Memory-Management/tree/main/chapter11`.

What do we mean by deferred reclamation?

Why would one want to resort to deferred reclamation? That's a valid question indeed, so thanks for asking!

The short answer is that it solves a real problem. Indeed, there are programs where it makes sense not to collect objects right after they stop being referred to by client code, or where it's unclear whether they can be collected at all until we know for sure the code that could use them concludes. These programs are somewhat rare in C++ because of the way we reason about code in our language, but they are not rare when looking at the programming world in general.

For example, consider a function in which there are circular references between some of the locally allocated objects, or one where there is a tree that one can navigate from the root node to its leaf nodes, but in which the leaves of the tree also have a reference to its root node. Sometimes, we can determine how to destroy the set of objects: for example, in the case of a tree, we could decide to start at the root and go down the branches. In other situations, if we know that a group of objects will not escape a given function, we can also use the knowledge that, at the end of that function, they all can be reclaimed as a group.

If you are familiar with garbage-collected languages, you probably know that in most of them, the collector "reclaims the bytes," freeing the underlying storage of the reclaimed objects (and sometimes compacting the memory as it proceeds), but does not finalize the objects. One reason for this is that it is difficult (in some cases, impossible) for an object in such a language to know which other objects still exist in the program since there is no order-of-finalization guarantee... and how could there be one if the garbage collector needs to deal with cycles of objects referring to each other? Not knowing which other objects still exist when an object reaches the end of its lifetime severely limits what finalization code can do.

The fact that reclamation does not mean finalization in many languages simplifies the task of collecting the objects: one can conceptually call $std::free()$ or some equivalent function and free memory without worrying about the objects therein. In languages that do guarantee finalization before reclamation, one often finds a class hierarchy rooted in a single, common base class (often called $object$ or $Object$), which makes it possible to call the equivalent of a $virtual$ destructor on each object and polymorphically finalize it. Of course, what one can do when finalizing an object under such circumstances is limited since the order in which objects are finalized is usually unknown.

What is more common in contemporary garbage-collected languages is to make finalization the responsibility of client code and leave the collection to the language itself. Such languages often use a special interface ($IDisposable$ in C# and $Closeable$ in Java come to mind) that is implemented by classes for which finalization is important (typically, classes that manage external resources), and client code will explicitly put in place the required mechanisms for the ordered finalization of objects. This moves part of the responsibility over resource management from the object itself (as is customary in C++ with the RAII idiom described in *Chapter 4*) to the code that uses it, which is a reminder that garbage collectors tend to simplify memory management but, at the same time, tend to complicate the management of other resources.

Examples of such client code-driven resource management include a try block accompanied by a $finally$ block, which serves as the locus of cleanup code applied regardless of whether the try block concluded normally or some $catch$ block was entered. There are also simplified syntaxes that perform the same thing in a less burdensome manner for client code. For example, Java uses try-with blocks and implicitly calls $close()$ on selected $Closeable$ objects at *end of scope*, and C# uses $using$ blocks likewise in order to implicitly call $Dispose()$ on selected $IDisposable$ objects.

C++ does not have $finally$ blocks, nor does it use intrusive techniques such as special interfaces known to the language that receive special treatment or a common base class to all types. In C++, objects are usually made responsible for the management of their resources through the RAII idiom; this leads to a different mindset and different programming techniques when compared to other popular languages.

In this chapter, we will face a similar yet different situation to the one faced in garbage-collected languages: if we want to use deferred reclamation of objects, we cannot guarantee that during destruction, one of the reclaimed objects will be able to access other objects reclaimed in the same group, so one should not try to do this. On the other hand, the fact that we will choose to apply deferred reclamation to *selected* objects (instead of doing so for all objects) means that objects not part of this group and known to survive that group's reclamation can still be accessed during the finalization of reclaimed objects. It's a benefit of not having a one-size-fits-all solution, really: C++ is nothing if not versatile, as you probably knew even before starting to read this book.

Not having a common base class to all types means that we will have to either forego finalization (and this can work if we limit ourselves to allocating objects of trivially destructible types, something we could validate at compile time) or that we will have to find some other way to remember the types of the objects we allocated and call the appropriate destructor when the time comes. In this chapter, we will show how one can implement both approaches.

Contrary to popular belief, some garbage collectors have been implemented for C++. One of the best-known ones (the Boehm-Demers-Weiser collector made by Hans Boehm, Alan Demers, and Mark Weiser) does not finalize objects in general but allows the registration of chosen finalizers from user code. This is done through a facility named `GC_register_finalizer`, but the authors warn users of this facility that what such a finalizer can do is limited, as is the case in garbage-collected languages (and discussed earlier in this section).

> **Further reading**
> To explore further, please check `https://www.hboehm.info/gc/`.

We will use other techniques in this chapter. As is always the case in this book, the intent is to present ideas from which you can experiment and build the kind of solution your code needs. We will show three different examples:

- Code that reclaims selected objects at the end of program execution but does not finalize them, limiting deferred reclamation to trivially destructible objects

- Code that reclaims and finalizes selected objects at the end of program execution

- Code that reclaims and finalizes selected objects at the end of selected scopes

We will proceed differently in each case, to give you a broader perspective on what can be done. In all three cases, we will store the pointers in a globally accessible object. Yes, a singleton, but that's the correct tool here as we are discussing a feature that impacts the whole program. Ready? Here we go!

> **Things we sometimes do to make examples readable...**
>
> The code in the following sections can seem strange to some readers. In an effort to focus on the deferred reclamation aspects of the code and keep the overall presentation readable, I chose not to go into aspects of thread safety, although this is essential in contemporary code. In the GitHub repository for this chapter, however, you will find both the code presented in this book and the thread-safe equivalent for each example.

Reclamation (without finalization) at the end of the program

Our first implementation will provide reclamation but not finalization at the end of program execution. For this reason, it will not accept managing objects of some type T if T is not trivially destructible since objects of that type have a destructor that might have to be executed to avoid leaks or other problems along the way.

With this example, as with the others in this chapter, we will start with our test code, and then go on to see how the reclamation mechanics are implemented. Our test code will go as follows:

- We will declare two types, NamedThing and Identifier. The former will not be trivially destructible as its destructor will contain user code that prints out debugging information, but the latter will be, as it will only contain trivially destructible non-static data members and offer no user-provided destructor.

- We will provide two g() functions. The first one will be commented out as it tries to allocate NamedThing objects through our reclamation system, something that would not compile as type NamedThing does not meet our requirement of trivial destructibility. The second one will be used as the objects it allocates are of a type that meets those requirements.

- The f(), g(), and main() functions will construct objects at various levels in the call stack of our program. However, the reclaimable objects will only be at the end of program execution.

The client code in this case would be as follows:

```
// ...
// note: not trivially destructible
struct NamedThing {
    const char *name;
    NamedThing(const char *name) : name{ name } {
        std::print("{} ctor\n", name);
    }
    ~NamedThing() {
        std::print("{} dtor\n", name);
    }
};
```

```
struct Identifier {
   int value;
};
// would not compile
/*
void g() {
   [[maybe_unused]] auto p = gcnew<NamedThing>("hi");
   [[maybe_unused]] auto q = gcnew<NamedThing>("there");
}
*/
void g() {
   [[maybe_unused]] auto p = gcnew<Identifier>(2);
   [[maybe_unused]] auto q = gcnew<Identifier>(3);
}
auto h() {
   struct X {
      int m() const { return 123; }
   };
   return gcnew<X>();
}
auto f() {
   g();
   return h();
}
int main() {
   std::print("Pre\n");
   std::print("{}\n", f()->m());
   std::print("Post\n");
}
```

With this code and the (so far missing) deferred reclamation code, this program will print the following:

```
Pre
123
Post
~GC with 3 objects to deallocate
```

Note that f() allocates and returns an object from which main() calls the m() member function without explicitly resorting to a smart pointer, yet this program does not leak memory. Objects allocated through the gcnew<T>() function are registered in the GC object, and the destructor of the GC object will ensure the registered memory blocks will be deallocated.

How does gcnew<T>() work, then, and why write such a function instead of simply overloading operator new()? Well, remember that operator new() intervenes in the overall allocation process as an allocation function – one that trades in raw memory, not one that knows what the type of object to create will be. In this example, we want (a) memory to be allocated for the new object, (b) the object to be constructed (hence the need for the type and the arguments that will be passed to the constructor), and (c) to reject types that are not trivially destructible. We need to know the type of object to construct, something operator new() is not aware of.

To be able to reclaim the memory for these objects at the end of program execution, we will need a form of globally available storage where we will put the pointers that have been allocated. We will call such pointers roots and store them in a singleton of the GC type (inspired by the nickname typically associated with garbage collectors, even though this is not exactly what we are implementing – that name will convey the intent well, and it's short enough not to get in the way).

The GC::add_root<T>(args...) member function will ensure that T is a trivially destructible type, allocate a chunk of sizeof(T) bytes, construct T(args...) at that location, store an abstract pointer (a void*) to that object in roots, and return a T* object to the newly created object. The gcnew<T>() function will allow user code to interface with GC::add_root<T>() in a simplified manner; since we want user code to use gcnew<T>(), we will qualify GC::add_root<T>() as private and make gcnew<T>() a friend of the GC class.

Note that the GC class itself is not a generic class (it's not a template). It exposes template member functions, but structurally only stores raw addresses (void* objects), which makes this class mostly type-agnostic. This all leads to the following code:

```
#include <vector>
#include <memory>
#include <string>
#include <print>
#include <type_traits>
class GC {
    std::vector<void*> roots;
    GC() = default;
    static auto &get() {
        static GC gc;
        return gc;
    }
    template <class T, class ... Args>
      T *add_root(Args &&... args) {
          // there will be no finalization
          static_assert(
              std::is_trivially_destructible_v<T>
          );
          return static_cast<T*>(
```

```
                roots.emplace_back(
                    new T(std::forward<Args>(args)...)
                )
            );
        }
    // provide access privileges to gcnew<T>()
    template <class T, class ... Args>
        friend T* gcnew(Args&&...);
 public:
    ~GC() {
        std::print("~GC with {} objects to deallocate",
                    std::size(roots));
        for(auto p : roots) std::free(p);
    }
    GC(const GC &) = delete;
    GC& operator=(const GC &) = delete;
};
template <class T, class ... Args>
    T *gcnew(Args &&...args) {
        return GC::get().add_root<T>(
            std::forward<Args>(args)...
        );
    }
```

As expected, `GC::~GC()` calls `std::free()` but invokes no destructor, as this implementation reclaims memory but does not finalize objects.

This example shows a way to group memory reclamation as a single block to be executed at the end of a program. In code where there is more available memory than what the program requires, this can lead to a more streamlined program execution, albeit at the cost of a slight slowdown at program termination (of course, if you want to try this, please measure to see whether there are actual benefits for your code base!). It can also help us write analysis tools that examine how memory has been allocated throughout program execution and can be enhanced to collate additional information such as memory block size and alignment: we simply would need to keep pairs – or tuples, depending on the needs – instead of single `void*` objects in the `roots` container to aggregate the desired data.

Of course, not being able to finalize objects allocated through this mechanism can be a severe limitation, as no non-trivially destructible type can benefit from our efforts. Let's see how we could add finalization support to our design.

Reclamation and finalization at the end of the program

Our second implementation will not only free the underlying storage for the objects allocated through our deferred reclamation system but will also finalize them by calling their destructors. To do so, we will need to remember the type of each object that goes through our system. There are, of course, many ways to achieve this, and we will see one of them.

By ensuring the finalization of reclaimed objects, we can get rid of the trivially destructible requirement of our previous implementation. We still will not guarantee the order in which objects are finalized, so it's important that reclaimed objects do not refer to each other during finalization if we are to have sound programs, but that's a constraint many other popular programming languages also share. This implementation will, however, keep the singleton approach and finalize and then deallocate objects and their underlying storage at the end of program execution.

As in the previous section, we will first look at client code. In this case, we will be using (and benefitting from) non-trivially destructible objects and use them to print out information during finalization: this will simplify the task of tracing program execution. Of course, we will also use trivially destructible types (such as `struct X`, local to the `h()` function) as there is no reason not to support these too. Note that, often (but not always), non-trivially destructible types will be RAII types (see *Chapter 4*) whose objects need to free resources before their life ends, but we just want a simple example here so doing anything non-trivial such as printing out some value (which is what we are doing with `NamedThing`) will suffice in demonstrating that we handle non-trivially-destructible types correctly.

We will use nested function calls to highlight the local aspect of construction and allocation, as well as the non-local aspect of object destruction and deallocation since these will happen at program termination time. Our example code will be as follows:

```
// ...
// note: not trivially destructible
struct NamedThing {
    const char *name;
    NamedThing(const char *name) : name{ name } {
        std::print("{} ctor\n", name);
    }
    ~NamedThing() {
        std::print("{} dtor\n", name);
    }
};

void g() {
    [[maybe_unused]] auto p = gcnew<NamedThing>("hi");
    [[maybe_unused]] auto q = gcnew<NamedThing>("there");
}
auto h() {
```

```
    struct X {
        int m() const { return 123; }
    };
    return gcnew<X>();
}
auto f() {
    g();
    return h();
}
int main() {
    std::print("Pre\n");
    std::print("{}\n", f()->m());
    std::print("Post\n");
}
```

When executed, you should expect the following information to be printed on the screen:

```
Pre
hi ctor
there ctor
123
Post
hi dtor
there dtor
```

As can be seen, the constructors happen when invoked in the source code, but the destructors are called at program termination (after the end of main()) as we had announced we would do.

> **On the importance of interfaces**
>
> You might notice that user code essentially did not change between the non-object-finalizing implementation and this one. The beauty here is that our upgrade, or so to say, is completely achieved in the implementation, leaving the interface stable and, as such, the differences transparent to client code. Being able to change the implementation without impacting interfaces is a sign of low coupling and is a noble objective for one to seek to attain.

How did we get from a non-finalizing implementation to a finalizing one? Well, this implementation will also use a singleton named GC where "object roots" will be stored. In this case, however, we will store semantically enhanced objects, not just raw addresses (void* objects) as we did in the previous implementation.

We will achieve this objective through a set of old yet useful tricks:

- Our GC class will not be a generic class, as it would force us to write GC<T> instead of just GC in our code, and find a way to have a distinct GC<T> object for each T type. What we want is for a single GC object to store the required information for all objects that require deferred reclamation, regardless of type.

- In GC, instead of storing objects of the void* type, we will store objects of the GC::GcRoot* type. These objects will not be generic either but will be polymorphic, exposing a destroy() service to destroy (call the destructor, then free the underlying storage) objects.

- There will be classes that derive from GC::GcRoot. We will call such classes GC::GcNode<T> and there will be one for each type T in a program that is involved in our deferred reclamation mechanism. These are where the type-specific code will be "hidden."

- By keeping GC::GcRoot* objects as roots but storing GC::GcNode<T>* in practice, we will be able to deallocate and finalize the T object appropriately.

The code for this implementation follows:

```
#include <vector>
#include <memory>
#include <print>
class GC {
    class GcRoot {
        void *p;
    public:
        auto get() const noexcept { return p; }
        GcRoot(void *p) : p{ p } {
        }
        GcRoot(const GcRoot &) = delete;
        GcRoot& operator=(const GcRoot &) = delete;
        virtual void destroy(void *) const noexcept = 0;
        virtual ~GcRoot() = default;
    };
    // ...
```

As can be seen, GC::GcRoot is an abstraction that trades in raw pointers (objects of the void* type) and contains no type-specific information, per se.

The type-specific information is held in derived classes of the GcNode<T> type:

```
    // ...
    template <class T> class GcNode : public GcRoot {
        void destroy(void* q) const noexcept override {
            delete static_cast<T*>(q);
```

```
        }
    public:
        template <class ... Args>
            GcNode(Args &&... args) :
                GcRoot(new T(std::forward<Args>(args)...)) {
            }
        ~GcNode() {
            destroy(get());
        }
    };
    // ...
```

As we can see, a GcNode<T> object can be constructed with any sequence of arguments suitable for type T, perfectly forwarding them to the constructor of a T object. The actual (raw) pointers are stored in the base class part of the object (the GcRoot but the destructor of a GcNode<T> invokes destroy() on that raw pointer, which casts the void* to the appropriate T* type before invoking operator delete().

Through the GcRoot abstraction, a GC object is kept apart from type-specific details of the objects it needs to reclaim at a later point. This implementation can be seen as a form of **external polymorphism**, where we use a polymorphic hierarchy "underneath the covers" to implement functionality in such a way as to keep client code unaware.

Given what we have written so far, our work is almost done:

- Lifetime management can be delegated to smart pointers, as the finalization code is found in the destructor of GcNode<T> objects. Here, we will be using std::unique_ptr<GcRoot> objects (simple and efficient).

- The add_root() function will create GcNode<T> objects, store them in the roots container as pointers to their base class, GcRoot, and return the T* pointing to the newly constructed object. Thus, it installs lifetime management mechanisms while exposing pointers in ways that look natural to users of operator new().

That part of the code follows:

```
    // ...
    std::vector<std::unique_ptr<GcRoot>> roots;
    GC() = default;
    static auto &get() {
        static GC gc;
        return gc;
    }
    template <class T, class ... Args>
        T *add_root(Args &&... args) {
```

```
            return static_cast<T*>(roots.emplace_back(
                std::make_unique<GcNode<T>>(
                    std::forward<Args>(args)...)
                )->get());
        }
    template <class T, class ... Args>
        friend T* gcnew(Args&&...);
public:
    GC(const GC &) = delete;
    GC& operator=(const GC &) = delete;
};

template <class T, class ... Args>
    T *gcnew(Args &&...args) {
        return GC::get().add_root<T>(
            std::forward<Args>(args)...
        );
    }
// ...
```

So, there we have it: a way to create objects at selected points, and destroy and reclaim them all at program termination, with the corresponding upsides and downsides, of course. These tools are useful, but they are also niche tools that you should use (and customize to your needs) if there is indeed a need to do so.

So far, we have seen deferred reclamation facilities that terminate (and finalize, depending on the tool) at program termination. We still need a mechanism for reclamation at the end of selected scopes.

Reclamation and finalization at the end of the scope

Our third and last implementation for this chapter will ensure reclamation and finalization at the end of the scope, but only on demand. By this, we mean that if a user wants to reclaim unused objects that are subject to deferred reclamation at the end of a scope, it will be possible to do so. Objects subject to deferred reclamation that are still considered in use will not be reclaimed, and objects that are not in use will not be reclaimed if the user code does not ask for it. Of course, at program termination, all remaining objects that are subject to deferred reclamation will be claimed, as we want to avoid leaks.

This implementation will be more subtle than the previous ones, as we will need to consider (a) whether an object is still being referred to at a given point in program execution and (b) whether there is a need to collect objects that are not being referred to at that time.

To get to that point, we will inspire ourselves from `std::shared_ptr`, a type we provided an academic and simplified version of in *Chapter 6*, and will write a `counting_ptr<T>` type that, instead of destroying the pointee when its last client disconnects, will mark it as ready to be reclaimed.

The client code for this example follows. Pay attention to the presence of objects of the `scoped_collect` type in some scopes. These represent requests made by client code to reclaim objects not in use anymore at the end of that scope:

```cpp
// ...
// note: not trivially destructible
struct NamedThing {
    const char *name;
    NamedThing(const char *name) : name{ name } {
        std::cout << name << " ctor" << std::endl;
    }
    ~NamedThing() {
        std::cout << name << " dtor" << std::endl;
    }
};
auto g() {
    auto _ = scoped_collect{};
    [[maybe_unused]] auto p = gcnew<NamedThing>("hi");
    auto q = gcnew<NamedThing>("there");
    return q;
} // a reclamation will occur here
auto h() {
    struct X {
        int m() const { return 123; }
    };
    return gcnew<X>();
}
auto f() {
    auto _ = scoped_collect{};
    auto p = g();
    std::cout << '\"' << p->name << '\"' << std::endl;
} // a reclamation will occur here
int main() {
    using namespace std;
    cout << "Pre" << endl;
    f();
    cout << h()->m() << endl;
    cout << "Post" << endl;
} // a reclamation will occur here (end of program)
```

The end of a scope where a `scoped_collect` object lives will lead to the reclamation of all objects allocated through `gcnew<T>()` that are not referenced anymore at that point; this holds regardless of whether they were allocated in that scope or somewhere else in the program. The intent here is that the end of such as scope is a point where we are willing to "pay" the time and effort required to collect a group of objects. Do not use a `scoped_collect` object in a scope where either speed or deterministic behavior is of the essence!

Executing this code, we end up with the following:

```
Pre
hi ctor
there ctor
hi dtor
"there"
there dtor
123
Post
```

As we can see, objects that are still being referred to remain available, and objects that are not being referred to are collected either when the destructor of a `scoped_collect` object is called, or at program termination if there are still some reclaimable objects in the program at that point.

The `scoped_collect` type itself is very simple, its main role being to interact with the GC global object. It is simply a non-copiable, non-movable RAII object that invokes a reclamation at the end of its lifetime:

```
// ...
struct scoped_collect {
   scoped_collect() = default;
   scoped_collect(const scoped_collect &) = delete;
   scoped_collect(scoped_collect &&) = delete;
   scoped_collect&
      operator=(const scoped_collect &) = delete;
   scoped_collect &operator=(scoped_collect &&) = delete;
   ~scoped_collect() {
      GC::get().collect();
   }
};
// ...
```

How does this whole infrastructure work? Let's take it step by step. We will inspire ourselves from the previous sections of this chapter, where we initially collect all objects at the end of program execution, and then add finalization for these objects. The novelty in this section is that we will add the possibility of collecting objects at various times in program execution and implement the required code to track references to objects.

To track references to objects, we will use objects of the `counting_ptr<T>` type:

```cpp
#include <vector>
#include <memory>
#include <string>
#include <iostream>
#include <atomic>
#include <functional>
#include <utility>
```

As can be seen, we can (and do!) implement this type solely through standard tools. Note that the count data member is a pointer as it might be shared between instances of `counting_ptr<T>`:

```cpp
template <class T>
   class counting_ptr {
      using count_type = std::atomic<int>;
      T *p;
      count_type *count;
      std::function<void()> mark;
   public:
      template <class M>
         constexpr counting_ptr(T *p, M mark) try :
            p{ p }, mark{ mark } {
               count = new count_type{ 1 };
         } catch(...) {
            delete p;
            throw;
         }
      T& operator*() noexcept {
         return *p;
      }
      const T& operator*() const noexcept {
         return *p;
      }
      T* operator->() noexcept {
         return p;
      }
      const T* operator->() const noexcept {
         return p;
      }
      constexpr bool
         operator==(const counting_ptr &other) const {
         return p == other.p;
      }
      // operator!= can be omitted since C++20
```

```cpp
constexpr bool
    operator!=(const counting_ptr &other) const {
    return !(*this == other);
}
// we allow comparing counting_ptr<T> objects
// to objects of type U* or counting_ptr<U> to
// simplify the handling of types in a class
// hierarchy
template <class U>
    constexpr bool
        operator==(const counting_ptr<U> &other) const {
        return p == &*other;
    }
template <class U>
    constexpr bool
        operator!=(const counting_ptr<U> &other) const {
        return !(*this == other);
    }
template <class U>
    constexpr bool operator==(const U *q) const {
        return p == q;
    }
template <class U>
    constexpr bool operator!=(const U *q) const {
        return !(*this == q);
    }
// ...
```

Now that the relational operators are in place, we can implement copy and move semantics for our type:

```cpp
// ...
void swap(counting_ptr &other) {
    using std::swap;
    swap(p, other.p);
    swap(count, other.count);
    swap(mark, other.mark);
}
constexpr operator bool() const noexcept {
    return p != nullptr;
}
counting_ptr(counting_ptr &&other) noexcept
    : p{ std::exchange(other.p, nullptr) },
      count{ std::exchange(other.count, nullptr) },
      mark{ other.mark } {
```

```
        }
    counting_ptr &
        operator=(counting_ptr &&other) noexcept {
        counting_ptr{ std::move(other) }.swap(*this);
        return *this;
    }
    counting_ptr(const counting_ptr &other)
        : p{ other.p }, count{ other.count },
          mark{ other.mark } {
        if (count) ++(*count);
    }
    counting_ptr &operator=(const counting_ptr &other) {
        counting_ptr{ other }.swap(*this);
        return *this;
    }
    ~counting_ptr() {
        if (count) {
            if ((*count)-- == 1) {
                mark();
                delete count;
            }
        }
    }
    };
namespace std {
    template <class T, class M>
        void swap(counting_ptr<T> &a, counting_ptr<T> &b) {
            a.swap(b);
        }
    }
}
// ...
```

Instead of destroying the counter and the pointee like a `shared_ptr<T>` would, `counting_ptr<T>` will delete the counter but "mark" the pointee, making it a candidate for ulterior reclamation.

The general GC, `GC::GcRoot`, and `GC::GcNode<T>` approach from the previous section remains, but is enhanced as follows:

- The `roots` container couples a `unique_ptr<GcRoot>` with a "mark" data member of type `bool`

- The `make_collectable(p)` member function marks the root associated with the `p` pointer as collectable

- The `collect()` member functions reclaim all the roots that are marked as collectable

What this implementation does is (a) associate a Boolean mark (collect or do not collect) with each reclaimable pointer, (b) use `counting_ptr<T>` object with each `T*` to keep track of how each pointee is being used, and (c) collect reclaimable pointees as a group whenever a collection request arrives. The easiest way to request such a collection is to reach the destructor of a `scoped_collect` object.

The code for this somewhat more sophisticated version is as follows:

```cpp
// ...
class GC {
    class GcRoot {
        void *p;
    public:
        auto get() const noexcept { return p; }
        GcRoot(void *p) : p{ p } {
        }
        GcRoot(const GcRoot&) = delete;
        GcRoot& operator=(const GcRoot&) = delete;
        virtual void destroy(void*) const noexcept = 0;
        virtual ~GcRoot() = default;
    };
    template <class T> class GcNode : public GcRoot {
        void destroy(void *q) const noexcept override {
            delete static_cast<T*>(q);
        }
    public:
        template <class ... Args>
            GcNode(Args &&... args)
                : GcRoot(new T(std::forward<Args>(args)...)) {
            }
        ~GcNode() {
            destroy(get());
        }
    };
    std::vector<
        std::pair<std::unique_ptr<GcRoot>, bool>
    > roots;
    GC() = default;
    static auto &get() {
        static GC gc;
        return gc;
    }
}
```

The collection functions in this case would be as follows:

```cpp
void make_collectable(void *p) {
    for (auto &[q, coll] : roots)
        if (static_cast<GcRoot*>(p) == q.get())
            coll = true;
}
void collect() {
    for (auto p = std::begin(roots);
            p != std::end(roots); ) {
        if (auto &[ptr, collectible] = *p; collectible) {
            ptr = nullptr;
            p = roots.erase(p);
        } else {
            ++p;
        }
    }
}
template <class T, class ... Args>
    auto add_root(Args &&... args) {
        auto q = static_cast<T*>(roots.emplace_back(
            std::make_unique<GcNode<T>>(
                std::forward<Args>(args)...
            ), false
        ).first->get());
        // the marking function is implemented as
        // a lambda expression that iterates through
        // the roots, then finds and marks for
        // reclamation pointer q. It is overly
        // simplified (linear search) and you are
        // welcome to do something better!
        return counting_ptr{
            q, [&,q]() {
                for (auto &[p, coll] : roots)
                    if (static_cast<void*>(q) ==
                        p.get()->get()) {
                        coll = true;
                        return;
                    }
            }
        };
    }
```

```
    template <class T, class ... Args>
        friend counting_ptr<T> gcnew(Args&&...);
    friend struct scoped_collect;
public:
    GC(const GC &) = delete;
    GC& operator=(const GC &) = delete;
};
// ...
template <class T, class ... Args>
    counting_ptr<T> gcnew(Args &&... args) {
        return GC::get().add_root<T>(
            std::forward<Args>(args)...
        );
    }
// ...
```

As you can see, dear reader, this last example would benefit from several optimizations, but it works and is meant to be simple enough to understand and improve.

We now know it is possible to reclaim objects in groups in C++, as it is in other popular languages. It might not be idiomatic C++ code, but deferred reclamation can be achieved with reasonable effort, on an opt-in basis. Not bad!

Summary

This chapter took us in the territory of deferred reclamation, a territory that's unfamiliar to many C++ programmers. We saw ways in which we can reclaim objects in groups at specific points in a program, discussed restrictions on what could be done when reclaiming such objects, and examined various techniques to finalize objects before freeing their associated memory storage.

We are now ready to look at how memory management interacts with C++ containers, an important topic that will occupy us in the next three chapters.

Indeed, we could write containers that handle memory explicitly, but in general, that would be counterproductive (for example, if we tied `std::vector<T>` to new and `delete`, how could `std::vector<T>` handle some type T for which allocation and deallocation have to be done through other means?).

There are, of course, quite a few ways to get there. Want to know some of them? Let's take a deep breath and dive in...

Unlock this book's exclusive benefits now

This book comes with additional benefits designed to elevate your learning experience.

Note: Have your purchase invoice ready before you begin.

https://www.packtpub.com/
unlock/9781805129806

Part 4:
Writing Generic Containers
(and a Bit More)

In this part, we will focus on writing efficient generic containers, doing so through explicit memory management, then through implicit memory management, and finally, through allocators, under the various guises these types have held over the years. Leveraging our deeper understanding of memory management techniques and facilities, we will express two types of containers (one that uses contiguous memory and another that uses linked nodes) in ways that can sometimes be much more efficient than a simpler, more naïve implementation would be. We end this part with a look to the near future in memory management with C++.

This part has the following chapters:

- *Chapter 12, Writing Generic Containers with Explicit Memory Management*
- *Chapter 13, Writing Generic Containers with Implicit Memory Management*
- *Chapter 14, Writing Generic Containers with Allocator Support*
- *Chapter 15, Contemporary Issues*

12

Writing Generic Containers with Explicit Memory Management

We have come quite a long way since the beginning of our journey into the wonders of memory management mechanisms and techniques in C++. From *Chapter 4* to *Chapter 7*, we built an interesting toolbox, one on which we can build and from which we can adapt to solve new problems we might face in the future. This toolbox now contains, among other things, the following:

- Techniques through which an object implicitly manages its resources

- Types that behave like pointers but encode responsibility over the pointee in the type system

- Various ways in which we can take over the behavior of memory allocation mechanisms of a program

One (important!) aspect of memory management we have not covered yet is how containers manage memory. This is actually quite an interesting topic, one that we will address through three different angles, in three different chapters.

The first angle is how to handle memory management *explicitly* yet efficiently in a container. This is what the current chapter is about. In some application domains, it is customary to implement (or maintain) one's own containers instead of using those provided by the standard library. There can be various reasons for this: for example, maybe your company has highly specialized needs. Maybe your company has been unsatisfied with standard library containers' performance in the past, perhaps because the implementations were less efficient than they hoped back then, and developed its own alternative containers in response. After years of writing code based on your own containers, moving back to standard library containers might seem too costly.

The second angle, which is somewhat shorter, is how to handle memory *implicitly* yet efficiently in a container, and will be covered in *Chapter 13* of this book, where we will revisit and simplify the implementations seen in the current chapter.

The third angle, which is more complex and subtle, is how to handle memory through an allocator in a container, and will form *Chapter 14* of this book.

In the current chapter, we will write a (naïve) `std::vector<T>` lookalike named `Vector<T>`. We will use that as an opportunity to discuss exception safety (an important issue, especially when writing generic code). Then, we will notice that we have been very inefficient up to that point, in the sense that `std::vector<T>` will be significantly more efficient than our `Vector<T>` alternative, at least for some types. Based on this realization, we will revisit our design with better memory management, seeing important improvements in many aspects, and discuss some important low-level standard facilities for memory management that can (and will) make our lives easier.

We will also write a homemade `std::forward_list<T>` lookalike named `ForwardList<T>`, as there are issues and considerations specific to node-based containers that a vector-like type does not really allow us to discuss. This chapter will write a "vanilla" version of a forward list, and we will revisit it briefly in *Chapter 13*, then in more detail in *Chapter 14*.

This means that after reading this chapter, you will be able to do the following:

- Write a correct and exception-safe container with naïve memory management techniques
- Understand the problems associated with `const` or reference data members
- Use standard-provided low-level memory management algorithms

More generally, you will know why `std::vector<T>` is so fast, and why that type is so difficult to beat at the resource management game. You will also get an idea of the challenges faced by node-based containers such as `std::forward_list<T>`, although later chapters will delve more deeply into this. That does not mean you should not write your own containers (for specific use cases, we can often do better than a general solution), but it does mean that you will know better why (and when) to do so, and how much effort you will need to invest.

Exhaustiveness or representativeness

This book does not in general aim for exhaustive representations or implementations (there are size limits to a physical object such as a book!), and this chapter will be no exception to that rule… far from it! Implementing the full set of member functions provided for two container types inspired by the standard library would require this book to grow immensely – and your standard library implementation covers many more corner cases (and offers many more cool optimizations) than a book such as this one could hope to present. For that reason, we will try to expose a core set of member functions from which you can build instead of trying to write every single one of them.

Technical requirements

You can find the code files for this chapter in the book's GitHub repository here: `https://github.com/PacktPublishing/C-Plus-Plus-Memory-Management/tree/main/chapter12`.

Writing your own vector<T> alternative

Suppose you get up one day and say: "Hey, I'm going to beat `std::vector` at its own game" and confidently start coding. Some words to the wise:

- This seemingly simple task is astonishingly difficult to accomplish: for one thing, `std::vector` is a work of art, and then there's the fact that your favorite standard library writers are spectacularly skilled individuals.

- You might still think you can do it, so it's fine to try, but make sure you test your ideas with both a type of element that is trivially constructible (for example, `int` or `double`) and one that is not (for example, `std::string`) and compare the results. For many, the former will lead to stellar performance, but the latter might bring …sadness.

- The reason for this difference is that a container such as `std::vector` is extremely efficient at… managing memory (I know, reading this in this book must come as quite a shock!). It is much better, in fact, than a homegrown alternative would be, unless you invest significant time and effort and (most probably) have a specific use case in mind, one for which the homegrown version would be optimized more specifically.

Your standard library vendor does invest such time and effort and does so for your very benefit, so it is possible that learning how to use `std::vector` optimally will end up being an avenue that brings better results than trying to write your personal equivalent container. Of course, in the end, which container to use is up to you, and you can often write code for custom situations that outperforms general solutions the way standard containers do.

> **A general note on how we will write our containers**
>
> We will be writing (and using) containers in this chapter and the ones that follow, so a brief explanation is needed if we want to have a common understanding of how we will proceed. For one thing, we will use type aliases in our containers that match those used in standard containers, as this helps toward a more fluid integration in other standard library tools, such as the standard algorithms. Then, we will strive to use the same public names for our member functions as those used in the standard library (for example, we will write `empty()` for the predicate used to test whether a container is empty or not, matching existing practice in the standard library, even though some might argue `is_empty()` would be preferable). Finally, we will adopt a gradual refinement approach: our first versions will be simpler but less efficient than later ones, so be patient, dear reader: we are following our own path to enlightenment!

Representational choices for a container of contiguous elements

Informally, a `std::vector` represents a dynamically allocated array that can grow as needed. As with any array, a `std::vector<T>` is a sequence of elements of type T arranged contiguously in memory. We will name our homemade version `Vector<T>` to make it visibly distinct from `std::vector<T>`.

To get a reasonably performant implementation, the first key idea is to *distinguish size from capacity*. If we do not do so, deciding to make size and capacity the same thing, our `Vector<T>` implementation will always conceptually be full and will need to grow, which means allocating more memory, copying the elements from the old storage to the new storage, getting rid of the old storage, and so on with every insertion of even a single element. To say such an implementation would be painful seems like a severe understatement.

There are two main approaches to the internal representation of a vector-like type. One is to keep track of three pointers:

- One to the beginning of the allocated storage

- One to the end of the elements

- One to the end of the allocated storage (note that we are referring to half-open ranges here, with the beginning included and the end excluded)

A simplified illustration would be as follows:

```
template <class T>
  class Vector {
    T *elems;
    T *end_elems;
    T *end_storage;
    // ...
```

Another is to keep a pointer to the beginning of the allocated storage as well as two integers (for the container's size and capacity, respectively). A simplified illustration in this case would be the following:

```
template <class T>
  class Vector {
    T *elems;
    std:size_t nelems; // number of elements
    std::size_t cap; // capacity
    // ...
```

These are equivalent representations in the sense that they both allow us to write a correct container, but they bring different trade-offs. For example, keeping three pointers makes computing the `end()` iterator fast but makes `size()` and `capacity()` require computing a pointer subtraction, whereas keeping a pointer and two integers makes both `size()` and `capacity()` fast but requires computing the addition of a pointer and an integer to get the `end()` iterator.

As far as size goes, the three-pointer representation makes `sizeof(Vector<T>)` equal to `3*sizeof(void*)`, thus probably 24 bytes on a 64-bit platform with an alignment of 8. The pointer and two integers might be of the same size or might be slightly different depending on the integer types used. For example, choosing 32-bit integers for the size and capacity on a 64-bit machine would lead to a 16-byte representation and an alignment of 8. These details may make a difference on a resource-constrained system, but as you have probably deduced already, the main memory consumption cost of something such as `Vector<T>` comes from the memory allocated for the `T` objects.

Different implementations will make different representational choices due to size considerations, estimates of which member functions will be called more often on average, and so on. We will need to make a choice too; in this book, we will choose the "one pointer and two integers" approach, but keep in mind it's one of a few reasonable options (you can even play with the idea and implement what follows through other representational choices and see where this leads you!).

The implementation of Vector<T>

We will walk through our initial (naïve) `Vector<T>` implementation step by step, building a gradual understanding of how this all works, and what makes us claim that this implementation is indeed naïve. Our initial step has mostly been covered already and consists of defining our abstractions through standard library-conforming type aliases and choosing our internal representation:

```
#include <cstddef>
#include <algorithm>
#include <utility>
#include <initializer_list>
#include <iterator>
#include <type_traits>
template <class T>
    class Vector {
    public:
        using value_type = T;
        using size_type = std::size_t;
        using pointer = T*;
        using const_pointer = const T*;
        using reference = T&;
        using const_reference = const T&;
    private:
        pointer elems{};
        size_type nelems{},
                  cap{};
        // ...
```

You will notice that this implementation makes the choice of using non-`static` data member initializers for the three data members of a `Vector<T>`, initializing them to their default values (integers are 0, the pointer is null), which is suitable in our implementation as it represents an empty container, which seems like a reasonable state for a default `Vector<T>`.

Some simple yet fundamental member functions follow:

```
// ...
public:
    size_type size() const { return nelems; }
    size_type capacity() const { return cap; }
    bool empty() const { return size() == 0; }
private:
    bool full() const { return size() == capacity(); }
// ...
```

💡 **Quick tip**: Enhance your coding experience with the **AI Code Explainer** and **Quick Copy** features. Open this book in the next-gen Packt Reader. Click the **Copy** button (**1**) to quickly copy code into your coding environment, or click the **Explain** button (**2**) to get the AI assistant to explain a block of code to you.

```
                                          Copy    Explain
function calculate(a, b) {                 1        2
  return {sum: a + b};
};
```

📕 **The next-gen Packt Reader** is included for free with the purchase of this book. Unlock it by scanning the QR code below or visiting `https://www.packtpub.com/unlock/9781805129806`.

Pay attention to the implementation of `empty()` and `full()`. Some people will prefer accessing data members (here: using `nelems` and `cap` instead of `size()` and `capacity()`) internally when implementing member functions, but consider reusing your more fundamental member functions to implement the more "synthetic" ones. This will make your code less sensitive to changes in the implementation, and C++ compilers are very good at function inlining, particularly when these functions are non-`virtual`.

At this point, the most useful set of members we could probably design is the iterator types and data members of our class, as this will help us use standard algorithms to cleanly and efficiently implement the rest of our member functions.

Iterators

C++ containers usually expose iterators as part of their interface, and ours will be no exception. We will define type aliases for the const and non-const iterator types, as this makes it simpler to implement alternatives such as bounds-checked iterators if we feel the need to do so, and implement both const and non-const versions of the begin() and end() member functions:

```cpp
// ...
public:
    using iterator = pointer;
    using const_iterator = const_pointer;
    iterator begin() { return elems; }
    const_iterator begin() const { return elems; }
    iterator end() { return begin() + size(); }
    const_iterator end() const {
        return begin() + size();
    }
    // for users' convenience
    const_iterator cend() const { return end(); }
    const_iterator cbegin() const { return begin(); }
    // ...
```

You might complain about the syntactic repetition that comes with writing a const and non-const version for begin() and end(), as these are syntactically similar yet semantically distinct. If you have a C++23 compiler at hand, you can simplify this somewhat through the handy "deduced this" feature:

```cpp
// alternative approach (requires C++23)
template <class S>
    auto begin(this S && self) { return self.elems; }
template <class S>
    auto end(this S && self) {
        return self.begin() + self.size();
    }
```

This is a slightly more complicated way of expressing these functions, but it lets us coalesce both versions of begin() and end() into one by leveraging the type deduction system through forwarding references.

Costructors and other special member functions

We now get to our constructors. The first two we will look at are the default constructor and a parametric constructor that takes as arguments a number of elements and an initial value, such that Vector<char>(3,'a') yields a container with three elements of value 'a'. Note that the default-ed default constructor (yes, I know) in this case is implicitly constexpr as all the non-static member initializers can be resolved in a constexpr context:

```
// ...
Vector() = default;
Vector(size_type n, const_reference init)
    : elems{ new value_type[n] },
      nelems{ n }, cap{ n } {
    try {
        std::fill(begin(), end(), init);
    } catch(...) {
        delete [] elems;
        throw;
    }
}
// ...
```

Pay attention to the exception-handling code in this constructor, as it will come back again and again. We are writing a generic container, so we are using some type T we have no prior knowledge of. When calling std::fill(), which assigns the value of the init argument to each of the T objects in the sequence, we are assigning a T value to a T object, but we do not know whether that assignment operator can throw.

Our responsibility is to elems, a dynamically allocated array of T, so if one of the assignment operators throws, we need to make sure that array is destroyed and deallocated before the Vector<T> constructor fails; otherwise, we will leak the memory and (even worse) the objects we had constructed in that array will not be finalized. The catch(...) block means "catch anything," without really knowing what you caught in this case, and the throw; expression means "re-throw whatever you had caught." Indeed, we do not want to handle the exception in such a case (we do not have sufficient knowledge of the execution context to do so: is this a console application? A graphical application? An embedded system? Something else?); we just want to make sure our failure to construct the Vector<T> object did not leak resources and let user code know exactly why it is that our constructor failed to meet its postconditions (failed to construct a valid object).

The copy constructor will follow a similar pattern, except that instead of filling the sequence with copies of a single value, it copies values from a source sequence (`other`) to a destination sequence (`*this` or `elems` depending on how you see it). The move constructor is, of course, quite different:

```cpp
// ...
Vector(const Vector &other)
   : elems{ new value_type[other.size()] },
     nelems{ other.size() }, cap{ other.size() } {
   try {
      std::copy(other.begin(), other.end(), begin());
   } catch(...) {
      delete [] elems;
      throw;
   }
}
// ...
Vector(Vector &&other) noexcept
   : elems{ std::exchange(other.elems, nullptr) },
     nelems{ std::exchange(other.nelems, 0) },
     cap{ std::exchange(other.cap, 0) } {
}
// ...
```

As you can see, the copy constructor is a costly beast for this type: an allocation for `other.size()` objects (with as many calls to the default constructor of type `T` accompanying this for non-trivially-constructible objects), then `other.size()` assignments, and exception handling thrown in.

The move constructor is simpler: it's a constant-time, `noexcept` function. You don't technically need move operations in most classes (C++ got along fine for years without move operations, after all), but when you can take advantage of them, you probably should do so. The speed improvements can be stupendous, and execution speed becomes more predictable.

On values and salient properties

If you read the copy constructor's code attentively, you might have noticed that `*this` did not copy `other.capacity()`, instead deciding to make `cap` a copy of `other.size()`. That's actually the correct thing to do in such a case: the `size()` of a container is what is called a **salient property** of the object, but `capacity()` is more of an artifact of that object's life, showing traces of how it has grown over time. What we want is that, after copying an object, the original and the copy compare equal with respect to `operator==` and, of course, `capacity()` does not intervene in that function: two arrays are generally considered equal if they have the same number of elements and each of these elements has the same value when compared to its counterpart in the other container. Copying the capacity would work in practice, but it would be wasteful for most use cases.

I added (for convenience) a constructor that accepts an `initializer_list<T>`, argument to allow for initializing a `Vector<T>` object with a sequence of values of type `T`. The destructor should be self-explanatory:

```
// ...
Vector(std::initializer_list<T> src)
    : elems{ new value_type[src.size()] },
      nelems {src.size() }, cap{ src.size() } {
    try {
        std::copy(src.begin(), src.end(), begin());
    } catch(...) {
        delete [] elems;
        throw;
    }
}
// ...
~Vector() {
    delete [] elems;
}
```

Implementing the copy assignment operator from a source object (here: `other`) to a destination object (`*this`) can be complicated if done in an... undisciplined manner, as it involves cleanup code (for the before-assignment contents of `*this`), duplication of the state of the source object, and ensuring we handle both self-assignment and potential exceptions thrown when duplicating the source object's state appropriately.

Luckily, there's a neat trick suggested by Scott Meyers (and re-proposed by countless others!) who noticed that copy assignment can be expressed as a combination of a copy constructor (the locus of object duplication), the destructor (where cleanup happens) and a `swap()` member function: you simply copy the argument into an anonymous object (to make its lifetime minimal), then swap the states of that unnamed temporary with those of `*this`, leading to `*this` becoming a copy of `other`. This programming idiom almost always works, which explains its success!

Move assignment can be expressed along the same lines as copy assignment, but replacing the copy constructor with a move constructor in the implementation of the assignment operator:

```
// ...
void swap(Vector &other) noexcept {
    using std::swap;
    swap(elems, other.elems);
    swap(nelems, other.nelems);
    swap(cap, other.cap);
}
Vector& operator=(const Vector &other) {
```

```
      Vector{ other }.swap(*this);
      return *this;
   }
   Vector& operator=(Vector &&other) {
      Vector{ std::move(other) }.swap(*this);
      return *this;
   }
   // ...
```

Basic services of a vector-like class

We have now implemented the special member functions that handle the internal representation of a Vector<T> object, but there is more to writing a convenient dynamic array type. For example, member functions that let you access the first() element, or the last (back()) element, or that let you access the element at a specific index in the array (using square brackets) are all to be expected:

```
      // ...
      reference operator[](size_type n) {
         return elems[n];
      }
      const_reference operator[](size_type n) const {
         return elems[n];
      }
      // precondition: !empty()
      reference front() { return (*this)[0]; }
      const_reference front() const { return (*this)[0]; }
      reference back() { return (*this)[size() - 1]; }
      const_reference back() const {
         return (*this)[size() - 1];
      }
      // ...
```

As can be expected, calling front() or back() on an empty Vector<T> is undefined behavior (you could make these functions throw if you prefer, but then everyone would pay the price for those few programs that are badly behaved maybe only in so-called **debug mode**?). Again, this set of six member functions can be reduced to only three through C++23's "deduced this" feature:

```
      // alternative approach, (requires C++23)
      // ...
      template <class S>
         decltype(auto) operator[](this S && self,
                                    size_type n) {
            return self.elems[n];
         }
```

```
// precondition: !empty()
template <class S>
   decltype(auto) front(this S &&self) {
      return self[0];
   }
template <class S>
   decltype(auto) back(this S &&self) {
      return self[self.size()-1];
   }
// ...
```

Some will want to add an `at()` member function in both `const` and `non-const` form that behaves like `operator[]` but throws an exception if an attempt to access the underlying array is out of bounds. Feel free to do so if you wish.

Comparing two `Vector<T>` objects for equivalence or lack thereof is a relatively easy matter if we use algorithms since we implemented iterators for our type:

```
// ...
bool operator==(const Vector &other) const {
   return size() == other.size() &&
          std::equal(begin(), end(), other.begin());
}
// can be omitted since C++20 (synthesized by
// the compiler through operator==())
bool operator!=(const Vector &other) const {
   return !(*this == other);
}
// ...
```

Finally, you might say, we reach the point that interests us the most in a book discussing memory management: how to add elements to our container, and how the underlying memory is managed. Without going through every mechanism client code could use to add elements to a `Vector<T>` object, we will at least examine the `push_back()` and `emplace_back()` member functions:

- In this version, there will be two `push_back()` member functions: one that takes `const T&` as argument and one that instead takes a `T&&`. The one that takes a `const T&` argument will copy that argument at the end of the container, and the one that takes a `T&&` will move it at that location.

- The `emplace_back()` member function will take a variadic pack of arguments, then perfectly forward them to the constructor of a `T` object that will be placed at the end of the container.

- A reference to the newly constructed object is returned by `emplace_back()` for convenience, in case user code would like to use it right away. This is not done by `push_back()`, which is called with a fully constructed object to which user code already has access.

In all three functions, we first check whether the container is full, in which case we call `grow()`, a private member function. The `grow()` function needs to allocate more memory than what the container currently holds, something that can, of course, fail. Note that if `grow()` throws, the addition of a new object never occurred and the container remains intact. Note that `grow()` takes into account the possibility of a `capacity()` of value 0, in which case an arbitrary default capacity is chosen.

Once `grow()` has succeeded, we add the new element after the last object in the container's storage. Note that the value is added through assignment, which implies an object to the left side of the assignment operation, meaning that `grow()` not only added storage but initialized it with (most probably) default objects of type T. Thus, we can infer that with this implementation of `Vector<T>`, type T needs to expose a default constructor:

```
    // ...
    void push_back(const_reference val) {
        if(full())
            grow();
        elems[size()] = val;
        ++nelems;
    }
    void push_back(T &&val) {
        if(full())
            grow();
        elems[size()] = std::move(val);
        ++nelems;
    }
    template <class ... Args>
    reference emplace_back(Args &&...args) {
        if (full())
            grow();
        elems[size()] =
            value_type(std::forward<Args>(args)...);
        ++nelems;
        return back();
    }
private:
    void grow() {
        resize(capacity()? capacity() * 2 : 16);
    }
    // ...
```

Note that the insertion code in `push_back()` and `emplace_back()` does, in both cases, the following:

```
elems[size()] = // the object to insert
++nelems;
```

You might be tempted to combine the incrementation of the number of elements and the actual insertion expression into one, as follows:

```
elems[nelems++] = // the object to insert
```

Do *not* do that, however. "Why are you stopping me?" you might ask. Well, this would lead to exception-unsafe code! The reason for this is that the suffix version of `operator++()` has a high (very high!) priority, *much* higher than assignment does. This means that in the combined expression, `nelems++` happens very early on (which might go unnoticed as that expression yields the old value of `nelems`), and assignment follows later, but assignment can throw: we are assigning from an object of some type `T` to another object of that same type, and we do not know whether `T::operator=(const T&)` will throw. Of course, if it does throw, the assignment will not have occurred, and no object will have been added at the end of the containers; but the number of elements will have been incremented, leading to an incoherent `Vector<T>` object.

There's a general trick here: do not modify your object until you know you can do so safely. Try to do the potentially throwing operations first, then do the operations that can mutate your object. You will sleep better, and the risks of object corruption will be alleviated somewhat.

Our `grow()` member function did its work by calling `resize()` and doubling the container's capacity (unless that capacity was 0, in which case it picked a default capacity). How does `resize()` work? With our implementation, it's a matter of allocating enough memory to cover the needs of the new capacity, copying or moving the objects from the old memory block to the new one, then replacing the old memory block with the new one and updating the capacity.

How do we know whether we should move or copy the objects? Well, since moving could destroy the original objects, we only do so if `T::operator=(T&&)` is explicitly `noexcept`. The `std::is_nothrow_move_assignable<T>` trait is our tool of choice to determine whether that is indeed the case (if it is not, then we copy the objects, which is the safe option as it leaves the original objects intact):

```
// ...
public:
    void resize(size_type new_cap) {
        if (new_cap <= capacity()) return;
        auto p = new T[new_cap];
        if constexpr(std::is_nothrow_move_assignable_v<T>){
            std::move(begin(), end(), p);
        } else try {
            std::copy(begin(), end(), p);
```

```
        } catch (...) {
            delete[] p;
            throw;
        }
        delete[] elems;
        elems = p;
        cap = new_cap;
    }
    // ...
```

There we go. It's not exactly trivial code, I agree, but it's not insurmountable either. Remember that this is only our first draft, and that it will be much slower than std::vector<T> for a wide array of types.

One last aspect of this container we should address is how to insert() elements into it and how to erase() elements from it. In industrial-strength containers such as those found in the standard library, there is a wide array of functions to perform these two tasks, so we will limit ourselves to one of each: inserting a sequence of values at a given location in the container and erasing an element at a given location from the container.

Our insert() member function will be a template that takes a pair of source iterators named first and last, as well as a const_iterator named pos representing a location within the Vector<T> object. Making it a template means that we will be able to use pairs of iterators from any container as a source of values to insert, a useful property indeed.

Within the function, we will use a non-const equivalent of pos named pos_, but only because we are writing a simplified and incomplete container where many member functions that would work on const_iterator objects are missing.

To perform the insertion, we will compute remaining, the space we will have available in the container (expressed as a number of objects), and n, which will be the number of objects to insert. If the available space remaining is insufficient, we will allocate more through our resize() member function. Of course, calling resize() will probably lead to pos_ becoming invalid (it pointed into the old block of memory, which will be replaced by another block once resize() has completed its task), so we take care of computing the relative index in the container before resizing, and recomputing the equivalent of pos_ in the new memory block after resizing.

An interesting twist in the insertion process is that we will want to copy (or move, but we will keep things simple here) the objects from pos_ to end() at the location *ending* at end()+n before performing the insertion of n objects at the pos_ location, but that copy has to be made *backward* (from the last to the first) if we are to avoid overwriting some of the objects we are trying to copy along the way. The std::copy_backward() algorithm is expressed this way: the third argument expressed where the destination of the copy stops, not where it begins.

Only then do we copy the sequence determined by `first` and `last` at position `pos_`, update the number of elements in the `Vector<T>` object, and return what the standard requires (an iterator to the first element inserted, or `pos` in the case where `first==last`, meaning that they determine an empty sequence):

```
template <class It>
iterator insert(const_iterator pos, It first, It last) {
    iterator pos_ = const_cast<iterator>(pos);
    // deliberate usage of unsigned integrals
    const std::size_t remaining = capacity() - size();
    const std::size_t n = std::distance(first, last);
    if (remaining < n) {
        auto index = std::distance(begin(), pos_);
        resize(capacity() + n - remaining);
        pos_ = std::next(begin(), index);
    }
    std::copy_backward(pos_, end(), end() + n);
    std::copy(first, last, pos_);
    nelems += n;
    return pos_;
}
```

Our `erase()` member function will take a `const_iterator` argument named `pos` representing the location of the element to erase from the `Vector<T>` object. We again resort to the trick of using a non-`const` iterator named `pos_` within the function. Erasing `end()` is a no-op (as it should); otherwise, we perform a linear copy from `next(pos_)` to `end()` into the location starting at `pos_`, effectively replacing each element from that point on with its immediate successor.

Finally, we replace the last element with some default value, something that might not seem necessary but actually is since the `T` object at the end could have been holding some resource that needed to be freed. For example, in a program where we use a `Vector<Res>` object and where `Res` is an RAII type that releases a resource on destruction, not replacing the object "lying around just past the end" might lead to the associated resource being closed only when the `Vector` object is destroyed, which might occur later, maybe much later, than client code would expect it to be.

We then update the number of elements in the `Vector<T>` object. Once again, this implementation means we are requiring that `T` exposes a default constructor, something that is not fundamentally necessary (and a requirement that we will alleviate later in this chapter):

```
iterator erase(const_iterator pos) {
    iterator pos_ = const_cast<iterator>(pos);
    if (pos_ == end()) return pos_;
    std::copy(std::next(pos_), end(), pos_);
    *std::prev(end()) = {};
```

```
    --nelems;
    return pos_;
}
```

I'm sure you're wondering how we could do better, but we will get back to this very soon. We will look at how to implement a simple node-based container (a homemade `std::forward_list<T>`-like type) in the meantime.

Writing your own forward_list<T> alternative

Writing a node-based container such as `std::list`, `std::unordered_map`, `std:: map`, and so on is an interesting exercise, but in this chapter, the fact that it is interesting will not necessarily "shine" right away. The points of interest for such classes will be more evident in *Chapter 13* and *Chapter 14*, but we will still write a basic, simplified version here to make the side-by-side evolution of our container types clearer in the pages and chapters to come.

A forward list is an exercise in leanness. We want the type to be small and do what it does well. Some forward lists occupy the size of a single pointer in memory (a pointer to the first node in the sequence); in our implementation, we will pay the price for an additional integer (the number of elements) in order to get a constant-time complexity guarantee for the `size()` member function.

Representational choices for a node-based container

In our implementation, `ForwardList<T>` will hold nodes, and each node will hold a pair made of a value (of type `T`) and a pointer to the next node in the sequence. The last node will have a null pointer as the `next` node.

The representation of a `ForwardList<T>` object will thus be a `Node*` and an unsigned integral (for the number of elements in the list). Our implementation will be very simple and will show a small set of member functions. Feel free to enrich it as you want, as long as you limit yourself to functions that can be written efficiently.

The implementation of ForwardList<T>

As we did for `Vector<T>`, we will walk through our initial (naïve) `ForwardList<T>` implementation in steps. Our initial step consists of defining our abstractions through standard library-conforming type aliases and choosing our internal representation, as is usually the case with containers:

```
#include <cstddef>
#include <algorithm>
#include <utility>
#include <iterator>
#include <initializer_list>
```

```
#include <concepts>
template <class T>
class ForwardList {
public:
    using value_type = T;
    using size_type = std::size_t;
    using pointer = T*;
    using const_pointer = const T*;
    using reference = T&;
    using const_reference = const T&;
    // ...
```

As mentioned earlier, a ForwardList<T>::Node object will hold a value and a pointer to the next node in the sequence. Initially, the next node will always be a null pointer; it is the list's responsibility to organize nodes, the nodes themselves being responsible for the ownership of the values stored therein:

```
    // ...
private:
    struct Node {
        value_type value;
        Node *next = nullptr;
        Node(const_reference value) : value { value } {
        }
        Node(value_type &&value)
            : value { std::move(value) } {
        }
    };
    Node *head {};
    size_type nelems {};
    // ...
```

The default state of a ForwardList<T> object will be equivalent to that of an empty list (a null pointer for head and no elements). That's a reasonable default for most containers as an empty container is usually what users expect in practice when asking for a default constructor.

The size() and empty() member functions are both trivial to write. I expressed empty() in terms of a null head rather than as a zero size() since in some (reasonable) forward list implementations, the size would be computed, not stored, which would make size() a linear complexity operation instead of a constant-time one. In practice, exposing a constant-time size() member function is a good idea as it matches most users' expectations:

```
    // ...
public:
    size_type size() const { return nelems; }
```

```
bool empty() const { return !head; }
// ...
```

Iterators on a linked list cannot be raw pointers, as the elements it stores are not contiguous in memory. We need a class whose instances can iterate over elements of the list, and that can take into account the const-ness of the elements (or lack thereof).

Our (private) `ForwardList<T>::Iterator` class will be a template on some type, U, where (in practice) U will be T for `ForwardList<T>::iterator` and const T for `ForwardList<T>::const_iterator`.

Standard iterators in C++ are expected to provide five aliases:

- `value_type`: The type of the pointed-to value.

- `reference`: The type that represents a reference to a pointed-to value.

- `pointer`: The type that represents a pointer to a pointed-to value.

- `difference_type`: The type that represents the distance between two iterators of this type (a signed integral).

- `iterator_category`: There are six categories as of C++20, and they guide the code generation by describing what an iterator can do. In our case, since we will provide ++ but not - -, we will describe our iterators as being part of `forward_iterator_category`.

An iterator is an object that describes how we can traverse a sequence of values, and `ForwardList<T>::Iterator` is no exception. The key operations exposed by an iterator are probably `operator++()` (advance one position in the sequence), `operator!=()` (compare two iterators to know whether we have attained the end of a sequence), as well as `operator*()` and `operator->()` (accessing the pointed-to element or its services). Note that we make `ForwardList<T>` our friend as that class will be responsible for the organization of nodes, which is easier done when you have full access privileges to private data members such as `cur`:

```
    // ...
private:
    template <class U> class Iterator {
    public:
      using value_type =
          typename ForwardList<T>::value_type;
      using pointer = typename ForwardList<T>::pointer;
      using reference = typename ForwardList<T>::reference;
      using difference_type = std::ptrdiff_t;
      using iterator_category =
          std::forward_iterator_tag;
      friend class ForwardList<T>;
    private:
```

```
            Node *cur {};
        public:
            Iterator() = default;
            Iterator(Node *p) : cur { p } {
            }
            Iterator& operator++() {
                cur = cur->next;
                return *this;
            }
            Iterator operator++(int) {
                auto temp = *this;
                operator++();
                return temp;
            }
            bool operator==(const Iterator &other) const {
                return cur == other.cur;
            }
            // not needed since C++20
            bool operator!=(const Iterator &other) const {
                return !(*this == other);
            }
            U& operator*() { return cur->value; }
            const U& operator*() const { return cur->value; }
            U* operator->() { return cur->value; }
            const U* operator->() const { return cur->value; }
        };
    public:
        using iterator = Iterator<T>;
        using const_iterator = Iterator<const T>;
        // ...
```

The preceding proposed implementation uses a template based on the type, U, of the elements that an Iterator<U> can traverse. We used U instead of T as T is the type of the values in a ForwardList<T> object. In ForwardList<T>, we then make aliases for types Iterator<T> and Iterator<const T> through iterator and const_iterator, respectively. We could also have written two distinct types had we preferred that approach, but a template seemed less verbose.

The begin() and end() set of member functions are essentially trivial; begin() yields an iterator to the head of the list, and the conceptual just-after-the-end node returned by end() is a null pointer, which is what the default constructor of our Iterator<U> gives us:

```
    // ...
    iterator begin() { return { head }; }
    const_iterator begin() const { return { head }; }
```

```
const_iterator cbegin() const { return begin(); }
iterator end() { return {}; }
const_iterator end() const { return {}; }
const_iterator cend() const { return end(); }
// ...
```

We will sometimes need to clear() a ForwardList<T> object, which will lead us to destroy that container's content. In this implementation, for simplicity, I made the destructor call the clear() member function, but we could have spared a tiny bit of processing time (the reinitialization of nelems, not needed in the destructor) by writing the destructor separately:

```
// ...
void clear() noexcept {
    for(auto p = head; p; ) {
        auto q = p->next;
        delete p;
        p = q;
    }
    nelems = 0;
}
~ForwardList() {
    clear();
}
// ...
```

One thing that might seem tempting would be to write a Node destructor that applies delete to its next data member; if we did so, clear() would simply be delete head; (which would call delete head->next and continue from that point on, recursively) followed by nelems=0;. However, I would not do that if I were you: on principle, the ForwardList<T> object should organize the nodes in a ForwardList<T>, and this responsibility should not be given to the numerous Node objects themselves. Then, there is a small technical problem: calling delete head; would call delete head->next;, which would then technically call delete on head-> next-> next; and so on. This leads to a very concrete risk of stack overflow if the list is long enough, something that a loop would avoid altogether.

There is a simple lesson here: life is easier when each class has a single responsibility. This is something that's been known for a while as the "single responsibility principle". That principle is the 'S' in the well-known SOLID principles of object-oriented programming. Let the container deal with the organization of nodes in a node-based container and let the nodes store values.

As far as constructors go, we will implement a small set for this class:

- A default constructor that models an empty list

- A constructor that accepts a std::initializer_list<T> as argument

- A copy constructor that duplicates each node from the source list in order

- A move constructor

- A sequence constructor that accepts two objects of some type, It, that satisfies the std::input_ iterator concept (essentially: that lets you make at least a single pass through the sequence and consume the elements, which is all we need to do the job)

It happens that this last constructor can be seen as a generalization of some of the others, and that only the default constructor and the move constructor really benefit from being written separately (we could technically compute the size of the sequence more efficiently if we did not delegate the work to a general constructor, so if this makes a difference in your code base, feel free to do so):

```
// ...
ForwardList() = default;
template <std::input_iterator It>
    ForwardList(It b, It e) {
        if(b == e) return;
        try {
            head = new Node{ *b };
            auto q = head;
            ++nelems;
            for(++b; b != e; ++b) {
                q->next = new Node{ *b };
                q = q->next;
                ++nelems;
            }
        } catch (...) {
            clear();
            throw;
        }
    }
ForwardList(const ForwardList& other)
    : ForwardList(other.begin(), other.end()) {
}
ForwardList(std::initializer_list<T> other)
    : ForwardList(other.begin(), other.end()) {
}
ForwardList(ForwardList&& other) noexcept
    : head{ std::exchange(other.head, nullptr) },
      nelems{ std::exchange(other.nelems, 0) } {
}
// ...
```

Unsurprisingly, assignment can be expressed through the safe assignment idiom that we applied in the case of type `Vector<T>` earlier:

```
// ...
void swap(ForwardList& other) noexcept {
   using std::swap;
   swap(head, other.head);
   swap(nelems, other.nelems);
}
ForwardList& operator=(const ForwardList& other) {
   ForwardList{ other }.swap(*this);
   return *this;
}
ForwardList& operator=(ForwardList&& other) {
   ForwardList{ std::move(other) }.swap(*this);
   return *this;
}
// ...
```

Some of the remaining operations can reasonably be said to be trivial, for example, `front()`, `operator==()`, and `push_front()`. As you could reasonably assume for a forward list, we will implement neither a `back()` nor a `push_back()` member function as there would not be an efficient way to do so with our representational choices (the only reasonable algorithm would require looping through the whole construct in order to find the last node, leading to a linear complexity algorithm):

```
// ...
// precondition: !empty()
reference front() { return head->value; }
const_reference front() const { return head->value; }
bool operator==(const ForwardList &other) const {
   return size() == other.size() &&
          std::equal(begin(), end(), other.begin());
}
// can be omitted since C++20
bool operator!=(const ForwardList &other) const {
   return !(*this == other);
}
void push_front(const_reference val) {
   auto p = new Node{ val };
   p->next = head;
   head = p;
   ++nelems;
}
void push_front(T&& val) {
```

```
        auto p = new Node{ std::move(val) };
        p->next = head;
        head = p;
        ++nelems;
    }
    // ...
```

As an example of value insertion into a container, consider the following `insert_after()` member function, which inserts a node with a value of `value` after the node pointed to by `pos`. With this function, we could easily build more complex ones, such as one that inserts a sequence of values after some position in the list (try it!):

```
    // ...
    iterator insert_after
        (iterator pos, const_reference value) {
        auto p = new Node{ value };
        p->next = pos.cur->next;
        pos.cur->next = p;
        ++nelems;
        return { p };
    }
    // ...
```

Offering the possibility of adding elements to a container is a useful feature indeed, and so is offering the option of removing an element from a container. As an example, see the following `erase_after()` member function implementation:

```
    // ...
    iterator erase_after(iterator pos) {
        if (pos == end() || std::next(pos) == end())
            return end();
        auto p = pos.cur->next->next;
        delete pos.cur->next;
        pos.cur->next = p;
        return { p->next };
    }
};
```

That should do the job for this class. For the rest of this chapter, there will be little room for improvement for `ForwardList<T>`, but we will return to this class in *Chapter 13*, and more so in *Chapter 14*.

For `Vector<T>`, however, we can do significantly better than we have so far... at the cost of some added complexity. But we are ready for this, are we not?

Better memory management

So, this humble writer claims our nice but simple Vector<T> type is no match for std::vector<T>. That may seem like a bold claim: after all, we seemed to do what was needed and, no less, we used algorithms instead of raw loops; we caught exceptions as we wanted to be exception-safe but limited ourselves to cleaning up the resources… What are we doing wrong?

If you run comparative benchmarks between a Vector<int> object and a std::vector<int> object, in fact, you will probably not notice much of a difference in the respective numbers of both tests. For example, try adding a million int objects (through push_back()) to each of these containers and you will think our container holds its own quite well. Cool! Now, change that to a comparative test between Vector<std::string> and std::vector<std::string> and you might be saddened a bit, seeing that we're "left behind in the dust," as they say.

> **A word about the small object optimization**
>
> This will show more if you add strings that are not too short (try at least 25 characters, say) as with "short" strings (for some indeterminate value of "short") most standard libraries will perform what is called the **Small String Optimization (SSO)**, a special case of the **Small Object Optimization (SOO)**. Through this optimization, when the data to store in an object is small enough, the implementation will use the storage for the so-called "control block" (the data members, really) of the object as raw storage, avoiding dynamic memory allocation altogether. Because of this, "small" strings do not allocate and are very, very fast in practice.

But why?

There is a clue in the type of element in both tests: int is a trivially constructible type, and std::string is not. This clue is an indication that std::vector might be calling fewer constructors than we are, essentially being more efficient than Vector<T> in the way it handles memory and the objects therein.

What's the problem? Well, let's look at one of the constructors of Vector<T> to get an appreciation of the problem with our implementation. Any constructor but the default constructor (defaulted in our implementation) and the move constructor would do, so let's take the one that accepts a number of elements and an initial value as arguments. Pay special attention to the highlighted code:

```
// ...
Vector(size_type n, const_reference init)
    : elems{ new value_type[n] }, nelems{ n }, cap{ n } {
    try {
        std::fill(begin(), end(), init);
    } catch(...) {
        delete [] elems;
        throw;
    }
}
// ...
```

The construction of the `elems` data member allocates a block of memory big enough to hold n objects of type T and calls the default constructor for each of these n elements. Obviously, if T is trivially constructible, then these default constructors are not a big source of worries, but you could question the virtue of so doing if T is not trivially constructible.

Still, you might want to argue that the objects need to be constructed, but then look ahead and you will notice that `std::fill()` replaces each of these default T objects with a copy of `init`, showing that the initial default construction of the objects was essentially a waste of time (we never used these objects!). This is the sort of thing that `std::vector<T>` does so much better than we do: it avoids wasteful operations, restricting itself to what is necessary.

We will now try to see how we could get closer in performance to what `std::vector<T>` achieves in practice.

A more efficient Vector<T>

The key to a more efficient `Vector<T>` is distinguishing allocation from construction, something we have discussed many times in this book, and, well, lying to the type system in adequate ways and in a controlled environment. Yes, those "evil" early chapters of this book will come in handy now.

We will not rewrite the entirety of `Vector<T>` in these pages, but we will look at selected member functions to highlight what needs to be done (a full implementation is available in the GitHub repository mentioned at the beginning of this chapter).

We could try to do this effort manually, using the language facilities we already know about, such as `std::malloc()`, to allocate a raw memory block and placement `new` to construct the objects in that block. Taking the same constructor that takes a number of elements and an initial value as arguments, we would then get the following:

```cpp
// ...
Vector(size_type n, const_reference init)
    // A
    : elems{ static_cast<pointer>(
        std::malloc(n * sizeof(value_type)
    ) }, nelems{ n }, cap{ n } {
    // B
    auto p = begin(); // note: we know p is a T*
    try {
    // C
        for(; p != end(); ++p)
            new(static_cast<void*>(p)) value_type{ init };
    } catch(...) {
    // D
        for(auto q = begin(); q != p; ++q)
            q->~value_type();
```

```
        std::free(elems);
        throw;
    }
  }
  // ...
```

Now that's... unpleasant. Pay attention to the sections marked with are **A** to **D** in this function:

- In **A**, we face our first lie as we allocate storage that can hold n objects of type T but limit ourselves to raw memory allocation (the constructor of no T object is being called at this point), yet we keep a T* to that block of memory for our own purposes. Our implementation needs to be aware, internally, that the type of the elems pointer is incorrect at this stage.

- In **B**, we call begin() knowing that iterator is the same thing as T* in our implementation. If our implementation used a class instead of a raw pointer to model an iterator, we would have to do some work here to get the underlying pointer to the raw storage in order to implement the rest of the function.

- In **C**, we construct the T objects in place within the block of memory we allocated. Since there are no objects there to replace, we construct these objects with the placement new, and use the fact that we lied to the type system (in the sense that we used a T* even though we allocated raw memory) to do the pointer arithmetic required to move from one object to another.

- In **D**, we handle potential exceptions thrown by the constructors of the T objects. Since we are the only ones who know that there are T objects therein, just as we are the only ones who know exactly where the first object that we failed to construct is, we need to destroy the objects manually, then free the (now raw) memory block and re-throw the exception. As a bonus, this implementation is not even standards-compliant; we should destroy the objects in reverse order of construction, something this example does not do.

By the way, this example shows a clear example of the reasons why you cannot throw from a destructor: if an exception is thrown during **D**, we cannot reasonably hope to recover (at least not without incurring prohibitive costs).

You, dear reader, are probably thinking right now that this is unreasonably complicated and way too error-prone for non-specialists to hope to be able to write a whole container that way. Indeed, this sort of complexity would creep into a significant number of member functions, making quality control much more difficult than you would hope.

But wait, there is hope! As you might imagine, your library vendors face the same challenges we do (and more!), so the standard library provides low-level facilities that make handling raw memory in homemade containers a reasonably achievable task as long as you know, well, what you have read in this book so far.

Using low-level standard facilities

The `<memory>` standard library header is a treasure trove of useful facilities for those who dabble in memory management. We have already discussed the standard smart pointers defined in that header (see *Chapter 5* for a reminder), but if you look a bit deeper, you will see some algorithms made to operate on raw memory.

Keeping as an example the `Vector<T>` constructor that takes a number of elements and an initial value as argument, we went from something rather simple that allocates an array of T objects and replaces them through a call to `std::fill()` to something significantly more complicated. The original version was both simple and inefficient (we constructed unneeded objects just to replace them); the replacement was much more efficient (doing minimal work) but required much more skill to write and maintain.

We will now examine the impact of these facilities on the implementation of our allocating member functions. The first such functions we will pay attention to are the constructors, as they make a nice starting point.

Impact on constructors

In practice, when you want to write a homemade container that manages memory explicitly, it's better to use the low-level facilities found in `<memory>`. Take the following example:

```
// ...
Vector(size_type n, const_reference init)
   : elems{ static_cast<pointer>(
       std:malloc(n * sizeof(value_type))
   ) }, nelems{ n }, cap{ n } {
   try {
      std::uninitialized_fill(begin(), end(), init);
   } catch(...) {
      std::free(elems);
      throw;
   }
}
// ...
```

This is much nicer than the version we entirely wrote ourselves, is it not? The two highlights of this version are as follows:

- We allocate a properly sized block of raw memory instead of an array of T objects, thus avoiding all of the unneeded default constructors the initial version had.

- We replaced the call to `std::fill()` (found in `<algorithm>`), which uses `T::operator=(const T&)` and thus supposes an existing object to the left side of the assignment with a call to `std::uninitialized_fill()`, which instead supposes that it is iterating through raw memory and initializes the objects through the placement new.

The beauty of this algorithm (and others of this family) is that it is exception-safe. If one of the constructors invoked by `std::uninitialized_fill()` ends up throwing, then the objects it had managed to create before the exception occurred will be destroyed (in reverse order of construction, as they should) before the exception leaves the function.

It's what we had written (clumsily) by hand, really. Apart from the fact that we now allocate and free raw memory, the rest of the code is very similar to the original, simple version. This probably makes you feel much better… and it should.

A similar approach can be taken with other constructors. Take, for example, the copy constructor:

```
// ...
Vector(const Vector& other)
   : elems{ static_cast<pointer>(
        std::malloc(n * sizeof(value_type))
     ) },
     nelems{ other.size() }, cap{ other.size() } {
   try {
     std::uninitialized_copy(
        other.begin(), other.end(), begin()
     );
   } catch (...) {
     std::free(elems);
     throw;
   }
}
// ...
```

As you can see, with the proper algorithms, the fast implementations that work on raw memory are very similar to the naïve and slower versions.

The key point here is to understand the boundaries of the API. A function such as `std::uninitialized_copy()` takes three arguments: the beginning and end of a source sequence (this sequence is presumed to contain objects) and the beginning of the destination sequence (this sequence is presumed to be appropriately aligned and made of raw memory, not objects). If the function concludes its execution because it met its postconditions and constructed the objects in the destination sequence, then that destination sequence contains objects. On the other hand, if the function fails to meet its postconditions, then there are no objects in the destination sequence as whatever the function has constructed, it will also have destructed.

Similar maneuvers can be done with other constructors, keeping in mind that the default constructor and the move constructor are implemented very differently and as such deserve a different treatment.

Impact on the destructor

The destructor in this implementation of `Vector<T>` is interesting: when the object reaches the end of its lifetime, we cannot simply call `delete[]` on the `elems` data member as it has not been allocated by `new[]` in the first place and it is made of a sequence of T objects, potentially followed by a sequence of raw bytes. We would not want to call `T::~T()` on an arbitrary sequence of bytes since this could cause quite a lot of damage in our program and incur **UB**.

The only entity that knows how many objects there are in the container is the `Vector<T>` object itself, which means that it will need to `destroy()` the remaining objects, and only then `free()` the (now devoid of objects) memory block that remains. Applying the `std::destroy()` algorithm on a sequence of T objects calls `T::~T()` on each of them, turning a sequence of objects into raw memory:

```
// ...
~Vector() {
   std::destroy(begin(), end());
   std::free(elems);
}
// ...
```

These low-level memory management algorithms really help in clarifying the intent of the code we write, as you can see.

Impact on per-element insertion functions

A similar situation happens in member functions `push_back()` and `emplace_back()` where we used to replace through an assignment some existing object at the end of our array; we now need to construct an object at the end of the array since there is no object there anymore (we do not construct objects needlessly; that's the point of our efforts!).

We could use placement `new` to do this, obviously, but the standard library offers a moral equivalent named `std::construct_at()`. This makes our intent even clearer from the source code:

```
// ...
void push_back(const_reference val) {
   if (full())
      grow();
   std::construct_at(end(), val);
   ++nelems;
}
void push_back(T&& val) {
   if (full())
```

```
        grow();
    std::construct_at(end(), std::move(val));
    ++nelems;
    }
    template <class ... Args>
        reference emplace_back(Args &&...args) {
            if (full())
                grow();
            std::construct_at(
                end(), std::forward<Args>(args)...
            );
            ++nelems;
            return back();
        }
```

Impact on growth functions

The grow() function we had implemented initially called resize() on our Vector<T>, but resize() is meant to initialize the storage with objects. To make the allocated storage grow in size without initializing it with objects, we need a different member function, namely reserve().

> **On the differences between resize() and reserve()**
>
> Expressed simply, resize() potentially adds objects to the container, and as such it can modify both size() and capacity(). On the other hand, reserve() adds no object to the container, limiting itself to potentially increasing the storage space being used by the container; in other words, reserve() can change capacity() but will not change size().

Following the example set by std::vector<T>, our Vector<T> class will offer both resize() and reserve(). A version of resize() adapted to the new reality of our part-objects, part-raw-memory container follows, accompanied by an implementation of reserve() that suits Vector<T>. We will discuss reserve() and resize() separately:

```
    // ...
private:
    void grow() {
        reserve(capacity()? capacity() * 2 : 16);
    }
public:
    void reserve(size_type new_cap) {
        if(new_cap <= capacity()) return;
        auto p = static_cast<pointer>(
            std::malloc(new_cap * sizeof(T))
        );
```

```
        if constexpr(std::is_nothrow_move_assignable_v<T>) {
           std::uninitialized_move(begin(), end(), p);
        } else try {
           std::uninitialized_copy(begin(), end(), p);
        } catch (...) {
           std::free(p);
           throw;
        }
        std::destroy(begin(), end());
        std::free(elems);
        elems = p;
        cap = new_cap;
     }
     // ...
```

The `reserve()` member function first ensures that the requested new capacity is higher than the existing one (otherwise there's nothing to do). If that is so, it allocates a new memory block and either moves or copies the existing elements of the `Vector<T>` object into that new memory (a copy will be made if moving T objects can throw: it pays to make move operations `noexcept`, dear readers!) using algorithms that construct objects into raw memory.

The T objects left in `elems` are then destroyed (even if they have been moved-from: they still need to be finalized), and we ensure that `cap` is updated and `elems` points to the new block of storage. Of course, `size()` does not change as no new object has been added to the container.

The procedure is similar for `resize()` (as follows), except that the locations in the memory block starting at the `size()` index are initialized with a default T instead of being left in their raw memory state. Consequently, `size()` is updated, leading to different semantics from those obtained following a call to `reserve()`:

```
     // ...
     void resize(size_type new_cap) {
        if(new_cap <= capacity()) return;
        auto p = static_cast<pointer>(
           std::malloc(new_cap * sizeof(T))
        );
        if constexpr(std::is_nothrow_move_assignable_v<T>) {
           std::uninitialized_move(begin(), end(), p);
        } else try {
           std::uninitialized_copy(begin(), end(), p);
        } catch (...) {
           std::free(p);
           throw;
        }
```

```
    std::uninitialized_fill(
        p + size(), p + capacity(), value_type{}
    );
    std::destroy(begin(), end());
    std::free(elems);
    elems = p;
    nelems = new_cap;
    cap = new_cap;
}
// ...
```

This more sophisticated structure we are implementing will obviously have an impact on the way we insert() or erase() elements.

Impact on element insertion and erasure functions

As expected, member functions such as insert() and erase() have to be updated to take into account the changes we have made to the internal organization of Vector<T> objects. That does not have to be painful (and, indeed, required changes, if any, can be tiny) as long as the semantics of every function are clear from the onset, but it does require care.

For example, using insert(pos,first,last) as an example, we are moving from the simple model described in *Figure 12.1*:

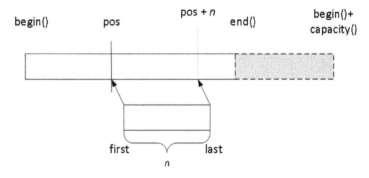

Figure 12.1 – Example of the naïve Vector<T> insertion model

Here, inserting a [first,last) sequence at position pos means copying (in reverse order) the elements in [pos,end()) at position pos + n, then overwriting the elements of [pos,pos+n) with [first,last) to the more complex model described in *Figure 12.2*:

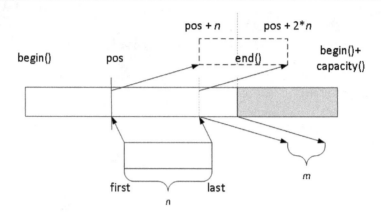

Figure 12.2 – Example of the current Vector<T> insertion model

The idea is that we need to insert [first,last) at position pos, which means that the elements in [pos,pos+n) have to be copied (or moved) to the right. This will require constructing some objects in raw memory (the gray area in the preceding figure) and replacing some other objects through copy (or move) assignment.

There are four steps to consider here:

- How many elements should be copied or moved from the [begin(),end()) sequence to the raw memory block at the end of the container, and where in that block should the resulting objects be constructed.

- If there are elements from the [first,last) sequence to insert in raw memory (there could be none), how many should there be? If there are any such objects, they will be inserted at end().

- If there are elements to copy or move from the [pos,end()) sequence to copy or move as a replacement to existing objects in the container (there could be none), how many should there be? The end of the destination range will be end() in this case.

- Finally, whatever remains to be inserted from the [first,last) sequence will be copied in the container starting at pos.

A possible implementation would be the following:

```
// ...
template <class It>
iterator insert(const_iterator pos, It first, It last) {
    iterator pos_ = const_cast<iterator>(pos);
    const auto remaining = capacity() - size();
    const auto n = std::distance(first, last);
    // we use cmp_less() here as remaining is an unsigned
    // integral but n is a signed integral
```

```cpp
if (std::cmp_less(remaining, n)) {
   auto index = std::distance(begin(), pos_);
   reserve(capacity() + n - remaining);
   pos_ = std::next(begin(), index);
}
// objects to displace (move or copy) from the
// [begin(),end()) sequence into raw memory
const auto nb_to_uninit_displace =
   std::min<std::ptrdiff_t>(n, end() - pos_);
auto where_to_uninit_displace =
   end() + n - nb_to_uninit_displace;
if constexpr(std::is_nothrow_move_constructible_v<T>)
   std::uninitialized_move(
      end() - nb_to_uninit_displace, end(),
      where_to_uninit_displace
   );
else
   std::uninitialized_copy(
      end() - nb_to_uninit_displace, end(),
      where_to_uninit_displace
   );
// objects from [first,last) to insert into raw
// memory (note: there might be none)
const auto nb_to_uninit_insert =
   std::max<std::ptrdiff_t>(
      0, n - nb_to_uninit_displace
   );
auto where_to_uninit_insert = end();
std::uninitialized_copy(
   last - nb_to_uninit_insert, last,
   where_to_uninit_insert
);
// objects to displace (copy or move) from the
// [pos,end()) sequence into that space (note:
// there might be none)
const auto nb_to_backward_displace =
   std::max<std::ptrdiff_t>(
      0, end() - pos_ - nb_to_uninit_displace
   );
 // note : end of destination
auto where_to_backward_displace = end();
if constexpr (std::is_nothrow_move_assignable_v<T>)
   std::move_backward(
```

```
            pos_, pos_ + nb_to_backward_displace,
            where_to_backward_displace
        );
    else
        std::copy_backward(
            pos_, pos_ + nb_to_backward_displace,
            where_to_backward_displace
        );
    // objects to copy from [first,last) to pos
    std::copy(
        first, first + n - nb_to_uninit_insert, pos
    );
    nelems += n;
    return pos_;
}
```

Make sure you do not move the elements in [first,last), however: that would be user-hostile as it would potentially destroy the data in the source range!

As for the erase() member function that we had written in a more naïve manner initially, the key adjustment we will need to make is in the way we handle the removed element: you might remember that in our naïve version, we assigned a default T to the erased element at the end of the container, and complained that this added the suspicious requirement of a default constructor in type T. In this version, we will quite simply destroy this object, ending its lifetime and turning its underlying storage back into raw memory:

```
iterator erase(const_iterator pos) {
    iterator pos_ = const_cast<iterator>(pos);
    if (pos_ == end()) return pos_;
    std::copy(std::next(pos_), end(), pos_);
    std::destroy_at(std::prev(end()));
    --nelems;
    return pos_;
}
```

Hopefully, this gives you, dear reader, a better idea of what it takes to write a more serious implementation of a homemade std::vector-like type and a better appreciation for the craftsmanship of the individuals behind your favorite standard library provider. Know that they do all this and more for your programs to be the wonderfully efficient things they are!

Const or reference members and std::launder()

Before we conclude this chapter, we need to say a few words on those oddities that are containers that hold objects of const types, as well as on containers whose elements are of a type with const or reference members.

Consider this seemingly innocuous program:

```
// ...
int main() {
    Vector<const int> v;
    for(int n : { 2, 3, 5, 7, 11 })
        v.push_back(n);
}
```

With the implementation we have, this will refuse to compile as our implementation calls a number of low-level functions (std::free(), std::destroy_at(), std::construct_at(), and so on) that take a pointer to a non-const type as an argument.

If we are to support such a program, it means we will have to "cast away" const-ness in some places in our implementation. For example, replacing the following line

```
std::free(elems); // illegal if elems points to const
```

with this:

```
using type = std::remove_const_t<value_type>*;
std::free(const_cast<type>(elems));
```

Likewise, if your container is to support insertion where there are already existing objects, assignment such as what will be done with the std::copy() or std::copy_backward() algorithms will not work on const objects or objects with const data members. You can make it work by replacing assignment with destruction followed by construction, but your code will be less exception-safe if the construction fails just after the destruction of the object that had to be replaced.

Of course, casting away const-ness leads us into tricky territory as we are bordering the frightening lands of undefined behavior. Standard library implementors can, of course, do what they want, having the ears of the compiler implementors, but we mere mortals do not share this privilege and, for that reason, must tread carefully.

A similar situation arises with composite objects that have data members of some reference type: you cannot make a container of references as references are not objects, but you sure can make a container of objects with reference-type data members. The problem, of course, is making sense of what happens when an object with a reference data member is being replaced.

Let's take a simpler example than `Vector<T>` to explain this situation. Suppose we have the following class, made to hold a reference to some object of type T:

```
#include <type_traits>
template <class T>
struct X {
    static_assert(std::is_trivially_destructible_v<T>);
    T &r;
public:
    X(T &r) : r{ r } {
    }
    T& value() { return r; }
    const T & value() const { return r; }
};
// ...
```

As is, this class is simple enough and seems easy to reason about. Now, suppose we have the following client code:

```
// ...
#include <iostream>
#include <new>
int main() {
    int n = 3;
    X<int> h{ n };
    h.value()++;
    std::cout << n << '\n'; // 4
    std::cout << h.value() << '\n'; // 4
    int m = -3;
    // h = X<int>{ m }; // nope
    X<int> *p = new (static_cast<void*>(&h)) X<int>{ m };
    std::cout << p->value() << '\n'; // -3
    // UB (-3? 4? something else?)
    std::cout << h.value() << '\n';
    std::cout << std::launder(&h)->value() << '\n'; // -3
}
```

Replacing an X<int> object through assignment is incorrect as having a reference data member deletes your assignment operator, at least by default (the default meaning would be ambiguous: should the reference be rebound to something else, or should the referred-to object be assigned to?).

One way to get around this problem is to destroy the original object and construct a new object in its place. In our example, since we ensured (through `static_assert`) that T was trivially destructible, we just constructed a new object where the previous one stood (ending the previous object's lifetime). The bits are then all mapped properly to the new object... except that the compiler might not follow our reasoning.

In practice, compilers track the lifetime of objects the best they can, but we placed ourselves in a situation where the original X<int> object has never been explicitly destroyed. For that reason, this original X<int> object could still be considered to be there by the compiler, but the bits of the original object have been replaced by the new object placed at that specific address through very manual means. There might be a discrepancy between what the bits say and what the compiler understands from the source code, because (to be honest) we have been playing dirty tricks with the explicit construction of an object at a specific address that happens to have been occupied by another object.

Accessing `value()` through p will definitely give you - 3 as it's obvious that p points to an X<int> object that holds a reference to m, and m has the value - 3 at that point. Accessing `value()` through h is undefined behavior (will the resulting code give you what the bits say or what the compiler thinks that code is saying?).

This sort of evil-seeming situation, where the code logic as understood by the compiler might not match the bits, happens with objects with `const` data members, objects with reference data members, and some `union` types crafted in weird ways, but these are the tools we use for the low-level manipulation of objects, and that can be found underneath `std::optional<T>`, `std::vector<T>`, and others. It's our fault, in the end, for using these weird types, but it's part of life.

When the bits do not necessarily align with what the compiler can understand, we have `std::launder()`. Use this cautiously: it's an optimization barrier that states "just look at the bits, compiler; forget what you know about source code when looking at this pointed-to object." Of course, this is a very dangerous tool and should be used with a lot of care, but sometimes it's just what is needed.

Summary

Whew, this was a long chapter! We implemented a naïve `vector`-like container, then a naïve `forward_list`-like container, and then took another look at the `vector`-like container (we will return to the `forward_list`-like container in the next two chapters) to show how tighter control over memory can lead to more efficient containers.

Our implementations in this chapter were "manual," in the sense that we did the memory management by hand. That involved writing a lot of code, something we will reconsider in *Chapter 13*. In *Chapter 14*, we will examine how allocators interact with containers, and will use this opportunity to revisit our `forward_list`-like container as there will be interesting aspects to examine as we continue our adventure through memory management in C++.

Unlock this book's exclusive benefits now

This book comes with additional benefits designed to elevate your learning experience.

Note: Have your purchase invoice ready before you begin.

https://www.packtpub.com/
unlock/9781805129806

13
Writing Generic Containers with Implicit Memory Management

In the previous chapter, we wrote a working (if simple) implementation of a `std::vector<T>`-like type in `Vector<T>`, as well as a working (if, again, simple) implementation of a `std::forward_list<T>`-like type in `ForwardList<T>`. Not bad!

In the case of our `Vector<T>` type, after an initial effort that led to a working but sometimes inefficient implementation, we made the effort to separate allocation from construction, something that reduced the amount of redundant effort required at runtime but came at the cost of a more subtle implementation. In this more sophisticated implementation, we distinguished parts of the underlying storage that are initialized from those that are not and, of course, operated on both parts appropriately (treating objects as objects and raw memory as such). For example, we used assignment (and algorithms that use the assignment operator) to replace the contents of existing objects but preferred placement new (and algorithms that rely on this mechanism) to create objects in raw memory.

Our `Vector<T>` implementation from the previous chapter is a class expressed with a sizable amount of source code. One of the reasons for this situation is the explicit memory management we have been doing. Indeed, we have made a `Vector<T>` object responsible for both the management of the underlying memory block and the objects stored therein, and this double responsibility came with a cost. In this chapter, we will revisit that design by making memory management *implicit* and we will discuss the consequences of this new approach. Hopefully, dear reader, this will lead you toward a possible simplification and refinement of your coding practices.

In this chapter, our goals will be as follows:

- To adapt a hand-written container such as `Vector<T>` in such a way as to significantly simplify its memory management responsibilities

- To understand the consequences of our design on source code complexity

- To understand the consequences of our design on exception safety

We will spend most of our energy on revisiting the `Vector<T>` container, but we will also revisit `ForwardList<T>` to see if we can apply the same kind of reasoning to both container types. By the end of this chapter, at least in the case of `Vector<T>`, we will still have a hand-written container that manages memory efficiently and distinguishes raw memory from constructed objects, but our implementation will be significantly simpler than the one we produced in *Chapter 12*.

Note that with respect to `Vector<T>`, this chapter will compare two versions. One will be named the "*naïve* version" and will be the initial implementation that uses objects of type `T` throughout the underlying storage. The other will be named the "*sophisticated* version" and will be the implementation that considers the underlying storage as being made of two (potentially empty) "sections," with objects of type `T` at the beginning and raw memory at the end.

Technical requirements

You can find the code files for this chapter in the book's GitHub repository here: `https://github.com/PacktPublishing/C-Plus-Plus-Memory-Management/tree/main/chapter13`.

> **Some words about the code excerpts in this chapter**
>
> This chapter will for the most part revisit and modify (hopefully simplifying!) the code examples from *Chapter 12*, using ideas from previous chapters (notably *Chapter 5* and *Chapter 6*) along the way. Since a lot of the code used for `Vector<T>` and `ForwardList<T>` will not change, we will not write the entire classes all over again to avoid undue repetition.
>
> Instead, we will concentrate on the most meaningful modifications made to the previous versions of those classes, sometimes comparing implementations "before" and "after" modifications have been made. Of course, the code samples in the GitHub repository are complete and can be used to "complete the picture."

Why explicit memory management complicates our implementation

Let's look for a moment at one of the constructors for `Vector<T>` as written in *Chapter 12*. For simplicity, we will use the constructor that accepts a number of elements and an initial value for these elements as arguments. If we limit ourselves to the naïve version where `elems` points to a sequence of

T objects and put aside for the moment the more sophisticated version where elems points to a block of memory that holds T objects at the beginning and raw memory at the end, we have the following:

```
// naïve version with elems of type T*
Vector(size_type n, const_reference init)
    : elems{ new value_type[n] }, nelems{ n }, cap{ n } {
    try {
        std::fill(begin(), end(), init);
    } catch (...) {
        delete [] elems;
        throw;
    }
}
// ...
```

This constructor allocates an array of T objects, initializes them through a sequence of assignments, "handles" exceptions, and so on. The try block and its corresponding catch block are part of our implementation, but not because we want to handle exceptions raised by the constructors of T objects. Indeed: how could we know what exceptions it could throw if we do not know what T is? We insert these blocks because we need to explicitly deallocate and destroy the array if we are to avoid leaks. The situation gets even more complicated if we look at the more sophisticated version that distinguishes allocation from construction:

```
// sophisticated version with elems of type T*
Vector(size_type n, const_reference init)
    : elems{ static_cast<pointer>(
        std::malloc(n * sizeof(value_type))
    ) }, nelems{ n }, cap{ n } {
    try {
        std::uninitialized_fill(begin(), end(), init);
    } catch (...) {
        std::free(elems);
        throw;
    }
}
// ...
```

As we can see, we do this work because we decided that Vector<T> would be the *owner* of that memory. And we are totally allowed to do so! But what if we made something else responsible for our memory?

Implicit memory management with a smart pointer

In C++, the simplest way to change our Vector<T> implementation from one that manually manages memory to one that does so implicitly is through a smart pointer. The idea here is, essentially, to change the type of the elems data member of Vector<T> from T* to std::unique_ptr<T[]>. We will look at this from two angles:

- How does this change impact the naïve version of Vector<T>? As a reminder, our naïve version from *Chapter 12* did not distinguish between objects and raw memory in the underlying storage, and thus only stored objects. This led to a simpler implementation, but also one that needlessly constructed objects on many occasions and was much slower than the more sophisticated implementation for non-trivially constructible types.

- How does this change impact the sophisticated version of Vector<T> that avoided the performance trap of constructing unnecessary objects at the cost of a somewhat more complicated implementation?

In both cases, we will examine selected member functions that are indicative of the impact of this change. The full implementations of both the naïve and the sophisticated implementations of Vector<T> are available to peruse and use in the GitHub repository associated with this book.

Impact on the naïve Vector<T> implementation

If we were basing our simplification effort on the initial, naïve version of *Chapter 12* where elems simply pointed to a contiguous sequence of T objects, this would be rather simple, as we could change:

```
// naïve implementation, explicit memory management
// declaration of the data members...
pointer elems{};
size_type nelems{}, cap{};
```

... to:

```
// naïve implementation, implicit memory management
// declaration of the data members...
std::unique_ptr<value_type[]> elems;
size_type nelems{}, cap{};
```

... and then change the implementation of the begin() member functions from this:

```
// naïve implementation, explicit memory management
iterator begin() {
    return elems; // raw pointer to the memory block
}
const_iterator begin() const {
```

```
    return elems; // raw pointer to the memory block
}
```

... to this:

```
// naïve implementation, implicit memory management
iterator begin() {
    return elems.get(); // raw pointer to the beginning
                        // of the underlying memory block
}
const_iterator begin() const {
    return elems.get(); // likewise
}
```

Just doing this would be sufficient to significantly simplify the implementation of type Vector<T> as deallocating memory would become implicit. For example, we could simplify each constructor by removing the exception handling altogether, changing, for example, the following implementation:

```
// naïve implementation, explicit memory management
Vector(size_type n, const_reference init)
    : elems{ new value_type[n] }, nelems{ n }, cap{ n } {
    try {
        std:: fill(begin(), end(), init);
    } catch (...) {
        delete [] elems;
        throw;
    }
}
// ...
```

... for this significantly simpler one:

```
// naïve implementation, implicit memory management
Vector(size_type n, const_reference init)
    : elems{ new value_type[n] }, nelems{ n }, cap{ n } {
    std:: fill(begin(), end(), init);
}
// ...
```

The reason for this simplification is the following:

- If the Vector<T> object is responsible for the allocated memory, then deleting the array will be done implicitly when the destructor is called, but for a destructor to be called, there needs to be an object to destroy: a Vector<T> constructor needs to have succeeded! That explains why we need to catch whatever exception was thrown, manually delete the array, and re-throw whatever exception was thrown: until the closing brace of a destructor is reached, there is no Vector<T> object to destruct and all resource management has to be done explicitly.

- On the other hand, if elems is a smart pointer, then it becomes responsible for the pointee as soon as the smart pointer itself has been constructed, and this occurs *before* the opening brace of the Vector<T> constructor. This means that once elems has been constructed, it *will* be destructed if an exception leaves the constructor, freeing the Vector<T> object-to-be from the task of destructing the array. To be clear: when we reach the opening brace of the constructor of Vector<T>, the data members of *this have been constructed, and for that reason, they will be destructed if an exception is thrown, even if the construction of *this itself does not conclude. The object model of C++ is truly wonderful in such situations.

The more astute among you, dear readers, will have noticed that even if one was writing code for a company where exceptions are disallowed or frowned upon, the exception-safety we gained from using a smart pointer remains. We have (discretely) written exception-safe code without writing the words try or catch.

Other examples of simplification through the introduction of implicit memory management would include move operations and the destructor of Vector<T>, which would change from this:

```
// naïve implementation, explicit memory management
   Vector(Vector &&other)
      : elems{ std::exchange(other.elems, nullptr) },
        nelems{ std::exchange(other.nelems, 0) },
        cap{ std::exchange(other.cap, 0) } {
   }
   Vector& operator=(Vector &&other) {
      Vector{ other }.swap(*this);
      return *this;
   }
   ~Vector() {
      delete [] elems;
   }
// ...
```

... to simply this:

```
// naïve implementation, implicit memory management
   Vector(Vector&&) = default;
   Vector& operator=(Vector&&) = default;
   ~Vector() = default;
// ...
```

Making move operations =default works because type std::unique_ptr does "the right thing" when moving and transfers ownership of the pointee from the source to the destination.

Something to be aware of

By making the move operations =default, we induced a slight semantic change in our Vector<T> implementation. The C++ standard recommends that a moved-from is in a valid yet unspecified state but does not go into detail as to what "valid" means. Our hand-written move operations restored the moved-from object to the equivalent of a default-constructed Vector<T> object, but the "defaulted" one leaves the moved-from object with a null elems but with potentially non-zero size and capacity. This still works in practice as long as user code does not use the moved-from object unless it has first been reassigned to, but it is a semantic change that deserves to be acknowledged.

Yet another interesting simplification would be the implementation of the resize() member function. In the original, naïve Vector<T> implementation, we had the following:

```
// naïve implementation, explicit memory management
   void resize(size_type new_cap) {
      if(new_cap <= capacity()) return;
      auto p = new T[new_cap];
      if constexpr(std::is_nothrow_move_assignable_v<T>) {
         std::move(begin(), end(), p);
      } else try {
         std::copy(begin(), end(), p);
      } catch (...) {
         delete[] p;
         throw;
      }
      delete[] elems;
      elems = p;
      cap = new_cap;
   }
```

Here, again, we are faced with the possibility of an exception being thrown from the copy assignment of a T object to a T object and need to handle exceptions in order to avoid leaking resources. Going from explicit resource handling to implicit resource handling, we get the following:

```
// naïve implementation, implicit memory management
void resize(size_type new_cap) {
    if(new_cap <= capacity()) return;
    auto p = std::make_unique<value_type[]>(new_cap);
    if constexpr(std::is_nothrow_move_assignable_v<T>) {
        std::move(begin(), end(), p.get());
    } else {
        std::copy(begin(), end(), p.get());
    }
    elems.reset(p.release());
    cap = new_cap;
}
```

As you can see, the entire exception handling code is gone. Object p owns the new array and will destroy it when the function concludes execution. Once the copies (or the moves, depending on whether the move assignment of type T is or is not marked as noexcept) are completed, elems lets go of the previously owned array through reset() (destroying it at the same time) and "steals" ownership of the array released by p through release(). Note that writing elems = std::move(p); would have had a similar effect.

Applying this simplification process throughout Vector<T>, source code gradually shrinks and, on a container like the naïve version of Vector<T> that only contains objects, no raw memory block at the end of the underlying storage, we can save almost 25% of the number of source code lines (going from roughly 180 lines to 140 lines for this academic implementation). Try it and see for yourself!

Impact on the sophisticated Vector<T> implementation

Applying the same technique to the more sophisticated Vector<T> will require a bit more work as the default behavior of the destructor of an object of type std::unique_ptr<T[]> will be to apply operator delete[] to the pointer it owns. As we know at this point, our sophisticated implementation can be conceptualized as being made of two (potentially empty) "sections": an initial section made of T objects manually placed into raw memory followed by another section of uninitialized, raw memory devoid of objects. As such, we need to handle each "section" in a different manner.

We will still use a std::unique_ptr<T[]> object to manage the memory, but we will need to use a custom deleter object (something we discussed in *Chapter 5* and in *Chapter 6*) to take into account the specifics of our implementation. This object will need knowledge of the runtime state of the Vector<T> object it will accompany since it will have to know where each "section" of the underlying storage starts as well as where it ends, and that is something that changes as the code is executing.

The first important point of this implementation, and this is a point that has been recurring but that we probably did not insist upon enough, is that we want our implementations to expose the same interface to client code, regardless of implementation variations. This is sometimes impossible or unreasonable to achieve, but it is nonetheless a meaningful and worthwhile target. This includes our choice of internal public types: for example, the fact that we use a smart pointer to manage the underlying memory does not change the fact that a pointer to an element is a `T*`:

```cpp
// ...
template <class T>
class Vector {
public:
   using value_type = T;
   using size_type = std::size_t;
   using pointer = T*;
   using const_pointer = const T*;
   using reference = T&;
   using const_reference = const T&;
   // ...
```

Now, since we want to define `elems` as being a smart pointer that owns and manages the underlying storage instead of being a raw pointer, we will need to define the custom deleter that will be used by that smart pointer.

An important aspect of this problem is that the custom deleter will need to know the state of the `Vector<T>` object to know what part of the underlying storage holds objects. For this reason, the custom deleter of our `std::unique_ptr<T[]>` will be stateful and store a reference named `source` to the `Vector<T>` object. Through `source`, The function call operator of the `deleter` object will have access to the sequence of objects in the container (the half-open sequence from `source.begin()` to `source.end()`) and will be able to `destroy()` these objects before freeing the underlying storage:

```cpp
   // ...
private:
   struct deleter {
      Vector& source;
      void operator()(value_type* p) {
         std::destroy(std::begin(source),
                      std::end(source));
         std::free(static_cast<void*>(p));
      }
   };
   std::unique_ptr<value_type[], deleter> elems;
   size_type nelems{},
             cap{};
   // ...
```

The `elems` data member knows that the type of the custom deleter will be `deleter`, but the actual object that will play the role of deleter will have to know what `Vector<T>` object it will interact with. The constructors of a `Vector<T>` will be responsible for providing this information, and we will need to be careful with the ways in which we implement our move operations in order to make sure we do not transfer the `deleter` object's state and make our code incoherent.

As mentioned with the naïve version, we need to adapt the `begin()` member functions to take into account the fact that `elems` is a smart pointer but that our `iterator` interface relies on raw pointers:

```cpp
// ...
using iterator = pointer;
using const_iterator = const_pointer;
iterator begin() { return elems.get(); }
const_iterator begin() const { return elems.get(); }
// ...
```

Our constructors will need to adapt to the fact that we have a custom deleter that will clean up if anything bad happens, or if the program concludes normally. Three examples of `Vector<T>` constructors follow:

```cpp
// ...
constexpr Vector()
    : elems{ nullptr, deleter { *this } } {
}
Vector(size_type n, const_reference init)
    : elems{ static_cast<pointer>(
        std::malloc(n * sizeof(value_type))
      ), deleter{ *this }
    } {
    std::uninitialized_fill(begin(), begin() + n, init);
    nelems = cap = n;
}
Vector(Vector&& other) noexcept
    : elems{ std::exchange(
        other.elems.release()), deleter{ *this }
      },
      nelems{ std::exchange(other.nelems, 0) },
      cap{ std::exchange(other.cap, 0) } {
}
// ...
```

Please note that we are not expressing the move constructor with `=default` in this case as we do not want to transfer the custom deleter, our implementation having associated this object with a specific `Vector<T>` object.

A small note is in order here: we are passing *this to the constructor of the deleter object, but we are doing so *before* the construction of *this has been completed, so *anything* done by the deleter object before the construction of *this concludes (before the closing brace of its constructor) deserves care and attention.

In our case, the deleter object will come into play if the destructor of elems comes into play, which will happen if the constructor of an object of type T throws. We need to make sure that the values of the data members of *this are coherent whenever there is a possibility that the deleter object intervenes.

In our case, since the begin() and end() member functions return iterators that define a half-open range of objects and, as we now know, std::uninitialized_fill() calls the constructors and (if an exception is thrown) destroys the objects that have been constructed, we have to make sure that nelems==0 until all of the objects have been constructed. Note that we defined the range to initialize as begin() and begin()+n, and waited until after the call to std::uninitialized_fill() to change nelems: this way, begin()==end() if an exception is thrown, and the deleter object will not try to destruct "non-objects."

Other constructors of class Vector<T> are likewise simplified; we will not show them here so consider them as not-so-dreaded "exercises left to the reader."

The simplification of Vector<T> is made evident with some of the special member functions that now require little or no effort on our part. Of note in this regard is the destructor, which can now be defaulted; as mentioned with the move constructor earlier in this section, we do not default the move assignment to avoid transferring the custom deleter's internal state, as can be seen in the following code excerpt:

```
// ...
~Vector() = default;
void swap(Vector& other) noexcept {
    using std::swap;
    swap(elems, other.elems);
    swap(nelems, other.nelems);
    swap(cap, other.cap);
}
Vector& operator=(const Vector& other) {
    Vector{ other }.swap(*this);
    return *this;
}
Vector& operator=(Vector&& other) {
    Vector{ std::move(other) }.swap(*this);
    return *this;
}
```

```
reference operator[](size_type n) { return elems[n]; }
const_reference operator[](size_type n) const {
    return elems[n];
}
```

Member functions swap() and operator[] have been shown to make it clear that std::unique_ptr<T[]> behaves in many ways like a "regular" array of T objects. Many other member functions of Vector<T> remain unchanged, such as front(), back(), operator==(), operator!=(), grow(), push_back(), and emplace_back(). Please refer to *Chapter 12* for details on these functions.

The reserve() and resize() functions can also be simplified through the use of smart pointers, as we can get rid of explicit exception management and yet remain exception-safe since std::unique_ptr<T[]> is an **RAII** type and handles memory for us.

In the case of reserve(), we now use smart pointer p to hold the allocated memory, then either move() or copy() the objects from elems to p. Once this is done, we destroy() the objects left in elems, after which p relinquishes its pointer and transfers it to elems, and the only thing left to do is to update the container's capacity:

```
// ...
void reserve(size_type new_cap) {
    if (new_cap <= capacity()) return;
    std::unique_ptr<value_type[]> p{
        static_cast<pointer>(
            std::malloc(new_cap * sizeof(T))
        )
    };
    if constexpr (std::is_nothrow_move_assignable_v<T>) {
        std::uninitialized_move(begin(), end(), p.get());
    } else {
        std::uninitialized_copy(begin(), end(), p.get());
    }
    std::destroy(begin(), end());
    elems.reset(p.release());
    cap = new_cap;
}
```

In the case of `resize()`, we now use smart pointer p to hold the allocated memory, then either `move()` or `copy()` the objects from `elems` to p and construct default T objects in the remaining part of the memory block. Once this is done, we `destroy()` the objects left in `elems`, after which p relinquishes its pointer and transfers it to `elems`, and the only thing left to do is to update the container's capacity:

```cpp
// ...
void resize(size_type new_cap) {
    if (new_cap <= capacity()) return;
    std::unique_ptr<value_type[]> p =
        static_cast<pointer>(
            std::malloc(new_cap * sizeof(T))
        );
    if constexpr (std::is_nothrow_move_assignable_v<T>) {
        std::uninitialized_move(begin(), end(), p.get());
    } else {
        std::uninitialized_copy(begin(), end(), p.get());
    }
    std::uninitialized_fill(
        p.get() + size(), p.get() + new_cap, value_type{}
    );
    std::destroy(begin(), end());
    elems.reset(p.release());
    nelems = cap = new_cap;
}
// ...
```

The magic of it all, or so to speak, is that our other member functions such as `insert()` and `erase()` are built on top of basic abstractions such as `reserve()`, `begin()`, `end()`, and so on, which means they do not have to be modified to take into account this representational change.

Consequences of this redesign

What are the consequences of this "redesign" of sorts? They have been mentioned along the way, but let's summarize:

- For user code, consequences are essentially none: an object of type `Vector<T>` occupies the same space in memory with the implicit memory management implementation and almost the same space with the explicit memory management implementation (where the custom deleter is stateful), and each exposes the same public interface.

- There are essentially no speed costs either, for reasons explained in *Chapter 5*: in code compiled with optimization levels other than the basic, made-for-debugging ones, going through `std::unique_ptr<T>` will, due to function call inlining, lead to code that is as efficient as going through a `T*`.

- The implementation is made significantly simpler: fewer instructions, no explicit exception handling code, more member functions that can be defaulted…

- An important aspect of this implicit memory management implementation is that it is exception-safe even in the absence of explicit `try` and `catch` blocks. This can make a difference in many situations: for example, you might be in a situation where exceptions are not allowed but find yourself using a library where exceptions are a possibility… or can simply call `operator new()` in a situation where memory is constrained. Our implementation with implicit memory management would be safe under such circumstances, but an implementation taking a manual memory management approach with no exception handling code would not be so "lucky."

The effort involved in implementing the custom deleter seems to be a sound investment with `Vector<T>`. Now, you might wonder whether the situation is similar with node-based containers, so we will explore this question by revisiting the naïve `ForwardList<T>` implementation from *Chapter 12*.

Generalizing to ForwardList<T>?

We now know that we can adapt the implementation of `Vector<T>`, transforming it from an explicit memory management model to an implicit one, and that so doing has lots of advantages. It is tempting to do the same with other containers, but before embarking on such an adventure, it might be wise to analyze the problem a little.

We implemented a node-based container with explicit memory management named `ForwardList<T>` in *Chapter 12*. What would be the impact of trying to change the implementation of this container to make it more implicit?

Attempt - making each node responsible for its successor

In our exploration of ways in which we could try to make memory management in a node-based container more implicit, one possible approach could be to change the definition of `ForwardList<T>::Node` such that the `next` data member becomes a `std::unique_ptr<Node>` instead of a `Node*`.

As a synopsis, we would get the following:

```
template <class T>
class ForwardList {
public:
    // ...
private:
```

```
struct Node {
   value_type value;
   std::unique_ptr<Node> next; // <--
   Node(const_reference value) : value{ value } {
   }
   Node(value_type&& value) : value{ std::move(value) }{
   }
};
Node* head{};
size_type nelems{};
// ...
```

This might seem like an improvement at first glance, since it would simplify the destructor of ForwardList<T> down to the following:

```
// ...
~ForwardList() {
   delete head; // <-- lots of work starts here!
}
// ...
```

This simplification would induce a kind of "domino effect": since the next data member of a node becomes the owner of its successor node in the list, and since this is true for every node in the chain (except for head itself), then destructing the first node ensures the destruction of its successor, and of that successor's successor, and so on.

This apparent simplification hides a tricky fact: when calling delete head; under this implementation, *we might be provoking a stack overflow*. Indeed, we replaced a loop that applied delete on each node in succession with something that's essentially a recursive call, meaning that the impact on stack usage changed from something that was fixed to something that is proportional to the number of nodes in the list. That's unpleasant news indeed!

At this point, dear reader, maybe you are thinking "Well, I was only going to use this ForwardList<T> type for small lists anyway, so I'm not worried." If that expresses your line of thinking, maybe we should explore other implications of this implementation decision in our ForwardList<T> class.

One such implication is that iterators get a little bit more complicated: we do not want an iterator over nodes to be the sole owner of the node it is traversing. That would be destructive indeed, as nodes would be destroyed as we are iterating over the list. For this reason, ForwardList<T>::Node<U> (where U is either T or const T) would still have a T* data member, meaning that operator++(), for example, would need to obtain the underlying pointer of the std::unique_ptr<T> data member in each node:

```
// ...
template <class U> class Iterator {
```

```
public:
    // ...
private:
    Node* cur{};
public:
    // ...
    Iterator& operator++() {
        cur = cur->next.get(); // <--
        return *this;
    }
    // ...
```

That's a slight complexity increase, but nothing that is impossible to manage.

In *Chapter 12*, we made most of our `ForwardList<T>` constructors converge towards the more general sequence constructor that takes a pair of forward iterators of some type `It` as arguments. This constructor would become in part more complex, as chaining nodes would now require knowledge that we are using smart pointers inside each node, but cleanup in case an exception is thrown would only require deleting the head node and letting the aforementioned "domino effect" take place:

```
// ...
template <std::forward_iterator It>
ForwardList(It b, It e) {
    try {
        if (b == e) return;
        head = new Node{ *b };
        auto q = head;
        ++nelems;
        for (++b; b != e; ++b) {
            q->next = std::make_unique<Node>(*b); // <--
            q = q->next.get(); // <--
            ++nelems;
        }
    } catch (...) {
        delete head; // <--
        throw;
    }
}
// ...
```

Most member functions of `ForwardList<T>` would remain unchanged. There would be slight adjustments to such things as `push_front()`, for example:

```
// ...
void push_front(const_reference val) {
```

```
    auto p = new Node{ val };
    p->next = std::unique_ptr<Node>{ head }; // <--
    head = p;
    ++nelems;
}
void push_front(T&& val) {
    auto p = new Node{ std::move(val) };
    p->next = std::unique_ptr<Node>{ head }; // <--
    head = p;
    ++nelems;
}
// ...
```

As can be seen, we need to distinguish code that uses the head data member from code that uses the other nodes in the chain. Similar adjustments would apply to any member function that modifies the structure of the list, including, notably, insertions and suppressions.

A more interesting, and probably more enlightening, member function would be the insert_after() member function that inserts one element after a given iterator in the list. Let's look at this function in detail:

```
// ...
iterator
    insert_after(iterator pos, const_reference value) {
    auto p = std::make_unique<Node>(value); // <-- A
    p->next.reset(pos.cur->next.get()); // <-- B
    pos.cur->next.release(); // <-- C
    pos.cur->next.reset(p.get()); // <-- D
    p.release(); // <-- E
    ++nelems;
    return { pos.cur->next.get() }; // <-- F
}
// ...
```

Hum, that's quite a lot of updated text! How did this function get so complicated? Looking at the "lettered" comments, we have the following:

- On line *A*, we create a std::unique_ptr<Node> object named p for the value to be inserted. We know the newly created node will not be the first node in the list since the function is insert_after(), and requires an iterator to an existing "before" node (named pos here), so that makes sense. For the same reason, we know that pos is not end(), which, by definition, does not point to a valid node in our container.

- On line *B*, we do what is required to make the successor of p the successor of pos. That requires some care since `pos.cur->next` is guaranteed to be a `std::unique_ptr<Node>` (it obviously cannot be `head` as `pos.cur` is "before" `pos.cur->next`) and we made p a `std::unique_ptr<Node>`. We are displacing responsibility over the successor node of `pos.cur` to `p->next`, effectively inserting `pos->next` after p (albeit in a complicated way).

- On line *C*, we are ensuring that `pos.cur` relinquishes its responsibility over `pos.cur->next`. This is important since, if we did not do so, then replacing that `std::unique_ptr<Node>` would destroy the pointee. Line *B* ensured that `pos.cur->next` and `p->next` would lead to the same object, which would have been disastrous had we stopped there (two objects responsible for the same pointee is a semantic problem we do not need).

- Once `pos.cur->next` has been disconnected, we move to line *D* where we make it point to the raw pointer underneath p. This would, again, lead to a shared responsibility over a `Node`, so we continue with line *E* where we disconnect p from its underlying pointer.

- Line *F* concludes the work in this function by returning the expected iterator to a raw (thus non-owning) pointer.

That is... complicated. The main reason why this is complicated is that most of the effort in this function is the transfer of ownership. A `std::unique_ptr<T>` object represents sole ownership over a `T*`, after all, and in a linked list, each and every insertion or suppression requires moving pointers around, thus transferring ownership between nodes. We simplified an occasional situation (deletion of the nodes) by complicating most of the operations in our type. That's... sad.

On meaning and responsibility semantics

Smart pointers are all about encoding meaning and responsibility in the type system. Simplifying user code is important, but it's not the main point of these types. In a `ForwardList<T>`object, the real owner of the T objects is the `ForwardList<T>` object, and the `ForwardList<T>::Node<U>` objects are (from the `ForwardList<T>` object's perspective) essentially a storage facility. Trying to change this can be made to work, but the ensuing complexity is an indication that something's suspicious.

When writing a class, especially a container class, it's essential that we have a clear view of the role intended for each type. We know that iterators are non-owning by nature (we could, however, envision `shared_ptr<T>` objects that co-own the pointee in some use cases). As far as containers and their underlying representation goes, the important point is that the responsibilities of each type need to be clear if our design is going to be manageable.

Okay, so making a node responsible for its successor did not work. Would simply making the `head` member of a `ForwardList<T>` object responsible for the other nodes in the list make our lives better?

Attempt: making the head pointer responsible for the other nodes

As seen in the previous section, making each node responsible for its successor is semantically incorrect. It leads to complex, involved, and error-prone code, and the aspects of the implementation that are simplified by this transformation are mostly outweighed by the added complexity in other places.

Maybe just making the head node a std::unique_ptr<Node> object with a custom deleter responsible for deleting the entire list would be beneficial? Well, we can assuredly try this approach.

As a synopsis, we would now get the following:

```cpp
template <class T>
class ForwardList {
    // ...
    struct Node {
        value_type value;
        Node* next = nullptr;
        Node(const_reference value) : value{ value } {
        }
        Node(value_type&& value) : value{ std::move(value) }{
        }
    };
    struct deleter { // <--
        void operator()(Node* p) const {
            while (p) {
                Node* q = p->next;
                delete p;
                p = q;
            }
        }
    };
    std::unique_ptr<Node, deleter> head;
    // ...
```

We now have a ForwardList<T> type that, when an object of that type is destroyed, implicitly ensures that the nodes in the list are destructed. The entire list remains built from raw pointers, such that nodes are not responsible for memory management, which is probably an upgrade from the previous attempt.

With this implementation, we would get a defaulted `ForwardList<T>` destructor, which is a good thing. There would be a tiny complexity increase in `clear()` where we need to distinguish the `head` smart pointer from the underlying pointer:

```
// ...
void clear() noexcept {
    for (auto p = head.get(); p; ) { // <--
        auto q = p->next;
        delete p;
        p = q;
    }
    nelems = 0;
}
// ...
```

The iterator interface needs to be adapted somewhat since `head` is not a `Node*` anymore, but iterators trade in non-owning resources:

```
// ...
iterator begin() { return { head.get() }; } // <--
const_iterator begin() const {
    return { head.get() }; // <--
}
// ...
```

The `ForwardList<T>` constructor that takes a pair of iterators and towards which most other constructors converge requires slight modifications:

```
// ...
template <std::forward_iterator It>
    ForwardList(It b, It e) {
        if(b == e) return;
        head.reset(new Node{ *b }); // <--
        auto q = head.get(); // <--
        ++nelems;
        for(++b; b != e; ++b) {
            q->next = new Node{ *b };
            q = q->next;
            ++nelems;
        }
    }
// ...
```

The exception handling side of this member function is indeed simplified, being made implicit from the fact that, should any constructor of a T object throw an exception, the previously created nodes will be destroyed.

As in the previous version, our `push_front()` member functions will require some adjustment as they interact with the `head` data member:

```
// ...
void push_front(const_reference val) {
    auto p = new Node{ val };
    p->next = head.get(); // <--
    head.release(); // <--
    head.reset(p); // <--
    ++nelems;
}
void push_front(T&& val) {
    auto p = new Node{ std::move(val) };
    p->next = head.get(); // <--
    head.release(); // <--
    head.reset(p); // <--
    ++nelems;
}
// ...
```

On the upside, no member function that does not interact with the `head` data member requires any modification.

Is this "implicitness" worth it? It probably depends on the way in which you approach writing code. We did gain something of value in implicit exception safety. There is value in separating concerns, and this implementation does free the container from the task of managing memory (for the most part). It is up to you, dear reader, to determine whether the reduced complexity "here" outweighs the added complexity "there."

Summary

In this chapter, we reexamined containers written in *Chapter 12*, seeking to use implicit memory management tools in such a way as to make our implementations simpler and safer. We did reach an improvement in `Vector<T>` but the results obtained with our node-based `ForwardList<T>` container were... not absent, but arguably less conclusive depending on your perspective.

In the next chapter, we will introduce the idea of allocators, objects that inform containers as to how memory should be obtained or liberated, and examine how they impact the ways in which we write code.

Unlock this book's exclusive benefits now

This book comes with additional benefits designed to elevate your learning experience.

Note: Have your purchase invoice ready before you begin.

https://www.packtpub.com/unlock/9781805129806

14

Writing Generic Containers with Allocator Support

We have come a long way since the beginning of this book. Recent chapters examined how one can write memory-efficient containers, describing how to do so when memory management is done explicitly (in *Chapter 12*) and when it is done implicitly, through smart pointers (in *Chapter 13*). Choosing a memory management approach is not an either/or proposition; each one is useful in its own way and solves real-life use cases depending on one's application domain.

However, none of the approaches we have covered so far match what standard library containers do. Indeed, standard library containers (as well as many other standard library types that can dynamically allocate memory) are **allocator-aware** and delegate low-level memory management tasks to specialized objects that can be supplied by client code. There is merit to this idea as it allows one to pick a container based on the way it organizes objects in memory and couple said container with an allocator, a "memory allocation specialist." This opens up a world of possibilities, some of them very popular, such as using a `std::vector` whose memory comes from an arena (see *Chapter 10*) or from a fixed-capacity buffer on the stack.

Allocators officially came to the C++ language, along with the standard library containers, in C++98, but they evolved and diversified themselves over time. Writing an allocator became significantly simpler with C++11, and C++17 introduced an entirely new approach to memory allocation with **polymorphic memory resource** (**PMR**) allocators and containers.

In this chapter, you will do the following:

- Understand and use traditional allocators
- Write a traditional allocator for a specialized application domain
- Learn how to manage the allocator lifetime when a container is moved or copied
- Clone an allocator's type
- Understand and use PMR allocators and containers

Equipped with a knowledge of allocators and how they interact with containers, this chapter will enrich your memory management toolbox and open up new ways to combine data organization with the way storage is obtained. Understanding allocators might even make writing new containers less of a necessity; sometimes, instead of trying to create an entirely new container, the solution is just a matter of combining the right data organization strategy with the right storage management approach.

Technical requirements

You can find the code files for this chapter in the book's GitHub repository here: `https://github.com/PacktPublishing/C-Plus-Plus-Memory-Management/tree/main/chapter14`.

> **A word about the examples in this chapter**
>
> As was the case with *Chapter 13*, this chapter will show incomplete examples to avoid redundancy with the excerpts found earlier, particularly those in *Chapter 12*. Allocators change the way in which containers interact with memory management facilities, but they do not require rewriting containers entirely, so a lot of code written for a given container remains stable regardless of how memory is managed. The code you will find in the GitHub repository is, of course, complete.
>
> Also note that this chapter discusses allocators in the context of containers, but the idea can be extended to many types that need to dynamically allocate memory. It is sometimes difficult to do so; for example, support for allocators in `std::function` was removed in C++17 as no known standard library implementation had managed to make it work. Still, allocators can be seen as a general idea, not something that is limited to containers, and you can envision using allocators in other contexts.

Why allocators?

Allocators tend to scare people, including some experts, but you will not be scared as you are already in possession of significant memory management knowledge and skills (and you are probably curious to know more about the topic given the fact that you are reading this book). Knowing this, the first question we need to address, before even expressing what an allocator is, is "Why do allocators exist?". Why would we concern ourselves with an additional layer of complexity in our memory management code?

Well, this is C++, and C++ is all about giving users *control*, so that's where our explanation begins. To make an analogy, think about iterators: why they are useful, and how they make your life as a programmer better. They decouple iterating over elements of a sequence from how the elements are organized in that sequence, such that you can write code that computes something such as the sum of the values in `std::list<int>` or `std::vector<short>` without having to know that in the first case, you are navigating through nodes linked to one another by pointers and in the second case, you are iterating through objects stored in contiguous memory.

The beauty of iterators is this decoupling between iteration and data organization. Similarly, allocators decouple data organization from the way the underlying storage is obtained or freed. This allows us to reason about the properties of containers independently from the properties of memory management and makes containers useful in even more situations than they would otherwise be.

A very, very thin layer…

To a container, an allocator (at least those in the "traditional" model that we are about to discuss) represents a thin (*very* thin) layer of abstraction over the hardware. To a container, an allocator expresses such things as "What is an address?", "How does one put an object somewhere?", "How does one destroy an object at some location?", and so on. In a way, for a container, the allocator essentially *is* the hardware.

Traditional allocators

As mentioned already, allocators have been a mainstay of C++ for decades now, but they have existed in a few different guises and shapes. In this chapter, we will adopt a sort of chronological approach, starting from the earlier (and more complicated) allocator types and progressing toward the simpler (and more versatile) ones.

To understand this chapter, one key idea to keep in mind is that a container type such as `std::vector<T>` does not really exist. What does exist is the `std::vector<T,A>` type where, by default, A is `std::allocator<T>`, which allocates through `::operator new()` and deallocates through `::operator delete()`. By **traditional allocator**, we mean an allocator type that is part of the type of a container (this is not the only possible approach to writing allocators today, as we will see when we discuss PMR allocators later in this chapter).

We will first examine what was required to write an allocator before C++11, and how a container such as `std::vector<T,A>` could use an object of the A type to abstract away its memory allocation tasks. Improvements to the way allocators are expressed will follow in later sections of this chapter.

Before C++11

Traditional allocators written before C++11 had to implement a wide array of members, which made the task of writing allocators seem daunting to many. Consider what one had to write in those days, and please note that not all of what follows remains true as of this writing since the API of allocators has evolved over time.

> **On the difficulty of tracking an evolving API**
>
> What is required of allocators changed with every version of C++ since C++03, and these days, it is not always easy (or relevant) to write examples that compile for C++11. For this reason, the examples we will write in a detailed manner will use C++11 allocators, to show what that actually meant, but will compile with the C++17 standard to make the code more pleasant to read (and write).

We will examine such an allocator, `small_allocator<T>`, and implement it in a way that resembles `std::allocator<T>` in order to highlight what it meant to write an allocator in the C++11 era, and then compare that with an equivalent expressed for a more recent version of the standard. We will use C++17 features in our implementation as we do not want to introduce unnecessary complexity in an already subtle topic.

After introducing `small_allocator<T>`, we will show how `Vector<T>` from *Chapter 12* and *Chapter 13* can be enhanced and become `Vector<T,A>`, and how A can be `std::allocator<T>`, `small_allocator<T>`, or any other conforming allocator type.

Type aliases

An allocator of the T type had to expose type aliases for `value_type`, `size_type`, `difference_type` (the type one would get from subtracting two `pointer` objects), `pointer`, `const_pointer`, `reference`, and `const_reference`. One way to think about this is that to a container, the allocator represents the underlying memory and consequently defines the types that best describe these low-level ideas. Containers could then map their own aliases to those of their allocator for conformity.

In our `small_allocator<T>` type, this would translate to the following:

```
template <class T>
struct small_allocator {
    using value_type = T;
    using pointer = T*;
    using const_pointer = const T*;
    using reference = T&;
    using const_reference = const T&;
    using size_type = std::size_t;
    using difference_type = std::ptrdiff_t;
    // ...
```

In practice, for an allocator of T, one could expect these type aliases to correspond to those shown here for `small_allocator<T>` in all but the strangest cases: as long as `value_type` is defined, we can almost always infer the others.

Member functions

An allocator of the `T` type had to expose a member function, `max_size()`, that was supposed to return the size of the largest block that this allocator could actually allocate.

In practice, that often proved to be unimplementable as, with some operating systems, allocation always succeeds (but usage of the allocated memory may fail if the program is over-allocated) so that function usually turned out to be implemented on a best-effort basis on a given platform. A possible implementation would be the following:

```
// ...
constexpr size_type max_size() const {
    return std::numeric_limits<size_type>::max(); // bah
}
// ...
```

💡 **Quick tip**: Enhance your coding experience with the **AI Code Explainer** and **Quick Copy** features. Open this book in the next-gen Packt Reader. Click the **Copy** button (**1**) to quickly copy code into your coding environment, or click the **Explain** button (**2**) to get the AI assistant to explain a block of code to you.

```
                                              Copy      Explain
function calculate(a, b) {
    return {sum: a + b};                       1          2
};
```

📖 **The next-gen Packt Reader** is included for free with the purchase of this book. Unlock it by scanning the QR code below or visiting `https://www.packtpub.com/unlock/9781805129806`.

An allocator of the `T` type also had to expose two overloads of a function that uses all the words this author's students "love" in a single signature (appreciate the irony!). Consider `pointer address(reference r)` as well as the equivalent for `const` objects, which is `const_pointer address(const_reference r)`. The intent here is to abstract the ways in which one would get the address of an object.

It would be tempting to implement each of these functions as `return &r;` but in practice, this is perilous as users are allowed to overload the unary `operator&()` for their types, and this means such an implementation would call arbitrary code, a scary prospect indeed... Avoid overloading something as fundamental as "taking the address of an object" unless you really, *really* have a good reason to do so, and even then, consider alternative approaches to solving your problem!

A better implementation technique is to express these functions through `return std::addressof(r);` where `std::addressof()` is a "magical" standard library function from `<memory>` (that is, `constexpr`) and returns the address of an object without going through an overloadable facility:

```
// ...
constexpr pointer address(reference r) const {
    return std::addressof(r);
}
constexpr
    const_pointer address(const_reference r) const {
    return std::addressof(r);
}
// ...
```

Obviously, an allocator needs to expose member functions to perform the actual memory allocation. The signatures for these are `allocate(size_type n)` and `deallocate(pointer p, size_type n)`. A simple implementation of these two functions could be the following:

```
// ...
pointer allocate(size_type n) {
    auto p = static_cast<pointer>(
        malloc(n * sizeof(value_type))
    );
    if (!p) throw std::bad_alloc{};
    return p;
}
void deallocate(pointer p, size_type) {
    free(p);
}
// ...
```

The `allocate()` member function used to take a second argument of the `void*` type named `hint`, which was initialized to `nullptr` by default. This argument was meant to inform the allocator of a location that could be used to provide storage, in case the container knew of such a location. That feature seemed rarely (if ever) used in practice, and was deprecated in C++17 and then removed in C++20.

These two functions are the essence of why allocators exist: `allocate()` returns a chunk of memory big enough to hold n contiguous elements of `value_type`, throwing `bad_alloc` on failure, and `deallocate()` deallocates a chunk of memory big enough to hold n contiguous elements of `value_type`. When one writes an allocator, one usually seeks to provide an answer to this specific problem.

> **Bytes or objects**
>
> Interestingly, contrary to `operator new()`, which takes a number of *bytes* as argument, `allocate()` and `deallocate()` both take as argument a number of *objects*. That is because traditional allocators are type-aware (they are allocators of some type T after all), whereas `operator new()` and friends are (mostly) type-agnostic. You will notice later in this chapter that PMR allocators (which one might call "a step back") use memory resources that are type-agnostic such as `malloc()` or `operator new()`.

Both `allocate()` and `deallocate()` deliberately lie to client code: they trade in raw memory and neither create nor destroy objects of type T, yet `allocate()` returns a `pointer` (a T*, essentially) and `deallocate()` accepts a `pointer` as argument even though all T objects are assumed to have been destroyed beforehand.

The fact that these functions lie to the type system is a good thing in a way, as it relieves the container from the task of doing so. Of course, the container has to be aware of what these functions do and should not assume the presence of objects in memory returned by `allocate()` or passed to `deallocate()`.

Finally, an allocator had to expose member functions to turn raw memory into objects and conversely. The `construct(pointer p, const_reference r)` and `destroy(pointer p)` functions are respectively meant to construct a copy of r at location p (which is assumed to have been allocated beforehand), and destroy the object at location p (without deallocating the underlying storage):

```
// ...
void construct(pointer p, const_reference r) {
    new (static_cast<void*>(p)) value_type(r);
}
void destroy(const_pointer p) {
    if(p) p->~value_type();
}
// ...
template <class U>
struct rebind {
    using other = small_allocator<U>;
};
};
```

One can expect that most implementations will do essentially what the preceding code does. There are alternatives, but they are rarely met in practice.

Again, these functions lie to the type system: `construct()` takes a `pointer` (a `T*`, in practice) as argument but when the function is called, that pointer points to raw memory, not to an object of type T.

> **What about rebind?**
>
> You will notice that we did not discuss the `rebind` public template type, but that is only because the idea behind this type is easier to understand when facing the kind of problem it is meant to solve. We will face such a situation when discussing allocator-aware node-based containers through our `ForwardList<T,A>` class later in this chapter.

Past this point, the requirement for an allocator is to define whether two allocator objects of different types are equal or not. A possible implementation would be the following:

```
// ...
template <class T, class U>
constexpr bool operator==(const small_allocator<T>&,
                          const small_allocator<U>&) {
   return true;
}
template <class T, class U>
constexpr bool operator!=(const small_allocator<T>&,
                          const small_allocator<U>&) {
   return false;
}
```

Expressed otherwise, two `small_allocator` specializations for distinct types describe the same strategy and are thus considered equal. "But wait!" you say, "Where do you take into account the state of the allocators in this computation?". But here's a revelation: pre-C++11 allocators were essentially assumed to be *stateless*.

Well, they were not, but it was unclear what would happen to an allocator if it was associated with a container object and that object was copied. You see, if an allocator has *state*, we have to know what to do with that state when the allocator is copied. Is the state copied? Is it shared? In the pre-C++11 era, we did not know what to do in such a situation, so unless a container was used in a context where it would not be copied, as in the case of a vector local to a function and associated with an allocator that uses stack space as storage, most people avoided stateful allocators altogether.

> **But what about stateful allocators?**
>
> As hinted, stateful allocators were a possibility back then (they existed, and they were used in practice). How is one expected to define allocator equality for stateful allocators (and for allocators in general)? The general idea is that two allocators should compare equally if memory allocated from one can be deallocated from the other. With an allocator that delegates allocation tasks to free functions such as `std::malloc()` or `::operator new()`, equality is trivially `true`, but stateful allocators require us to think about how to define this relation.

Before we look at how we could write allocator-aware containers, we will take a step back and see how we could adapt some of the uninitialized memory algorithms used in *Chapter 12* and *Chapter 13* to use the services of an allocator. This will reduce the refactoring effort required later in the process.

Some allocator-aware support algorithms

Since we are using allocators to bridge the gap between raw storage and objects, we will not be able to use the raw memory algorithms seen in *Chapter 12* and *Chapter 13* in our allocator-aware implementations.

We have the option of writing our own versions of these algorithms in detail at each call site within our containers, but that would be tedious (and bug-prone). Instead, we will write somewhat simplified versions of these low-level memory management algorithms and make these simplified versions use an allocator passed as an argument. In so doing, we will reduce the impact of making containers allocator-aware on our implementation.

The first three of these algorithms will be allocator-aware versions of algorithms that initialize a range of values, as well as one that destroys such a range. To minimize the impact on the existing implementations, we will essentially use the same signature as their non-allocator-aware counterpart, but with an added argument that is a reference to the allocator. For the algorithm that fills a block of raw memory with some value, we have the following:

```
template <class A, class IIt, class T>
void uninitialized_fill_with_allocator(
    A& alloc, IIt bd, IIt ed, T init
) {
    // bd: beginning of destination
    // ed: end of destination
    auto p = bd;
    try {
        for (; p != ed; ++p)
            alloc.construct(p, init);
    } catch (...) {
        for (auto q = bd; q != p; ++q)
            alloc.destroy(q);
        throw;
    }
}
```

Then, for the algorithm that copies a sequence of values to a block of raw memory, we have the following:

```
template <class A, class IIt, class OIt>
void uninitialized_copy_with_allocator(
    A& alloc, IIt bs, IIt es, OIt bd
) {
    // bs: beginning of source
    // es: end of source
    // bd: beginning of destination,
    auto p = bd;
    try {
        for (auto q = bs; q != es; ++q) {
            alloc.construct(p, *q);
            ++p;
        }
    } catch (...) {
        for (auto q = bd; q != p; ++q)
            alloc.destroy(q);
        throw;
    }
}
```

For the algorithm that moves a sequence of values to a block of raw memory, we have the following:

```
template <class A, class IIt, class OIt>
void uninitialized_move_with_allocator(
    A& alloc, IIt bs, IIt es, OIt bd
) {
    // bs: beginning of source
    // es: end of source
    // bd: beginning of destination,
    auto p = bd;
    try {
        for (auto q = bs; q != es; ++q) {
            alloc.construct(p, std::move(*q));
            ++p;
        }
    } catch (...) {
        for (auto q = bd; q != p; ++q)
            alloc.destroy(q);
        throw;
    }
}
```

Finally, for the algorithm that transforms a sequence of objects into a block of raw memory, we have the following:

```
template <class A, class It>
    void destroy_with_allocator(A &alloc, It b, It e) {
        for (; b != e; ++b)
            alloc.destroy(b);
    }
```

Note that in each case, the implementation would be more conformant if, when an exception occurs, objects were destroyed in reverse order of construction. Feel free to implement this slight adjustment; it's not difficult but it would introduce some noise in our example.

The other standard facility we will rewrite is `cmp_less()`, which allows comparing a signed value with an unsigned value without getting caught by the integer promotion rules of the C language. It's not directly memory-related, but we need it in our `Vector<T>` implementation, and it's a C++20 feature, which makes it unavailable when we compile for C++17:

```
template<class T, class U>
    constexpr bool cmp_less(T a, U b) noexcept {
        if constexpr (std::is_signed_v<T> ==
                        std::is_signed_v<U>)
            return a < b;
        else if constexpr (std::is_signed_v<T>)
            return a < 0 || std::make_unsigned_t<T>(a) < b;
        else
            return b >= 0 && a < std::make_unsigned_t<U>(b);
    }
```

Both the `std::is_signed<T>` trait as well as the `std::make_unsigned<T>()` function can be found in header `<type_traits>`.

Conditional compilation and feature test macros

As an aside, if you find yourself having to maintain code where a feature such as `std::cmp_less()` might or might not be available, such as a source file that is sometimes compiled for C++20 and sometimes compiled for C++17, consider conditional inclusion of your "homemade workaround" version by testing the associated feature test macro.

For this specific case, one could wrap the definition of our personal version of `cmp_less()` with `#ifndef __cpp_lib_integer_comparison_functions` to make sure it is only provided if there is no version provided by one's standard library implementation.

Now, let's see how these allocators and our support algorithms can be used by a container, first with a container that uses contiguous storage (our Vector<T, A> class) and then with a node-based container (our ForwardList<T, A> class).

An allocator-aware Vector<T,A> class

We are now ready to look at how introducing allocator awareness in a container that uses contiguous memory (more specifically, our Vector<T> class) impacts the implementation of that container. Note that we will use the explicit memory management approach from *Chapter 12* as a baseline in this case since we want to explore the impact of allocator awareness and this will help us make the implementation changes more apparent. Feel free to adapt the code in this chapter with an implicit approach to memory management if you are so inclined.

Starting with the template's signature itself, we now have a two-type template with T being the type of the elements and A being the type for the allocator, but with a reasonable default type for A such that casual users will not need to worry about such technical details:

```
template <class T, class A = std::allocator<T>>
class Vector : A { // note: private inheritance
public:
   using value_type = typename A::value_type;
   using size_type = typename A::size_type;
   using pointer = typename A::pointer;
   using const_pointer = typename A::const_pointer;
   using reference = typename A::reference;
   using const_reference = typename A::const_reference;
private:
   // deliberately self-exposing selected members
   // of the private base class as our own
   using A::allocate;
   using A::deallocate;
   using A::construct;
   using A::destroy;
   // ...
```

Note some techniques here:

- Since we expect A to be stateless, we used private inheritance and made A a base class of Vector<T, A>, enabling the empty base optimization. Alternatively, we could also have used a data member of type A inside each Vector<T, A> object (perhaps incurring a small size penalty).

- We deduced the type aliases of the container from those of its allocator. This probably changes nothing in practice with respect to the aliases we used in previous chapters, but A might be doing some "fancy tricks" (one can never be too careful).

- In a private section of our class, we expose some selected members of our base class as our own. This will make the code less verbose later on, allowing us to write `allocate(n)` instead of `this->A::allocate(n)`, for example.

The non-allocating members of our class do not change, unsurprisingly. Data members stay the same, and so do basic accessors such as `size()`, `empty()`, `begin()`, `end()`, `front()`, `operator[]`, and so on. Even the default constructor remains unchanged since it does not allocate memory and so does not need to interact with its allocator.

There is a new constructor needed, one that accepts as argument an allocator. This one is particularly useful in the case of stateful allocators:

```
// ...
Vector(A &alloc) : A{ alloc } {
}
// ...
```

Of course, when reaching the constructors that do need to allocate memory, the situation becomes more interesting. Take, for example, the constructor that takes as argument a number of elements and an initial value:

```
// ...
Vector(size_type n, const_reference init)
   : A{},elems{ allocate(n) },
     nelems{ n }, cap{ n } {
   try {
     uninitialized_fill_with_allocator(
        *static_cast<A*>(this), begin(), end(), init
     );
   } catch (...) {
     deallocate(elems, capacity());
     throw;
   }
}
// ...
```

There is a lot to say here:

- The memory block that will serve as the underlying storage for our container is allocated through a call to our base class's `allocate()` member function. Remember that even though this yields a `pointer` (a `T*`), that is a lie and there are no `T` objects in the newly allocated block.

- We fill that uninitialized memory block with T objects through our homemade allocator-aware version of std::uninitialized_fill() (see the _with_allocator suffix). Note how we pass the allocator as an argument to the algorithm: the inheritance relationship between Vector<T,A> and A is private, but the derived class is aware of it and can use that information through static_cast.

- If one of the constructors used in the process of initializing that memory block throws, the algorithm destroys the objects it had created, as usual (no one else really could do it anyway), after which we intercept that exception and deallocate the storage before re-throwing said exception in the interest of exception neutrality.

Similar maneuvers are used in other allocating constructors, with different algorithms used to initialize the allocated storage. The move constructor and the swap() member function do not allocate memory and, for that reason, remain unchanged, and the same goes for the assignment operators: they are built from other member functions and do not need to allocate or deallocate memory by themselves.

As you probably suspected already, the destructor of our container will use the allocator to destroy the objects and deallocate the underlying storage:

```cpp
// ...
~Vector() {
    destroy_with_allocator(
        *static_cast<A*>(this), begin(), end()
    );
    deallocate(elems, capacity());
}
// ...
```

The push_back() and emplace_back() member functions do not allocate by themselves, delegating to our private grow() member function, which, in turn, delegates to reserve() for the allocation, but they do need to construct() an object at the end of the container:

```cpp
// ...
void push_back(const_reference val) {
    if (full()) grow();
    construct(end(), val);
    ++nelems;
}
void push_back(T&& val) {
    if (full()) grow();
    construct(end(), std::move(val));
    ++nelems;
}
template <class ... Args>
reference emplace_back(Args &&...args) {
```

```
        if (full()) grow();
        construct(end(), std::forward<Args>(args)...);
        ++nelems;
        return back();
    }
    // ...
```

The principal tools for memory allocation in our class are probably `reserve()` and `resize()`. In both cases, the algorithm remains as it was, but the low-level memory management tasks are delegated to the allocator. For `reserve()`, this leads us to the following:

```
    // ...
    void reserve(size_type new_cap) {
        if (new_cap <= capacity()) return;
        auto p = allocate(new_cap);
        if constexpr (std::is_nothrow_move_assignable_v<T>) {
            uninitialized_move_with_allocator(
                *static_cast<A*>(this), begin(), end(), p
            );
        } else {
            auto src_p = begin();
            auto b = p, e = p + size();
            try {
                uninitialized_copy_with_allocator(
                    *static_cast<A*>(this), begin(), end(), p
                );
            } catch (...) {
                deallocate(p, new_cap);
                throw;
            }
        }
        deallocate(elems, capacity());
        elems = p;
        cap = new_cap;
    }
    // ...
```

Whereas, for `resize()`, we now have the following:

```
    // ...
    void resize(size_type new_cap) {
        if (new_cap <= capacity()) return;
        auto p = allocate(new_cap);
        if constexpr (std::is_nothrow_move_assignable_v<T>) {
            uninitialized_move_with_allocator(
```

```
            *static_cast<A*>(this), begin(), end(), p
        );
    } else {
      uninitialized_copy_with_allocator(
          *static_cast<A*>(this), begin(), end(), p
      );
    }
    try {
      uninitialized_fill_with_allocator(
          *static_cast<A*>(this),
          p + size(), p + new_cap, value_type{}
      );
      destroy_with_allocator(
          *static_cast<A*>(this), begin(), end()
      );
      deallocate(elems, capacity());
      elems = p;
      nelems = cap = new_cap;
    } catch(...) {
      destroy_with_allocator(
          *static_cast<A*>(this), p, p + size()
      );
      deallocate(p, new_cap);
      throw;
    }
  }
}
// ...
```

In previous implementations of the Vector<T> class, we had implemented one version each of insert() and erase(), as implementing the whole set of these functions would make this book unreasonably large. Since both functions meddle with initialized and uninitialized memory, they need to be adapted to use the services of the allocator rather than doing their own memory management.

In the case of insert(), the key aspects of the function that need to be adjusted are those that copy or move objects into raw memory:

```
// ...
template <class It>
iterator insert(const_iterator pos, It first, It last) {
    iterator pos_ = const_cast<iterator>(pos);
    const auto remaining = capacity() - size();
    const auto n = std::distance(first, last);
//      if (std::cmp_less(remaining, n)) { // needs C++20
    if(cmp_less(remaining, n)) {
```

```
        auto index = std::distance(begin(), pos_);
        reserve(capacity() + n - remaining);
        pos_ = std::next(begin(), index);
    }
    const auto nb_to_uninit_displace =
        std::min<std::ptrdiff_t>(n, end() - pos_);
    auto where_to_uninit_displace =
        end() + n - nb_to_uninit_displace;
    if constexpr (
        std::is_nothrow_move_constructible_v<T>
    )
        uninitialized_move_with_allocator(
            *static_cast<A*>(this),
            end() - nb_to_uninit_displace, end(),
            where_to_uninit_displace
        );
    else
        uninitialized_copy_with_allocator(
            *static_cast<A*>(this),
            end() - nb_to_uninit_displace, end(),
            where_to_uninit_displace
        );
    // note : might be zero
    const auto nb_to_uninit_insert =
        std::max<std::ptrdiff_t>(
            0, n - nb_to_uninit_displace
        );
    auto where_to_uninit_insert = end();
    uninitialized_copy_with_allocator(
        *static_cast<A*>(this),
        last - nb_to_uninit_insert, last,
        where_to_uninit_insert
    );
    // note : might be zero
    const auto nb_to_backward_displace =
        std::max<std::ptrdiff_t>(
            0, end() - pos_ - nb_to_uninit_displace
        );
    auto where_to_backward_displace = end();
    if constexpr (std::is_nothrow_move_assignable_v<T>)
        std::move_backward(
            pos_, pos_ + nb_to_backward_displace,
            where_to_backward_displace
```

```
        );
    else
        std::copy_backward(
            pos_, pos_ + nb_to_backward_displace,
            where_to_backward_displace
        );
        std::copy(
            first, first + n - nb_to_uninit_insert, pos_
        );
        nelems += n;
        return pos_;
    }
    // ...
```

In the case of `erase()`, what we do is copy all objects after the erased one "to the left" by one position; the object at the end of the sequence after this copying has been performed has to be destroyed, and for this, we need to use the allocator's services. An example follows:

```
    // ...
    iterator erase(const_iterator pos) {
        iterator pos_ = const_cast<iterator>(pos);
        if (pos_ == end()) return pos_;
        std::copy(std::next(pos_), end(), pos_);
        destroy(std::prev(end()));
        --nelems;
        return pos_;
    }
};
```

As you have probably gathered at this point, we could optimize or simplify these functions in numerous ways, such as the following:

- There is a common core functionality between `reserve()` and `resize()`, so we could essentially claim that `resize()` is in large part like `reserve()` followed by an uninitialized fill and express it as such.

- In the case of `erase()`, at compile time, we could test the value of the `std::is_nothrow_move_assignable_v<T>` trait and, if that condition holds, replace the call to `std::copy()` with a call to `std::move()`.

- We could make `insert()` and `erase()` more exception-safe than they are, although this would make the code a bit long for a book such as this one.

At this point, we have an allocator-aware container that manages contiguous memory. It will now be interesting to see what the impacts of allocator awareness will be on a node-based container, something we will address through an allocator-aware version of the `ForwardList<T>` class.

An allocator-aware ForwardList<T,A> class

A funny thing happens when writing allocator-aware node-based containers. Pay attention to the beginning of our `ForwardList<T,A>` class:

```
template <class T, class A = std::allocator<T>>
class ForwardList {
public:
    using value_type = typename A::value_type;
    // likewise for the other aliases
private:
    struct Node {
        value_type value;
        Node *next = nullptr;
        Node(const_reference value) : value { value } {
        }
        Node(value_type &&value)
            : value { std::move(value) } {
        }
    };
    Node *head {};
    size_type nelems {};
    // ...
```

Did you notice something interesting about type A? Think about it...

Yes, that's it: A *is the wrong type*! A node-based container such as `ForwardList<T,A>` never allocates objects of type T: it allocates *nodes* that (most probably) contain T objects and other things such as, in this case, a pointer to the next Node in the sequence.

Knowing this, if we were supplied some allocator A that modeled a size-aware allocation strategy akin to what we used in our arena for `Orc` objects in *Chapter 10*, making the allocator aware of T (and thus, of `sizeof(T)`) would lead to an arena that manages objects of the wrong size. This is not good!

We are faced with an interesting conundrum: user code provides us with an allocator because it wants our container to put an *allocation strategy* to good use. That allocation strategy appears as a template parameter of our container, which is why it is associated with the type of its elements (we do not know what the nodes will be at this point in the definition of our container class). Only later, when we have defined what a node will be for our container, are we really ready to say what will need to be allocated, but then A already exists and is already associated to T, not to the type we really need, which is `ForwardList<T,A>::Node`.

Note that we have instantiated type A but have not constructed any object of that type. Lucky for us, as that would have been wasteful (we would never use it!). What we do need is a type that is just like A, but able to allocate objects of our Node type instead of objects of type T. We need a way to *clone the allocation strategy* described by A and apply it to another type.

This is exactly what `rebind` is for. Remember that we mentioned this template type when writing `small_allocator<T>` earlier but said we would return to it when we could put it to good use? There we are, dear reader. As a reminder, in the context of an allocator, `rebind` presents itself as follows:

```
template <class T>
  class small_allocator { // for example
  // ...
  template <class U>
    struct rebind {
      using other = small_allocator<U>;
    };
  // ...
};
```

You can see `rebind` as some kind of weird code poetry: it is a way for the allocator to say "If you want the same type as myself but applied to some U type instead of T, here's what that type would be."

Returning to our `ForwardList<T,A>` class, now that we know what `rebind` is for, we can create our own internal allocator type, `Alloc`. This will be "like the allocator type A but applied to Node, not to T" and create an object of that type (incidentally named `alloc` in our implementation), which we will use to perform the memory management tasks in our container:

```
// ...
using Alloc = typename A::rebind<Node>::other;
Alloc alloc;
// ...
```

It's a nice trick, isn't it? Remember that we cloned the *strategy*, the type, not an actual object so any state some hypothetical A object would have had would not necessarily be part of our new `Alloc` type (at least not without performing some non-trivial acrobatics). This is yet another reminder that with traditional allocators as they were originally designed, copying and moving allocator state was a complex problem.

As was the case for the transformation from `Vector<T>` to `Vector<T,A>`, a significant portion of our `List<T>` implementation involved no memory allocation and thus needs not change with `List<T,A>`. This includes the `size()`, `empty()`, `begin()`, `end()`, `swap()`, `front()`, and `operator==()` member functions, among others, as well as most of the `List<T,A>::Iterator<U>` class definition. As our implementation of `ForwardList<T,A>` will need to access private data member `cur` of its iterators on occasion, we give it `friend` privileges over `Iterator<U>`:

```
// ...
template <class U> class Iterator {
    // ...
private:
    Node *cur {};
    friend class ForwardList<T,A>;
    // ...
};
// ...
```

There are, of course, member functions of `ForwardList<T,A>` that use memory allocation mechanisms. One of them is `clear()`, whose role is to destroy the nodes in the container. The destruction and deallocation of `Node` objects have to be performed through the allocator, replacing the call to `operator delete()` with a pair of function calls:

```
// ...
void clear() noexcept {
    for(auto p = head; p; ) {
        auto q = p->next;
        alloc.destroy(p);
        alloc.deallocate(p, 1);
        p = q;
    }
    nelems = 0;
}
// ...
```

In `ForwardList<T>`, we made all of the allocating constructors converge toward a single sequence constructor that accepted a pair of iterators (type `It`) as arguments. This localizes the changes required for constructors in `ForwardList<T,A>` to that single function, something that simplifies our task.

In `ForwardList<T>`, we had constrained template parameter `It` by the `std::forward_iterator` concept, but concepts are a C++20 feature and we are compiling this implementation in C++17 so we will (sadly) let go of this constraint for the time being.

Having to perform allocation and construction in separate steps complicates our implementation a little, but I think you esteemed readers, will not find this to be unsurmountable:

```cpp
// ...
template <class It> // <std::forward_iterator It>
    ForwardList(It b, It e) {
        if(b == e) return;
        try {
            head = alloc.allocate(1);
            alloc.construct(head, *b);
            auto q = head;
            ++nelems;
            for(++b; b != e; ++b) {
                auto ptr = alloc.allocate(1);
                alloc.construct(ptr, *b);
                q->next = ptr;
                q = q->next;
                ++nelems;
            }
        } catch (...) {
            clear();
            throw;
        }
    }
// ...
```

We also had written insertion member functions for ForwardList<T>, so these will also need to be adapted to use allocators in ForwardList<T,A>. We had two overloads of push_front():

```cpp
// ...
void push_front(const_reference val) {
    auto p = alloc.allocate(1);
    alloc.construct(p, val);
    p->next = head;
    head = p;
    ++nelems;
}
void push_front(T&& val) {
    auto p = alloc.allocate(1);
    alloc.construct(p, std::move(val));
    p->next = head;
    head = p;
    ++nelems;
}
// ...
```

We also had two overloads of `insert_after()`, one that inserted a single value and one that inserted the elements in a half-open range. In the latter case, we will need to put aside the `std::forward_iterator` constraint on type `It` again as we are compiling for C++17:

```
// ...
iterator
    insert_after(iterator pos, const_reference value) {
    auto p = alloc.allocate(1);
    alloc.construct(p, value);
    p->next = pos.cur->next;
    pos.cur->next = p;
    ++nelems;
    return { p };
}
template <class It> // <std::input_iterator It>
    iterator insert_after(iterator pos, It b, It e) {
        for(; b != e; ++b)
            pos = insert_after(pos, *b);
        return pos;
    }
// ...
```

Our `erase_after()` member function is similarly adjusted:

```
// ...
iterator erase_after(iterator pos) {
    if (pos == end() || std::next(pos) == end())
        return end();
    auto p = pos.cur->next->next;
    alloc.destroy(pos.cur->next);
    alloc.deallocate(pos.cur->next, 1);
    --nelems;
    pos.cur->next = p;
    return { p->next };
}
};
```

That concludes our transformation of `ForwardList<T>` into an allocator-aware `ForwardList<T,A>` class. I hope, dear reader, that this was not as difficult as some might have feared: given our understanding of the principles and fundamental techniques presented in this book, integrating allocator awareness in a container should make some sort of sense to most of us at this point.

Now that we have seen how to write a "traditional" iterator as well as examples of how one can make a container allocator-aware, you might be wondering about the benefits of using allocators. We know that allocators give use code control over the ways in which containers manage memory, but what can we gain from that control?

Example usage – a sequential buffer allocator

A classical example of allocator usage is one that, instead of allocating memory from the free store, manages a pre-allocated chunk of memory. That memory does not have to come from the execution stack of a thread, but that's often what is done in practice, so that's what our example code will do.

What you need to know before reading the following example is this:

- This sort of allocator is a specialized tool for specialized users. We expect users to know what they are doing.

- The pre-allocated buffer that will be managed by the allocator in our example has to be properly aligned for the objects that will be stored therein. If you want to adapt this example to handle memory allocation for any naturally aligned object, some additional effort will be required (you will want the allocator to yield addresses aligned on a `std::max_align_t` boundary, something our example allocator does not do).

- Some care will need to be taken if client code tries to "over-allocate," asking for more memory than what the managed buffer could provide. In this example, we will throw `std::bad_alloc` as usual, but alternatives exist.

> **When bad_alloc is not an option…**
>
> For some applications, throwing or otherwise failing to allocate is not an option. The fact that a specialized allocator cannot meet an allocation request should not, for these applications, result in throwing an exception as throwing means "I cannot meet the postconditions of this function."
>
> One thing that some applications do when a sequential buffer allocator runs out of memory is simply call `::operator new()` and take the indeterministic allocation time "hit" but leave a trace somewhere (a log, maybe) that this happened. This means the program will leak memory, but for some applications (say, a stock market exchange program that is restarted every day), one can expect those leaks to be relatively low in number, and the fact that there is a trace that something leaked will let programmers look at the problem and (hopefully) fix it before the next day. The "lesser of two evils," as some might say.

Our sequential buffer allocator will look like this:

```
#include <cstdint>
template <class T>
struct seq_buf_allocator {
    using value_type = T;
```

```
    // pointer, reference and other aliases are as
    // usual, and so is max_size()
private:
    char *buf;
    pointer cur;
    size_type cap;
public:
    seq_buf_allocator(char *buf, size_type cap) noexcept
        : buf{ buf }, cap{ cap } {
        cur = reinterpret_cast<pointer>(buf);
    }
    // ...
```

As you can see, the state for this allocator resembles what we did for the size-based arena in *Chapter 10*: we know where the buffer to manage starts (`buf`), how big it is (`cap`), and where we are at in our sequential allocation process (`cur`).

We make `cur` a `pointer`-type object to simplify computation later, in the `allocate()` member function, but it's a convenience, not a necessity.

The `allocate()` member function is very simple in the sense that it performs a constant-time computation, returning contiguously allocated objects from the underlying storage without even having to reuse that memory after it has been deallocated. Part of the work done in `allocate()` requires avoiding over-allocating, and to do this, we will compare pointers, but we might have to compare a pointer within the allocated memory block with one that is not within that block (it all depends on the value of our arguments). This would lead us into undefined behavior, something we need to avoid, so we cast our pointers to `std::intptr_t` objects and compare the resulting integral values instead.

> **What if std::intptr_t is not offered on my platform?**
>
> Types `std::intptr_t` and `std::uintptr_t` are conditionally supported in C++, which means that there might be vendors that do not offer these type aliases. If you find yourself in this unlikely but not impossible situation, you can simply keep track of the number of objects allocated and compare this with the `cap` data member to achieve the same effect.

We end up with the following `allocate()` implementation, accompanied by the corresponding `deallocate()` member function, which is, in this case, effectively a no-op:

```
    // ...
    // rebind, address(), construct() and destroy()
    // are all as usual
    pointer allocate(size_type n) {
        auto
            request = reinterpret_cast<
```

```
            std::intptr_t
         >(cur + n),
         limit = reinterpret_cast<
            std::intptr_t
         >(buf + cap);
      if(request >= limit)
         throw std::bad_alloc{};
      auto q = cur;
      cur += n;
      return q;
   }
   void deallocate(pointer, size_type) {
   }
};
// ...
```

As this allocator is stateful, we need to give some thought to allocator equality. What we will do in this case is the following:

```
template <class T, class U>
  constexpr bool operator==(const seq_buf_allocator<T> &a,
                            const seq_buf_allocator<U> &b) {
      return a.cur == b.cur; // maybe?
  }
template <class T, class U>
  constexpr bool operator!=(const seq_buf_allocator<T> &a,
                            const seq_buf_allocator<U> &b) {
      return !(a == b);
  }
```

These equality operators make sense at a specific moment in time only, but then this allocator type is not really meant to be copied in practice; if you plan to use a buffer such as this and share its internal state, you will need to give some thought to the way the original and the copy share their internal state and remain coherent with one another – something we do not need to do in this case.

As you can see, we test for overflow on allocation and throw std::bad_alloc if an allocation request would lead to a buffer overflow, but that's only one option among others, as we have discussed earlier in this chapter:

```
#include <chrono>
#include <utility>
template <class F, class ... Args>
   auto test(F f, Args &&... args) {
      using namespace std;
```

```
      using namespace std::chrono;
      auto pre = high_resolution_clock::now();
      auto res = f(std::forward<Args>(args)...);
      auto post = high_resolution_clock::now();
      return pair{ res, post - pre };
   }
#include <iostream>
#include <vector>
struct Data { int n; };
int main() {
   using namespace std::chrono;
   enum { N = 500'000 };
   {
      std::vector<Data> v;
      auto [r, dt] = test([](auto & v) {
         v.reserve(N);
         for(int i = 0; i != N; ++i)
            v.push_back({ i + 1 });
         return v.back();
      }, v);
      std::cout << "vector<Data>:\n\t"
                << v.size()
                << " insertions in "
                << duration_cast<microseconds>(dt).count()
                << " us\n";
   }
   {
      alignas(Data) char buf[N * sizeof(Data)];
      seq_buf_allocator<Data> alloc{ buf, sizeof buf };
      std::vector<Data, seq_buf_allocator<Data>> v(alloc);
      auto [r, dt] = test([](auto & v) {
         v.reserve(N);
         for(int i = 0; i != N; ++i)
            v.push_back({ i + 1 });
         return v.back();
      }, v);
      std::cout
         << "vector<Data, seq_buf_allocator<Data>>:\n\t"
         << v.size()
         << " insertions in "
         << duration_cast<microseconds>(dt).count()
         << " us\n";
   }
```

```
    // do the same replacing std::vector with Vector
}
```

Here are a few things you might want to note at this point:

- The test code is the same irrespective of the chosen allocator.

- When using a stateful allocator, we need to use a parametric constructor that accepts the allocator as argument.

- The responsibility with respect to the size and alignment of the buffer used by the seq_buf_allocator<T> falls on the (metaphorical) shoulders of user code. Again, remember that this is a specialized tool, so users are expected to know what they are doing.

- If you run this test on a conforming compiler, you might notice interesting performances with the sequential buffer allocator, and you might notice that Vector<T,A> outperforms std::vector<T,A>, but Vector<T,A> is not as complete and rigorous as its std::counterpart. Prefer the standard facilities in practice.

- There are limitations to the size of the buffer provided to a sequential buffer allocator as stack space is a limited resource (often one or two megabytes overall, so we have less than this to work with). Still, this technique is useful and used in practice in low-latency systems.

- If you apply this sort of allocator with a node-based container list ForwardList<T,A>, remember that there is a size overhead to each node so plan the size of the buffer to provide accordingly.

Of course, that was an implementation that respects C++17 standards. What has changed with respect to allocators since then?

Traditional allocators with contemporary standards

As mentioned already, the traditional approach of ensconcing the allocator type in the associated container type still exists as of this writing, but the way allocators themselves are expressed has changed over time, and the allocators from the previous section, whether small_allocator<T> or seq_buf_allocator<T>, do not compile as written on a C++20 compiler. Before thinking this is sad, know that we can still write these allocators, but we have to write them in a simpler manner. Whew!

Simplification and the advent of a traits-based implementation

The first step in a simplification effort of allocators was the recognition that in most cases, a significant part of the code written in an allocator is what we call "boilerplate code," code that is the same from class to class and could be qualified as "noise."

To that effect, C++11 introduced std::allocator_traits<A>. The idea is that given some typename A::value_type type, one can generate a reasonable and efficient default implementation for most allocator services (including type aliases such as pointer or size_type) as long as one provides implementations for allocate() and deallocate().

Using `small_allocator<T>` as an illustration, we would now be able to simply express that entire allocator type with the following:

```
template <class T>
struct small_allocator {
    using value_type = T;
    T* allocate(std::size_t n) {
        auto p = static_cast<T*>(
            malloc(n * sizeof(value_type))
        );
        if (!p) throw std::bad_alloc{};
        return p;
    }
    void deallocate(T *p, std::size_t) {
        free(p);
    }
};
// ... insert the equality operators here
```

As you can see, this is quite a simplification! This way, a container such as `Vector<T,A>` could now use `std::allocator_traits<A>` instead of A directly when referring to some allocator A's members. With traits being this very thin layer of abstraction that brings no runtime cost to speak of, what they do for some member M is essentially "If A exposes member "M, then use `A::M`; otherwise, here is some reasonable default implementation instead." Of course, there will be no branching here in practice as everything is determined at compile time.

For example, based on our previous `small_allocator<T>` type, given that `small_allocator<T>::allocate()` returns T*, then we can determine that `std::allocator_traits<small_allocator<T>>::pointer` will be equivalent to T*, and a container such as `Vector<T,A>` will make its `pointer` type alias correspond to the type expressed by `std::allocator_traits<A>::pointer`.

For another example, `seq_buf_allocator<T>` would now be expressed as follows:

```
template <class T>
struct seq_buf_allocator {
    using value_type = T;
    using pointer = T*;
    using size_type = std::size_t;
    char* buf;
    pointer cur;
    size_type cap;
    seq_buf_allocator(char* buf, size_type cap) noexcept
        : buf{ buf }, cap{ cap } {
        cur = reinterpret_cast<pointer>(buf);
```

```
    }
    pointer allocate(size_type n) {
        auto request =
            reinterpret_cast<std::intptr_t>(cur + n),
            limit =
            reinterpret_cast<std::intptr_t>(buf + cap);
        if (request > limit) {
            throw std::bad_alloc{};
        }
        auto q = cur;
        cur += n;
        return q;
    }
    void deallocate(pointer, size_type) {
    }
};
// ... insert equality operators here
```

In this case, even though it was not necessary, type seq_buf_allocator<T> exposes the pointer and size_type aliases, which means that for this type, the std::allocator_traits will use the allocator-provided versions instead of trying to synthesize an alternative. As you can see, the contemporary traits-based approach to allocators is very convenient.

What services does type std::allocator_traits<A> provide exactly? Well, as could be expected, this type exposes the usual type aliases of value_type (itself being an alias for A::value_type), pointer, const_pointer, size_type, and difference_type. For convenience, it also exposes aliases allocator_type (equivalent to A): void_pointer and const_void_pointer (respectively equivalent to void* and const void* in most cases). Remember that traits can be specialized, and for that reason, these seemingly evident type aliases could map to more exotic constructs on occasion.

Type std::allocator_traits<A> also exposes the traditional services of an allocator, but in the form of static member functions that take the allocator as first argument, including construct(), destroy(), allocate(), deallocate(), and max_size(). C++23 adds another static member function to this set: allocate_at_least(). This function returns a std::allocation_result object made of the allocated pointer and the actual size of the allocated chunk, expressed as a number of objects (even though, as usual, there is no object in that memory block after allocation has completed).

The rebind mechanism is expressed through types `std::rebind_alloc<A>` and `std::rebind_traits<T>`. When cloning an allocation strategy (for node containers, mostly), the equivalent of `typename A::rebind<T>::other` through these facilities is somewhat more verbose:

```
// ...
    typename std::allocator_traits<
        A
    >::template rebind_alloc<Node>;
// ...
```

Note the presence of the `template` keyword required for grammatical disambiguation Yes, I know what you are thinking now: what a complex language! But we rarely need to use that keyword in practice, and only in those strange situations where the compiler would get confused looking at the following < and not knowing whether it's part of a template signature or whether it's the less-than operator.

There are also new facilities that come with `std::allocator_traits<A>` and deal with allocator lifetime management, something we learned to do over the years:

- Three type aliases that inform containers as to what should be done with the allocator at key moments in the container's life. These types are `propagate_on_container_copy_assignment` (also known as **POCCA**), `propagate_on_container_move_assignment` (also known as **POCMA**), and `propagate_on_container_swap` (also known as **POCS**). All three can be instantiated and behave like `constexpr` functions that yield `true` or `false` (they are equivalent to `std::false_type` by default as, by default, allocators are not meant to be copied or moved). For example, if an allocator exposes type alias POCMA equivalent to `std::true_type`, then a container with that allocator should move the allocator along with the allocated data. Note that in all three cases, this trait being equivalent to `std::true_type` implies a `noexcept` copy, move, or swap (respectively) operation for the allocator.

- Type alias `is_always_equal`; which means that allocators of that type will compare equally irrespective of the type of object to allocate (this alleviates the need for `operator==()` and `operator!=()`, which compare two allocators of the same template but different `value_type` aliases). Don't spend too much time on this one though; it has been deprecated in C++23 and will most likely be removed in C++26.

- The `select_on_container_copy_construction()` member function. This is a `static` member function that takes an allocator and copies it if its allocator traits express that this is the right thing to do, or returns the original allocator otherwise.

Okay, this allocator lifetime management is new and might be surprising. What do we do with this information?

Managing traditional allocator lifetime

What should a container do with allocators within a move or a copy operation? Well, here are the details.

In a container's copy constructor, the best thing to do is probably to use `select_on_container_copy_construction()`. It is that function's purpose, after all. Please do not use that function elsewhere: it is really meant for the copy constructor of a container. Once the container under construction has obtained its allocator, this allocator can be used to perform the remainder of the memory allocation tasks.

In a container's move constructor, the thing to do is move construct the allocator and steal the resources from the source container.

In a container's copy assignment operator, if type alias `propagate_on_container_copy_assignment` is equivalent to `std::true_type` and both allocators compare unequally, the destination container first has to deallocate all memory (that might not be possible later on in the process). Past this point, if `propagate_on_container_copy_assignment` is equivalent to `std::true_type`, then the allocators should be copy-assigned. Only once this is all done should the elements be copied.

The container's move assignment operator is trickier (remember that *move* is an optimization, and we want it to pay off!). The options we face are as follows:

- Type alias `propagate_on_container_move_assignment` is equivalent to `std::true_type`. In this situation, the steps to perform are (a) ensure that the destination container deallocates all memory under its responsibility (it might not be able to do so later on), (b) move-assign the allocator, and then (c) transfer memory ownership from the source container to the destination container.

- Type alias `propagate_on_container_move_assignment` is equivalent to `std::false_type` and the allocators compare equally. In this situation, you can do the same steps as in the previous case but do not move the container.

- Type alias `propagate_on_container_move_assignment` is equivalent to `std::false_type` and the allocators compare unequally. In this case, ownership cannot really be transferred, so the best one can do is move the objects themselves from the source container to the destination container.

Luckily, all of these allocator properties can be tested at compile time so the decision-making process does not need to incur any runtime cost.

> **Things we do for concision…**
>
> You will notice our Vector<T,A> and ForwardList<T,A> types do not do the entire "allocator lifetime management dance" in order to keep our examples reasonably short, and because the way in which we manage allocator copy and movement is an interesting design aspect that would require adding at least one chapter to this already rather big book. Please be tolerant, dear reader.

Using traits-based allocators in allocator-aware containers

The remaining question with traditional allocators in a traits-based approach is: how do containers use them?

The first thing we will need to do is to adapt our allocator-aware adaptation of the standard uninitialized memory algorithms. For example, our personal adaptation of std::uninitialized_copy() becomes the following:

```
template <class A, class IIt, class OIt>
void uninitialized_copy_with_allocator
   (A &a, IIt bs, IIt es, OIt bd) {
   auto p = bd;
   try {
      for (auto q = bs; q != es; ++q) {
         std::allocator_traits<A>::construct(a, p, *q);
         ++p;
      }
   } catch (...) {
      for (auto q = bd; q != p; ++q)
         std::allocator_traits<A>::destroy(a, q);
      throw;
   }
}
```

As you can see, we are now using std::allocator_traits<A> instead of A directly, opening up customization opportunities, and passing the allocator as first argument since the std::allocator_traits<A> member functions are all static. The same adjustment can be applied to the other allocator-aware versions of the algorithms we wrote, with the same calling pattern and passing the allocator as first argument.

Then, we reach our Vector<T,A> type. How do we adjust its implementation to use the contemporary traits-based allocators? The first thing to do is to adjust the source of the container's type aliases:

```
template <class T, class A = std::allocator<T>>
class Vector : A { // note: private inheritance
public:
```

```
using value_type =
    typename std::allocator_traits<A>::value_type;
using size_type =
    typename std::allocator_traits<A>::size_type;
using pointer =
    typename std::allocator_traits<A>::pointer;
using const_pointer =
    typename std::allocator_traits<A>::const_pointer;
using reference = value_type&;
using const_reference = const value_type&;
// ...
```

You might be surprised that type aliases `reference` and `const_reference` are not taken from `std::allocator_traits<A>`, but there is a reason for this. In C++, as in this writing, we can design types that behave like "smart pointers" (we have even done so in this book; see *Chapter 6*), so an abstraction is useful in case the allocator provides pointers that are not raw pointers, but there is no known way to write "smart references" (that would require being able to overload `operator.` `()` and proposals to that effect have so far failed to be accepted).

The only reference type that behaves like a reference to `T` is... well, `T&`. For that reason, these type aliases were deprecated in C++17 and removed in C++20. We can still provide them to clarify our type's member function signatures, but they are no longer required by the standard.

As far as the member functions of `Vector<T, A>` go, the general idea is that all calls to member functions of `A` are replaced with calls to `static` member functions of `std::allocator_traits<A>` that take a reference to the `A` object as argument (remember that in our `Vector<T, A>` implementation, `A` is a `private` base class of the container). Here is an example:

```
Vector(size_type n, const_reference init)
    : A{},
      elems{ std::allocator_traits<A>::allocate(
        static_cast<A&>(*this), n)
      },
      nelems{ n }, cap{ n } {
    try {
        uninitialized_fill_with_allocator(
            static_cast<A&>(*this), begin(), end(), init
        );
    } catch (...) {
        std::allocator_traits<A>::deallocate(
            static_cast<A&>(*this), elems, capacity()
        );
        throw;
    }
}
```

If you feel discomfort with the use of `*this` in the data member initializers, you can relax as we are only using the A part of `*this` and that base class sub-object has been fully initialized at that point. It's a safe part of `*this` to use.

The same adjustment has to be applied throughout the container (in dozens of places) and obviously makes the source code more verbose, but the good news is that this has gained us a zero-cost-at-runtime layer of abstraction and helped everyone who actually writes allocators.

For a node-based container such as `ForwardList<T,A>`, the situation is similar yet slightly different. For one thing, the type aliases are tricky; some of them are meant for user code and should be expressed with respect to the `value_type` of the container, and others should be based on the types of the allocator as expressed through its traits:

```cpp
template <class T, class A = std::allocator<T>>
class ForwardList {
public:
    // note: these are the forward-facing types, expressed
    // in terms where T is the value_type
    using value_type = T;
    using size_type =
        typename std::allocator_traits<A>::size_type;
    using pointer = value_type*;
    using const_pointer = const value_type*;
    using reference = value_type&;
    using const_reference = const value_type&;
    // ...
```

Within the container, we need to rebind A to an allocator of our internal Node type:

```cpp
    // ...
private:
    struct Node {
        value_type value;
        Node *next = nullptr;
        Node(const_reference value) : value { value } {
        }
        Node(value_type &&value) : value{ std::move(value) }{
        }
    };
    using Alloc = typename std::allocator_traits<
        A
    >::template rebind_alloc<Node>;
    Alloc alloc;
    // ...
```

Past this point, what we will do to perform memory management tasks is use static member functions from the std::allocator_traits<Alloc> type, passing the alloc data member as argument, as in this example:

```
// ...
void clear() noexcept {
    for(auto p = head; p; ) {
        auto q = p->next;
        std::allocator_traits<Alloc>::destroy(alloc, p);
        std::allocator_traits<Alloc>::deallocate(
            alloc, p, 1
        );
        p = q;
    }
    nelems = 0;
}
template <std::forward_iterator It>
    ForwardList(It b, It e) {
        if(b == e) return;
        try {
            head = std::allocator_traits<
                Alloc
            >::allocate(alloc, 1);
            std::allocator_traits<Alloc>::construct(
                alloc, head, *b
            );
            auto q = head;
            ++nelems;
            for(++b; b != e; ++b) {
                auto ptr = std::allocator_traits<
                    Alloc
                >::allocate(alloc, 1);
                std::allocator_traits<
                    Alloc
                >::construct(alloc, ptr, *b);
                q->next = ptr;
                q = q->next;
                ++nelems;
            }
        } catch (...) {
            clear();
            throw;
        }
```

```
        }
    // ...
```

The same technique needs to be applied throughout the container, of course, but the complexity remains the same.

Now that we have seen how traditional allocators, ensconced in the type of their container, have evolved from their original (rather involved) contract to their contemporary traits-based and simplified implementation (with somewhat more verbose containers), it's tempting to think that we have reached some form of optimality. This is both right and wrong.

Irritants with traditional allocators

The traditional approach to allocators is optimal at runtime in the sense that the services of such an allocator can be called without any overhead, and if an allocator is stateless, the introduction of an allocator in a container can be achieved without any costs in terms of space. Not bad!

Of course, the absence of runtime costs is not the absence of costs altogether:

- A container's implementation can become somewhat complex due to the additional (compile-time) layering, and there is a cost to writing, understanding, and maintaining source code. This sort of expertise is not universal; you have it, of course, dear reader, but others do not necessarily share that upside with you.

- Two containers that are identical in essentially every respect but differ in the way they manage memory (two containers that use different allocators) will in practice be different types, which might slow down compile times in programs that have multiple container-allocator combinations.

- Some operations that should probably be simple become more complicated. For example, if one seeks to compare containers v0 and v1 for equality, and if v0 is a Vector<T,A0> while v1 is a Vector<T,A1>, then one needs to write an operator==() function that deals with two different types... even though the allocator of a container is probably not one of its salient properties and, as such, should not be a concern when comparing two containers with respect to their sizes and values.

The same reasoning goes for many other container-related operations: an allocator is (traditionally) part of its container's type with the traditional approach, but many operations are value_type-related and have nothing to do with allocators. We are runtime optimal, but we have additional costs with respect to code generation complexity (which might lead to bigger binaries, which might have runtime speed impacts), and increasing the maintenance effort (including understanding code from its source) has a price.

Even something as seemingly simple as making allocators type-aware (traditional allocators are allocators of T for some type T after all) is sometimes controversial. Low-level memory allocation functions such as `std::malloc()` or `::operator new()` deal in raw bytes after all, so is it a sign that our traditional allocator model is perfectible?

Polymorphic memory resource allocators

With C++17, the C++ language added so-called PMR allocators. A PMR container stores allocator information as a runtime value, not as a compile-time part of its type. In this model, a PMR container holds a pointer to a PMR allocator, reducing the number of types required but adding virtual function calls whenever using memory allocation services.

This is again not a no-cost decision, and there are trade-offs with the traditional model:

- This new allocator model supposes that containers store a pointer to an allocation strategy, which generally (not always) makes PMR containers larger than their non-PMR counterparts. Interestingly, it also means that a `std::pmr::vector<T>` is a different container from a `std::vector<T>`, which sometimes causes very real annoyances. For example, there is no implicit way to copy the contents of a `std::pmr::string` into a `std::string`, but luckily, writing such a function is very easy.

- Every allocation or deallocation service call incurs a polymorphic indirection cost. This will be minor to unnoticeable in programs where the called function performs some significant computation, but the same costs can be painful when the called function performs little computation.

- PMR containers are parameterized on memory resources, and PMR memory resources trade in bytes, not in objects. It's unclear whether this is a good thing or a bad thing (it's probably a matter of perspective), as both approaches work, but trading in bytes (the simplest common denominator) makes it easier to reduce the number of types in a program.

There are also advantages to the PMR approach:

- The type of a container is not influenced by the type of its allocator. All PMR containers simply hold a pointer to the base class of all PMR memory resources named `std::pmr::memory_resource`.

- The work required to implement a PMR allocator is very small as one only needs to override three virtual member functions. This opens up avenues to express reusable allocator libraries, for example.

Under the PMR model, a `std::pmr::polymorphic_allocator<T>` object uses a `std::pmr::memory_resource*` to determine how memory is managed. In most cases, when designing a memory allocation strategy, what one does is write a class that specializes `std::memory_resource` and determines what it means to allocate or deallocate memory with that strategy.

Let's look at a simple example of a PMR container with a sequential buffer memory resource, as we just implemented such a mechanism with traditional allocators:

```cpp
#include <print>
#include <vector>
#include <string>
#include <memory_resource>
int main() {
    enum { N = 10'000 };
    alignas(int) char buf[N * sizeof(int)]{};
    std::pmr::monotonic_buffer_resource
        res{ std::begin(buf), std::size(buf) };
    std::pmr::vector<int> v{ &res };
    v.reserve(N);
    for (int i = 0; i != N; ++i)
        v.emplace_back(i + 1);
    for (auto n : v)
        std::print("{} ", n);
    std::print("\n {}\n", std::string(70, '-'));
    for (char * p = buf; p != buf + std::size(buf);
         p += sizeof(int))
        std::print("{} ", *reinterpret_cast<int*>(p));
}
```

That's quite simple, isn't it? You might want to pay attention to the following:

- This program aims to "allocate" objects in a byte buffer located on the thread's execution stack. With these objects being of type `int`, we ensure that buffer `buf` is appropriately aligned and is of sufficient size to hold the objects that are meant to be stored therein.

- A `std::pmr::monotonic_buffer_resource` object named `res` knows where the buffer to manage starts and how big it is. It represents a perspective on contiguous memory.

- The `std::pmr::vector<int>` used in this program knows about `res` and uses that resource to allocate and deallocate memory.

That's all there is to it. In practice, this program does not allocate even a single byte from the free store in order to store the `int` objects. Compared to what we had to do to achieve similar effects in the past, this might seem rejoiceful somewhat. At the end of the program, iterating through the byte buffer and iterating through the container yield the same results.

That works nicely and requires very little coding effort, but what if we wanted to express something like a vector of `string` objects but wanted both the vector and the `string` objects it stores to use the same allocation strategy?

Nested allocators

Well, it so happens that PMR allocators propagate allocation strategies by default. Consider the following example:

```cpp
#include <print>
#include <vector>
#include <string>
#include <memory_resource>
int main() {
   auto make_str = [] (const char *p, int n) ->
      std::pmr::string {
      auto s = std::string{ p } + std::to_string(n);
      return { std::begin(s), std::end(s) };
   };
   enum { N = 2'000 };
   alignas(std::pmr::string) char buf[N]{};
   std::pmr::monotonic_buffer_resource
      res{ std::begin(buf), std::size(buf) };
   std::pmr::vector<std::pmr::string> v{ &res };
   for (int i = 0; i != 10; ++i)
      v.emplace_back(make_str("I love my instructor ", i));
   for (const auto &s : v)
      std::print("{} ", s);
   std::print("\n {}\n", std::string(70, '-'));
   for (char c : buf)
      std::print("{} ", c);
}
```

This example also uses a buffer on the stack, but that buffer is used both for the std::pmr::vector object and its metadata and for the std::string objects therein. Propagation of the allocation strategy from the enclosing container to the enclosed containers is implicit.

Do note that the make_str lambda expression in that program is used to convert std::string (formatted to end with an integer) to a std::pmr::string. As mentioned earlier, the integration of types from namespace std and types from namespace std::pmr sometimes requires a little bit of effort, but the APIs of classes in these namespaces are sufficiently similar for this effort to remain reasonable.

If you use this program, you will notice that the std::pmr::string objects contain the expected text, but you will also probably notice from the last loop that buffer buf contains (among other things) the text in the strings. That's because our strings are rather short and, in most standard library implementations, the **small object optimization** will be applied, leading to the actual text being inscribed *within* the individual std::pmr::string instead of being allocated separately. This shows clearly that the same allocation strategy, represented by our object of type std::pmr::monotonic_buffer_resource, has propagated from the std::pmr::vector object to the enclosed std::pmr::string objects.

Scoped allocators and the traditional model

It is possible to use a scoped allocator system with the traditional allocator approach, even though we did not do so in this book. If you are curious, feel free to explore type std::scoped_allocator_adapter for more information.

We will now look at one last example that uses allocators to track the memory allocation process.

Allocators and data collection

As we saw in *Chapter 8* when we wrote our own humble yet functional leak detector, memory management tools are often used to gather information. For a non-exhaustive list, know that some companies use them to track memory fragmentation or otherwise assess where objects are placed in memory, maybe in a quest to optimize cache usage. Others want to evaluate when and where allocations occur in the course of program execution to know whether a reorganization of the code could lead to better performances. Of course, detecting leaks is useful, but we already knew that.

As our third and last example of PMR allocation usage, we will implement a *tracing resource*, in the sense that we will track allocation and deallocation requests from a container to understand some implementation choices made by that container. For the sake of this example, we will use a standard library's std::pmr::vector and try to understand its approach to increasing its capacity when trying to insert objects into a full container. Remember that the standard mandates an amortized constant complexity for operations such as push_back(), meaning that capacity should grow rarely and most insert-at-end operations should take constant time. However, it does not impose a specific growth policy: for example, one implementation could grow by a factor of 2, another by a factor of 1.5, and another could prefer 1.67. Other options exist; each one has trade-offs, and each library makes its own choices.

We will express this tool as class `tracing_resource`, which derives from `std::pmr::memory_resource` as expected by `std::pmr` containers. This lets us show how easy it is to add a memory resource type to this framework:

- The base class exposes three member functions that we need to override: `do_allocate()`, which is meant to perform an allocation request, `do_deallocate()`, whose role is, unsurprisingly, to deallocate memory that is presumed to have been allocated through `do_allocate()`, and `do_is_equal()`, which is meant to let user code test two memory resources for equality. Note that "equality" in this sense means that memory allocated from one could be deallocated from the other.

- Since we want to trace allocation requests but do not want to implement an actual memory allocation strategy ourselves, we will use an `upstream` resource that will do the allocation and deallocation for us. In our test implementation, that resource will be a global resource obtained from `std::pmr::new_delete_resource()` that calls `::operator new()` and `::operator delete()` to achieve this objective.

- For this reason, our allocation functions will simply "log" (in our case, print) the requested allocation and deallocation sizes, then delegate the allocation work to the `upstream` resource.

A complete implementation follows:

```cpp
#include <print>
#include <iostream>
#include <vector>
#include <string>
#include <memory_resource>
class tracing_resource : public std::pmr::memory_resource {
    void* do_allocate(
        std::size_t bytes, std::size_t alignment
    ) override {
        std::print ("do_allocate of {} bytes\n", bytes);
        return upstream->allocate(bytes, alignment);
    }
    void do_deallocate(
        void* p, std::size_t bytes, std::size_t alignment
    ) override {
        std::print ("do_deallocate of {} bytes\n", bytes);
        return upstream->deallocate(p, bytes, alignment);
    }
    bool do_is_equal(
        const std::pmr::memory_resource& other
    ) const noexcept override {
        return upstream->is_equal(other);
    }
    std::pmr::memory_resource *upstream;
```

```
public:
   tracing_resource(std::pmr::memory_resource *upstream)
      noexcept : upstream{ upstream } {
   }
};
int main() {
   enum { N = 100 };
   tracing_resource tracer{
      std::pmr::new_delete_resource()
   };
   std::pmr::vector<int> v{ &tracer };
   for (int i = 0; i != N; ++i)
      v.emplace_back(i + 1);
   for (auto s : v)
      std::print("{} ", s);
}
```

If you run this very simple program, you will develop an intuition for the growth strategy of your standard library `std::pmr::vector` implementation.

Upsides and costs

As we have seen, there's a lot to love about the PMR model. It is simple to use, relatively simple to understand, and easy to extend. In many application domains, it is fast enough to meet most programmers' needs.

There are, of course, also domains that need the increased control over execution time and runtime behavior that the traditional allocator model allows: no indirection that stems from the model, no overhead in terms of object size… Sometimes, you just need all the control you can get. This means that both models work and have their own valid reasons for being.

One very real benefit of PMR allocators is that they make it easier to build allocator and resource libraries that one can combine and build from. The standard library offers a few useful examples from the `<memory_resource>` header:

- We have already seen function `std::pmr::new_delete_resource()`, which provides a system-wide resource where allocation and deallocation are implemented through `::operator new()` and `::operator delete()`, just as we have seen class `std::pmr::monotonic_buffer_resource`, which formalizes the process of sequential allocation within an existing buffer.

- The `std::pmr::synchronized_pool_resource` and `std::pmr::unsynchronized_pool_resource` classes model the allocation of objects from pools of blocks of some sizes. Use the synchronized one for multithreaded code, of course.

- There are `std::pmr::get_default_resource()` and `std::pmr::set_default_resource()` functions that respectively obtain or replace the default memory resource of a program. The default memory resource is, as could be expected, the same as what is returned by function `std::pmr::new_delete_resource()`.

- There is also a function `std::pmr::null_memory_resource()` that returns a resource that never allocates (its `do_allocate()` member function, when called, throws `std::bad_alloc`). This is interesting as an "upstream" measure: consider a sequential buffer allocator system implemented through `std::pmr::monotonic_buffer_resource` in which a request for memory allocation leads to a possible buffer overflow. Since, by default, the `upstream` of a memory resource uses another resource that calls `::operator new()` and `::operator delete()`, this potential overflow will lead to an actual allocation, which could have an undesirable impact on performance. Choosing a `std::pmr::null_memory_resource` for the `upstream` resource ensures no such allocation will occur.

As we have seen and done, it is simple to add to this small set of memory resources and customize the behavior of your containers to suit your needs with the PMR model.

Summary

This has been an eventful chapter, has it not? After venturing into explicit and implicit memory allocation implementations in *Chapter 12* and *Chapter 13*, this chapter explored allocators and how these facilities let us customize the behavior of memory allocation in containers to match our needs.

We saw how a traditional allocator, ensconced in the type of its enclosing container, can be implemented and used. We did so with a container that trades in contiguous memory as well as with a node-based container. We also looked at how the task of writing (and using) such allocators evolved through the years to become the contemporary traits-based allocators that implicitly synthesize default implementations for most allocator services.

We then looked at the more recent PMR allocator model that represents a different take on memory allocation and discussed its upsides and downsides. Equipped with the knowledge in this chapter, you should have ideas of ways in which containers can be customized to meet your needs.

We are nearing the end of our journey. In our next (and last) chapter, we will look at some contemporary problems of memory allocation in C++ and start to think about what awaits us in the near future.

15
Contemporary Issues

We are reaching the end of our journey, dear reader. Over the course of this book, we have examined fundamental aspects of the C++ object model and discussed dangerous aspects of low-level programming. We have looked at the fundamentals of resource management in C++ through the RAII idiom, looked at how smart pointers are used, and explored how to write such a type. We also took control of the memory allocation functions at our disposal (and we did that in many ways!), and we wrote containers that manage memory themselves as well as through other objects or types, including allocators.

That was quite an experience!

What do we still have to cover? Well, so much… but there's a limit to what we can put in a single book. So, to conclude our discussion of memory management in C++, I thought we might have a chat (yes, dear reader, just you and I) about some of the interesting topics in contemporary memory management in C++. Yes, things that were so recently standardized (as of this writing) that most, if not all, libraries still do not implement them, and things the standards committee is actively working on.

It's important to look at C++ as it is today and how it might be in the near future because the language continues to evolve, and at quite a quick pace: a new version of the C++ standard is issued every three years, and this has been the case since 2011. The evolution of C++ is too slow for some and too quick for others, but it is unrelenting (we call this publishing rhythm the "train model" to highlight its sustained pace) and brings regular progress and innovation to this language that we love so much.

As of this writing, in the early weeks of 2025, C++23 is a freshly adopted standard, having been officialized in November 2024 (yes, I know: the ISO process does take some time), and the committee is discussing proposals meant for C++26 (yes, already!) and C++29.

The memory management-related topics we will discuss in this chapter are either aspects of the C++23 standard that we have not discussed in this book yet or are some that, as this chapter is being written, are under discussion for upcoming standards. Be aware, dear reader, that what you will now read may become reality in the form you will read about, but it might also come along in another form after discussions and debates in the C++ standards committee… or it might, in the end, never come to be.

Even if these topics do not end up entering the C++ standard in the form in which they were initially discussed, you will know that they will have been discussed, along with the problems they were meant to solve, and that these features might become part of the language at some point. Who knows; maybe you will have an epiphany and find the words to turn one of these ideas into a proposal that the C++ standards committee will discuss, and then adopt.

In this chapter, we will cover the following topics:

- Explicitly starting the lifetime of one or many objects without resorting to their constructors

- Trivial relocation: what it means and in what ways the standards committee is trying to address it

- Type-aware allocation and deallocation functions: what they would do and how to benefit from them

Our approach in this chapter will be to present these new features (or features-to-be) through the perspective of the problems we are trying to solve. The intent behind this approach is to make it clear that these features address actual issues and will help real programmers do their jobs better.

I hope this chapter will give you insights into an interesting (albeit non-exhaustive) set of contemporary issues in memory management and associated facilities as they pertain to C++.

> **A note on code examples for this chapter**
>
> If you try to compile the examples in this chapter, esteemed reader, you might find yourself saddened by the fact that some will not compile yet and others might not compile for a while, or ever. This situation is normal for a chapter such as this one: we will be discussing a combination of features that have been very recently added to the C++ language (recently enough that they have not yet been implemented at the time of authoring this book) and features that are under discussion by the C++ standards committee. Take the examples as illustrations, then, and adjust them as the features take a more formal shape.

Technical requirements

You can find the code files for this chapter in the book's GitHub repository: https://github.com/PacktPublishing/C-Plus-Plus-Memory-Management/tree/main/chapter15.

Starting object lifetime without constructors

Consider the case of a program that consumes serialized data from a stream and that seeks to make objects from that data. Here's an example:

```
#include <fstream>
#include <cstdint>
#include <array>
```

```cpp
#include <memory>
#include <string_view>
struct Point3D {
    float x{}, y{}, z{};
    Point3D() = default;
    constexpr Point3D(float x, float y, float z)
        : x{ x }, y{ y }, z{ z } {
    }
};
// ...
// reads at most N bytes from file named file_name and
// writes these bytes into buf. Returns the number of
// bytes read (postcondition: return value <= N)
//
template <int N>
    int read_from_stream(std::array<unsigned char, N> &buf,
                         std::string_view file_name) {
    // ...
}
// ...
```

As you can see, in this example, we have the Point3D class. An object of this type represents a set of *x,y,z* coordinates. We also have a read_from_stream<N>() function that consumes bytes from a file. The function then stores at most N bytes into argument buf, which is passed by reference and returns the number of bytes read (which might be zero but will never be more than N).

For the sake of this example, we will suppose that the file from which we plan to read is known to contain the binary form of serialized Point3D objects, equivalent to objects of type float serialized in binary format by groups of three. Now, consider the following program, which consumes the byte representation of at most four objects of type Point3D from a file named some_file.dat:

```cpp
// ...
#include <print>
#include <cassert>
using namespace std::literals;
int main() {
    static constexpr int NB_PTS = 4;
    static constexpr int NB_BYTES =
        NB_PTS * sizeof(Point3D);
    alignas(Point3D)
        std::array<unsigned char, NB_BYTES> buf{};
    if (int n = read_from_stream<NB_BYTES>(
            buf, "some_file.dat"sv
        ); n != 0) {
```

```
        // print out the bytes: 0-filled left, 2
        // characters-wide, hex format
        for (int i = 0; i != n; ++i)
            std::print("{:0<2x} ", buf[i]);
        std::println();
        // if we want to treat the bytes as Point3D objects,
        // we need to start the lifetime of these Point3D
        // objects. If we do not, we are in UB territory (it
        // might work or it might not, and even if it works
        // we cannot count on it)
        const Point3D* pts =
            std::start_lifetime_as_array(buf.data(), n);
        assert(n % 3 == 0);
        for (std::size_t i = 0;
             i != n / sizeof(Point3D); ++i)
            std::print("{} {} {}\n",
                       pts[i].x, pts[i].y, pts[i].z);
    }
}
```

This example program reads bytes from a file into a `std::array` object big enough to contain the bytes of four objects of type `Point3D`, having first ensured that this array would be aligned appropriately if it were to hold objects of that type. This alignment consideration is essential as we plan to treat the bytes as objects of that type once those bytes have been read.

The point of this example is that once the bytes have been read, the programmer is confident (well, as confident as one could be) that *all the bytes are correct* for some hypothetical `Point3D` objects but still cannot use these objects as *their lifetime has not yet started*.

This sort of situation traditionally makes many C programmers smile and some C++ programmers cringe: the C++ object model imposes constraints on programs that make it **UB** (see *Chapter 2*) to use objects outside of their lifetime, even if all the bytes are right and alignment constraints have been respected, whereas C is less restrictive. To use the contents of the buffer we just used to read from that file, our options are traditionally as follows:

- To loop through the array of bytes, write appropriately-sized subsets of those bytes into objects of type `float`, then call the constructors of `Point3D` objects and put them in another container.

- To `reinterpret_cast` the array of bytes into an array of `Point3D` objects and hope for the best, leading to code that might or might not work and, being UB, would not be portable anyway (not even between versions of a given compiler). With our `Point3D` objects, it will probably give the results one would hope for, but replace these with, say, `std::complex<float>` objects from the standard library (a type that probably has a similar inner structure as our `Point3D` type) and… well, who knows what might happen?

- To `std::memcpy()` the array of bytes into itself, casting the return value to type `Point3D*` and using the resulting pointer as if it were an array of `Point3D` objects. That's actually valid (the `std::memcpy()` function is part of a select set of functions that are allowed to start the lifetime of objects). There is, of course, the risk of creating an actual copy of the bytes (which would be wasted execution time); some standard libraries are said to recognize that pattern and just behave as if the call was a no-op, but a special kind of no-op that can start the lifetime of objects.

None of these options seems truly satisfactory, however, so a cleaner solution that does not rely on compiler-specific optimizations is needed. To that effect, the C++23 standard introduces a set of `constexpr` functions (accompanied by a number of overloads) that are called `std::start_lifetime_as_array<T>(p,n)` and `std::start_lifetime_as<T>(p)`. Both are portable forms of magical no-op functions that inform the compiler that the bytes are OK and to consider the lifetime of the pointees as having begun.

Of course, if for some reason the pointees have non-trivial destructors, you should make sure that your code calls these destructors when appropriate. Expect this situation to be rare and unusual. Since we consumed raw bytes from some source of data and turned these bytes into objects, the probability that the resulting objects own resources is somewhat slim. Of course, these objects can acquire resources once their lifetimes have begun. Let's be honest, dear reader; C++ programmers are nothing if not creative!

This set of `std::start_lifetime_...` functions is expected to be a boon to network programmers everywhere, in particular. These individuals often receive data frames of well-formed byte sequences that they need to turn into objects for the purpose of further processing. These functions are also expected to be useful to programs that consume bytes from files in order to form aggregates. Many programmers think that just reading bytes into an array of bytes and casting that array to an intended type (or array thereof) suffices to get access to the (hypothetical) object (or objects) therein and are surprised when their C++ code starts behaving unexpectedly. C++ is a systems programming language, and the set made of these `std::start_lifetime_...` functions closes a gap where it could be said to be underperforming.

Of course, these functions form a very sharp toolset due to the risks involved: non-trivially destructible objects whose lifetime starts this way are especially suspicious, and you have to be highly trusting of whatever facility provided the bytes in which an object's lifetime is manually and explicitly started. Thus, these facilities should be used with utmost care.

A note to complete this section: as of this writing, no major compiler yet implements these functions, even though they have been standardized and are part of C++23. Maybe they will be implemented by the time you get to read this, who knows?

Trivial relocation

As you know, dear reader, C++ is known in the programming community as one of those languages that we use when we need to get the most out of our computer or whatever hardware platform interests us. Some of the language's credos can be paraphrased as "you shall not pay for what you do not use" and "there shall be no room for a lower-level language (except for the occasional bit of assembly code)", after all. The latter explains the importance of the `std::start_lifetime_...` functions of the previous section.

That's probably why, when it becomes evident that we could do even better than we are already doing in terms of execution speed, that becomes a subject of interest to the C++ programmer community in general, and more specifically to members of the C++ standards committee. We all take these core credos of the language to heart.

One case where we could do better is when we encounter types for which moving a source object to a destination object, followed by destroying the original object, could in practice be replaced by a call to `std::memcpy()`: directly copying an array of bytes is faster than performing a series of moves and destructors (and if it isn't, there's probably some work required on your `std::memcpy()` implementation), even though move assignments and destructors make for a fast combination.

It turns out that there are many types for which such an optimization could be considered, including `std::string`, `std::any`, and `std::optional<T>` (depending on what type T is), classes such as `Point3D` from the previous section, any type that does not define any of the six special member functions seen in *Chapter 1* (including fundamental types), and so on.

To understand the impact, consider the following `resize()` free function, which mimics a `C::resize()` member function for some container, C, that manages contiguous memory such as our `Vector<T>` type in the various incarnations seen in this book. This function resizes `arr` from `old_cap` (the old capacity) to `new_cap` (the new capacity), filling the space at the end with default T objects. The highlighted lines of the function are what interests us here:

```
//
// This is not a good function interface, but we want to
// keep the example relatively simple
//
template <class T>
  void resize
    (T *&arr, std::size_t old_cap, std::size_t new_cap) {
    //
    // we could deal with throwing a default constructor
    // but it would complicate our code a bit and these
    // added complexities, worthwhile as they are, are
    // besides the point for what we are discussing here
    //
```

```
static_assert(
  std::is_nothrow_default_contructible_v<T>
);
//
// sometimes, there's just nothing to do
//
if(new_cap <= old_cap) return arr;
//
// allocate a chunk of raw memory (no object created)
//
auto p = static_cast<T*>(
  std::malloc(new_cap * sizeof(T))
);
if(!p) throw std::bad_alloc{};
// ...
```

At this point, we are ready to copy (or move) objects:

```
// ...
//
// if move assignment does not throw, be aggressive
//
if constexpr(std::is_nothrow_move_assignable_v<T>) {
  std::uninitialized_move(arr, arr + old_cap, p);
  std::destroy(arr, arr + old_cap);
} else {
  //
  // since move assignment could throw, let's be
  // conservative and copy instead
  //
  try {
    std::uninitialized_copy(arr, arr + old_cap, p);
    std::destroy(arr, arr + old_cap);
  } catch (...) {
    std::free(p);
    throw;
  }
}
//
// fill the remaining space with default objects
// (remember: we statically asserted that T::T() is
// non-throwing)
//
```

```
    std::uninitialized_default_construct(
      p + old_cap, p + new_cap
    );
    //
    // replace the old memory block (now without objects)
    // with the new one
    //
    std::free(arr);
    arr = p;
  }
```

Looking at the highlighted lines of that function, even though the combination of `std::uninitialized_move()` followed by `std::destroy()` makes for a fast path, we could be even faster than this and replace a linear number of move assignment operators followed by a linear number of destructor calls with a single call to `std::memcpy()`.

How do we achieve this? Well, there are many competing proposals by Arthur O'Dwyer, Mingxin Wang, Alisdair Meredith, and Mungo Gill, among others. Each of these proposals has merits, but these proposals have in common the following factors:

- Providing a way to test a type for "trivial relocatability" at compile time, for example, a `std::is_trivially_relocatable_v<T>` trait.

- Providing a function that actually relocates the objects, for example, `std::relocate()` or `std::trivially_relocate()`, which take a source pointer and a destination pointer as arguments and relocate the source object to the destination location, concluding the lifetime of the original object and then starting the lifetime of the new one

- Providing a way to mark a type as being trivially relocatable, for example through a keyword or an attribute

- Providing rules to deduce trivial relocatability for a type at compile time

The details can vary depending on the approach, but if we suppose these tools, the same `resize()` function could benefit from trivial relocation by a slight adjustment to the previously presented implementation:

```
template <class T>
  void resize
    (T * &arr, std::size_t old_cap, std::size_t new_cap) {
    static_assert(
        std::is_nothrow_default_contructible_v<T>
    );
    if(new_cap <= old_cap) return arr;
    auto p = static_cast<T*>(
        std::malloc(new_cap * sizeof(T))
```

```
    );
    if(!p) throw std::bad_alloc{};
    //
    // this is our ideal case
    //
    if constexpr (std::is_trivially_relocatable_v<T>) {
        // equivalent to memcpy() plus consider the
        // lifetime of objects in [arr, arr + old_cap)
        // finished and the lifetime of objects in
        // [p, p + old_cap) started
        //
        // note: this supposes that the trait
        // std::is_trivially_relocatable<T>
        // implies std::is_trivially_destructible<T>
        std::relocate(arr, arr + old_cap, p);
    //
    // if move assignment does not throw, be aggressive
    //
    } else if constexpr(
        std::is_nothrow_move_assignable_v<T>
    ){
        std::uninitialized_move(arr, arr + old_cap, p);
        std::destroy(arr, arr + old_cap);
    } else {
        // ... see previous code example for the rest
    }
}
```

This seemingly simple optimization has been reported to provide considerable benefits, with some having claimed up to 30% speedup in common cases, but this is experimental work, and more benchmarks are expected to come if proposals coalesce (as we expect them to) into something that will be integrated into the C++ standard.

Such potential speedups are part of what the C++ language aims to make possible, so we can reasonably expect trivial relocatability to become reality in the foreseeable future. The question is "how": how should compilers detect the trivial relocatability property? How should programmers be able to indicate that property on their own types when the default trivial relocatability deduction rules are not met?

As of February 2025, the standard committee voted trivial relocation into what will become C++26 standard. This means we can expect that some programs that compiled with previous standards of the C++ language and are recompiled with C++26 could just run faster without changing a single line of source code.

Type-aware allocation and deallocation functions

Our last topic for this chapter on new approaches to memory management and optimization opportunities that pertain to object lifetime is type-aware allocation and deallocation functions. This is a novel approach to allocation functions for cases where user code might want to somehow use information with respect to what type is undergoing allocation (and eventual construction) to guide the allocation process.

We saw one facet of such features in *Chapter 9* when describing the **destroying delete** mechanism made possible by C++20, where a member-function version of `T::operator delete()` is passed `T*` instead of the abstract `void*` as an argument, and is for that reason made responsible for both the finalization of the object and the deallocation of its underlying storage. We saw that there are cases where this reveals interesting optimization opportunities.

What is under discussion for C++26 is a new family of `operator new()` and `operator delete()` member functions, as well as free functions that take a `std::type_identity<T>` object as the first argument for some type `T`, guiding the selected operator towards some specialized behavior for that type `T`. Note that these type-aware allocation functions are really allocation functions: they do not perform construction, nor does their deallocation counterpart perform finalization.

> **What is the std::type_identity<T> trait?**
>
> The expression `typename std::type_identity<T>::type` corresponds to T. OK, that seems trivial enough. So, what role does this trait play in contemporary C++ programming? It happens that trait `std::type_identity<T>`, introduced with C++20, is a tool that is typically used to provide additional control over argument type deduction in generic functions.
>
> For example, with the function signature `template <class T> void f(T,T)`, you could call `f(3,3)` as both arguments are of the same type, but not `f(3,3.0)` as int and double are distinct types. That being said, by replacing either argument type with `std::type_identity_t<T>`, you could call `f(3,3.0)`, and since T would be deduced with the other argument (the one of type T), that type would be used for the other (the argument for which the type is `std::type_identity_t<T>`). That would lead to both arguments being int or double, depending on which argument is of type T.
>
> The idea of using `std::type_identity<T>` (not `std::type_identity_t<T>`) instead of plain T as the type of the first argument in type-aware allocation functions is to make it clear that we are using this specific specialized overload of `operator new()` and that this is not an accident or a call to some other specialized form of this allocation function, such as those described in *Chapter 9*.

This means that you could provide specialized allocation functions for a specific class, X, through the following function signatures:

```
#include <new>
#include <type_traits>
void* operator new(std::type_identity<X>, std::size_t n);
void operator delete(std::type_identity<X>, void* p);
```

In such cases, when calling new X, for example, the specialized form will be preferred to the usual form of operator new() and operator delete(), being assumed to be more appropriate unless the programmer takes steps to prevent it.

It also means that, given a specialized allocation algorithm that applies to type T only if special_alloc_alg<T> is satisfied, you could provide allocation functions that use this specialized algorithm for type T through the following function signatures:

```
#include <new>
#include <type_traits>
template <class T> requires special_alloc_alg<T>
  void* operator new(std::type_identity<T>, std::size_t n);
template <class T> requires special_alloc_alg<T>
  void operator delete(std::type_identity<T>, void* p);
```

This provides new avenues for optimizations such as those described in *Chapter 10*, for example. Consider this simple example where we have a cool allocation algorithm for types X and Y, but that algorithm does not apply to other classes, such as Z:

```
#include <concepts>
#include <type_traits>
class X { /* ... */ };
class Y { /* ... */ };
class Z { /* ... */ };
template <class C>
  concept cool_alloc_algorithm =
    std::is_same_v<C, X> || std::is_same_v<C, Y>;
template <class T> requires cool_alloc_algorithm<T>
  void* operator new(std::type_identity<T>, std::size_t n){
    // apply the cool allocation algorithm
  }
template <class T> requires cool_alloc_algorithm<T>
  void operator delete(std::type_identity<T>, void* p) {
    // apply the cool deallocation algorithm
  }
```

```
#include <memory>
int main() {
    // uses the "cool" allocation algorithm
    auto p = std::make_unique<X>();
    // uses the standard allocation algorithm
    auto q = std::make_unique<Z>();
} // uses the standard deallocation algorithm for q
    // uses the "cool" deallocation algorithm for p
```

The type-aware allocation functions can also be member function overloads, leading to algorithms that apply to the class where these functions are defined, as well as to derived classes thereof.

Consider the following example, inspired by a more complex example found in the proposal for the feature that is described at `https://wg21.link/p2719`:

```
class D0; // forward class declaration
struct B {
  // i)
  template <class T>
  void* operator new(std::type_identity<T>, std::size_t);
  // ii)
  void* operator new(std::type_identity<D0>, std::size_t);
};
// ...
```

As expressed, i) applies to B and its derived classes, but ii) applies to the specific case of the forward-declared class D0 and will only be used if D0 is indeed a derived class of B.

Continuing this example, we now add three classes that each derive from B, with D2 adding iii), which is a non-type-aware member function overload of operator new():

```
// ...
struct D0 : B { };
struct D1 : B { };
struct D2 : B {
  // iii)
  void *operator new(std::size_t);
};
// ...
```

Given these overloads, here are some examples of expressions calling overloads `i)`, `ii)`, and `iii)`:

```
// ...
void f() {
  new B;        // i) where T is B
  new D0;       // ii)
  new D1;       // i) where T is D1
  new D2;       // iii)
  ::new B;      // uses appropriate global operator new
}
```

As you can see, dear reader, type-aware allocation functions will, if accepted into the C++ standard, provide new ways to control what memory allocation algorithm will be used (depending on the circumstances) while still leaving user code in control, leaving it able to defer to the global `operator new()` function if that is the preferred option, as the last line of the `f()` function in the previous example shows.

Contrary to the destroying delete feature of C++20, which performs both the finalization of the object and the deallocation of the underlying storage, the type-aware versions of `operator new()` and `operator delete()` are only allocation functions, and as of this writing, there is no plan to provide a type-aware version of destroying delete.

Summary

In this chapter, we have had a glimpse of the future with the `std::start_lifetime_...` functions that are part of C++23 but, as of this writing, have not been implemented by any major compiler. We have also looked at probable (but not yet official) parts of the future of C++ with the potential support of trivial relocatability and the possibility of introducing type-aware versions of `operator new()` and `operator delete()`.

With every step, C++ becomes a richer and more versatile language with which we can do more and express our ideas in more precise ways. C++ is a language that provides ever more significant control over the behavior of our programs. As powerful as C++ is today, and as powerful as it makes programmers like us, this chapter shows we can still continue to get better.

We are at the end of our journey, at least for now. I hope the trip was just eventful enough to be pleasant and entertaining to you, esteemed reader, and that you have learned a thing or two along the way. I also hope that some of the ideas discussed here will help you in your tasks and enrich your perspective of C++ programming.

Thanks for accompanying me. I hope the journeys ahead for you will be enjoyable, just as I hope this book will make your toolbox better and that you will continue exploring on your own. Safe travels.

Unlock this book's exclusive benefits now

This book comes with additional benefits designed to elevate your learning experience.

Note: Have your purchase invoice ready before you begin.

https://www.packtpub.com/
unlock/9781805129806

16
Unlock Your Book's Exclusive Benefits

Your copy of *C++ Memory Management* comes with the following exclusive benefits:

- Next-gen Packt Reader
- AI assistant (beta)
- DRM-free PDF/ePub downloads

Use the following guide to unlock them if you haven't already. The process takes just a few minutes and needs to be done only once.

How to unlock these benefits in three easy steps

Step 1

Have your purchase invoice for this book ready, as you'll need it in *Step 3*. If you received a physical invoice, scan it on your phone and have it ready as either a PDF, JPG, or PNG.

For more help on finding your invoice, visit `https://www.packtpub.com/unlock-benefits/help`.

> **Note**
> Bought this book directly from Packt? You don't need an invoice. After completing *Step 2*, you can jump straight to your exclusive content.

Step 2

Scan the following QR code or visit `https://www.packtpub.com/unlock/9781805129806`:

Step 3

Sign in to your Packt account or create a new one for free. Once you're logged in, upload your invoice. It can be in PDF, PNG, or JPG format and must be no larger than 10 MB. Follow the rest of the instructions on the screen to complete the process.

Need help?

If you get stuck and need help, visit `https://www.packtpub.com/unlock-benefits/help` for a detailed FAQ on how to find your invoices and more. The following QR code will take you to the help page directly:

> **Note**
>
> If you are still facing issues, reach out to `customercare@packt.com`.

Annexure
Things You Should Know

This book supposes readers possess some technical background that some might not consider to be "common knowledge". In the following sections, you might find the complementary information that will help you get the most out of this book. Refer to it as needed, and enjoy!

Feel free to skim through the following sections if you think you know their contents well and take a closer look at those you're less comfortable with. You could even skip this entire section and come back if you realize while reading this book that these topics are not things you know as well as you thought you did.

The overall goal is to get the most out of this book after all!

struct and class

In C++, the words `struct` and `class` essentially mean the same thing, and code such as the following is perfectly legal:

```
struct Drawable {
    virtual void draw() = 0;
    virtual ~Drawable() = default;
};
class Painting : public Drawable {
    void draw() override;
};
```

Here are some details to note:

- C++ has no `abstract` keyword like some other languages do. An abstract member function in C++ is `virtual` and has `=0` instead of a definition. The `virtual` keyword means *can be specialized by derived classes* (the `=0` part essentially means *must be specialized...*). We often talk of **overriding** the function when specializing a `virtual` member function. Functions that must be overridden are said to be **pure virtual** functions.

Providing a default implementation for a pure virtual function

One can provide a definition for an abstract member function: it's not typical, but it's possible. That can be useful in cases where the base class wants to provide a default implementation of a service but requires that the derived classes at least consider providing their own. Here is an example:

```cpp
#include <iostream>
struct X { virtual int f() const = 0; };
int X::f() const { return 3; }
struct D : X { int f() const override {
   return X::f() + 1; }
};
void g(X &x) { std::cout << x.f() << '\n'; }
int main() {
   D d;
   // X x; // illegal: X has a pure virtual member function
   g(d);
}
```

- C++ classes have destructors that handle what happens when an object reaches the end of its lifetime. Contrary to many other popular languages, automatic and static objects in C++ have deterministic lifetimes, and using destructors efficiently is idiomatic in that language. In a **polymorphic** class (a class with at least one `virtual` member function), it is customary to have a `virtual` destructor (here, `virtual ~Drawable()`) to indicate that in a situation such as the following, destroying an object used through an indirection such as p should effectively destroy the pointed-to object (`Painting`), not the one denoted by the pointer's static type (`Drawable`):

```cpp
//
// the following supposes that Painting is a public
// derived class of Drawable as suggested earlier in
// this section
//
Drawable *p = new Painting;
// ...
delete p; // <-- here
```

- A `class` can derive from a `struct` just as a `struct` can derive from a `class` as both are structurally equivalent. The main differences are that for a `struct`, inheritance is `public` by default (but that can be changed using `protected` or `private`) and the same goes for members, whereas for a `class`, inheritance and members are `private` by default (but again, that can be changed).

Note, in passing, that it's perfectly fine in C++ to have a member function with an access qualifier in the base class (for example, `Drawable::draw()`, which is `public`) and in a derived class (for example, `Painting::draw()`, which is `private`). Some other popular languages do not allow this.

std::size_t

Type `std::size_t` is an alias for some unsigned integral type, but the actual type can vary from compiler to compiler (it could be `unsigned int`, `unsigned long`, `unsigned long long`, and so on).

One frequently encounters type `std::size_t` when discussing container sizes and the space occupied in memory by an object as expressed by operator `sizeof`.

The sizeof operator

The `sizeof` operator yields the size in bytes of an object or a type. It is evaluated at compile time and will be used extensively throughout this book as we will need that information to allocate properly sized blocks of memory:

```
auto s0 = sizeof(int); // s0 is the number of bytes in an
                       // int (parentheses required)
int n;
auto s1 = sizeof n; // s1 is the number of bytes occupied
                    // by s1, which is identical to s0.
                    // Note: for objects, parentheses are
                    // allowed but not mandated
```

Object size is one of the key components of memory management and influences the speed at which programs will execute. For that reason, it is a recurring theme throughout this book.

Assertions

Assertions are statements of fact that programmers think should be upheld by code. Some are dynamic, based on information known at runtime, for example, "*The following pointer should not be null at this point.*" Others are static, based on information known at compile time, for example, "*This program has been written with the non-portable assumption that an* `int` *occupies four bytes of storage.*" In the latter case, we have a program that has been written based on a non-portable assumption and we have to live with this choice, but we do not want our code to compile on platforms where that assumption does not hold.

For dynamic assertions, it is customary to use the `assert()` macro from the `<cassert>` header. That macro takes as argument a boolean expression and halts program execution if it evaluates to `false`:

```
void f(int *p) {
    assert(p); // we hold p != nullptr to be true
    // use *p
}
```

Note that many projects disable `assert()` from production code, something that can be done by defining the NDEBUG macro before compilation. As such, make sure never to put expressions with side effects in `assert()` as it might be removed by compiler options:

```
int *obtain_buf(int);
void danger(int n) {
    int *p; // uninitialized
    assert(p = obtain_buf(n)); // dangerous!!!
    // use *p, but p might be uninitialized if assert()
    // has been disabled. This is very bad
}
```

Contrary to `assert()`, which is a library macro, `static_assert` is a language feature that prevents compilation if its condition is not met. Based on the example mentioned previously where a company might have built software based on a non-portable assumption such as `sizeof(int)==4`, we could make sure that code does not compile (and do bad things) for platforms that are not really supported:

```
static_assert(sizeof(int)==4); // only compiles if the
                               // condition holds
```

Fixing bugs before shipping a software product is significantly better for developers and users alike than fixing bugs after the software has been sent "in the wild." Consequently, `static_assert` can be seen as a powerful tool for delivering higher-quality products.

In this book, we will use `static_assert` regularly: it has no runtime cost and documents our assertions in a verifiable manner. It's the sort of feature that essentially has no downsides.

Undefined behavior

Undefined behavior, often abbreviated to **UB**, results from a situation in which the standard does not prescribe a specific behavior. In the C++ standard, UB is behavior for which no requirements are imposed. It can lead to the problem being ignored, just as it can lead to a diagnostic or program termination. The key idea is that if your program has undefined behavior, then it's not playing by the rules of the language and is broken; its behavior is not guaranteed on your platform, it's not portable between platforms or compilers, and it cannot be relied upon.

A correctly written C++ program has no undefined behavior. When faced with a function that contains undefined behavior, the compiler can do just about anything with the code in that function, which makes reasoning from source code essentially impossible.

Undefined behavior is one of the preeminent "things to be careful with" listed in *Chapter 2*. Strive to avoid undefined behavior: it always comes back to bite you if you leave it in.

Type traits

Over the years, C++ programmers have developed various techniques to reason about the properties of their types, mostly at compile time. Inferring such things as *"Is the* T *type const?"* or *"Is the* T *type trivially copyable?"* can be very useful, particularly in the context of generic code. The constructs resulting from these techniques are called **type traits**, and many of those that came into common practice over time (as well as some that require compiler support to be implemented) were standardized and can be found in the `<type_traits>` header.

The ways in which standard type traits are expressed have standardized over time, going from complex beasts such as `std::numeric_limits<T>`, which provide a lot of different services for type T, to more specific services such as `std::is_const<T>` (*Is the* type T *actually* const*?*) or `std::remove_const<T>` (*Please give me the type that's like* T *but without the* const *qualification if there was one*), which yield either a single type or a single value. Practice has shown that small, unitary type traits that yield either a type (named `type`) or a compile-time-known value (named `value`) can be considered "best practices," and most contemporary type traits (including standard ones) are written this way.

Since C++14, the traits that yield types have aliases that end with `_t` (for example, instead of writing the rather painful `typename std::remove_const<T>::type` incantation, one can now write `std::remove_const_t<T>` instead) and since C++17, the traits that yield values have aliases that end with `_v` (for example, instead of writing `std::is_const<T>::value`, one can now write `std::is_const_v<T>`).

> **What about concepts?**
> Type traits are a programming technique that's been part of C++ for decades, but since C++20, we have had **concepts**, and concepts are sort of like traits (often, they are expressed *through* traits) but are stronger in the sense that they are part of the type system. This book does not use concepts much, but you (as a programmer) really should get acquainted with them. They are extremely powerful and extremely useful to contemporary C++ programming.

The std::true_type and std::false_type traits

When expressing type traits, the standard library applies the common practice of using the names type for types and value for values, as in this example:

```
// hand-made is_const<T> and remove_const<T> traits
// (please use the standard versions from <type_traits>
// instead of writing your own!)
template <class> struct is_const {
    static constexpr bool value = false; // general case
};
// specialization for const types
template <class T> struct is_const<const T> {
    static constexpr bool value = true;
};
// general case
template <class T> struct remove_const {
    using type = T;
};
// specialization for const T
template <class T> struct remove_const<const T> {
    using type = T;
};
```

It happens that many type traits have Boolean values. To simplify the task of writing such traits and to ensure that the form of these traits is homogeneous, you will find types std::true_type and std::false_type in the <type_traits> header. These types can be seen as the type system counterparts of constants true and false.

With these types, we can rewrite traits such as is_const as follows:

```
#include <type_traits>
// hand-made is_const<T> (prefer the std:: versions...)
template <class> struct is_const : std::false_type {
};
template <class T>
    struct is_const<const T> : std::true_type {
    };
```

These types are both a convenience and a way to express ideas more clearly.

The std::conditional<B,T,F> trait

It's sometimes useful to choose between two types based on a condition known at compile time. Consider the following example where we seek to implement a comparison between two values of some type T that behave differently for floating-point types and for "other" types such as int all grouped together for simplicity:

```cpp
#include <cmath>
// we will allow comparisons between exact representations
// or floating point representations based on so-called tag
// types (empty classes used to distinguish function
// signatures)
struct floating {};
struct exact {};
// the three-argument versions are not meant to be called
// directly from user code
template <class T>
    bool close_enough(T a, T b, exact) {
        return a == b; // fine for int, short, bool, etc.
    }
template <class T>
    bool close_enough(T a, T b, floating) {
        // note: this could benefit from more rigor, but
        // that's orthogonal to our discussion
        return std::abs(a - b) < static_cast<T>(0.000001);
    }
// this two-argument version is the one user code is
// meant to call
template <class T>
    bool close_enough(T a, T b) {
        // OUR GOAL: call the "floating" version for types
        // float, double and long double; call the "exact"
        // version otherwise
    }
```

You might notice that we did not name the arguments of type exact and floating in our close_enough() functions. That's fine as we are not using these objects at all; the reason for these arguments is to ensure both functions have distinct signatures.

There is a `std::is_floating_point<T>` trait in the `<type_traits>` header with the value of `true` for floating-point numbers, and `false` otherwise. If we did not have this trait, we could write our own:

```
// we could write is_floating_point<T> as follows
// (but please use std::is_floating_point<T> instead!
template <class> struct is_floating_point
    : std::false_type {}; // general case
// specializations
template <> struct is_floating_point<float>
    : std::true_type {};
template <> struct is_floating_point<double>
    : std::true_type {};
template <> struct is_floating_point<long double>
    : std::true_type {};
// convenience to simplify user code
template <class T>
    constexpr bool is_floating_point_v =
        is_floating_point<T>::value;
```

We can use this to make our decision. However, we do not want to make a runtime decision here since the nature of type T is fully known at compile time, and nobody wants to pay for a branch instruction when comparing integers!

The `std::conditional<B,T,F>` trait can be used to make such a decision. If we wrote our own, it could look like this:

```
// example, home-made conditional<B,T,F> type trait
// (prefer the std:: version in <type_traits>)
// general case (incomplete type)
template <bool, class T, class F> struct conditional;
// specializations
template < class T, class F>
    struct conditional<true, T, F> {
        using type = T; // constant true, picks type T
    };
template < class T, class F>
    struct conditional<false, T, F> {
    using type = F; // constant true, picks type F
};
// convenience to simplify user code
template <bool B, class T, class F>
    using conditional_t = typename conditional<B,T,F>::type;
```

Given this trait, we can choose, at compile time, one of two types based on a compile-time Boolean value, which is exactly what we were trying to do:

```
// ...
// this version will be called from user code
template <class T>
   bool close_enough(T a, T b) {
      return close_enough(
         a, b, conditional_t<
            is_floating_point_v<T>,
            floating,
            exact
         > {}
      );
   }
```

The way to read this is that the third argument in the call to close_enough() (found within our two-argument, user-facing close_enough() function) will either be an object of type floating or an object of type exact , but the exact type will be picked at compile time based on the value of the is_floating_point_v<T> compile-time constant. The end result is that we instantiate an object of one of these two empty classes, call the appropriate algorithm, and let function inlining do the rest and optimize the entire scaffolding away.

Algorithms

The C++ standard library contains, among other gems, a set of algorithms. Each of these functions performs the tasks that a very well-written loop would do but with specific names, complexity guarantees, and optimizations. As such, let's say we write the following:

```
int vals[]{ 2,3,5,7,11 };
int dest[5];
for(int i = 0; i != 5; ++i)
   dest[i] = vals[i];
```

It is idiomatic in C++ to write the following instead:

```
int vals[]{ 2,3,5,7,11 };
int dest[5];
std::copy(begin(vals), end(vals), begin(dest));
```

The important thing to know here is that C++ sequences are of the form [begin, end), meaning that for all algorithms, the beginning iterator (here, begin(vals)) is included and the ending iterator (here, end(vals)) is excluded, making [begin, end) a half-open range. All algorithms in <algorithm> and in its cousin header, <numeric>, follow that simple convention.

> **What about ranges?**
>
> The <ranges> library is a major addition to the C++ standard library since C++20 and can sometimes be used to lead to even better code than the already tremendous <algorithm> library. This book does not use ranges much, but that does not mean this library is not wonderful, so please feel free to use it and investigate ways through which it can be used to make your code better.

Functors (function objects) and lambdas

It is customary in C++ to use **functors**, otherwise called **function objects**, to represent stateful computations. Think, for example, of a program that would print integers to the standard output using an algorithm:

```cpp
#include <iostream>
#include <algorithm>
#include <iterator>
using namespace std;
void display(int n) { cout << n << ' '; }
int main() {
    int vals[]{ 2,3,5,7,11 };
    for_each(begin(vals), end(vals), display);
}
```

This small program works fine, but should we want to print elsewhere than on the standard output, we would find ourselves in an unpleasant situation: the for_each() algorithm expects a unary function in the sense of "function accepting a single argument" (here, the value to print), so there's no syntactic space to add an argument such as the output stream to use. We could "solve" this issue through a global variable, or using a different function for every output stream, but that would fall short of a reasonable design.

If we replace the display function with a class, which we'll name Display to make them visually distinct, we end up with the following:

```cpp
#include <iostream>
#include <algorithm>
#include <iterator>
#include <fstream>
using namespace std;
class Display {
    ostream &os;
public:
    Display(ostream &os) : os{ os } {
    }
```

```
    void operator()(int n) const { os << n << ' '; }
};
int main() {
    int vals[]{ 2,3,5,7,11 };
    // display on the standard output
    for_each(begin(vals), end(vals), Display{ cout });
    ofstream out{"out.txt" };
    // write to file out.txt
    for_each(begin(vals), end(vals), Display{ out });
}
```

This leads to nice, readable code with added flexibility. Note that, conceptually, lambda expressions are functors (you can even use lambdas as base classes!), so the previous example can be rewritten equivalently as follows:

```
#include <iostream>
#include <algorithm>
#include <iterator>
#include <fstream>
using namespace std;
int main() {
    int vals[]{ 2,3,5,7,11 };
    // display on the standard output
    for_each(begin(vals), end(vals), [](int n) {
        cout << n << ' ';
    });
    ofstream out{"out.txt" };
    // write to file out.txt
    for_each(begin(vals), end(vals), [&out](int n) {
        out << n << ' ';
    });
}
```

Lambdas are thus essentially functors that limit themselves to a constructor and an operator() member function, and this combination represents the most common case by far for such objects. You can, of course, still use full-blown, explicit functors if you want more than this.

Friends

C++ offers an access qualifier that's not commonly found in other languages and is often misunderstood: the friend qualifier. A class can specify another class or a function as one of its friends, giving said friend qualifier full access to all of that class's members, including those qualified as protected or private.

Some consider `friend` to break encapsulation, and indeed it can do this if used recklessly, but the intent here is to provide privileged access to specific entities rather than exposing them as `public` or `protected` members that were not designed to that end, leading to an even wider encapsulation breakage.

Consider, for example, the following classes, where `thing` is something that is meant to be built from the contents of a file named `name` by a `thing_factory` that's able to validate the file's content before constructing the `thing`:

```
class thing {
   thing(string_view); // note: private
   // ... various interesting members
   // thing_factory can access private members of
   // class thing
   friend class thing_factory;
};
// in case we read an incorrect file
class invalid_format{};
class thing_factory {
   // ... various interesting things here too
   string read_file(const string &name) const {
      ifstream in{ name };
      // consume the file in one fell swoop, returning
      // the entire contents in a single string
      return { istreambuf_iterator<char>{ in },
               istreambuf_iterator<char>{ } };
   }
   bool is_valid_content(string_view) const;
public:
   thing create_thing_from(const string &name) const {
      auto contents = read_file(name);
      if(!is_valid_content(contents))
         throw invalid_format{};
      // note: calls private thing constructor
      return { contents };
   }
};
```

We do not want the whole world to be able to call the `private`-qualified `thing` constructor that takes an arbitrary `string_view` as an argument since that constructor is not meant to handle character strings that have not been validated in the first place. For this reason, we only let `thing_factory` use it, thus strengthening encapsulation rather than weakening it.

It is customary to put a class and its friends together when shipping code as they go together: a friend of a class, in essence, is an external addition to that class's interface. Finally, note that restrictions apply to friendship. Friendship is not reflexive; if A declares B to be its friend, it does not follow that B declares A to be its friend:

```
class A {
    int n = 3;
    friend class B;
public:
    void f(B);
};
class B {
    int m = 4;
public:
    void f(A);
};
void A::f(B b) {
    // int val = b.m; // no, A is not a friend of B
}
void B::f(A a) {
    int val = a.n; // Ok, B is a friend of A
}
```

Friendship is not transitive; if A declares B to be its friend and B declares C to be its friend, it does not follow that A declares C to be its friend:

```
class A {
    int n = 3;
    friend class B;
};
class B {
    friend class C;
public:
    void f(A a) {
        int val = a.n; // Ok, B is a friend of A
    }
};
class C {
public:
    void f(A a) {
        // int val = a.n; // no, C is not a friend of A
    }
};
```

Last but not least, friendship is not inherited; if A declares B to be its friend, it does not follow that if C is a child class of B, A has declared C to be its friend:

```cpp
class A {
   int n = 3;
   friend class B;
};
class B {
public:
   void f(A a) {
      int val = a.n; // Ok, B is a friend of A
   }
};
class C : B {
public:
   void f(A a) {
      // int val = a.n; // no, C is not a friend of A
   }
};
```

Used judiciously, friend solves encapsulation problems that would be difficult to deal with otherwise.

The decltype operator

The type system of C++ is powerful and nuanced, offering (among other things) a set of type deduction facilities. The best-known type deduction tool is probably auto, used to infer the type of an expression from the type of its initializer:

```cpp
const int n = f();
auto m = n; // m is of type int
auto & r = m; // r is of type int&
const auto & cr0 = m; // cr0 is of type const int&
auto & cr1 = n; // cr1 is of type const int&
```

As you might notice from the preceding example, by default, auto makes copies (see the declaration of variable m), but you can qualify auto with &, &&, const, and so on if needed.

Sometimes, you want to deduce the type of an expression with more precision, keeping the various qualifiers that accompany it. That might be useful when inferring the type of an arithmetic expression, the type of a lambda, the return type of a complicated generic function, and so on. For this, you have the decltype operator:

```cpp
template <class T>
   T& pass_thru(T &arg) {
```

```
        return arg;
    }
int main() {
    int n = 3;
    auto m = pass_thru(n); // m is an int
    ++m;
    cout << n << ' ' << m << '\n'; // 3 4
    decltype(pass_thru(n)) r = pass_thru(n); // r is an int&
    ++r;
    cout << n << ' ' << r << '\n'; // 4 4
}
```

The use of auto has become commonplace in C++ code since C++11, at least in some circles. The decltype operator, also part of C++ since C++11, is a sharper tool, still widely used but for more specialized use cases.

> **When the types get painful to spell**
>
> In the preceding decltype example, we spelled pass_thru(n) twice: once in the decltype operator and once in the actual function call. That's not practical in general since it duplicates the maintenance effort and… well, it's just noise, really. Since C++14, one can use decltype(auto) to express "the fully qualified type of the initializing expression."
>
> Thus, we would customarily write decltype(auto) r = pass_thru(n); to express that r is to have the fully qualified type of the expression pass_thru(n).

Perfect forwarding

The advent of variadic templates in C++11 has made it necessary to ensure there is a way for the semantics at the call site of a function to be conveyed throughout the call chain. This might seem abstract but it's quite real and has implications on the effect of function calls.

Consider the following class:

```
#include <string>
struct X {
    X(int, const std::string&); // A
    X(int, std::string&&); // B
    // ... other constructors and various members
};
```

This class exposes at least two constructors, one that takes an `int` and `const string&` as argument and another that takes an `int` and a `string&&` instead. To make the example more general, we'll also suppose the existence of other X constructors that we might want to call while still focusing on these two. If we called these two constructors explicitly, we could do so with the following:

```
X x0{ 3, "hello" }; // calls A
string s = "hi!";
X x1{ 4, s }; // also calls A
X x2{ 5, string{ "there" } }; // calls B
X x3{ 5, "there too"s }; // also calls B
```

The constructor of x0 calls A, as `"hello"` is a `const char(&)[6]` (including the trailing `'\0'`), not a `string` type, but the compiler's allowed to synthesize a temporary `string` to pass as a `const string&` in this case (it could not if the `string&` was non-`const` as it would require referring to a modifiable object).

The constructor of x1 also calls A, as s is a named `string` type, which means it cannot be implicitly passed by movement.

The constructors of x2 and x3 both call B, which takes a `string&&` as an argument, as they are both passed temporary, anonymous `string` objects that can be implicitly passed by movement.

Now, suppose we want to write a factory of X objects that relays arguments to the appropriate X constructor (one of the two we're looking at or any other X constructor) after having done some preliminary work; for the sake of this example, we'll simply log the fact that we are constructing an X object. Let's say we wrote it this way:

```
template <class ... Args>
   X makeX(Args ... args) {
      clog << "Creating a X object\n";
      return X(args...); // <-- HERE
   }
```

In this case, arguments would all have names and be passed by value, so the constructor that takes a `string&&` would never be chosen.

Now, let's say we wrote it this way:

```
template <class ... Args>
   X makeX(Args &... args) {
      clog << "Creating a X object\n";
      return X(args...); // <-- HERE
   }
```

In this case, arguments would all be passed by reference, and a call that passed a `char` array such as `"hello"` as an argument would not compile. What we need to do is write our factory function in such a way that each argument keeps the semantics it had at the function's call site, and is forwarded by the function with the exact same semantics.

The way to express this in C++ involves **forwarding references** and a special library function called `std::forward<T>()` (from `<utility>`), which behaves as a cast. A forwarding reference superficially and syntactically looks like the `rvalue` references used for move semantics, but their impact on argument semantics is quite different. Consider the following example:

```
// v passed by movement (type vector<int> fully specified)
void f0(vector<int> &&v);
// v passed by movement (type vector<T> fully specified
// for some type T)
template <class T>
    void f1(vector<T> &&v);
// v is a forwarding reference (type discovered by
// the compiler)
template <class T>
    void f2(T&& v);
```

With a forwarding reference, the argument semantics depend on the call site. For example, let's say we have the function `f2()`:

```
// T is vector<int>&& (pass by movement)
f2(vector<int>{ 2,3,5,7,11 });
vector<int> v0{ 2,3,5,7,11 };
f2(v0); // T is vector<int>& (pass by reference)
const vector<int> v1{ 2,3,5,7,11 };
f2(v1); // T is const vector<int>& (pass by ref-to-const)
```

Returning to our factory of X objects, in this case, the appropriate signature for `makeX()` would be as follows:

```
template <class ... Args>
    X makeX(Args &&... args) {
        clog << "Creating a X object\n";
        return X(args...); // <-- HERE (still incorrect)
    }
```

This version of our function almost works. The signature of `makeX()` is correct as each argument will be accepted with the type used at the call site, be it a reference, a reference to `const`, or an `rvalue` reference. What's missing is that the arguments we are receiving as `rvalue` references now have a name within `makeX()` (they're part of the pack named `args`!), so when calling the constructor of X, there's no implicit move involved anymore.

What we need to do to complete our effort is to *cast back each argument to the type it had at the call site*. That type is inscribed in `Args`, the type of our pack, and the way to perform that cast is to apply `std::forward<T>()` to each argument in the pack. A correct `makeX()` function, at long last, would be as follows:

```
template <class ... Args>
    X makeX(Args &&... args) {
        clog << "Creating a X object\n";
        return X(std::forward<Args>(args)...); // <-- HERE
    }
```

Whew! There are simpler syntaxes indeed, but we made it.

The singleton design pattern

There are many design patterns out there. Design patterns are a topic of their own, representing well-known ways of solving problems that one can represent in the abstract, give a name to, explain to others, and then reify within the constraints and idioms of one's chosen programming language.

The **singleton** design pattern describes ways in which we can write a class that ensures it is instantiated only once in a program.

Singleton is not a well-liked pattern: it makes testing difficult, introduces dependencies on global state, represents a single point of failure in a program as well as a potential program-wide bottleneck, complicates multithreading (if the singleton is mutable, then its state requires synchronization), and so on, but it has its uses, is used in practice, and we use it on occasion in this book.

There are many ways to write a class that is instantiated only once in a program with the C++ language. All of them share some key characteristics:

- The type's `copy` operations have to be deleted. If one can copy a singleton, then there will be more than one instance of that type, which leads to a contradiction.

- There should be no `public` constructor. If there were, the client code could call it and create more than one instance.

- There should be no `protected` members. Objects of derived classes are also, conceptually, objects of the base class, again leading to a contradiction (there would, in practice, be more than one instance of the singleton!).

- Since there is no `public` constructor, there should be a `private` constructor (probably a default constructor), and that one will only be accessible to the class itself or to its friends (if any). For simplicity, we'll suppose that the way to access a singleton is to go through a `static` (obviously) member function of the singleton.

We'll look at ways to implement an overly simplistic singleton in C++. For the sake of this example, the singleton will provide sequential integers on demand. The general idea for that class will be the following:

```cpp
#include <atomic>
class SequentialIdProvider {
   // ...
   std::atomic<long long> cur; // state (synchronized)
   // default constructor (private)
   SequentialIdProvider() : cur{ 0LL } {
   }
public:
   // service offered by the singleton (synchronized)
   auto next() { return cur++; }
   // deleted copy operations
   SequentialIdProvider(const SequentialIdProvider&)
      = delete;
   SequentialIdProvider&
      operator=(const SequentialIdProvider&) = delete;
   // ...
};
```

The following subsections show two different techniques to create and provide access to the singleton.

Instantiation at program startup

One way to instantiate a singleton is to create it before `main()` starts by actually making it a `static` data member of its class. This requires *declaring* the singleton in the class and *defining* it in a separate source file in order to avoid ODR problems.

> **ODR, you say?**
>
> The **One Definition Rule (ODR)** and associated issues are described in *Chapter 2* of this book, but the gist of it is that in C++, every object can have many declarations but only one definition.

A possible implementation would be as follows:

```cpp
#include <atomic>
class SequentialIdProvider {
   // declaration (private)
   static SequentialIdProvider singleton;
   std::atomic<long long> cur; // state (synchronized)
   // default constructor (private)
   SequentialIdProvider() : cur{ 0LL } {
   }
```

```
public:
    // static member function providing access to the object
    static auto & get() { return singleton; }
    // service offered by the singleton (synchronized)
    auto next() { return cur++; }
    // deleted copy operations
    SequentialIdProvider(const SequentialIdProvider&)
        = delete;
    SequentialIdProvider&
        operator=(const SequentialIdProvider&) = delete;
    // ...
};
// in a source file somewhere, say SequentialIdProvider.cpp
#include "SequentialIdProvider.h"
// definition (calls the default constructor)
SequentialIdProvider SequentialIdProvider::singleton;
```

This works fine and is efficient as long as there is no dependency between separate global objects. For example, if another singleton in the same program needed access to the services of SequentialIdProvider, we could run into trouble as C++ does not guarantee the order in which global objects from multiple files are instantiated.

Possible client code for this implementation would be as follows:

```
auto & provider = SequentialIdProvider::get();
for(int i = 0; i != 5; ++i)
    cout << provider.next() << ' ';
```

This would display monotonically increasing integers, maybe consecutively (as long as there is no other thread concurrently calling the singleton's services).

Instantiation of the first call

Another way to instantiate a singleton is to create it the first time its services are solicited by making it a static variable of the function that provides access to the singleton. This way, as static local variables are created the first time the function is called and keep their state thereafter, a singleton could provide services to other singletons as long as this does not create cycles.

A possible implementation would be the following:

```
#include <atomic>
class SequentialIdProvider {
    std::atomic<long long> cur; // state (synchronized)
    // default constructor (private)
    SequentialIdProvider() : cur{ 0LL } {
```

```
    }
public:
    // static member function providing access to the object
    static auto & get() {
        static SequentialIdProvider singleton; // definition
        return singleton;
    }
    // service offered by the singleton (synchronized)
    auto next() { return cur++; }
    // deleted copy operations
    SequentialIdProvider(const SequentialIdProvider&)
        = delete;
    SequentialIdProvider&
        operator=(const SequentialIdProvider&) = delete;
    // ...
};
```

Possible client code for this implementation would be as follows:

```
auto & provider = SequentialIdProvider::get();
for(int i = 0; i != 5; ++i)
    cout << provider.next() << ' ';
```

This would display monotonically increasing integers, maybe consecutively (as long as there is no other thread concurrently calling the singleton's services).

Note that this version has a hidden cost: `static` variables local to functions are called **magic statics** in C++ as the language guarantees that they will be constructed only once, even if two or more threads call the function concurrently. This property implies that access to that `static` variable involves some synchronization and that this synchronization is paid on every call to that function. The preceding client code alleviates that cost by calling `SequentialIdProvider::get()` once, then reusing the reference obtained through that call afterward; it's the call to `get()` that introduces the synchronization cost.

The std::exchange() function

There are (at least) two very useful and fundamental functions hidden in the `<utility>` header file. One is well-known and has been there for a long time: `std::swap()`, which is used for many purposes throughout the standard library as well as throughout user code.

The other, more recent one is `std::exchange()`. Where `swap(a,b)` swaps the values of objects `a` and `b`, expression `a = exchange(b,c)` changes the value of `b` with the value of `c`, returning the old value of `b` (to assign it to `a`). This might look strange at first but it's actually a very useful facility.

Consider the move constructor for the following simplified `fixed_size_array`:

```cpp
template <class T>
   class fixed_size_array {
      T *elems{};
      std::size_t nelems{};
   public:
      // ...
      fixed_size_array(fixed_size_array &&other)
         : elems{ other.elems }, nelems{ other.nelems } {
         other.elems = nullptr;
         other.nelems = 0;
      }
      // ...
   };
```

You might notice that this constructor does two things: it grabs the data members from `other`, and then replaces the members of `other` with default values. That's the posterchild for `std::exchange()`, so this constructor can be simplified as follows:

```cpp
template <class T>
   class fixed_size_array {
      T *elems{};
      std::size_t nelems{};
   public:
      // ...
      fixed_size_array(fixed_size_array &&other)
         : elems{ std::exchange(other.elems, nullptr) },
           nelems{ std::exchange(other.nelems, 0) } {
      }
      // ...
   };
```

With `std::exchange()`, this common two-step operation can be reduced to a function call, simplifying code and making it more efficient (in this case, turning assignments into constructor calls).

Index

www.packtpub.com

Subscribe to our online digital library for full access to over 7,000 books and videos, as well as industry leading tools to help you plan your personal development and advance your career. For more information, please visit our website.

Why subscribe?

- Spend less time learning and more time coding with practical eBooks and Videos from over 4,000 industry professionals

- Improve your learning with Skill Plans built especially for you

- Get a free eBook or video every month

- Fully searchable for easy access to vital information

- Copy and paste, print, and bookmark content

Did you know that Packt offers eBook versions of every book published, with PDF and ePub files available? You can upgrade to the eBook version at packtpub.com and as a print book customer, you are entitled to a discount on the eBook copy. Get in touch with us at customercare@packtpub.com for more details.

At www.packtpub.com, you can also read a collection of free technical articles, sign up for a range of free newsletters, and receive exclusive discounts and offers on Packt books and eBooks.

Other Books You May Enjoy

If you enjoyed this book, you may be interested in these other books by Packt:

C++ High Performance

Björn Andrist, Viktor Sehr

ISBN: 978-1-83921-654-1

- Write specialized data structures for performance-critical code
- Use modern metaprogramming techniques to reduce runtime calculations
- Achieve efficient memory management using custom memory allocators
- Reduce boilerplate code using reflection techniques
- Reap the benefits of lock-free concurrent programming
- Gain insights into subtle optimizations used by standard library algorithms
- Compose algorithms using ranges library
- Develop the ability to apply metaprogramming aspects such as constexpr, constraints,
- and concepts
- Implement lazy generators and asynchronous tasks using C++20 coroutines

Refactoring with C++

Dmitry Danilov

ISBN: 978-1-83763-377-7

- Leverage the rich type system of C++ to write safe and elegant code
- Create advanced object-oriented designs using the unique features of C++
- Minimize code duplication by using metaprogramming
- Refactor code safely with the help of unit tests
- Ensure code conventions and format with clang-format
- Facilitate the usage of modern features automatically with clang-tidy
- Catch complex bugs such as memory leakage and data races with Clang AddressSanitizer
- and ThreadSanitizer

Packt is searching for authors like you

If you're interested in becoming an author for Packt, please visit `authors.packtpub.com` and apply today. We have worked with thousands of developers and tech professionals, just like you, to help them share their insight with the global tech community. You can make a general application, apply for a specific hot topic that we are recruiting an author for, or submit your own idea.

Share Your Thoughts

Now you've finished *C++ Memory Management*, we'd love to hear your thoughts! Scan the QR code below to go straight to the Amazon review page for this book and share your feedback or leave a review on the site that you purchased it from.

https://packt.link/r/1805129805

Your review is important to us and the tech community and will help us make sure we're delivering excellent quality content.

www.ingramcontent.com/pod-product-compliance
Lightning Source LLC
Chambersburg PA
CBHW060647060326
40690CB00020B/4547